BLACK DEATH TO INDUSTRIAL REVOLUTION

WITHDRAWN

Hatfield Polytechnic
Wall Hall Campus
LIBRARY

Hatfield Polytechnic
Wall Hall Campus
Aldenham, Watford
Herts WD2 8AT

This book must be returned or renewed on or before the last date stamped below. The library retains the right to recall books at any time.

-8 NOV 1989
-4 DEC 1989
13 FEB 1992
10 NOV 1993
22 APR 1994
29 SEP 1995
8 DEC 1995
12 JAN 1996
-8 FEB 1996
11 NOV 1997
14 DEC 1998

By the Same Author

A Social and Economic History of Britain 1760–1972

The Chain of History

Free-Born John: a Biography of John Lilburne

The Welfare State

BLACK DEATH TO INDUSTRIAL REVOLUTION

A social and economic history of England

PAULINE GREGG
Ph.D. B.Sc. (Econ.)

HARRAP LONDON

For Barry and Sylvia

HATFIELD POLYTECHNIC
CONTROL— X44017200 3
CLASS 941 Gre
ITEM— 1201240138

First published in Great Britain 1976
by George G. Harrap & Co. Ltd
182–184 High Holborn, London WC1V 7AX

© *Pauline Gregg* 1976

All rights reserved. No part of this publication may be reproduced in any form or by any means without the prior permission of George G. Harrap & Co. Ltd

ISBN 0 245 52324 3

Photoset, printed and bound in Great Britain by
REDWOOD BURN LIMITED
Trowbridge & Esher

Preface

This book, which covers the period from the Black Death to the Industrial Revolution, is intended as a companion volume to my *Social and Economic History of England from 1760 to the Present Day*. In writing it I have incurred three main debts: the Bodleian Library has been my spiritual home throughout, and the unfailing kindness and quiet efficiency of the staff has considerably lightened my labours; in the final stages I owe much to the keen eye and shrewd judgment of Mr Roy Minton of Harrap's Editorial Department, and I am very grateful to him; in its early stages the book was piloted by Mr R. O. Anderson, the Chairman and Managing Director of Harrap's, who has handled all my books. As this was one of the last that he dealt with before his retirement, I should particularly like to associate it with his name, and at the same time to thank him for his encouragement and enthusiasm over the years.

But above all my thanks, as always, must go to my husband, Russell Meiggs, whose commitment to the simple life makes my task of writing much easier.

Garsington,
January 1976

PAULINE GREGG

Acknowledgments

I should like to thank Macmillan, London and Basingstoke, for permission to use items quoted in the table 'English Wool Prices' on p. 117; the Editors of *Economica* for the use of figures quoted in the table on *Inflation in Tudor and Stuart England* on p. 206; the Cambridge University Press for permission to use items for two tables on 'English Overseas Trade' on p. 219; and the Editors of *The Economic History Review* for the use of items for the table 'East India Imports' on the same page.

NOTE

In footnote references a date of publication is given when it is necessary to indicate the volume to which page reference is made. This is not necessarily a first edition. Quotations from early sources are given in the original where these seemed immediately intelligible.

062893

Contents

Illustrations

MAPS AND DIAGRAMS

TABLES

CHAPTER I

The Black Death

Epidemic plague can be traced back to the earliest recorded history. It struck the Philistines after their capture of the Ark of the Covenant. There was plague in ancient Athens and in the Roman Empire. There was plague in Britain when Saxon and Celt were fighting each other after the departure of the Romans. But the plague which hit Europe in the fourteenth century aroused a degree of horror if not greater, at least more articulate, than previous visitations. The name Black Death (referring, perhaps, to the black pustulae often observed on the bodies of victims) was not applied to it until much later, but the designation was apt, grimly expressing the mood of the time. With about a third of the population of Europe wiped out by sudden, ugly, unaccounted-for death, the effect on the living was bound to be cataclysmic, and all the more so since life in the Middle Ages was close-knit and gregarious.

This fourteenth-century pandemic can with some certainty be traced to the Near East, but probably originated in Central Asia, reaching Europe over the trade routes. When it was realized that ships from the East were bringing the plague they were driven away from ports where they attempted to make harbour, but it was too late to prevent the trail of infection and the pestilence spread, fanning out on every side from the coasts and the trade routes, its progress assisted by the insanitary conditions of towns and houses. The plague reached Sicily, parts of the Adriatic coast, Marseilles by the autumn of 1347. In January 1348 it was in Venice and Genoa; in April it was in

Florence, by the summer in Northern France and Central Europe, Jersey and Guernsey. In the summer of 1348 it was in England. It appeared to have come in ships' cargoes, perhaps through contact with the Channel Islands or, as some said, brought by refugees fleeing the plague at Calais, then in English hands. From its probable point of entry (Melcombe Regis, now part of Weymouth) it spread rapidly through Dorset and Somerset to Devonshire and up to Bristol, where mortality was probably the worst in the whole country. Cornwall and all the south-western counties were infected by the end of the year. The men of Gloucester tried to protect themselves by barring their city to Bristol people, but to no avail. The plague spread to Oxford. It was in London by November, lasting there for some seven or eight months. Here again, as in all ports, the sources of infection were numerous. In the eastern counties there were enormous ravages during the summer of 1349. In Ireland it was first seen in 1348 on the shores of Dublin Bay at Howth and Dalkey. By the following year it was raging in Dublin, on the Drogheda coast and in many other places. By the autumn of 1349 it was in the south of Scotland, and spread over the whole country during the following year, when the mortality was very high. By that time it had also reached Wales, and had extended to the northern countries of the Baltic and North Seas, brought, it was alleged, by a ship with a cargo of woollen cloth which sailed from London.

The rapid spread of the disease, the seemingly inevitable mortality, were appalling, and contemporaries were stunned by it. In villages entire communities were wiped out. When it came to Bristol 'there died as it were the whole strength of the town, taken by sudden death'.[1] Many shut themselves in their houses, refusing entry to the afflicted, only to find that the pestilence had broken out in their midst. It was noticed that the incidence of death varied from district to district without seeming reason, a few areas being comparatively free, while about them the mortality was heavy. In the bad areas the rich and the poor, the high and the low, perished. Though it was sometimes noted that the poor died first, and that the rich fled from the worst areas, all over Europe the toll was indiscriminate. Petrarch lost both his noble patron and Laura, the inspiration of his poems. Alfonso XI of Castile was a plague victim; and Joan, daughter of King Edward III of England, was struck down and died of the pestilence at Bordeaux on the way to her wedding with

Alfonso's son. Graveyards rapidly became full, and huge trenches were dug to take the bodies of victims, which were piled up, hundreds at a time, 'like merchandise stowed in the hold of a ship, tier upon tier, each covered with a little earth, until the trench would hold no more'.[2] In London graveyards of this kind were dug at Smithfield and at Spitalfields. The living shunned them for their stench of putrefaction.

Some physicians did what they could, tending the sick and recording the symptoms and course of the disease, though many were themselves struck down. Others behaved no differently from the rest of the population. 'Doctors dared not visit the sick for fear of infection' wrote the French physician Gui de Chauliac. He himself did not leave his post, and contracted the pestilence, but was one of the few who recovered. How many doctors died, how many of the clergy tended the living, how many gave the last rites to the dying and buried the dead will never be known. There was high mortality among the monks, but this could have been due to the communal life of the monasteries. Some accounts accused them of being as frightened of the plague as any others, and as anxious to shut themselves away. Even the Pope withdrew from the horror. He did, it is true, grant indulgences, pay doctors to care for the poor, and he purchased a large field for the plague pits. But at the same time he shut himself up in his chamber at Avignon and gave access to none. From England a monastic chronicler reported that parish churches remained altogether unserved and that beneficed parsons turned aside from the care of their benefices for fear of death. Some chaplains and hired priests demanded higher pay if they remained. The Bishop of Bath and Wells kept away from Bristol, and retired to his manor at Wiveliscombe until the worst was over. From this safe distance, he lamented the shortage of priests and authorized laymen to hear confessions. The Bishop of Exeter, on the other hand, never deserted his post, and remained throughout the epidemic available in his diocese. The Bishop of Lincoln likewise, steadily visiting his flock, remained faithful throughout.

Frightened monks in their cloisters strove to write down what they saw—Henry Knighton, Canon of St Mary's, Leicester, Geoffrey le Baker, a clerk in the Abbey of Osney, near Oxford, Robert de Avesbury, a monk of Malmesbury, a monk of Meaux Abbey, in Yorkshire. In Kilkenny, in Ireland, Friar John Clyn of the Friars Minor was writing in his monastery, sadly recording the repeated tale of death, and conscious of his own mortality. 'That pestilence', he wrote,

> deprived of human inhabitant villages and cities, and castles and towns, so that there was scarcely found a man to dwell therein; the pestilence was so contagious that whosoever touched the sick or dead was immediately infected and died; and the penitent and the confessor were carried together to the grave. I, waiting for death till it come, have reduced these things to writing; and lest the writing should perish with the writer, and the work fail together with the workman, I leave parchment for continuing the work, if haply any man survive, and any of the race of Adam escape this pestilence and continue the work which I have commenced.

There follows a brief record of another death, and the words *magna karistia* (great famine). After this another hand has added: *Videtur quod Author hic obit*—here it seems the author died.[3]

There was no lack of medical discussion. Some twenty treatises from physicians appeared in Europe within five years of the epidemic, fifty or sixty more before 1400. The number is remarkably high for an age before printing, when the process of writing and publication was laborious. But there was then no knowledge of how to deal with the plague. Its origins were shrouded in stories of pestilence, flood and horror which came out of the East. The more credulous imbibed stories of pollution caused by the foul breath of demons or invoked by avenging gods.[4] Some held that certain combinations of stars in their courses could bring about evil such as pestilence and death. Sirius, the Dog Star, in particular was held to enhance any pestilential quality in the air. The more scientific believed that a miasma might arise from pollution of the air by swamps and stagnant waters, from dead animals and fish, from the unburied dead on the field of battle. The understanding of both contagion and infection was vague. People imagined that all who had contact with the sick themselves became affected. It was also thought that the plague might be contracted visually and that to catch the eye of one sick of the plague was to develop the disease immediately. There were other beliefs, the result of hysteria as the plague panic grew: that evil people smeared doors and houses with virulently poisonous ointments; that the Jews had poisoned the world by infecting wells and by other means; that the deformed were taking their vengeance on the rest of mankind. As a result people found with ointments about their persons were often maltreated, the deformed were driven away from the places in which they dwelt, and there were frequent pogroms of the Jews. A few saw in the dirty streets of medieval towns where roads were fouled and waterways made putrid by the effluent of privies, the off-scourings of animal slaughtering, by trade refuse and domestic garbage, a cause of both the spread and the origin of the plague. Gentile da Foligno actually advised the cleansing of the streets of Florence and the making of bonfires in the streets.

For those afflicted there was little hope and little time, almost the only treatment prescribed being bleeding. For prevention, advice to leave infected areas was frequently given first place in the plague tractates, but prayer and the wearing of an amulet were also recommended. As far as possible, people should stay indoors and keep fires burning. As bad odours were thought to bring the plague, so pleasant ones could avert it: juniper and ash, vine and rosemary, young oak and pine, cypress and laurel should be burned for their aroma; the smoke of aloes, the perfume of amber and musk were recommended for those who could afford them; the cheaper mastic[5] was recommended for the poor. Various fumigatory troches[6] to be thrown on the fire were prescribed, for which precise recipes were given. Recipes also abound for 'smelling-apples'. The leading of a temperate life, with a plain diet of little meat and many vegetables, was advised. Certain herbs and spices were particularly beneficial, such as pills of aloes, myrrh and saffron; a powder of black pepper and cummin which could be sprinkled on foods; and, for the poor, the common scabious. Many theriacs,[7] sometimes compounded of as many as two hundred ingredients, were likewise recommended.

The number of plague deaths could be only guessed. Nine out of ten, four out of five, three out of four, seventy out of a hundred were contemporary estimates of the number of deaths; that the living were scarce sufficient to care for the sick or bury the dead was a common observation. One record spoke of 50 000 persons being buried in the plague year in Spitalfields in London, and another of 200 being buried each day in Smithfield. Monastic chroniclers left records of their dead. A monk of Meaux, in Yorkshire, says that four-fifths of the monks and lay brethren of his House died; Geoffrey le Baker says that at Osney only one-tenth survived. The Bishop of Rochester, from a small household, lost four priests, five gentlemen, ten serving men, seven young clerks, and six pages. From Leicester Henry Knighton wrote that 'many churches were widowed' because of the mortality among priests, but does not mention numbers. The Abbot of Westminster died, and twenty-seven of his monks were buried in a common grave; at St Albans the Abbot, the prior and the sub-prior, as well as many monks, succumbed.[8] Many monastic chronicles contain only the words *magna mortalitas*.

The most precise figures are those for a small section of the population given by a study of the episcopal registers in which bishops' clerks noted every change of incumbency in a parish, sometimes adding the cause—death, or resignation, or even death by plague. Frequently, however, no cause is given, and a change cannot be assumed to be a death. Moreover, any use of figures or calculation in the Middle Ages must remain suspect. For one thing, the use of numbers did not then imply the accuracy and finality assigned to them to-day. For another, Roman figures were rarely replaced by arabic, and the enormous difficulty of making calculations in Roman figures could lead to the wildest inaccuracies. But allowing for these difficulties, and using the records of some of the largest dioceses of medieval England, calculations have been made to show that plague deaths among incubents of parishes amounted to between 44 and 50 per cent. It would not be wide of the mark to say that perhaps nearly half the English parish clergy died of plague.[9]

The *inquisitiones post mortem* provide a rough indication of mortality among another class, for they are a record, made for the king, of property left at the death of a landowner. They provide eloquent testimony of the state of the manor: the mill is of no value because the miller is dead and none are left alive who want their corn ground; no-one uses the cloth mill; it stands idle and no-one will rent it. The *inquisitiones* indicate that perhaps 25 per cent of the principal landowners died of plague. Beside these stand the manorial records, where would normally be recorded changing tenancies, names of tenants, fines of admission to holdings, and the important item of heriots received—the heriot being the best beast of a tenant taken at his death by the lord of the manor. Such records as have been studied tell a melancholy tale. There is, for example, the Hundred and Manor of Farnham, comprising ten other villages besides Farnham itself and its suburbs. The reeve, William Waryn, died of plague, and his brother Robert took over his duties as reeve as well as his little farm of about thirty acres. In 1348–9 the number of heriots received numbered some 200; in the previous seven years twelve had been the highest number, seven the average. In 1348–9 fine on entry brought in the large sum of £101 14*s*. 2*d*.; no total for any year between 1340 and 1346 had exceeded £13 4*s*. 2*d*. Not only did heriots and fines increase, showing that new tenants were taking over from old, but a new heading appears in the manor records: *defectus per pestilentiam*—vacant because of the plague. The vacancies were greater than the supply of new tenants, possibly because whole families were wiped out. Forty times in 1349 it was recorded by the Reeve of the manor of Farnham that relatives had not made fine because there were none left. The plague lasted for two and a half years. In the Hundred of Farnham in that time deaths have been estimated, on the basis of the Manor rolls, at 1 376—one-third to one-half of the population.[10]

On the basis of such imperfect evidence, it is generally concluded that, in Britain as in Europe, one-third of the population died of the Black Death, a number amounting in England to at least a million persons. A modern estimate of 35 or 40 per cent in Bristol, a town which was badly hit,[11] is in line with this. From contemporary accounts, it would seem that the middle-aged were the first to succumb, and that children and those of child-bearing age fared better. This would account for the fact that there was a high birth-rate after 1348. But plague struck again and again within a few years—in 1361, 1369 and 1379. Though the earlier epidemic caused more deaths and generated greater horror, the later visitations attacked mostly younger people, and their effect on the birth-rate was therefore more severe. It has been estimated that by the end of the century the population was 50 per cent smaller than at the beginning.[12]

Yet the effects upon society as a whole were not nearly so striking as these figures and contemporary stories suggest. It was formerly assumed that the Black Death decimated a growing population and retarded an expanding economy.[13] Modern study has diminished the Black Death in this respect by showing that the population was already in decline and the economy already contracting before the epidemic struck: the Black Death did, in fact, hasten existing developments rather than initiate anything new. But economic generalizations cannot obscure the impact of the pestilence upon people alive at the time as death in horrific form ravaged their families and crippled their close-knit communities; nor can it hide the fact that Europe by the fourteenth century, however disunited in many ways, was sufficiently united by trade and other contacts to be vulnerable throughout her length and breadth to a major pandemic. Yet neither cause, nor origin, nor method of infection, nor means of contagion was known. Five hundred years, punctuated by repeated outbreaks of plague, were to pass before the cause was discovered in a flea and the agent in a black rat.

CHAPTER II

Land and People

How many of these people were living before the plague thus lopped off one-third of them, wiping out families and breaking up homes? What kind of country did they inhabit? How did they live? In what way did the Black Death alter the lives of the survivors?

The matter of total population itself creates difficulties. Between Domesday Book in 1086 and the poll-tax returns of 1377 there is nothing to go on, and both these estimates were very imperfect. The generally accepted view is that the twelfth and thirteenth centuries were a period of expansion, that from the middle of the twelfth century and right through the thirteenth there was great land hunger, the population pressing forward the margin of cultivation by taking in fresh tracts of forest and waste in a great 'colonizing' movement. This view assumed that the population would at least have doubled between Domesday Book and 1300, there being, perhaps, some $3\frac{1}{2}$ million persons in England at the beginning of the fourteenth century.

It was for a long time believed that expansion continued until it received a rude shock with the Black Death. More recently it has been argued that the turn of the century was, in fact, the peak of the expansion, that population was already declining in the first decades of the fourteenth century, and that the Black Death delivered a further blow to an economy and a population already on the decline. The reason for the decline, according to this view, was basically the simple one of marginal lands becoming more marginal, of yielding too little to support growing families, of stabilization or retrenchment both in colonizing and in size of family. Add to this the bad seasons of the second decade of the fourteenth century and the mortality of livestock, particularly among the valuable sheep of the south of England, and there is ample reason for a declining population. Evidence of the decline, runs the argument, is given by a continual rise in agricultural wage-rates, while other prices fell or remained steady, accompanied by a fall in agricultural output and a shrinkage of the area under cultivation.[1]

The retort to this line of reasoning has been that perhaps the amount of labour available for agricultural work declined because it was going to the towns, and that what is seen is a redistribution of labour not necessarily associated with an overall reduction of population. This view would regard the population as no longer expanding but fairly stable.[2] An intermediate view is indicated by an attempt to use modern demographic techniques on the few figures which are known for the period, such as the age of men making testaments or mentioned in Inquisitiones Post Mortem. This has produced some figures for expectation of life and size of family which indicate a declining rate of population growth, though not an overall decline.[3]

The most populous part of the country was the area of lowland south-east of a line from York to Exeter, though even here Surrey, Sussex and Hampshire were thinly peopled; Norfolk, Lincolnshire and parts of the Midlands had the highest population densities. London, capital city, biggest port, and largest town, had a population of some 35 000 towards the end of the fourteenth century. York, with a population of only 10 800, was the second city in size. Bristol, the second port, came next in size with a population of 9 500. Plymouth and Coventry each had some 7 000 inhabitants; Norwich, with a population of about 6 000, had still not made up the numbers lost in the Black Death.[4] Of the older centres of cloth-production—Stamford, Leicester, Lincoln, Beverley and York—York was the only town to maintain its size.

It is no easier to describe Britain topographically than to estimate her population. The medieval chronicler had, it seems, little interest in his physical surroundings. There was a monk of St Werburgh's, Chester, who wrote a world history in Latin in the first half of the fourteenth century, prefaced by a geographical survey which included Britain.[5] Like all his contemporaries, Higden is more concerned with the remarkable and the miraculous than with the ordinary. But the translation made towards the end of the century by a Cornish monk, John Trevisa, under the title *Descrypcion of Englonde* speakes of 'many faire wodes and grete with wel many bestes tame and wylde', of a land 'noble, copious, and riche of nobil welles and of nobil ryveres with plente of fische', of salt wells and hot wells which the inhabitants diverted into baths for men and women, of sheep 'that bereth good wolle', of 'many citees and townes, faire and noble and riche', of fine roads that crossed the country. This description may be supplemented by that of a Byzantine Emperor who visited the country in 1400 and found it destitute of vines, not abounding in fruit trees yet fertile in wheat and barley, in honey and wool. It may be concluded more specifically from manorial evidence and other records that central England was a land of open-field communities in the pattern of nucleated villages; that round the settlements spread the open, arable fields, the meadowland, the commonable waste, the fringes of the forest and scrubland that had been partly tamed, while beyond stretched the dense forests and untouched heath that were the area's natural covering. To the east, round the coasts of Norfolk, ran the Fenland, some of it reclaimed from the sea for profitable farming, much of it still unclaimed or slipping back beneath the waters. In Shropshire, Lincolnshire, Yorkshire, on the Cotswolds and other downland rolled the great pasture farms that provided grazing for the sheep whose fleece was already famous. In the far north, in Wales and in remote Cornwall, moors and uplands provided a tough living for a handful of farmers grazing a few animals and tending small crofts round their homesteads. In Devon the moors were bleak, but there were many little farms in the softer areas providing both pasture and arable. Of the impenetrable mountains of Scotland and Wales little was known.

Part of the forest and waste comprised the Royal Forests, preserved for hunting by the Norman kings of England and their successors—the New Forest ('new' in the Conqueror's time), Savernake, Arden, Sherwood, Wychwood, the forests of Essex (of which Epping Forest is the remnant), and many more. A Royal Forest did not mean an area of forest land without habitation, nor an area consisting only of trees, but included within its boundaries villages and clearings, scattered hamlets and open scrub or common land. Part of the outcry against these royal hunting preserves was the fact that all within their bounds were subject to forest law. This was not merely a matter of the king's pleasure against his subjects'. It deprived them of appurtenances which were of the greatest importance to a community living on the edge of subsistence. The resentment over afforestation was deep and long-lasting, in spite of actual disafforestation and various modifications in forest law which were made over the centuries for political or economic reasons. There were, for example, the privileges known as 'rights of warren' which had been granted for the killing of rabbits and small animals within the forests in return for a money rent. Though the benefits thus obtained accrued more to the king's feudatories than to small peasants, it is possible that some advantage rubbed off on to the poor man. By the middle of the fourteenth century, although much land was still under forest law—such as the forest of Rossendale in Lancashire, large parts of Essex including Epping forest, parts of the Midlands, of North Yorkshire, of the Welsh borderlands—the modifications had been sufficient to blunt the edge of resentment.

Rivers at the end of the Middle Ages were of great importance for irrigation, for driving the mill-wheel, for their fish, for the wild fowl that nested on their banks, as ways of communication, for the transport of heavy goods, for trade in general. Many travellers used the boats that plied the rivers, and sometimes took to the rougher coastal waters to reach some port less accessible by road. By Thames from London to Gravesend, and south round the coast and up the Medway, overland to the Stour and so on to Canterbury and the Kentish towns was a much-used route; the journey from Boston to York could be made in four days by using the ancient Foss Dyke; the coastal voyage from London to Newcastle or some intermediate town was often easier than travel by land; journeys across the Bristol Channel and round the Somerset or Welsh coasts were quicker than land travel. Generally speaking, however, there was less to attract the traveller on the waterways than on the roads; risks of robbery or ambush were less but natural dangers were greater, sea-sickness was a real hazard in the flimsy craft in use round the coasts, and there was less opportunity for the convivial comradeship of the road and the merrymaking of the inn at night.

It was for the transport of goods that the waterways were most popular, and by the end of the Middle Ages there was much general trade coastwise and by river. London brought corn and flour on a thirty-day journey by sea from the West Riding of Yorkshire in 1351. Newcastle coal, salt and salmon went to the Humber towns, to East Anglia and to London. East Anglia supplied grain round the English coast; Scotland sent fish to the South; Yarmouth sent herrings all round the coast and up the inland waterways. London distributed luxury imports, such as wine, coastwise and up the Thames. Bristol collected exports from Bath, from the Avon towns and the towns of the Bristol Channel and Welsh coast, and distributed her imports in return. Southampton was similarly the pivot of the South. Distribution centres also grew at important river junctions and where road and river transport met, an inland town which commanded good river communications being frequently referred to as a port. Lynn was even made a staple port (or official port of exchange) in 1373 because of her position linking her by river to the various towns of the Midlands and eastern counties, to which wool and other goods were regularly conveyed by water. Many other towns, like Cambridge and Oxford and York, owed much of their importance to their river communications.

Water was particularly important for the transport of heavy building materials. Small loads might be carried by pack-horses or wagon over short distances, but the heavier loads, and those brought from farther away, were almost invariably carried by water wherever this was available. While coastal transport was provided by a variety of craft under sail, on the rivers barges were drawn by teams of horses, sometimes of oxen, whose progress depended upon the condition of the towpath as well as the weight of the cargo. Not only was it possible to transport heavier loads by water than by land—the weight drawn by a comparable team of animals being greater by barge than by wagon or cart—but it was cheaper: a horse drawing a barge could move twelve times as much freight as a pack-horse at less than half the cost. Kentish stone came from the Medway and up the Thames to the Tower of London, to Westminster and to Windsor. Stone was carried from Northamptonshire along the rivers Welland and Nene and by Fens waterways to the Fenland Abbeys. Stone for York Minster came down the rivers Wharfe and Aire and Ouse from the inland quarries. Oaks from Sherwood Forest went by the river Trent to Norfolk for house-building. Iron was carried down the river Severn from the iron-mines of the Forest of Dean. There were exceptions, and when no water was available recourse was necessarily had to the roads. Richard, Lord Scrope, in building Bolton Castle in 1378 brought timber from Engleby, in Cumberland, by relays of oxen placed along the route. In the Pennine lead region the local pit-ponies were adept at treading the difficult ways. In almost every lead-mining field of the Pennines ore was carried from the mines to the smelt mills by these pack-animals, and often from the mills to the nearest town, whence they brought back timber and other supplies to the mines. They could carry two to three hundredweight each. In Derbyshire ponies carried lead from the mills to the town of Bawtry, on the river Idle, where it was put on ship for Hull, thus making economic use of both forms of transport.[6]

Yet, in spite of the importance of river and coastal transport, there was great difficulty in keeping rivers navigable and harbours open. On rivers there were the natural obstacles of rapids, changing levels, weed and mud, as well as the effects of gale and storm in blowing down trees and bridges or sweeping the waters to dangerous levels. River-banks were neglected, towpaths overgrown and deep in mud. In addition, there were rival users and the catching of fish frequently interfered with transport. In particular, the use of kiddles or weirs for trapping fish were a cause of great anxiety. Magna Carta had, indeed, contained a clause that all kiddles be removed from all rivers. But vested interests were strong, and complaints continued. Water-mills, again, created hazards for shipping, and were the subject of repeated objection; or bridges might be constructed in such a way that they interfered with navigation—like the bridge at Rochester, which hindered the passage of the barge carrying stone to Westminster. Nor was this all. Individual owners claimed toll for the use of the river, toll for the use of the towpath, and toll for the use of the locks which accommodated the various levels. Fish weirs were a danger to vessels at river-mouths and on sea-coasts, the tin-workers of Cornwall constantly blocked harbours with the waste of their working, while silt accumulated and uncleared wrecks were perilous to shipping. Canals as a supplement to water transport were not even considered until the beginning of the eighteenth century.

While there remained, in spite of all disadvantages, a balance in favour of sending heavy goods by water, the chief means of communication was by the roads—there was, indeed, in many

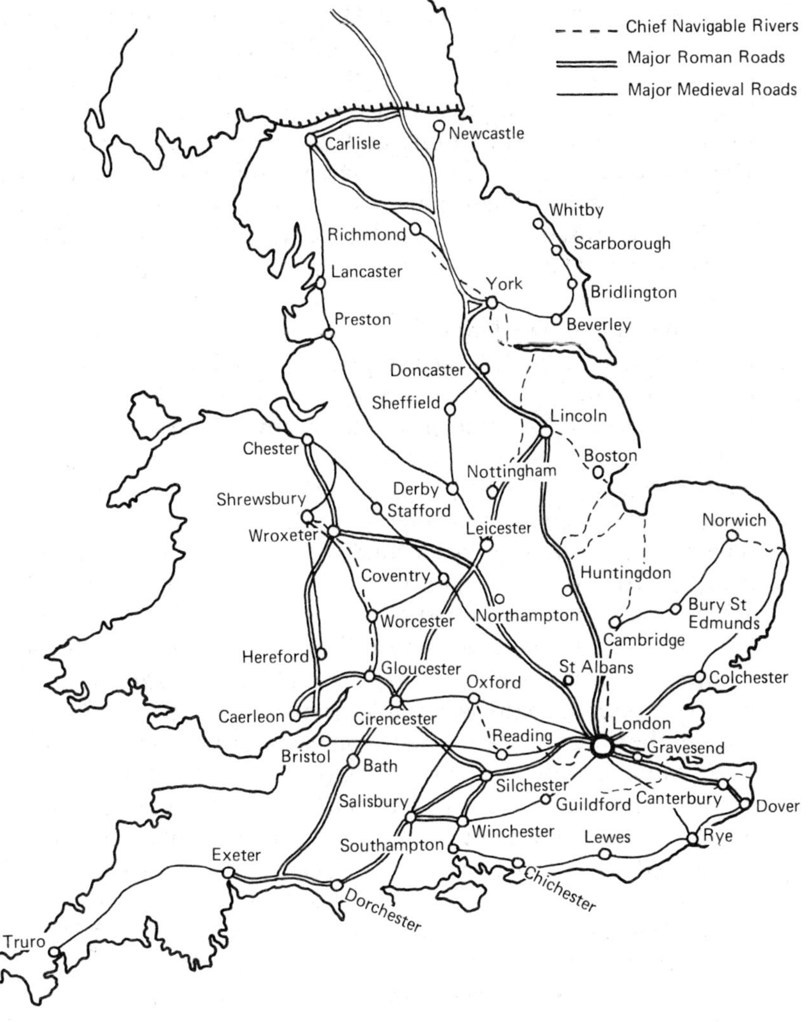

Fig. 1 Communications in the Late Middle Ages

cases no alternative—and the skeletal system of the Romans still remained in the straight roads radiating from London; but the Roman roads were primarily concerned with keeping London in touch with the outposts of the province—with York and Colchester and Lincoln—and ran straight to their objective. In the Middle Ages the need for transport between manor and manor, between manor and town, and between small towns brought also into existence many secondary roads, not made with solid foundations and cambered surface like the Roman roads, but for the most part simply developing along well-worn tracks. These newer ways, together with the old roads, constituted a network of highways and subsidiary ways which was still substantially the same in the seventeenth century.

At the time of the Black Death the roads were in bad condition, and it is likely that the plague contributed, in loss of morale and in loss of manpower, to a further slackening of maintenance. Their upkeep rested upon no central authority, but generally devolved upon the various landlords through whose property the road ran. Actual maintenance was done by a variety of local inhabitants who were bound by law to give six days of unpaid labour a year for the purpose. It is hardly surprising that, unsupervised and probably resentful, their work for the most part amounted to no more—and probably even less—than clearing verges and filling up the holes which the medieval citizen assumed it was his right to dig. No general law for the repair of roads was made until the sixteenth century, though the king, or a busy town, sometimes issued instructions concerning the repair or upkeep of stretches of road that were of special importance. Edward I, to help the passage of equipment for his Welsh wars, issued instructions for the enlargement of roads and passes into Wales and Derbyshire. Edward III in 1353 gave orders for the paving of the highroad from Temple Bar to Westminster, which was 'so full of holes and bogs' that it was dangerous for men and for carts. Each landowner on each side of the road was to make up a footway of seven feet and the middle of the road was to be paved, the expense being covered by a tax on all merchandise going to the staple at Westminster. This was a special road; paving was not generally used. In 1356 the City of London laid a road-repair tax on all carts and horses bringing goods to the town. In a special position were the Royal Ways, roads which had come to be of special importance for trade, or defence, or the king's pleasure. On these roads the King's Peace ran and malefactors could be brought to instant justice. No encroachment was allowed on the king's highway, any offender being bound to make immediate restitution as well as suffering punishment. But even these roads were not in good condition, and could be impassable in winter.

Yet miraculously the roads managed to accommodate a considerable traffic of great variety. The Norman kings remained in close touch with Northern France, and this necessitated much traffic on the roads to the south-coast ports. On roads all over the country Justices of the Shire and Hundred Courts proceeded on their business. The paraphernalia of the king's peripatetic court passed along the roads. Edward I, in the twenty-eighth year of his reign, changed his place of residence seventy-five times—about three times each fortnight—and feudal lords, like the king, moved from manor to manor with their retinue. As government and justice and finance became increasingly centred upon Westminster the flow of travellers to the capital increased. Supplies for the Hundred Years' War in France, for the Welsh wars and for the Wars of the Roses in England—victuals, tents and equipment, munitions, arms, accoutrements of all kinds—were carried over the roads.

Wool and woollen cloth, England's biggest exports, were taken to the ports over her roads; Crusaders off to the Holy Land began their journeys by riding over English roads to the ports. Itinerant masons, builders of the churches and the great cathedrals, were also there, the heavy materials of their craft occasionally going with them though more often being conveyed by water. Mendicant friars and other holy men begged their way through village after village; wandering priests made their way from church to church or from market-place to market-place. Seneschals or stewards executing their duties between manor and manor were regular users of the roads; poor villeins, carrying for their lord as part of their customary service, if they enjoyed the excursion into the world beyond the manor, regretted all the same the hours lost from their fields. Occasionally they met a fellow-villein on the run from manor to town in an effort to win his freedom. Pilgrims, like those of the *Canterbury Tales*, sought the shrines of their saints; buyers and sellers rode to the fairs, tinkers mended pots and pans by the roadside, there was a brisk, if surreptitious, trade in rabbit-skins and rabbits, its origin unquestioned; pedlars peddled their wares while wandering from town to town, as described officially in the early sixteenth century, selling 'pynnes, poyntes, laces, gloves, knyves, glasses, tapes'. Itinerant quacks and doctors proffered their cures, in spite of the law's severity against them. Tumblers, acrobats, musicians and players, bear-baiters and others typical of medieval England wandered along her roads to the towns, fairs, villages and manor houses where they would find hospitality and an audience. It was in the sixteenth century that John Heywood described the four P's who met together on the road, but it could have happened much earlier: a palmer, a pardoner, a pothecary, and a pedlar.

Many ordinary people travelled on foot; a traveller of moderate means would be likely to go by horseback, managing, perhaps, twenty miles a day. Pilgrims, like Chaucer's, took a more comfortable amble. Important journeys were serviced by relays of horses along the route, king's messengers provided for in this way achieving as much as forty or fifty miles a day. Carriages were a rarity, being used generally for some great personage, and were very expensive: one for the sister of Edward III cost £1 000—as much as a herd of 1 600 oxen. Naturally, such vehicles were prized and handed down from generation to generation. Lighter goods were carried by pack-horse in panniers slung across the horse's saddle. More bulky goods went by cart or wagon, drawn, perhaps, by one poor beast; but generally two or more oxen or horses toiled at the heavy burden. That carts, particularly, were in much demand is clear from contemporary accounts of carts being made, repaired, purchased, or even hired, and some of the treatises on husbandry give details of cart-making on the manor. Wagons were less often to be met with than carts, the four-wheeled vehicle being more clumsy, less easy to manoeuvre on difficult roads and more likely to be stuck on bad stretches than the two-wheeled cart. Any of these vehicles might be hindered by droves of geese, flocks of sheep, herds of cattle or by other animals being conveyed from one manor to another or between manor and market. But all were at the mercy of the weather, and even Members of Parliament failed to get to their destination; the Parliament of 1339, for example, was constrained to postpone its opening 'because the prelates, earls, barons, and other lords and knights of the shires, citizens and burgesses of cities and boroughs were so troubled by the bad weather that they could not arrive that day'.

The construction and repair of bridges and causeways devolved, like the upkeep of the roads, upon the landlord or the community concerned, but the responsibility was generally taken more seriously. Abbeys and monasteries, for example, had a particular interest in building and maintaining bridges, since their houses were frequently built by streams and rivers and depended for communications upon a crossing. The Bishop of Durham was even prepared to remit forty days of penance for help in building a causeway. The king had a particular concern with the upkeep of bridges, apart from trade and war, and his own method of achieving it, as when Henry III in 1234 directed all bridges on the Avon, Test, and Itchen to be repaired so that he might freely pass for his hunting. The interest of ordinary travellers is reflected in the small chapel they frequently built upon the bridge, like that dedicated to St Catherine on Bow Bridge, near London, and that on London Bridge dedicated to St Thomas of Canterbury.

Natural dangers were not the only ones to which the traveller was liable. Thieves and robbers lurked in ditch and coppice; in the forests swarmed the outlaws proper. Not all were Robin Hoods to mete out courteous treatment to the stranger. The solitary traveller was himself regarded with suspicion, and could be taken and held in custody until he could show his *bona fides*. Little travel was done after dark, the roads were too bad, the danger of apprehension as a stranger or molestation by bandits was too great. So the company of the road would gather at an inn or rest-house, generally on the outskirts of a town. Many of the travellers whom Langland saw in his 'fielde full of folke' were here: harmless minstrels, making an honest living by their music; babblers and vulgar jesters who invented fantastic tales about themselves; tramps and beggars hastening on their rounds, living by their wits and, according to Langland, with their bellies and packs crammed full of bread; pilgrims and palmers banding together, full of clever talk; hermits, whom Langland regarded as lazy, pretending to religion for the sake of an easy life; the four Orders of friars, a pardoner, barons, burgesses and peasants; bakers, brewers and butchers; linen-weavers and tailors, tinkers and toll-collectors, masons and miners and many other tradesfolk. Then the minstrels would come into their own, entertaining the company with pipe and song, the minstrels' galleries at many inns and manor-houses indicating that they were regular performers, specially catered for; or the tumblers and jugglers would practise the act they were to perform at the fair; or the ballad-monger, with his stock-in-trade of tale and romance, would entertain the company, bringing news and homely literature that the people could understand. Then, after the eating and drinking and entertainment, plans would be made for banding together the next day, both for companionship and to avoid the many hazards of the road.

CHAPTER III

The Manor and the Open Fields

Within the bounds set by nature, the artificial framework of man's life in England was nearly everywhere, at the time of the Black Death, the organization known as the manor. The term had a political, an economic and a legal connotation. Politically it represented the feudal hierarchy wherein all land belonged to the king and was farmed out to others in return for tribute; it governed the economic life of all who dwelt on the manor by an elaborate system of rights and obligations, all of which, reinforced by the 'custom of the manor', were interpreted in manor courts in which the lord of the manor had supreme authority. The king dealt in manors as other people dealt in commodities, except that instead of selling them he 'granted' them, his grant embodying a form of rent for their use. To his great fighting barons after the Conquest William had granted tracts of land consisting of many manors, and he had placated some native English on similar terms. Apart from what he kept himself, a large part of the country had been in this way parcelled out. But some regions still remained outside manorial organization. There were the villages of old Norse settlement in the north-east and in East Anglia which maintained their independence after the Conquest; districts remote from the centre of government or difficult of access where the king's writ did not run; little settlements too small for anyone but themselves to trouble about. The great untamed forest, scrub, marsh and waste that covered the rest of the country might, or might not, be within the organization of a manor.

A manor might be small or large, part of a big holding of many manors or held on its own; it might be a small farm supporting a single household or it could be the centre of many thousands of acres of land supporting several hundred people. It might be in the king's possession or it might be held by a simple knight many removes from the royal bequest. It could be held by a great ecclesiastical house or be part of the holding of a powerful baron. It could comprise several villages, or one only, or its bounds might bisect a centre of population. A town, or part of a town, might be within its borders. A town, or even a village, might be divided between more than one manor. It could represent the political and jurisdictional aspects of the manor without being an organized economic unit; it could be merely a centre for receiving the tribute of scattered homesteads without further interest or control. According to its natural features, it would produce crops or graze sheep, support many people or few, be richer or poorer. Geography and history jointly determined the relation of its inhabitants to the lord and to the king, their obligations, their rights, their status.

Within the variety it is possible to pick out certain strongly marked areas where the way of life formed a distinct pattern. Such were the plains of the Midlands. Here, on the fertile arable land of central England, cultivation was carried out on great fields, often several hundred acres in extent. No hedge, wall or fence broke their continuity, but where an edge abutted on a road or any area from which animals might stray it was fenced between seed-time and harvest by means of wooden stakes driven into the ground a few feet apart and interlaced with the branches of trees. The absence of enclosure within them gave rise to the name 'open fields'. Characteristic of the open fields were the high ridge and furrow, formed by centuries of ploughing on the same furrow lines, and the pattern of strips and 'lands' into which they were divided. These were immediately apparent after the ploughing or when the crops were low on the ground; but when the harvest was ready the open field was an undulating sea of waving corn, the surface rising and falling with the ridge and furrow of the earth beneath, with little perceptible break, save possibly where some access way caught the eye with a darkening of the colour.

In some parts of the country strip farming was associated with the division of land between heirs or the apportionment of land taken in from the waste, and it was probably carried on as an individual enterprise. The strips of the open fields of the Midlands, however, were subject to a common pattern of farming associated with a common way of life which governed the activities of all the inhabitants, from the lord of the manor to the poorest serf. The origins, the extent, the precise workings of common-field farming are being reappraised. Like all living organisms, the system was never static, and there was never a copy-book manor or open-field village that fitted all the evidence. Moreover, the evidence of common-field farming that comes from manor records like account rolls and proceedings of the manor court, from treatises on husbandry, legal pronouncements or literary reference is evidence of the working of the system in its maturity, and throws but uncertain light upon its origins and first form. For these, in the Midlands at least, the most likely explanation is based upon the plough and the need to apportion land between the settlers concerned.[1]

Ploughing with the fixed mouldboard plough in use over most of the Midlands was not an operation which continued up and down a field from edge to edge until the whole area was finished. The action of the mouldboard plough cut a great slice of earth along the line of the ploughing, lifted it, and laid it to the right of the plough. This, continued up and down a field, would simply lay a series of furrow slices, first one way and then the other, over unploughed earth. So the ploughman worked instead on a seemingly complicated but basically simple and intelligent pattern. First he 'opened a top'. He ploughed a long, straight furrow, as long as his team would go without resting or until some obstacle was reached, and as he proceeded a furrow slice would be laid to the right (Fig. 2*a*(i)). Returning in the same track, the furrow slice, again to the right, would this time be lying away from the first (Fig. 2*a*(ii)). He then proceeded to form a ridge by returning along the outer edge of the second furrow slice, so throwing it inwards (Fig. 2*a*(iii)); turning and continuing along the furrow edge of the first furrow slice, he likewise turned this inwards so that the ridge was formed (Fig. 2*a*(iv)). The ploughman then ploughed round this ridge, throwing the furrow-slices on each side in towards the ridge (Figs 2*a*(v–viii)). The width of each 'land' was limited by reason of natural features or the requirements of drainage, and also by the fact that the ploughman did not wish his animals to walk too far before beginning each new furrow. When one of these 'lands' was finished the ploughman would leave a space and proceed to the next once more starting with the four long furrows that first opened a top and then formed the ridge. As the furrow slices would again be turned inwards towards the new ridge, it is clear that there would be a well-marked boundary between two 'lands', both in the small space left unploughed between them and particularly in the way the furrow slices of adjacent 'lands' turned away from each other. The dividing line would be less clearly marked when the crops were high and the harvest about to be reaped.

A good average length for the medieval furrow was 220 yards, which came to be referred to as the furlong—the *furrow long*—but topography frequently caused it to be shorter, occasionally longer, than this. Convenience generally dictated the width of the 'land' as 22 yards, eleven on each side of the original furrow. Although, again, there could be variation the standard area might be taken as 220 yards by 22 yards—an acre. This also coincided roughly with the area which could be ploughed in a day's ploughing or in a long morning's work, for the animals were taken to pasture in the afternoon. A modern German word for acre, *Morgen* (actually well under an acre), meaning literally morning, implies this. But it is likely that an acre represented a very good morning's work indeed, and on good soil, and that in many fields an area corresponding to the German *Morgen* rather than the English acre was the result of a morning's work. Topographical considerations, too, affected the area of the 'land', and in practice there were many of half an acre or even less. An occasional variant of the straight furrow was the curved furrow, snaking over the field like a reversed letter S. This entailed no difference in the method of ploughing, but was quite likely easier in some situations. It was, for example, simpler to take the turn at the end of a field with a distinct boundary by approaching at an angle; it also saved on headland space, a big plough requiring a much larger area in which to turn if it approached on the straight than if it came in at an angle.

This, then, was the 'land', the high ridge with the furrows falling away on either side of it; the ridge providing the all-important drainage while the earth itself was well turned. A series of parallel 'lands', roughly equal in size, was continued until some configuration of the land, generally concerned with the vital question of drainage, was considerable enough to cause the plough team to start on a completely new set of 'lands'

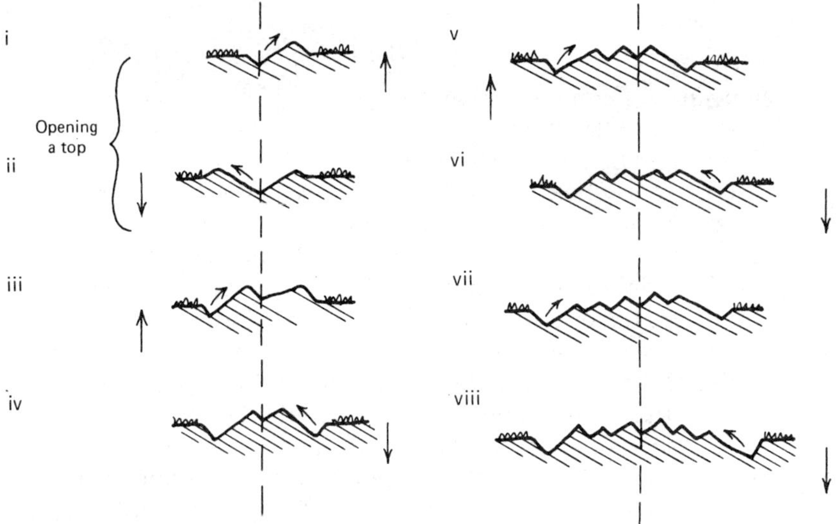

Fig. 2a Ploughing a Ridge (after Orwin)

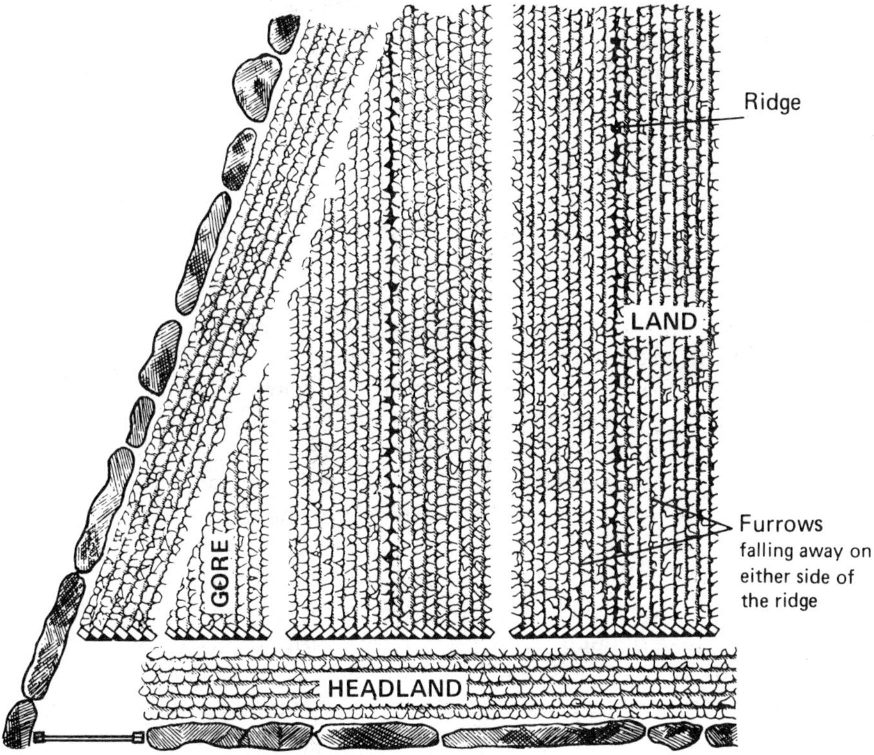

Fig. 2b Open-field ploughing, showing lands, headlands and gore (after Orwin)

lying in a different direction and possibly of different size. Each group of parallel 'lands' was generally called a shot or a flat, but there might be other local names.

When the whole field was worked over into shots there was always some small area unploughed. A slanting edge to the field, for example, could leave a triangular portion that fitted no 'land', and the edges of the field where the plough turned at the top of the furrows remained unploughed. Land was too precious to waste, and so the open-field farmer ploughed straight round the edges of his fields, like hemming a handkerchief (except that he was bound to leave some access space) with a series of headlands. He also ploughed up the odd three-cornered piece by the field's edge into what he termed a gore. The whole effect was of a patchwork, each patch being represented by a shot patterned by the distinctive rise and fall of the 'lands' of which it was composed, and having, like many a patchwork quilt, odd corners filled with odd-shaped pieces, the whole being bordered by the straight lines of the headlands. But, even with the greatest care, some 5 per cent of the land was unploughed in awkward corners, stony or rocky patches, wet bottoms and the access ways which were necessary to allow the passage of farmers and their implements from one part of the field to another. Little of it was wasted, however, since the grass that was allowed to grow on the uncultivated patches served as cattle feed after the harvest.[2]

Two, three or four—most commonly three—of these big fields lay around the open-field village, one of them lying fallow each year. So, amid the cultivation, a portion of the land might always be seen standing out bare and richly brown. This was not wasteful. In the virtual absence of manure, of clover and other cleansing crops, a period of rest or fallow was essential to allow the land to repair naturally what the harvests of two or three seasons had taken from it. Lime was sometimes used to break down heavy clays or to destroy moss, but was too difficult to obtain and too expensive to be generally employed. Marl was known, but, again, its price limited its use. Sea-sand was used near the coast, and sand was sometimes dug on the waste to mix with heavy soils; soot was a good fertilizer but its limited quantity made it useful for the croft rather than the open field. Even street and household refuse was brought in to attempt to replace the goodness in the soil. But more effective than anything else was animal manure. The big fields and the meadowland received some after the harvest when they were open to grazing animals, but at other times the lord could claim that animals be folded within his pens or on his land for the purpose of the nourishment they gave his crops; one of the duties of his tenants was the collection of manure from the manor yard for the lord's fields. The manure produced on commons and waste was jealously taken up by all who could do so, but frequently, again, it was the lord who claimed it as his right.

The fields bore different crops within the range of those known to the open-field farmer, changing each year and taking their turn with the fallow. A three-year rotation of crops was normal. One field would be sown in the autumn with crops like wheat or rye (the bread crops) that require a long, slow, growing season, which would be reaped in August and left in stubble; another would be sown in February or March with quick-maturing crops like barley (the drink crop) or with oats, spring beans, peas or vetches—perhaps with some of each—and also be reaped in August. Thus, subject to the weather, the village was provided with the varied harvest necessary to its simple standard of life. If there were only two fields one would generally lie fallow and the other be divided between the spring and autumn crops, or a similar arrangement would be made to accord with the number of fields under the plough.

It was normally rye rather than wheat that provided the autumn sowing in the big field. Rye is hardier, it grows on poor soils, it makes tough straw. So it was rye bread rather than wheaten that formed the staple diet of the villager. Rye bread keeps moister than wheaten, and labourers were said to like it because it 'abode longer in the stomach and was not so soon digested with their labour'.[3] Sometimes a mixture of wheat and rye formed the popular 'maslin'. Barley was the source of malt for brewing the ale which was the universal drink of the Middle Ages.

The tools and implements used by the open-field farmer were simple—effective on easy soils, entailing much hard labour on difficult ground or on land newly assarted, or broken in. The big, heavy wooden plough with its iron coulter (cutting edge) and iron mouldboard was by far the most expensive, and was drawn by as many as eight oxen or horses. Oxen were preferred to horses for draught. The wide, heavy shoulders shown in contemporary pictures indicate strength and staying power, and they were steadier, although sometimes slower, than the horses, who were inclined to pull erratically and jerk and even break the harness. They did not require to be shod, and, moreover, there was an expression which said that horse dead was fit for nothing but its hide, but that ox dead would feed a family. After the ploughing the larger clods might be broken up with wooden mallets or hammers, and then came the harrowing, the further breaking up of the clods. The harrow might be simply a piece of hawthorn-tree, its prickles made to dig into the earth by the weight of logs on its upper side. More commonly it was a wooden frame with a lattice of sharp teeth made from ash or willow hardened by fire which could be attached to an animal by a rein or dragged over the earth by the human hand. Beans would sometimes be dibbled with the help of a wooden dibble, but most seed was sown broadcast. Rakes were improvised from bush or tree, sometimes crudely constructed of wood with teeth shaped from fire-hardened ash or willow; hoes and forks were similarly made. Flails for threshing were simply holly or thorn fastened with thongs to staves; shovels and spades were made of wood. The important scythe for cutting the ripened crops was made of iron attached to a wooden handle; axe and billhook similarly had striking and lopping blades made of iron.

Like a thread running through the open fields, the village street supported on either side the little houses or crude huts of the men and women who worked the land and attended to the various tasks of the village. Another thread through the patchwork was frequently the stream with its mill. Meadowland, pond, manor-house and church were somewhere near these central threads of village life. Occasionally the pattern differed. Houses surrounded a village green and the central motif became not a line but a rectangle of green grass, perhaps with its pond. In either case the dwellings were compactly together, away from the fields, a situation which gave protection in case of danger. The open- or common-field village (if it is named after its husbandry) or nucleated village (if reference is made to its compact design) was generally co-extensive with the manor, embracing the whole of the inhabited area and any of the land over which any of the inhabitants had rights. The size of a village could vary from fifty to perhaps five hundred people, and the big open fields varied accordingly, generally being several hundred acres in extent. It is possible that open-field and common farming such as this was practised in any fertile arable area, with variations based upon geographical and practical considerations. The full extent of the system and its variants must wait upon the results of detailed and laborious research, but there is little doubt that central England, including Berkshire and Oxfordshire, Warwickshire and Northamptonshire, Middlesex and Buckinghamshire, Leicestershire and Nottinghamshire were all areas of open-field and common-field farming.[4] In Nottinghamshire, ten miles north of Newark, ten miles south of East Retford and four miles to the west of the river Trent lies Laxton, a common-field village whose open fields and strip farming survived many centuries of change, to be preserved at last by the Ministry of Agriculture, which in 1952 acquired the manor of Laxton and continues still the old farming system based upon the open fields as a living example of a once common way of life. Their reconstruction was made easier by the existence of a detailed survey and map of the manor of Laxton which was made in 1635.[5]

The inhabitants of the open-field village farmed communally in the sense that the fields were treated as one unit, subject to the same rotation, each ploughed as one piece, sown with one crop, harvested at the same time, the larger and more expensive implements shared between either the whole village or several families. Yet within this communal system each family worked its own share of the fields, and harrowing and sowing, weeding, manuring and fencing, in most cases reaping, were family responsibilities. A family holding was not held compactly in one piece but in strips scattered over the big fields, so that a shot consisted of many strips belonging to different people. It sometimes happened that 'land' and strip coincided in size, approximating to the standard acre, but two or even more smaller 'lands' might make up a strip. How the original apportionment was made is matter for speculation—the system was certainly ancient by the time of the Black Death. But basically the reason for strip farming and for the division of the strips between the big fields was undoubtedly practical. In the first place, it was simply a method of sharing out the land. Using the plough and draught animals that were the joint property of a group, a team of villagers would plough as much as they could in one day, allot this to one member of the team and the following day proceed to more ploughing and another allotment. There was probably also some reference to size of strip, as well as time spent, since a day's ploughing on difficult ground would yield far less than on easy ground. The members of the ploughing team might have been given equal portions of land in compact areas rather than in strips, but this would have had the disadvantage of delaying the farming of the last man to receive his share, or perhaps allotting all the good, or all the bad or all the awkward land to one family, of alloting one person his land in fine weather, another at a rainy time when sowing was difficult. All these factors were of vital importance where the soil varied, drainage was dependent largely upon the slope of the land, and farm buildings and farm implements were at the village, which could be a considerable distance from the farthest point of a 500-acre field. Division between the different fields ensured that each family had its share of each crop and took its turn with the fallow.[6]

The provision of access ways to the various parts of the big fields required some ingenuity. They were difficult to maintain, easily confused with the strips themselves, liable to be brought into cultivation whether by accident or design, and cultivators were frequently at a loss to gain access to their own land without trampling other people's. That there was much trouble in this respect is clear from repeated cases in the manor court and from some interesting by-laws like the one made at Halton, in Buckinghamshire, in 1329: 'No-one shall make paths to his neighbour's damage by walking or by driving [his beasts] or by carrying grain, be it his own or another's, whether by night or any other time'.[7] The open fields were separated from each other by earthern banks or balks. But it is unlikely that in the fields themselves anything more served as marker between the strips than the slope of their furrows and the minimal space left by the plough as it proceeded from one 'land' to another. To have provided a balk would have been an unwonted encouragement to weeds, and at variance with the way the open-field farmer nursed each yard of precious land for cultivation. Moreover, if balks were common it is unlikely that so many cases of confused boundaries would have come before the manor court. Nor would it have made sense of the repeated castigation of the 'false husbandmen who falsely plough away men's lands, and take and plough away a furrow of land through and through'[8] or that Langland should have pilloried in *Piers Plowman* the dishonest peasant:

> If I went to the plough I pinched so narrowly that I would steal a foot of land or a furrow, or gnaw the half-acre of my neighbour; and if I reaped, I would over-reap, or gave counsel to them that reaped to seize for me with their sickles that which I never sowed.

With land so intermingled it was essential that certain rules be observed by each for the good of all. There was the obligation, for example, to fence between seed-time and harvest the end of each strip that abutted on a common way so that straying animals would not trample the crops; and to keep open access to the furthest point of the open fields; and to observe the regulations concerning the grazing of animals. Above all, it was necessary that the same rotation of crops should be adopted by all, the times of ploughing, sowing, reaping be agreed. No-one, not even the lord himself, could withstand the recognized unfolding of the agricultural year; and upon this core of common practice was built a series of rights, regulations, duties and obligations which constituted the custom of the manor.

At the apex of the organization stood the lord of the manor, who might be lay or ecclesiastical, a private person, some great lord, a large monastic house or even the king himself. He might own one manor or many, but, whoever he was, however many manors he held—unless he was the king—he held 'of' someone to whom he owed fealty and rent in service, kind or money. Like his tenants, he held strips in the open fields, and he also kept for himself an area round the manor-house, larger in extent but similar in kind to the gardens or crofts which lay around the villagers' dwellings. His total holding, known as the demesne, was generally about one-third of the whole of the cultivated area. As the lord held of a higher lord, so the villagers, according to their degree, held their land of him in return for rent in some form, the whole system of landholding thus being woven together on a legal, easily ascertainable basis in which each knew his rights and his duties and his relationship with everyone else. Occasionally a few freemen lived on the manor. Their land was not held in the open fields but may have been acquired through assart from the waste at some earlier time in return for a small lump sum or annual rent. Though free of servile dues, they were by custom expected to give their labour to the lord of the manor at busy times like harvest, to lend him animals, or even a plough, according to their ability. Their land was frequently difficult, on the margin of cultivation, and carried with it none of the rights that went with the open-field holdings. In practice the freemen, therefore, might be less well off than the villeins below them in the village hierarchy. These villeins formed the bulk of the village population.

The usual full villein holding was thirty strips in the open fields. Known collectively as 'husbandland', a 'living', a 'yardland' (from the measuring-rod or yard), or 'virgate' (from the Latin word for measuring-rod), it would be roughly thirty acres in area. As the size of each strip varied with custom, the nature of the soil, the lie of the land, so a man's total acreage varied slightly. There were also on the manor less prosperous villeins who worked, perhaps, only half a yardland, known as a bovate, whose duties were correspondingly less, whose status was lower, but whose standard of living might be little different. For, with a smaller area of land to work, and fewer seigneurial duties to perform, they would be able to undertake for payment some other of the numerous tasks of the manor. The name of their holding—*bovate*—comes from the Latin word for ox, (*bos, bovis*) the roughly fifteen acres of the bovate being about as much as one ox could plough in a year. On this basis the villein would hold as much land as two oxen could plough in a year, and the assumption might be made that the villein was the owner of two oxen.

The animals of the medieval farmer were almost as important to him as his crops and fields. The oxen and horses went with him to the plough, and carried his burdens or drew his carts; the ox in his old age served as food. Sheep provided wool for the home spinning and weaving of cloth as well as a little meat, and the milk of the ewes. His cows gave him meat and milk. The hides of his animals had a dozen uses, from the harness of his plough team to the shoes on his feet. Their manure was as valuable as their flesh and their hides. They were all as carefully and as equitably provided for as the scant resources of medieval farming allowed. The meadowland was fenced off into separate lots, each open-field farmer taking his appropriate share of the valuable hay crop. After the harvest the right of common of shack allowed the animals to graze, and at the same time to manure the stubble of the open fields and the meadow. On the common land which lay beyond the open fields communal grazing was jealously regulated. Rights of common were carefully related to the holdings in the open fields, no stranger's animals were permitted to graze, and only 'commonable beasts'—oxen or horses used in actual cultivation and sheep whose manure was highly valued—were normally allowed there. Swine were allowed in strictly limited numbers in a carefully defined area. Fines were frequent in the manor court against villagers who had put out to pasture more animals than their share. When the meadow, the commonable waste and the arable fields were all open the animals were not ill fed. But they never had a chance of making much fat, and with winter bringing little beyond dry straw and tree loppings—for winter feed in the form of root crops was unknown—they were open to murrain in cattle and scab and rot in sheep.

Because of their poor condition, many animals were killed at Michaelmas, and their carcases were salted down to provide a somewhat unpalatable form of human food in the winter months. Fresh meat from such animals as died, or could be spared, was not particularly good at the best of times. Pig was the most tasty, for the pig had no carrying duties to wear him down, he was happy to eat the scavengings of the village and, on the whole, his food was as good as any animal got. The milk of cow and ewe and goat, some of it made into butter or cheese, was an important part of the diet of the open-field farmer; geese and poultry gave flesh and eggs; rabbits and other wild creatures often went home to the pot under the tunic of an enterprising villein or his son. Fish from pond, lake and stream sometimes taken as a right, often by poaching, were an important addition to the villager's diet. From the forest or waste he gathered wild fruit and nuts, he cut turf for fire, for byre, or for cottage wall or roof, he collected furze for firing, roofing or bedding. The cutting of wood from the forest was permitted but carefully regulated, a peasant often being allowed no more than he could 'by hook or by crook' knock off or pull down from the trees or bushes. Both villeins and half-yardlanders owned also small crofts round their dwellings, where roamed the chickens, the geese when they were not out with the goose-girl, the goat when not tethered away on the waste. Bees clustered into the hive, making from the blossom of apple, pear, quince and cherry the honey which was the only form of sweetening available to the poor[9] and which made the mead and metheglin[10] which, with ale and cider, were the chief drinks of the Middle Ages. Onions, mustard, cabbages, garlic, leeks were grown in the croft, together with peas and beans for the universal pottage and the herbs that flavoured many a stew of stringy or salted meat or went to the making of homely medicines.

Homespun undoubtedly provided part of the peasant's attire, and gloves and boots came from the skins of his animals. The pictures of ploughmen and other agricultural labourers in the Luttrell Psalter of the early fourteenth century show peasant men and women well clad, with good gauntlet gloves on their hands, and boots or clogs on their feet—except when, as was customary at the threshing, they worked barefoot with their breeches rolled up. The Luttrell Psalter is so precise in its illustrations of tools and implements that it might be expected to be accurate with attire also. On the other hand, nothing could exceed the pathos of the picture of the ploughman given in *Pierce the Ploughman's Creed*, written about the year 1394:

> And as I went by the way weeping for sorrow
> I saw a poor man by me on the plough hanging
> His coat was of a clout that cary[11] was called
> His hood was full of holes and his hair cut
> With his knobby shoes patched full thick
> His tongue peeped out as he the earth trod
> His hosen overhung his gaiters on every side
> All beslobbered in mire as he the plough followed.
> Two mittens so scanty made all of patches
> The fingers were worn and full of mud hung.
> This fellow wallowed in the muck almost to the ankle.
> Four heifers before him that weak had become
> You could count all their ribs so wretched they were.
> His wife walked by him with a long goad
> In a coat cut short cut full high
> Wrapped in a winnowing sheet to cover her from the weather
> Barefoot on the bare ice that the blood followed.
> And at the field end lay a little bowl
> And on it lay a little child wrapped in rags
> And two of two years old on another side
> And all they sang a song that was sad to hear
> They all cried a cry a note full of care.
> The poor man sighed sore and said 'Children be still'.

The open-field farmer held his strips and exercised his rights in return for certain defined labour services, for payments in kind, and sometimes for money rent, the labour services constituting normally the main part of his obligation. These varied from manor to manor but generally a villein was obliged to give to his lord 'week work' on two or three days of the week, not necessarily for the whole day; and 'boon work', which was work at times of special need, like harvest, when he and possibly his whole family would be summoned to the 'great bedrip[12] or the 'great precaria'.[13] If the need were great the lord would sometimes provide 'love meals' as an encouragement to extra work. Week work was not necessarily an enormous hardship, for only one member of the family need give it. More onerous was harvest work, which could denude a man's own land of labour at a critical time. Equally burdensome was the villein's obligation to provide a pair of oxen or a single beast to join with the lord's own team in ploughing the demesne. He might have to supply seed as well, and a richer villein be called upon to lend his plough. Tenants were also required to act as carriers for their lord, a service which involved providing horses and cart, and throws into relief the difficulty of conveyance and the degree to which it was prized. They had also to provide the lord with payments in kind—honey and ale, poultry at Christmas, eggs at Easter, grain at Martinmas.

But, apart from anything that might be called a rent, villein tenure was burdened with obligations that underlined its servile nature. The villein was subject to the arbitrary annual tax of tallage levied by, and for the benefit of, the lord. It was a tax on the unfree peasantry, and was one of the most hated marks of servitude: to be 'tallaged high and low' was the mark of the slave. Villeins were obliged to use, for a monopoly payment, the lord's mill for grinding their corn, the lord's brewery for brewing their ale; they could not sell animals without the lord's permission, because of the danger of reducing the common stock; nor sell more grain than the lord allowed. A villein could not sell, assign or part with all or any of his land without his lord's consent duly recorded in the manor court. On his death the lord claimed as heriot his best beast, and when the succession had been approved in the manor court an entry fine had to be paid by the new tenant. The villein could neither educate his son at home, send him away to be educated, set him to a craft, or enter him into the Church without the lord's consent because of the danger of depleting the labour supply. His daughter, sometimes even his son, could not marry without payment of a fine known as merchet—regarded as the most degrading of all payments, and as a mark of villein status. Fornication was punishable by the fine of 'leyrwite'. Above all, the villein could not leave his land nor live away from the manor without his lord's permission. If he ran away the hue and cry could be raised, and he would be hunted like an outlaw. The marks of servitude were severe and to be of villein status was legally and politically to be little more than a chattel in the power of the lord of the manor.

Yet in practice the villein had rather more freedom than might be supposed. He could generally gain his freedom if he succeeded in living in a chartered borough without detection for a year and a day, and many boroughs, anxious to obtain a good labour force, had clauses to this effect embodied in their charters. Also, although in theory a villein could not buy his freedom because he possessed nothing that did not belong to his lord, in practice he could and did purchase emancipation in this way. Other evidence, again, shows the villein with a degree of independence at variance with theory. The reeve, for example, though normally of villein status elected by his fellow villeins, often, like Chaucer's reeve, wielded great authority:

> His lordes sheep, his neet, his dayerye,
> His swyn, his hors, his stoor and his pultrye
> Was hooly in this Reves governying; . . .
> He koude bettre than his lord purchace;
> Ful riche he was astored pryvely.

Other people who performed various common tasks were also appointed by and from the ranks of the villeins. The lord or his representative might also choose from among the villeins some more substantial or more efficient than the rest to supervise the services given on the demesne—contemporary pictures show these villeins at work, identifiable by the white rods of authority they carry. Villeins also had the duty—or the right—to serve as jurors in the manor court. Nor was the ordinary, daily life of the villein always one of degradation. He lived with his family in his own house with his own garden and his own animals. The members of his family could work with him in the open fields or take service on the lord's demesne, in the lord's house or the lord's dairy, or in any of the communal tasks of village life, or they could work for another villein who might be wealthier or short of family labour. The villein did not own his strips in the common fields; the lord *could* transfer him from his holding, he *could* deny his eldest son the right of succession, but for this to happen was rare, and meanwhile the produce of his strips, no less than that of his garden, was his own. It was equally difficult for his rights in meadow, pasture, waste and wood to be taken from him. These might be pared down, obligations to the lord seem more onerous, tallage become more heavy, the marks of servitude bite more deeply, yet always there remained a core of economic security. Moreover, there was an inescapable community of interest in that all relied on the weather, that all repeated the same processes of farming at the same time, that the state of the land, the condition of the animals, was of equal concern. And, as a kind of general security over all, was the custom of the manor, enforced by the manor court, which it was difficult for anyone to infringe. The villein, in the terms of the medieval lawyer, was *adscriptus glebae*—bound to the soil—but he was far from being a slave and his economic freedom was greater than his legal and political position implied.

The half-yardlanders and quarter-yardlanders were related to the lord in the same kind of way, with commensurately fewer obligations but carrying the same marks of servitude. Lower in the scale were the bordars and cottars, who were most likely the same class of people. In Domesday Book both terms are used, apparently indifferently, but the Norman-French 'bordar' is rarely found outside Domesday Book, while the Anglo-Saxon 'cottar' survived in common usage. The bordars and cottars normally did not hold strips in the open fields but farmed plots of some three to five acres round their tofts, for which they paid labour service; they had varying rights of common, waste and woodland and, like the half- and quarter-yardlanders, undertook many of the communal tasks of the village and manor. In economical terms, members of any of these classes might be as well off, or even better off, than a villein, with fewer obligations, and with greater opportunities of wages from service.

Below these again were the serfs, with no legal rights and no measurable obligations. They laboured at the lord's will, they received what recompense he cared to make. Yet, though legally unfree, in practice many of them occupied land, owned cattle, shared in the common rights of the village.

Many of the tasks necessary to the community as a whole were so important that they were the full-time occupation of special persons appointed by the villagers themselves. There was the pinder, who collected stray animals, keeping them in the pound until they were claimed. There was the hayward, whose task it was to see that no damage was done on the manor, particularly that no animals broke down fences or trampled the growing crops: he 'must go round early and late spying upon the woods, the farmyard, the meadows and fields'. There was the swineherd, who looked after the pigs of the village, including those of the lord himself, as they routed for acorns and mast on the edge of the forest land and on the waste. There was the goose-girl, generally the child of a villein, the cowherd, the shepherd—who all included in their care the animals of the whole community.

The lord's demesne was cultivated partly by the labour services of his tenants, partly by hired labour, and partly by full-time, often hereditary, demesne servants, or *famuli*, who were generally unfree and who worked on the land and also in and about the manor-house itself. The duties which these men and women performed, preparing for guests, salting the meat and laying up other stores for the winter, making cheese and cream, cider and mead, caring for the animals in the yard, making up fires in the hall, repairing the linen, making inventories, were common to any manor-house all over the country. Demesne work was generally under the supervision of a full-time bailiff, a free man appointed and paid by the lord of the manor who in the absence of the lord might live in the manor-house and more effectively exercise his authority from that eminence. Originally there was no inducement to a manorial lord to produce more than would provide handsomely for his family, for in an age when nearly everyone lived off the produce of his own land there was little scope for marketing agricultural produce. A lord of a single manor would live on it; if he owned more than one manor he would either travel round living on each in turn or receive the produce of all at a specified place. Even after the development of a money economy landlords at first demanded no more than a fixed return in kind or money from their lands. But from the end of the twelfth century, with rising prices and an increasing use of money, the management of the manor demesne became increasingly professionalized. By the fourteenth century self-sufficiency had developed into surplus, a fixed return had been abandoned in favour of profit, and the bailiff began to probe and to regularize much that had previously been taken for granted or left to chance. From this period, mainly in the thirteenth century, date the Estate Treatises, with their elaborate advice on all aspects of management, which give so much detail of English manorial life. The annual account and the twice-yearly 'views of the estate' which the bailiff rendered became very detailed. It was common practice to set down the costs and receipts of the manor on the front, the stock account, including animals, livestock of all kinds, and all the produce of the soil, on the back. So specialized did the compilation of these manorial accounts become that professional scribes went from manor to manor drawing them up.

The bailiff's job was to oversee the condition of the whole manor, but in particular the lord's demesne: he was a lord's man. The Estate Treatises explained in elaborate detail what he should do. The bailiff needed, indeed, to be vigilant, hard-working and all-seeing, as well as knowledgeable. He must 'see that the ploughs are yoked in the morning, and unyoked at the right time, so that they may do their proper ploughing every day'. He must be sure 'that the lands are well ploughed . . . and properly cropped, and well sown with good and pure seed, and cleanly harrowed' and 'he must cause the land to be marled, folded, manured, improved, and amended as his knowledge may approve'. He 'must see that there be good watch at the granges over the threshers, and that the corn be well and cleanly threshed' and 'the straw be well saved in good stacks or cocks well covered'.[14] He must ensure the good condition of the livestock, and must even 'answer for the issue of the mares of the court, that is to say, for each mare one foal in the year, and if there be any which has no foal let it be inquired if it be by bad keeping, or want of food, or too hard work, or want of stallion, or because it was barren, that she bare no foal'.[15]

The tenants had their representative in the person of the reeve or provost, generally elected by the villagers themselves, whose duties were similar to those of the bailiff. Generally, it seems, the reeve was held in high regard and, again, it says something for the practical fairness of the system that the villeins' interest, as well as the lord's, should be preserved. When the lord held more than one manor he was likely to put overall authority in the hands of a seneschal or steward, who was probably also a lawyer. The steward, riding between manor and manor two or three times a year, was the man to whom the bailiff and reeve were immediately responsible. His knowledge of the law enabled him to settle disputes, and he presided over the manor court in the lord's absence, the manor records were in his care. He inspected the accounts of the manor, noted deficiencies in organization and suggested improvements. The seneschal in the operation of his duties, said one of the Estate Treatises, 'ought to be prudent and faithful and profitable, and he ought to know the law of the realm, to protect his lord's business and to instruct and give assurance to the bailiffs who are beneath him in their difficulties'.[16] To a largish manor would come, finally, the auditors, to check the accounting, to question any omissions, reveal any slackness and unmask any dishonesty.

An impression is given of authority percolating downwards from auditors to seneschal to bailiff and finally to the reeve or provost, who was the whipping-boy. He was held responsible for the shortcomings of the tenants in the performance of their duties. He was asked to make good any deficiency, and if he could not do so then the whole manor was held responsible: 'if the lord receive any damage by the provost, and the provost cannot make good the damage, all those of the township who elected him shall make up for him the amount he cannot pay'.[17] Small wonder that Chaucer's reeve, caught between the upper and lower millstone, was 'a sclendre, colerik man', or that the office of reeve was by no means always welcomed. Thomas Smith, chosen by the steward of the manor of Brightwaltham in 1293 from a list of names submitted by the villagers, who bought himself out for the sum of 40*s*., was but one of many. On the other hand, Chaucer indicates that there could be opportunities for the right man. The reeve of the *Canterbury Tales*, besides being a knowledgeable farmer, was astute enough to meet the auditors on their own level, and subtle enough to retain his lord's favour over the years. As a result his life, though unostentatious, was comfortable, and his standard of living was high.

The seriousness with which manor accounting was taken, and the development of a new and almost scientific attitude towards farming, is apparent from the Estate Treatises. Sections were devoted to *The Return for Seed Sown; How Land Ought to be Measured; The Return from the Products of the Grange; The Yield from the Dairy; The Return from Cows, Heifers and their Milk.* Exact quantities were given: 'one can in many places reasonably sow four acres with a quarter of seed . . . in many places it requires a quarter and a half to sow five acres with wheat, rye, and beans and peas, and two acres with a quarter of barley and oats'; ten quarters of apples and pears should yield seven tons of cider; a quarter of nuts should yield four gallons of oil; each hive of bees ought to yield two gallons of honey. Beyond that, the manor must aim at the greatest degree of self-sufficiency. Its own wood and timber must be used, and it would be well to 'have carters and ploughmen who should know how to work all their own wood, although it should be necessary to pay them more'. Similarly, rope should be made on the manor from the hair of the avers or domestic animals and from hemp sown for the purpose, and an allowance should be paid to anyone on the manor who would make it. The smith must likewise be kept busy on the manor providing the iron parts of the plough and shoeing the horses and avers. All servants must be kept constantly occupied threshing corn, making walls, ditches, hedges, and anything else that would keep the manor in good condition and save money. In the fields it was very carefully calculated that five bands of five men (a woman counting as half a man) could reap and bind ten acres a day, working all day. 'If they have not reaped so much', was the stern admonition, do not pay them, 'for it is their fault that they have not reaped the amount and have not worked so well as they ought'.[18]

If the affairs of the manor were satisfactorily managed by his bailiff and seneschal, the lord of the manor might rarely be seen. In any case, his outlook and way of life was far removed from that of the peasants. The parson was different. He was generally a poor man like themselves, often of villein family, and could frequently be seen farming his glebe, which generally consisted of strips in the open fields like the land of any other villager: he was expected to preach to his parishioners at least four times a year. Agricultural settlements quite early had also their craftsmen, whose work on the land was subordinate to some other occupation, as many village names testify. The open-field community required the varied services given by such people as Alexander Carpenter, John Smith, Robert Miller, Robert Mason, Adam Baker and Geoffrey Weaver. But although these names indicate a division of labour, and although buying and selling quite early entered the life of the villager, this does not signify that the villein's wife was no longer spinning and weaving her own cloth, or that her husband was no longer using his hands in the long winter evenings.

The custom of the manor was propounded and enforced by the manor court, which met every two or three weeks, often in the great hall of the manor-house. If the lord was absent the seneschal would preside, and attendance was compulsory on all the villagers, though they might be able to compound for absence by payment of a fine. In the manor court were chosen the village officers, here were made detailed arrangements for the agricultural year; new tenants were registered, land transfers noted, fines and heriots and other payments were received and entered in the court roll. Charges against tenants were heard, such as failure to appear for boon work or to observe the custom of the manor; tenants brought charges against each other for infringement of one another's strips, for taking corn, implements, animals that belonged to someone else; for trampling someone else's land; quarrels and brawls were considered and verdicts given. More important cases were heard by jury, which it was customary by the fourteenth century for the lord to appoint from among the more substantial villeins.

Frequently associated with the custom of the manor was the manor court's administration of the wider law of the land. In this function it would try various offences against the King's peace, such as theft, assault, disturbance, and it would enforce such regulations as the Assize of Ale and the Assize of Bread.[19] Transgressions were punished by fine, by cucking-stool, pillory and the stocks. Fines were levied wherever possible, and almost certainly for offences concerning the custom of the manor, for these went into the coffers of the lord. But tradition was strong in the use, for example, of the cucking-stool for such offences as nagging and scolding and of both cucking-stool and stocks for bad quality or poor measure. The records of all cases were jumbled together in the manor rolls, and wander from trespass to assault to breaking the Assize of Bread to failure to appear for boon-work in a fine, shifting kaleidoscope of manor life.

It is these court rolls which bring the inhabitants most vividly to life. Their foibles, peccadilloes, their quarrels, sometimes their more serious crimes are there, illumined always by their names. They take hay from the lord's rick for their beasts, sow sedge before the general date, sometimes, like John the Herd, fail to reap the lord's corn promptly. Mabel Bencosin not only would not reap the corn of her lord but quitted the village, and could not be found. Like William Noah's son, a 'born bondman and a fugitive', she must be sought. John Witrich's foal is in the lord's corn, beasts were caught by night in the lord's meadow, four men have carried off geese not belonging to them, the whole community is appalled (probably because they will have to pay) at the action of Hugh Belde, the reeve, who made a stack of wheat on top of the stack of best barley in the lord's barn, so turning it rotten. Henry Shepherd made a way through the middle of the croft of John Tepito. The brethren of the Hospital of St John were guilty of pasturing sheep in autumn before the gleaners had done their work. Richard Guest and Ragenilda, widow of William Andrewsguard, quarrelled over possession of a certain headland, two more villagers were at feud over half a virgate of land. There were accusations of contracts not kept, goods not according to specification, payments which had not been made.

The court rolls take us, too, into the more personal side of village life. Alvena Leofred of Ruislip, Middlesex, is at law against Isabella of Hayes to prove she did not take a certain knife from her. Gilbert Vicar's wife and William of Stanbridge beat Hugh of Stanbridge and 'unlawfully struck him and dragged him by his hair out of his own proper house', to his damage and distress. We do not know why Gilbert Vicar's wife and William of Stanbridge struck up such a partnership, but Hugh was awarded 40*s*. for his 'damage' and 20*s*. for his 'distress'; most likely the money went into the manor chest and Hugh received nothing but the satisfaction of the verdict. Another unresolved story is given by the terse entry that William Fowler carried off the goods and chattels of Walter Albion 'against his will but with the consent of his wife, which consent he obtained by frequently kicking her'. An interesting insight into values is provided by the case of Rohese Bindebere, who called Ralph Bolay a thief. He called her a whore. 'And for that the trespass done to the said Ralph exceeds the trespass done to the said Rohese', recorded the court, she was saddled with the larger fine. Perhaps the villagers were not censorious, probably not so curious as we are, to know the story of Amice Hubert, who incurred a leyrwite with a certain stranger. The records are no more informative concerning Alice Balle, who 'defaced' the lord's corn so that people would not buy it.

Poignancy and sadness are often conveyed by these records of the manor court. But the touchingly beautiful perceptiveness, as well as the human suffering behind the account, make the story of Walter of the Moor most compelling of all.

The record reports the proceedings:

Walter of the Moor, thou art attached to answer in this court wherefore by night and against the lord's peace thou didst enter the preserve of the lord and didst carry off at thy will divers manner of fish. . . . How wilt thou acquit thyself or make amends?

Sir, by thy leave I will imparl . . . for God's sake do not take it ill of me if I tell thee the truth, how I went the other evening along the bank of this pond and looked at the fish which were playing in the water, so beautiful and so bright, and for the great desire that I had for a tench I laid me down on the bank and just with my hands quite simply, and without any other device, I caught that tench and carried it off; and now I will tell thee the cause of my covetousness and my desire; my dear wife had lain abed a right full month, as my neighbours who are here know, and she could never eat or drink anything to her liking, and for the great desire that she had to eat a tench I went to the bank of the pond to take just one tench; and that never other fish from the pond did I take, ready am I to do by way of proof whatever thou shalt award me.

Walter, saith the steward, at least thou hast confessed in this court a tench taken and carried away in other wise than it should have been, for thou mightest have come by it in fairer fashion. Therefore we tell thee that thou art in the lord's mercy, and besides this thou must wage us a law six-handed that thou didst not take at that or any other time any other manner of fish.[20]

Walter, it seems, had simply to bring six approved witnesses (to 'wage a law six-handed') to testify that he had not at any time taken any other fish and on that condition the charge against him was dismissed—even with the suggestion that had he asked he might have been given the fish for his wife.

The actual standard of living of the open-field farmer is difficult to estimate, and cannot be measured against a sophisticated and multi-choice modern economy. There was certainly a difference between the standard of the lord of the manor and that of his poorest serf. There was a great difference, for one thing, between the manor-house with its high-timbered hall and tapestry hangings and the simple tofts of the peasants, consisting of one or two rooms with turf or wood, wattle or daub for walls, furze for roofing and bracken for bedding. Their flimsy nature is demonstrated by the ease with which they were moved. 'William Found had departed and carried off his cottage' was a form of entry not uncommon in the court rolls.

But the open-field farmer was protected from destitution by

his share in the harvest of the big fields, by the product of his croft, by his animals and poultry, by his rights in various parts of the manor. In bad years these might all amount to little more than mere subsistence, and winters would always be hard, but there was generally something to fall back upon. In good years a villein could be quite prosperous. But the advantages of community, of the ownership of the product of the land he farmed, were offset by certain material disadvantages inherent in the open-field method of husbandry. Much time was wasted between village and strip and between strip and strip, and the implements of production were housed for safety in farm buildings at the village. Speed and efficiency gained no bonus, for each process on the big fields had its agreed starting date: the slow or lazy ploughman might delay his team, but even the quickest could do little to advance the date of sowing. The open fields suffered from the man who neglected his weeding and fouled his neighbour's strip, from the careless villager who walked over another's land, from the man who, late with his own sowing, turned his implements on his neighbour's seeds, from the lazy farmer who neglected to fence the ends of his strips so that animals trampled the growing crops, from the dishonest neighbour who filched pieces of another's land. At the same time unhealthy animals commoned with healthy and dragged down the condition of all. Apart from such evils, inherent in the system itself, was the lack of farming knowledge which kept the standard of farming low. Rejuvenating crops like clover were unknown, seed was wastefully sown, implements were crude, lack of winter feed for the animals meant a constant straining of resources to keep any animals alive at all for draught, for manure or for providing next year's stock. The careful precepts of the Estate Treatises often accord strangely with the reality of open-field farming.

CHAPTER IV

Wool, Wood and Leather

Any description of medieval Britain is sure at many points to touch the common-field system of agriculture and the nucleated village, but the manor with its open fields, strip farming and villein tenure was by no means typical of the whole country. There were other methods of farming, other kinds of landholding, and villages were frequently dispersed hamlets. In the east and north-east of England were many mixed farms of little arable and much pasture. In the difficult hill country of the North of England, little mixed farms eked out a precarious existence as independent units, relying as much upon sheep as upon arable. In parts of Kent the arable land was not held in strips but in compact plots. In parts of Norfolk and Suffolk the land was worked continuously on a one-field system—the 'whole year lands'—with no period of fallow. In north-west England a system known as 'run-rig' dominated. The custom here prevailed of working intensively one lot of land, the 'infield', near the settlement, while at the same time using an 'outfield' less intensively and moving on to another when its yield declined. Sometimes a system of inheritance, like gavelkind in Kent, divided the land continuously among co-heirs with the result that it was broken up into very small units. There were also small manors in many parts of the country which seemed to fit no pattern, like Swyncombe in Oxfordshire. Here there were two hides of demesne arable (about 240 acres), ten villeins each farmed eight acres, and there were eleven cottars with little crofts. Each villein, besides his holding, could keep a horse, six oxen and fifty sheep upon the common pasture.[1]

But the outstanding contrast to the open-field manors were the big pastoral farms where the famous English sheep of the golden fleece and the little golden hoof carried all before them. The sheep farms spread over the dales of Yorkshire, over the rolling Lincolnshire wolds, on the short, sweet grass of the Cotswolds, the limestone of North Oxfordshire, in Shropshire, Herefordshire and the Welsh border country, on the chalk downland of Wiltshire and Sussex, round the marshes of the Welsh and Kentish coasts, on the moors of Devonshire and Cornwall. As the open-field village was a natural development in fertile country where big stretches of arable land had been farmed for centuries and the proportion of people to farmland was comparatively high, so thinly settled areas, never under the plough, were the natural location of the big sheep-farms. Hill country, in particular, whose contours made cultivation difficult but whose grass was sweet, was a natural home for sheep. On sheep-farms fewer people were required than on arable, and the amount of land under the plough was only as much as was necessary to produce food for them. The lord of an open-field manor made his profit from the sale of consumption crops that met everyday needs—with few exceptions, from the same crops that fed the villagers; the lord of a sheep-farming manor made his profit from something other than the immediate source of subsistence. The lord of an open-field manor took his dues largely in labour services because labour was abundant and the tasks to be performed were many; the owner of a pastoral estate took his rents mainly in produce because there were comparatively few tasks to perform, the number of workmen was small, and the fact that the main economy of the manor was directed to pasture enhanced the value of the fruits of the soil. One economy was built on a high proportion of people to land; the other on a high proportion of land to people.

The protective value of a sheepskin had been obvious from earliest times. The whole fleece covered primitive man. The felted wool lined the helmets and breastplates of Greek and Roman soldiers. It made protective cloaks and leggings and other garments for simple people all over the world. Tents, floor coverings, wall hangings were crudely made from felted wool. At the same time, the arts of spinning the fleece of the sheep and weaving the yarn into crude cloth were among the earliest known to man, and peasants the world over were clothed in 'home spun'. By the thirteenth century the production of cloth had reached a very high standard in parts of Europe, and had become a specialized production for the market, notably in Flanders and in Lombardy. England, after an early start in the twelfth century, lagged behind.[2] This was in spite of—perhaps almost because of—the supremely high quality of her raw wool. Her wool was such an inestimable asset, providing the means of exchange for her imports, profit for her landowners and her merchants, a source of taxation for her kings and employment for her population, that until the middle of the fourteenth century she had little need to look further. It was a golden fleece, indeed, that grew upon the backs of the sturdy animals that grazed in larger or smaller flocks, or even in ones and twos, on the grasslands of England and Wales, and the fact that the fleece renewed itself year after year throughout the animal's life was a natural bonus.

English wool was prized for its fineness and its high felting quality, and countries making finer cloth used English wool in large quantities: the Low Countries, particularly Flanders and Brabant, and Italy, in particular Florence, not only imported English wool but were dependent upon it for their fine cloth and their large export trade.

Top-grade English wool was the very fine, short fleece of the Welsh border sheep, particularly those from Shropshire and Herefordshire; running these close was the longer-haired but still fine wool of the Lincolnshire (especially the Lindsey) and the Cotswold sheep. By the fifteenth century the Cotswold sheep were, in fact, the chief source of fine wool. Yorkshire wool too was much sought after, even if it were not so fine as the others. Midland wool constituted a middle grade, while the wools of the south and south-east of England were coarser. The sheep of Devon and Cornwall produced a coarser kind still, used for native industry and not exported. Those of East Anglia grew a long fleece, particularly suited to the making of worsted[2] but not generally used in export. But there were always particular clips of special graziers which had their own contacts and their regular customers.[3]

The organization of the big pasture farm was less complex than that of the open-field farm, yet, being directly dependent upon the market for its profit, it was far more highly professionalized, and relied upon an accounting system that was even more detailed and more precise than that of the open-field manor. Biggest lay farmers were the Dukes of Lancaster, whose estates were spread about England from the South Downs to Lincolnshire and Yorkshire. Their rivals were the Cistercian monks who, early in the twelfth century, began to settle in England. Their Order prescribed work and solitude: sheep-farming on the uninhabited stretches of the Yorkshire Dales and in the Welsh valleys was a natural way of life. Here there were no manorial ties and the whole organization was naturally based upon central estate management. Sometimes the manors of a big sheep-farmer were divided into groups for easier administration, or they might specialize with breeding ewes on one, hoggets (yearlings) on another, wethers on a third. In any case, total flocks could be very large. The Bishop of Winchester kept some 29 000 sheep in 1259 on his Hampshire manors. The nearby Priory of St Swithins owned 20 000 at the beginning of the fourteenth century. A Duchy of Lancaster farm in the Peak District of Derbyshire boasted probably the largest single flock, where some 5 500 sheep grazed on one 'ranch' alone.[4]

Of the workers who were required to ensure the smooth running of these big sheep-farms, washers and shearers might be temporarily hired, but others were needed all the year round to preserve and renew farm buildings and stone sheepcotes, to attend to the dairy, to maintain supplies that the estate could not provide, such as tar to ward off the scab and ruddle for marking the sheep. Above all, there was the shepherd. Where the sheep pastures stretched, he was in sole charge, and a thirteenth-century Estate Treatise set out his qualifications:

> It profiteth the lord to have discreet shepherds, watchful and kindly, so that the sheep be not tormented by their wrath but crop their pasture in peace and joyfulness; for it is a token of the shepherd's kindliness if the sheep be not scattered abroad but browse around him in company. . . . Let him provide himself with a good barkable dog and lie nightly with his flock.[5]

Such a person was obviously important. He was a free man, who pastured his own sheep with the flocks he was attending, who folded his lord's flock on his own land at Christmas, who received a lamb at weaning time and a fleece at shearing.[6]

On lay sheep-farms scattered settlements usually grew enough food to feed the population who tended the sheep. The religious houses generally had their granges, compact areas of arable land cultivated by some of the brethren. Over all whether lay or ecclesiastical, were the bailiffs and the seneschal, maximizing the lord's profit, overseeing the processes of the sheep's life, from its conception to its shearing and its ultimate fate as provider of food and leather, often ensuring that the destiny of its fleece was arranged before it was born, or at least as soon as a sample of its fleece could be run through the appraising fingers of the Fleming or the Lombard who would give the best price. The climax came when the sheep were driven in from the pastures for washing and shearing. Then came the winding, and then the sale to the merchant or his factor who was frequently present to make sure the quality was as good as that of the specimen upon which he had based his purchase. For the big estates all this is clearly documented in the estate accounts. Like those of the open-field manors, these were rendered annually at Michaelmas (September), with an intermediate view of the estate in spring, and they were subject to the same checks of visiting auditors.

Although not nearly as impressive as the big pasture farm with hundreds of sheep coming together at the annual climax, innumerable small sheep and mixed farms all over the country grazed a number which in total might well have exceeded them. On the standard open-field farm sheep were an adjunct to arable, valued largely for their manure, only secondarily for wool and meat and milk. On poorer arable land the lord might own a considerable flock, and the villagers themselves might depend as much on sheep as upon crops. In the Wiltshire villages of South Domerham and Merton, Tisbury and West Hatch, Dinton and Teffont, for example, villagers grazed thousands of sheep.[7] The tenant sheep-farmer on these smaller manors probably managed his flocks as a family concern, his wool probably going with that of other peasant flocks to the wool market of the nearby town.

In open-field, arable country the outline of village and manor is generally clear. The village is nucleated, manor-house and church stand out clearly, the manor court is a perpetual reminder of the common purpose of farming, and of the interdependence of the inhabitants. The small, mixed manor might be not dissimilar. On a wide-spreading sheep-farm with fewer people there is a less integrated agricultural life, the centre of the organization is farther away and less obvious, there are fewer customs to interpret, less work to do jointly. This is reflected geographically in the fact that there is no central village, but merely farmsteads or crofts spread over the area. The bigger the pastoral farm the vaguer the form of manor and village. It is vaguest of all on the sheep-farming estates of the big religious houses, particularly the Cistercians. Here all the estate was demesne land, there were no tenants, no villeins, for all the estate was kept by the monastery and even the granges were farmed almost entirely by the brethren.

The big upland sheep-farms were, perhaps, the areas of greatest freedom in the land. There was no immediate supervisor to give a feeling of personal bondage; the open spaces, the height, were evocative of liberty. Contact with the outer world was at once greater and less—less in the lonely wandering with flocks over the pastures, greater in the sight of merchants or their agents come from distant parts to bargain for the fleece. On upland farms the standard of living is generally lower than in the fertile valleys. In spite of the shepherd's bonus, life could be hard, and in a bad season there was less to fall back on. But sheep vary less than crops with the seasons, and it was a tough and independent breed of men who inhabited the pastures. While wool remained the basis of the country's prosperity everyone connected with the sheep-farm had a measure of security. The standard of living of the part-time workers might be low indeed, but they would not face complete destitution.

Besides the cultivated arable land, the sheep pastures, the difficult mixed hill farms, the waste and scrub, were the forests proper, ranging from dense regions of mighty trees to mixed areas of trees and shrubs. Throughout the Middle Ages, although the uses of wood and timber were appreciated, the forests were regarded as enemies of society who would advance and envelop the works of man unless held at bay. They were so vast that they were expendable, inexhaustible, and in no way in need of protection—except in so far as they harboured animals of the chase. Until the sixteenth century this emphasis upon clearing them, rather than preserving them, barely changed. The area they covered appeared infinite compared with the little space where man was beating out a living, and any clearing that could be made was land gained rather than timber lost.

Trees were felled unquestioningly for a multitude of reasons and an infinity of uses. They were felled to enlarge the area under cultivation, or because they interfered with passage or with grazing or with hunting—small trees and shrubs by individual peasants, large trees by a joint effort of the village community. The felled trees were put to a variety of uses. Every implement used by medieval man—spades, rakes, hoes, axes, hammers, bellows—was made partly or entirely of wood. Wood of various kinds was used for furniture—cradles and beds, chairs and stools, tables and cupboards. There were wooden platters, wooden mugs, wooden spoons, wooden pots and bowls. The timber frame and roof timbers of manor-house and peasant's hut were made from wood. The lady's carriage and the peasant's cart were made of wood. Small branches made staves and switches. Miners lined their pit shafts with wood, and brought up the ore in wooden buckets. The tanners used bark, preferably oak bark, for tanning animal hides. Sap from the bark was used for pitch and tar. The blacksmith required wood for his forge, the cloth-dyer needed wood for the dyeing vat. The farmer's fields were fenced with wooden palings—frequently renewed, for they were not perennial like a growing hedge. The sheepcote, if not of stone, was made of wood; so was the movable sheep-pen.

Animals, especially pigs, grew fat on the seeds and mast of trees, particularly upon acorns and beech-mast. All who required heat used wood in the days before pit coal was an acceptable alternative. It was used for evaporating salt, and in the making of bricks. Wood-ash was used for potash, soap, glass, saltpetre. The lime-burners and the smelters of metals used wood in the form of charcoal, the iron-workers used charcoal for calcining the ore before it came to the smelting forge. The smith in his smithy used charcoal as well as wood, and both were widely used as domestic fuel. The lime-burners were the first to substitute pit coal for charcoal, which they did at the end of the thirteenth century, but as a domestic fuel wood and charcoal were the only acceptable forms of heat until the chimneys of Elizabethan times made pit coal a viable alternative by carrying away the fumes and smell to which people objected. In the iron-smelting furnace pit coal was rejected until an even later date: charcoal required less heat to ignite it, was required to be in contact with the ore for a shorter time and, above all, contained fewer impurities than coal. This was of supreme importance to the smelting of iron, because the process involves an absorption by the ore of some of the qualities of the heating agent. Only when coal was reduced first to coke did it become a practicable alternative to charcoal, and, although Dud Dudley professed to have achieved this towards the end of the seventeenth century, it did not become practicable until the work of Abraham Darby in the first decades of the eighteenth century. Only then did the smelters of iron cease to draw upon British forests for their furnaces.

Beechwood was used for the lighter kind of furniture. In 1240, for example, orders were given for the delivery of a good beech-tree from Windsor Forest to Master Simon, the Carpenter, for tables for the King's kitchen at Westminster.[8] Alder and ash were used for scaffolding: in Westminster in 1324, 25 pieces of alder 20 feet long, 400 pieces of alder 38 feet long and 61 pieces of ash 42 feet long were requisitioned for the uprights of scaffolding required for building purposes.[9] Ash, being pliant, tough and resilient, was also excellent for the handles of tools—as it still is today. When hardened in fire it could become a sharp and effectively pointed tool or weapon, even an arrow-head or the point of a spear.

Elm was sufficiently hard for the making of chopping-blocks, work-benches and hatters' moulds. It hardened still further in water, and was therefore fitted for piles that were sunk in river-beds or harbours, for water-wheels and water-mills, for piers and jetties, bridges and ships' planks. It was used for a variety of other purposes, from the supporting beams of a roof to the tables in a great hall or the chest in a lady's closet. But for most purposes—except for under-water work—elm was used only when oak was scarce.

The oak, which combined size, strength, and toughness, was the king of the forest:

> so tough, and extreamly compact that our sharpest tools will hardly enter it, and scarcely the very fire itself, in which it consumes but slowly . . . Houses, and Ships, Cities and Navies are built with it . . . It is doubtless of all Timber hitherto known, the most universally useful and strong; for though some trees be harder . . . yet we find them more fragil and not so well qualified to support great incumbencies and weights, nor is there any Timber more lasting which way soever us'd.[10]

It was as a bearer that oak was above all prized. For the high timbered roofs of castles, palaces and cathedrals with their curved rafters, long tie beam and supporting pendants, oak was supreme. It has survived for centuries, and superb examples of oak hammer-beam roofing can still be seen in, for example, the fourteenth-century Westminster Hall and the sixteenth-century great hall of Hampton Court. For building operations at Windsor Castle in the middle of the fourteenth century a whole wood containing over three thousand oaks was bought. But it was not always so easy to meet the demand. Building on the scale of Westminster Hall and many of the cathedrals required beams of at least 50 feet in length and of a comparable diameter. This implies a tree of very great size, and by the middle of the fourteenth century there was difficulty in obtaining such lengths, or lengths of 40 or even of 30 feet.

The selection of trees for felling was a skilled task requiring an eye for size, for strength, and for the appropriate natural curve of a great branch. The woodcutter, the sawyer, the carpenter, were expert in the matter of choice, as well as in the arts of felling and cutting, and it was frequently the carpenter himself who selected the tree he wished to use, as when Sir Thomas Lucas in 1505 paid 6*s*. 8*d*. 'to Loveday, carpenter, for felling and chosing of xxvj okes'. The carpenters became skilled, independent workmen at an early date. While most countrymen fashioned wooden articles in the enforced cessation of field work during winter, each village of any size also had its carpenter, while in the towns the craft gild of carpenters was strongly established by the fourteenth century.

Right through the Middle Ages, for one use or another, the country continued to be prodigal of its wood, and there seemed no reason why it should be otherwise. Yet in areas where the demand was high the problem quite early became on of protection rather than of destruction. A letter written as early as the beginning of the twelfth century shows that in one area at least the owner of woodland is thinking in terms of conservation: 'Concerning Thorpe wood', writes Bishop Herbert de Losinga of Norwich to one of his officials, 'I appointed thee guardian not uprooter, of that wood. To the sick I will give not wood but money. . . Meanwhile do thou guard the wood'.[11] In 1430, when Thomas Langley, Bishop of Durham, farmed out forests in a certain part of Weardale for seven years to Robert Kirkhous, 'ironburner', he expressly excluded oak, ash, holly and crabtree,[12] presumably because he required these timbers for other purposes.

The 'ironburner' would have been a charcoal-burner, making charcoal from wood, presumably for an iron-smelter's furnace. Vast quantities of charcoal were consumed by the ironworks. Though oak was generally believed to make the best charcoal, any wood served the purpose, one authority even maintaining that for some purposes beech charcoal was about 10 per cent better than that from oak, ash or hornbeam. Some idea of the large quantities of wood consumed by the charcoal-burners is given by the estimate that two Sussex ironworks consumed charcoal representing some 2 700 000 cubic feet of timber in less than two years.[13]

The charcoal-burners were important people, yet they pass through history shadowy and insubstantial. To provide fuel on such a large scale burning must in many cases, especially near ironworks, have quite early been a full-time occupation. Where the ironworks were not near habitation the charcoal-burners' huts were doubtless set up in some forest clearing. At other times they may have formed part of a village community, living possibly on the outskirts of the inhabited area and supplementing their wages by the produce of a garden patch and an animal or two. Sometimes they were itinerant, moving from place to place in the forests. The equipment they needed to take with them was simple enough—axes and knives for felling and cutting, stakes and poles which they could procure from the trees as they went. They needed to clear a level space for a hearth, to drive a stake down into the earth at the centre of this hearth, to mark out a rough circle, perhaps 40 feet in diameter, which would accommodate the amount of charcoal they were about to produce. Then would begin the elaborate building up of the wood, which already would have been cut and stacked into pieces about three feet long. These were now built into a pyramid, some eight feet high, and the pieces crossed and criss-crossed to allow plenty of draught for burning. The whole would then be covered with turf, straw, fern, clay or animal dung so that all cracks were stopped. This done, vent holes were made through the outer covering as far as the wood. Finally, the pole would be withdrawn from the centre and a lighted charcoal dropped down the hole which it left. The vent holes were then stopped or closed as necessary to make the whole pyramid burn slowly and evenly. Perhaps some five or six days were required to produce the charcoal, and a further two or three days for cooling.

Charcoal-burning was a primitive occupation which had remained virtually unchanged for centuries. Were the simple people who practised it free men, working for themselves in a small way? Sometimes, perhaps. This was most likely when they were producing charcoal to supply a town. At other times they worked for their feudal lord, providing for his domestic needs and any industry established within the bounds of the manor. In the bigger ironworks the charcoal-burners were generally employed by the ironmaster, their charcoal pits close to the forge, forming an integral part of the ironworks, and they themselves in the position of wage-earners.

Wool, wood, leather—leather was the third of the trio of natural resources virtually indispensable to medieval society. Leather was as obvious a commodity to use as wool or wood, the hides of dead animals forming a plentiful supply of tough material which had been used for innumerable purposes from earliest times. The steps from the raw hide—covered with hair, hard, dirty—to a soft, pliable, yet still tough and strong leather had to be learned, but the Ancient Britons already knew something of the art of leather-making, and the Romans used leather widely. By the Middle Ages the curing and tanning of hide into leather and the making of leather articles of innumerable kinds was widely practised all over England. Leather was used for boots and shoes and slippers; for jerkins, coats and leggings; for hats and caps and gloves; for boxes and chests and cases of all kinds and sizes; for bags and purses, book-covers, tassels for decoration, sheaths for weapons, bellows in the forge; for straps and harness and saddles and horse trappings; for the construction of litters and coaches and the coverings of wagons; for the seats of chairs and the tops of tables; and had even been used as coinage. It could carry liquid. The leather bucket was lighter in weight and more convenient than the wooden, while the leather bottle and the bouget (two bottles joined at the neck) were indispensable. So also were the famous black-jack, the drinking mug of medieval Britain, and its larger version, the bombard. Leather was even used for protective purposes, the fighting man's 'cuirass'—cuir-asse or quir-asse—being named from the French *cuir* or *quir* for leather. 'Boiled leather'—*cuir bouilli* or *quirboilly* as it was then called—was leather which had been soaked, moulded and probably embossed, and was very popular in the Middle Ages in being both protective and decorative. Chaucer says of the knight in his 'Rime of Sir Thopas', 'Hise jambeux [shin or leg guards] were of Quirboilly'. The 'buff-coat', the name given to the serving soldier for centuries, arose from the fact that his surcoat or jerkin was frequently made of the hide of the American buffalo, imported for the purpose. The leather was treated in such a way that it became a pale brown, and the name 'buff' attached itself also to the colour, even when native hides were used.

Correctly treated leather has all the qualities which these many articles require. It can be porous yet remain warm to the touch, it can become hard as a bone yet remain supple; it can be sealed to such perfection that buckets and black-jacks have endured for centuries without leaking their contents. It can be softened to take the impression of decorative motifs, and hardened again to retain them; it receives and retains colouring and gilding. Originally, it seems, a gild of Cordwainers—who took their name from the leather of Cordova, which early became famous—covered many of the leather crafts. By the fourteenth century, however, the specialist crafts had emerged, the cordwainers were associated especially with the shoemakers, and there were in addition gilds of skinners, curriers, tanners, leather-sellers, bottlers, pursers, pouch-makers, girdlers, saddlers, cobblers and many more, as well as the tawyers—often referred to as the white tawyers, because their work produced a perfectly white leather.

The tawyer dressed the raw skins by steeping them in an astringent mixture of common salt, sometimes potash as well, and of alum, a whitish, transparent mineral salt found in many parts of the country. In contrast to this mineral treatment, the tanner tanned his hides in a vegetable distillate from oak bark. The hides of deer, sheep and horses were usually tawed, those of oxen, cow and calf were generally tanned. So distinct were the two trades that from early times tanners and tawyers were forbidden to work each other's skins. Tanned leather was the stouter, used particularly for footwear; the softer tawed leather made such articles as gloves and purses and girdles. In both processes the quality of the leather depended much upon the skill and patience of the workmen. Tanning in the 'woozes' of oak-bark solution was, in particular, a very long process. A year was generally considered an appropriate time for tanning, but only the master himself could determine this. The proportions of bark and water were under his control, too, but he was prohibited by law from tanning twice in the same solution.

Whichever process was used, the raw hides had first to be soaked, then treated with lime to remove the hair and the outer skin, then washed again in water. After the tawing or tanning the skins were treated with oil to make them supple, a process again which could not be hurried. With tanned leather this process was generally in the hands of the curriers, who were known to demand a high quality in the tanned skins they treated.

Water was an essential requirement of the leather-workers, and they were never far from rivers or streams. Other requirements were oak bark for tanning, which frequently brought them to the same district as charcoal-burners or iron-miners, or alum for tawing, in the use of which they rubbed shoulders with other alum-using industries, such as dyeing. The other essential was the hides themselves, and it was in the big towns, particularly London, where there were abundant hides from animals slaughtered for meat-consumption that the industry became established. In the south of London, in Bermondsey and Southwark, where many little streams ran into the Thames, close to the forests of Kent and Surrey, where alum was already used for a variety of purposes, there was early established the most important leather industry in the country. Leicestershire and Northamptonshire, both sheep- and cattle-raising areas, were also centres of the leather industry. It tended, whenever possible, to be relegated to the outskirts of inhabited areas, for the smell of both tanning and tawing was most unpleasant, and the effluent of both processes fouled rivers and streams.

The capital equipment required by the leather-worker was not great. The tanner needed, besides his raw material, vats and tubs, some means of grinding the bark, knives for cutting, poles for stirring, and other small tools. The tawyer's requirements were similarly simple. The shoemakers and others who made up the leather likewise needed no elaborate tools—the poor shoemaker was a traditional character, and even when he prospered like Simon Eyre and had several apprentices his was still the 'gentle craft'; it was not one associated with capitalist exploitation. In the light leather industry it was not uncommon for several occupations to be combined—glover, purser, maker of belts—but in so far as any monopoly grew it was the tanner who held supplies for the small handicraftsman, and a Leathersellers' Company was one of the first to emerge. But this was chiefly in the towns. In the villages there is no doubt that the small man continued to obtain his own skins and work them up for himself from start to finish: the making of simple leather articles of general use from the animals he killed at Michaelmas, or who died through some mishap, was as natural as eating their flesh. The village shoemaker was as much part of village life as the carpenter or the potter.

CHAPTER V

Quarrying and Mining

Man made use of the land; of the forests which covered it, of the animals which grazed it, of the crops which grew on it. He also dug into it and extracted coal, iron and tin, lead, silver, copper, and many kinds of stone, from hardest granite and marble to alabaster and soft chalk and malleable clay. For coal and iron, tin, copper, lead and silver it was generally necessary to dig deep or to mine. Building stone, marble, alabaster, chalk and clay were often obtained by quarrying near the surface.

Of all the raw materials stone is, perhaps, the most obviously useful. Neolithic Britons used stone for such gigantic monuments as Stonehenge. The Romans built stone houses, temples and city walls. The Saxons, though building mainly in wood, built sturdy stone churches, like St Peter on the Wall at Bradwell in Essex, or the monumental Brixworth parish church. The Normans were greater builders in stone. For defence, for religion, for beauty, for utility, their towers and castles, churches, abbeys and cathedrals, palaces and manor-houses covered much of the habitable land. The Conqueror built the Tower of London and strengthened Westminster Palace. The thirteenth century was the age of the great cathedrals. By the fourteenth century the towns were expanding with the ambitious stone houses of their wealthier burgesses. The proximity of good local stone was often reflected in buildings: in the Cotswolds the wealth of the wool merchants utilized the pale golden stone to produce houses, wool halls and churches of great beauty; the green sandstone of Eastbourne was used for

Pevensey Castle, as it had been for its Roman walls; the founder of a religious house would sometimes bequeath a nearby quarry for its building.

For cathedrals and other important buildings, however, the use of local stone could matter less than getting the right stone. It was not only a question of colour. The very hard stone of Purbeck, the high-quality, easily worked Reigate stone, and the tough, rough 'Kentish rag' had their special uses. Purbeck stone was used for Westminster in 1278; Portland stone in the following century for Exeter Cathedral. Kentish rag was widely used for walls and wharfs and other rough work. It was not uncommon for it to form the core of a wall or building which was faced with superior stone. Rochester Castle, in Kent, drew on many quarries. It used stone from Fairlight near Hastings in Sussex, from quarries at Reigate in Surrey and Maidstone in Kent and from Stapleton in Yorkshire. The stone of Barnock in Northamptonshire was widely quarried by all the Fenland Abbeys. York drew upon the quarries of Thevesdale, Huddleston and Tadcaster for its Minster. London, Westminster and Windsor used stone from Merstham and Reigate in Surrey as well as from Maidstone.[1]

Stone was also used for many articles of church furniture, such as fonts, lavers and urns. Benches, cattle troughs and other farm pieces, boundary stones and posts were made of stone. Stone was used for missiles to be hurled from catapults, and later on for cannon-balls. When split it was suitable for roofing, though it generally had first to be exposed to frost.

Stone was not only functional but served a variety of decorative uses. Carving, window tracery and sculpture came naturally to the medieval mason. Patterns cut into the stone of doorways, gargoyles at the top of rain-spouts, angels' heads on roofs and the bosses of vaulting, birds and beasts, flowers and foliage formed under the mason's chisel, together with biblical scenes, the saints, the bishops, the Annunciation, plentiful representations of the Devil in Hell and, above all, the Last Judgment. Early medieval sculpture was normally in relief, an integral part of a wall or a pillar such as the beautiful example of the raising of Lazarus in Chichester Cathedral, which consists of eight figures, each about three feet high, bearing expressions of sorrow and compassion rarely equalled in any medium. Free-standing sculpture in stone developed later, encouraged by the demand of noble patrons for tombs and effigies. By the thirteenth century figure sculpture representing the great or the wealthy, particularly the recumbent portrait-effigy of the deceased, was very popular. Throughout the thirteenth century the cross-legged knight was, indeed, the stock-in-trade of the stone mason, although the figures were for the most part unmistakeably individual. Early in the following century a recumbent (but far from reposeful) knight in Dorchester Abbey makes to draw his sword, the curvilinear effect of the whole and the curving folds of the tunic being almost modern in conception. Rather different were several female statues made about the same time whose similarity could point to the work of a fashionable portrait sculptor.

Marble and alabaster are two kinds of stone whose qualities suit them to carving and statuary rather than to building. Marble is the harder of the two, it is capable of taking a high polish, and it was worked into columns and capitals, tombs and effigies, as well as into urns and bowls and such smaller articles. Purbeck marble was the most famous and Corfe the centre of a flourishing industry where, from the end of the twelfth century, the marble was not only quarried but cut to order and sent to many parts of the kingdom.

Alabaster is similar to marble and although it is softish when taken from the earth it hardens when exposed to the air. Like marble, it can be polished, but it is easier to work and it has a warm translucence which is lacking in marble. It was dug in the Derbyshire quarries of Chellaston, in parts of Nottinghamshire, at Tutbury in Staffordshire, and, like marble, was frequently quarried and cut at the same place. There was, for example, the table of alabaster bought in 1367 for the high altar of St George's, Windsor, which was made at Nottingham by Peter Mason and required ten carts, each with eight horses, to transport it from Nottingham to Windsor, a journey which took seventeen days.[2] Nottingham was, indeed, famous not only over Britain but in Europe for its alabaster work.

Alabaster was also in much demand for smaller, probably domestic, images, a number of which have been found hidden under floors—hidden obviously at some period of image-breaking—while many are mentioned as bequests in wills. They were generally gilded or painted, were 28 to 38 inches high and represented such subjects as the Trinity or Our Lady. Even more interesting is the evidence of the mass-production at Nottingham of alabaster tablets called St John's Heads. They measured anything from 4½ inches to 18 inches in height, were oblong in shape, and consisted of the head of John the Baptist on a charger with smaller supporting figures of saints or angels. Large numbers of these were apparently carved and painted in the same workshop. On 31st October 1491, for example, Nicholas Hill brought an action against William Bott for failing to pay for 58 St John's Heads which Bott had taken to sell at tabernacles and houses. In January 1495 Nicholas Hill, 'alabasterman', is himself sued by Robert Tull for failing to pay for transporting 'divers images and heads of John the Baptist' from Nottingham to London. Four years later Hill is again sued—this time because he has not paid Thomas Grene 'playsterer' for a head of St John the Baptist, price 16 pence.[3]

Builder's plaster, obtained by burning gypsum, was produced in large quantities at Buttercrambe in Yorkshire, where there was a large deposit of gypsum. It was also made by burning marble or alabaster not suitable for carving, quantities of plaster being produced, for example, at the Purbeck quarries. Lime, which was required for mortar, was obtained by burning chalk, kilns were frequently dug at or near building-sites, and the lime-burner himself was a well-known figure up and down the country.

Of the people who quarried the stone there is little record, but they were no doubt sufficiently important to be free men. The records show women at work, too, carrying the hewn stone from the quarry. The tools used by most quarry-workers were simple enough, an inventory made in 1400 including iron wedges, iron rods, crowbars, iron hammers, axes of various kinds, and shovels. Another account written a little later speaks of 'an iron tool for breaking stones in the quarry, called a polax, weighing 16½ lbs'.[4] Of the masons more is known, a skilled mason being in high demand. There were obviously degrees of refinement in his work, from cutting the stone into crude blocks at the quarry to the skilled work at the building-site and the making of tombs and statuary. Wherever a cathedral, a big house, a public building required the work of these men a master mason or overseer would be seen travelling the countryside to recruit their services. Robert Spilsbury, chief mason of York, rode for twenty-eight days round the country to secure carvers, and searched for workmen in 'divers places'. Once settled on a job (which might take months or years) the masons organized themselves in lodges, which were the equivalent of trade gilds, and they might even have livery provided for them, as at Canterbury, or working clothes such as gloves and aprons, as at York; it is evident that where the work was important every effort was made to keep the masons on the job.[5] The King, naturally, had an easier way of obtaining labour. For his Welsh castles Edward I in 1282 commanded the sheriffs of English counties to impress masons, ordering particularly fifteen good ones from Somerset and twenty, with a foreman, from Rutland. For building at Windsor Castle Edward III in 1360 ordered as many as 320 masons from twelve different shires, as far away as Northampton, Leicester and Warwick.[6]

Pottery was made in medieval Britain, as it was all over the world and as it had been since prehistoric times. There was nothing distinctive about either the clay or the potting and, apart from a few specialized centres, it was most likely for immediate local use. The process of potting is essentially one of shaping suitable clay by hand or on a potter's wheel and baking the article in a kiln. Sometimes the firing would consist of little more than putting the pot in a fire of brushwood; at other times a more sophisticated combination of kiln and furnace, based on methods learned from the Romans, was in use, in which the vessels to be baked stood on a clay table pierced with holes, underneath which ran hot air from the furnace. The whole process from start to finish could be the occasional occupation of a family as need arose, but there is no reason to doubt that here, as with most products, a division of labour occurred in which the potter's craft became a full-time occupation.

Another specialized craft was that of the tilers, who also used clay for their work. Tiles were made in Roman times, their manufacture probably ceased when the Romans left but by the thirteenth century the hazard of fires from thatched roofs had become so considerable that an effort was made by town authorities to secure the use of tiles for roofing. Throughout the century and thereafter the use of tiles, not only for roofs but for floors and pavements, was of growing importance. Unlike the clay used for pottery, the clay used for tiling had to undergo a rigid seasoning, and rules were early laid down, first by the tilers themselves and later, in 1477, by Act of Parliament, that clay to be made into tiles should be dug by 1st November, stirred and turned until the beginning of February to imbibe the frost, and not made into tiles before March. Chalk, marl and stones had to be rigidly cast out of the clay, and searchers were appointed to check the product. There were tileries in many parts of the country, one of the biggest being the tileworks at Wye in Kent, where ten kilns were turning out thousands of tiles in the middle of the fourteenth century.[7]

Bricks, like tiles, are baked from clay, but although the Romans used them, there was little brick-making in medieval England, and no real revival until the fifteenth century, possibly because of the wide availability of stone. The Flemish weavers, however, imported bricks for building into East Anglia, partly because of the comparative scarcity of building stone in that flat, open countryside and partly, no doubt, to remind them of home. The association for long caused bricks to be known in Britain as 'Flanders' tiles'. There was a general import into Britain from the Low Countries, from Burgundy and from Normandy until the British brick kilns were able to meet the heavy demand of the later fifteenth and sixteenth centuries. The warm red brick of Tudor manor-houses and of palaces like Hampton Court was the sixteenth-century equivalent of the stone cathedral. For domestic architecture its beauty is unsurpassed. Some of the finest examples are in the east of the country, possibly again because good building stone is not so plentiful there as elsewhere.

Glass, again, had been manufactured in England in Roman times. The art died out, it was reintroduced in Anglo-Saxon times, again declined, but in the thirteenth-century it was once more developing. Chiddingfold on the Surrey-Sussex border in particular was, from the beginning of the thirteenth century, one of the main locations of the industry. In the making of glass one part of clean sand was mixed with two parts of wood ash, bracken or beech ash being considered the best. The mixture was put in pots in a clay oven heated by dry wood. When the mixture was molten and thoroughly fused a long, hollow iron rod was inserted into it and a globule was withdrawn. While this globule hung on the one end of the rod the glass-blower blew down the other end, and by blowing and beating fashioned the molten glass into the required shape. For private use glass in any form remained a luxury until the end of the Middle Ages, but English glass—even English stained glass—for churches and cathedrals was not uncommon by the fourteenth century. Thereafter although it became more common for the rich, it was still unknown in the houses of the poor.

Of the extractive industries, coal was perhaps the least considered in the Middle Ages. It had been known as a fuel in Roman Britain, but after the Romans' departure it was hardly used until the beginning of the thirteenth century. By the fourteenth century coal was being mined in many parts of the country—in Northumberland, particularly round Newcastle; in Yorkshire, the Midlands, Lancashire and Shropshire as well as in many areas of small deposits. But, although pits were occasionally dug, it was all small-scale, much of it outcrop mining from surface deposits.

Difficulties of transport precluded the wide use of coal, except for districts near rivers or the sea, and its smoke and smell were considered too unpleasant to make it popular as a domestic fuel: Queen Eleanor in 1275 moved from Nottingham Castle because of the unpleasant fumes of coal burned in the town below. In 1306 the use of coal was prohibited in London by proclamation, although not long after ten shillingsworth was used in the royal palace at the King's coronation.[8] It was probably used more in the north than elsewhere, and Italian visitors sent home accounts of the marvellous stones that burned in the north country. Its wide domestic use was nevertheless impossible until chimneys became common in Elizabethan times. Nor was it an acceptable alternative to charcoal for iron-smelting until the eighteenth century, when it became possible, by coking, to rid it of impurities.[9] The only people actually preferring coal to wood or charcoal were the lime-burners, preparing lime for plaster and other building purposes. Their close connection with coal is borne out by a small street in London variously known as Sacoles Lane or Lime Burner's Lane (which still exists as Seacoal Lane). The common reference to coal as sea-coal probably arose because of the outcrops of coal on sea-shores, the transport of coal by sea—notably from Newcastle to London—later giving a further point to the name.

The first coal-pits dug were of the 'bell pit' type. Where a seam was expected a narrow shaft was sunk which, when the coal was actually struck, was enlarged at the bottom. Here the miner or miners would dig the coal, another worker would convey it to the shaft bottom, loading it in corves to be raised to the surface by a man working a winch. By the fourteenth century various simple methods of drainage were in operation, and by the fifteenth century a pump worked by horsepower was known. A viewer was frequently in charge of underground work, while an overman was in control at the surface.

The law governing the right to dig and the ownership of the coal was very uncertain. Manorial tenants often had the right to dig in waste and forest, but the Lord of the Manor sometimes charged a fee or rent, which could be inordinately large. Moreover, the Lord himself frequently had the right to dig on any of his land, even when farmed by a tenant, without paying compensation. The right to mine coal might come with the grant of the land, as when Edward III in 1351 granted possession of Castle Field to the burgesses of Newcastle-on-Tyne with liberty to dig for coals. A group of men searching for a fresh vein in a coal area would frequently prospect under an overseer, either for themselves or for an employer. In the latter case they might contract to sink the pit, timber it, drain and ventilate it as far as they knew how, erect the windlass to wind up the corves, protect the pit head by a thatch-and-wattle 'hovel' and provide the pickaxes, shovels, ropes and buckets which were a coal-miner's simple and customary tools. These prospectors were most likely free men, and perhaps not badly paid. But the actual face workers, whether free or bond, seem for the most part to have worked as unskilled labourers. Only in the Forest of Dean, where they rubbed shoulders with the iron-miners, did they attain to anything like privilege. Why the coal-miners should have kept such lowly status, in contrast to the iron, lead and tin miners, and to what degree they continued to combine farming and fishing with their mining, is largely guesswork. It is likely that the smaller demand for coal was the chief reason. It is evident, however, that apart from the very simplest collection of coal from outcrops some joint effort, some organization, and some locking up of capital was required for the enterprise.

With the iron-miners the picture is clearer. In the Forest of Dean, the Sussex Weald, in Derbyshire and Yorkshire iron deposits had been worked by the Romans. There was probably a running-down after their departure, but iron-mines and iron-workers figure in Domesday Book, and there was a considerable expansion of the industry in the twelfth and thirteenth centuries. The virtually continuous mining of iron is due to several factors. It is found in many locations—in rock, embedded with seams of coal, in bogs, in beds of lakes. It has had a wide and varied use since early times. The Ancient Britons used iron bars as currency, it was made into beads and other forms of personal adornment, it was used for nails, bolts, bars; for hammers, anvils, horseshoes and much more pertaining to the smithy; for spades, axes and other tools and implements of agriculture which, though rarely made entirely of iron, were frequently iron-tipped—the very plough itself was provided with iron cutting-edges from early times. It was used for arrowheads and much more of the paraphernalia of war and most importantly, for the body-armour of the fighting man. For countless domestic implements, such as pots and pans; for boxes and chests, often of great beauty, iron was used in whole or in part. The hinges of doors, often enlarged and elaborately wrought, were made of iron. The railings or protective grilling round tombs, on windows and over doors, the great decorative iron screens of medieval cathedrals, came from the smith's forge or from his bench. The scale of production can be gauged from the 50 000 iron horseshoes provided by the Forest of Dean for a Crusade of Richard I, or the 30 000 horseshoes and 60 000 nails which the sheriff of Sussex was called upon to supply to the royal army in 1254, or the size of the screen made by John Tresilian about the year 1479 for St George's Chapel at Windsor, which was $11\frac{1}{2}$ feet wide and 9 feet high.

The Forest of Dean was the most important centre of iron-production until the Wealds of Sussex and Kent regained the importance they had had in Roman times. In the Weald, as in Dean, there were deposits of iron and there were forests to provide charcoal. But the Weald had the added advantage of proximity to London and the south-coast ports, and by the fourteenth century its pre-eminence was established. Farther north iron deposits, particularly in Yorkshire and Derbyshire, were being worked on a scale indicated by the fact that at the end of the thirteenth century the Abbey of Furness alone operated some forty forges, compared with seventy-two in the whole of Dean at that time.[10] Most of the northern iron seems to have been absorbed locally, and little came south.

By the fourteenth century iron-mines were on the whole deeper and more elaborate than coal-mines. Besides men hewing iron at some depth, others were employed on timbering, there were bearers to bring the ore to the shaft bottom, winders to bring it to the surface, a man with a horse to carry the ore to workers who gave it a rough washing, then a preliminary heating and beating to rid it of slag and other impurities before breaking it up ready for the actual smelting. Smelting consisted basically of continuing to remove impurities from the ore, and reducing it to a purer and softer state than when it was mined. This was done by placing alternate layers of iron and burning charcoal upon a clay bed in a conical-shaped oven or cauldron with vents near the bottom for the passage of air. A simple fire beneath of wood and charcoal helped combustion. The fires were kept burning by huge bellows, often one at each side of the furnace, which could be worked by hand or by foot, and later were operated by water-power on the same principle as the mill-wheel. In the process of combustion the impurities were expelled and the pure iron sank to the bottom of the cauldron in a malleable lump of the consistency of putty known as a 'bloom'. To assist the formation of the bloom the whole cauldron was stirred with an iron bar, and the mass of iron several times lifted from the forge and vigorously beaten with a hammer. Like the bellows, the hammer was quite early harnessed to water: the term 'hammer-pond' (still in use) may refer to this practice, though the water may also have been used for the cooling of hammers and other tools. The bloom would sometimes go to a second furnace to be reheated and beaten into bars of suitable size and shape for the blacksmiths to forge into saleable commodities. Otherwise the blacksmith was himself involved in this additional labour.

By the fourteenth century many large and sophisticated forges existed on manorial estates in the Weald and in the North of England where the lord of the manor either produced iron himself or leased the right to a tenant. The Wealden ironworks of Tudely in Kent, for example, were variously worked by the lord or let out on lease. All the processes of production, from the mining of the ore to the production of the bloom, were part of the same enterprise: the ore was brought straight into the forge from the mines; charcoal was brought in from the manor woods; there were four skilled smiths (known as bloomsmiths to distinguish them from blacksmiths) in direct charge of the smelting; there was a keeper of works who controlled the men and women employed at the bellows and at other less skilled work. There was only one forge, and the blooms produced, averaging about two hundred a year before the Black Death, were sold directly to the blacksmiths. Payment to the workpeople was partly in kind, the smiths receiving every seventh bloom. There was a clothes allowance and drink money, and there is a record of a bonus payment for good work. The charcoal-burners also were paid by the ironmaster, and received transport charges as well if they brought their product direct to the forge. The ironmaster had also to make payments for timber, for implements like hammers and tongs and pots and pans, and for the great bellows.[11]

Tudeley is an example of a small ironworks with one furnace. Half a century later at Byrkeknott in Weardale, county Durham, an ironworks belonging to and worked by the Bishops of Durham demonstrated a larger type. The main forge was made of timber roofed with turf. Within it were two furnaces. The stream was dammed and the considerable force of water was led to a water-wheel by means of a stone channel and wooden pipes. There were two furnaces at Byrkeknott, one for smelting or blooming, the other for beating the bloom into bars. Labourers brought the ore to the forge from the iron-mines, charcoal was brought in by the charcoal-burners, who burned the underbrush in the Bishop's near-by park at Bedburn. The workers, who included two women, were under the control of a foreman, they were all paid by the piece, and beer was distributed each week. The product was either used on the manor or sold to various blacksmiths.[12]

In the Forest of Dean it is the iron-miners themselves who spring most vividly to life. They still formed in the fourteenth century, as they had for hundreds of years, a close corporation of free miners which had been recognized and given a charter by Edward I in 1286. Within the bounds of the Forest of Dean the resident free miners formed a close monopoly, and exercised many rights from which outsiders were excluded. They, and only they, could dig for iron anywhere in the Forest. They had right of access from the mine to and from the highway, and the right to timber for propping their mines. They exercised such control over persons who bought the ore that all who carried it down the river Severn were bound to pay duty to the miners under penalty of forfeiting their boats. The restraints upon their enterprise were few, though the landlord had the right to a share of the ore and the king claimed special dues.

Iron left the ironworks either in the form of bloom or of the more convenient bars. The blacksmith's work was done at the forge, where he reduced the iron once more to red-hot heat, and on the anvil, where he fashioned the burning metal with hammer and tongs. The heyday of pure blacksmithery, when the blacksmith worked with red-hot metal at the forge, lasted until the end of the thirteenth century. Even when making commonplace articles for everyday use he developed his art to an amazing degree of beauty and intricacy, pulling and beating, shaping and twisting the live metal with the implements he grasped in his hands. Beautiful and elaborate door-hinges were made of wrought iron. The hinge served the double purpose of enabling a door to open and shut, and, if it were sufficiently enlarged, of joining firmly together the timbers of which the door was made. With the double object in view, the blacksmiths expressed themselves with verve and imagination. Fortunately, many doors have been preserved, and it is possible still to see beautiful twelfth-century hinge-work like that on a door of St Albans Abbey—which binds the whole door together in a series of scrolls of simple yet infinitely satisfying design.[13]

A thirteenth-century smith, known from his native town as Thomas of Leghtone (the modern Leighton Buzzard), fashioned a magnificent grille to protect the tomb of Queen Eleanor in Westminster Abbey. It stands on the top of her stone tomb, projecting well over each end and above it to a height equal to that of the tomb itself. It consists of eleven vertical panels each filled with a simple, different pattern of scrolls or flowers or leaves which are so arranged as to cover the welded joints of the design. Twenty-six candle prickets surmount the whole length of the grille.

From the end of the thirteenth century ironwork was increasingly wrought cold, at the bench, and not at the forge. It was cut and fitted together often like timber joinery and frequently fretted with patterns. One of the most beautiful examples of wrought-iron bench-work is the screen in the chantry of Henry V's Chapel in Westminster Abbey, probably of 1428 or a little later. But greatest of all was the wrought ironwork of the chantry gates and screen of St George's Chapel, Windsor, made about 1479 by John Tresilian, the 'chief smith' of Windsor Castle. It is remarkable not only for its size and overall beauty but for the detail of the design, the fine quality of the workmanship, and the accuracy with which the smith, working entirely by hand and eye, fitted together the intricate pieces of his design.

All over the country, meanwhile, the local blacksmith

continued to turn out the objects of utility which were his stock-in-trade. Part of a trade jingle demonstrates his pride and his indispensability:

> How can the ships upon the sea sail,
> If Ankor prove nought, and do not prevail;
>
> How can the Shooemaker work at all,
> But first the Smith must make his Aul
>
> How can the Post-masters carry news,
> But first the Smith puts on the Shooes
> With Spurs and Stirrup for man's use
>
> How can they go to Plow or Cart,
> But first the Smith must play his part
> His Coulters and Shairs made well by art
>
> Your Pattern-Irons great and small,
> To support your Women long and tall;
> As to keep you out of the Dirt withall,
>
> Oh! what trade, Oh! can you name!
> But first the Smith supplies the same,
> For he is the honour of the Game.[14]

The casting of iron was a development whose full potential was not reached until much later. Casting consists of pouring white-hot liquid metal into a prepared mould or cast whose form it takes and keeps when cold; it requires a furnace capable of heating beyond boiling-point and one which is larger than the bloom furnace. Iron was cast in a foundry, and the man responsible was not a smith but a founder. The result depended upon bringing the ore to the required heat and liquidity and pouring the molten mass into the right mould at the right time and in the right way. 'A Furnace', wrote John Fuller the Sussex ironfounder in 1754 'is a fickle mistress and must be humoured and her favours not to be depended upon. The excellency of a Founder is to humour her dispositions, but never to force her inclinations.'[15]

The widest and most important use of cast iron was in the making of ordnance. Gunpowder, which made possible the first guns, was known by the early fourteenth century and the first ordnance in Britain were perhaps those used in 1333 at the siege of Berwick. But these early guns were of wrought-iron pieces welded together and kept more secure by iron rings shrunk round them, or else they were bronze, cast probably by bell founders. The earliest iron gun (a mortar) was not cast until the fifteenth century. Thereafter the industry of gun casting or founding grew rapidly, and by the time of Elizabeth I Sir Walter Raleigh could speak of it as 'a Jewel of great value'.

There were other uses to which cast iron was eminently suited, such as grave slabs and firebacks. Grave slabs may have been cast as early as the middle of the fourteenth century, firebacks came into general use when wall fires became common at the end of the fifteenth century; they could not, indeed, have had much purpose without the wall fire. Once this was established the cast-iron fireback, more resistant to heat than forged iron, was almost an essential for protecting the wall behind the fire and for giving back heat from its surface more effectively than the wall itself. For other domestic purposes—railings, balconies, gates, balustrades—the real importance of cast iron came later.

The blacksmith is generally pictured as a cheerful man, physically fit, singing at his forge as he wields his hammer with superhuman energy, making the sparks fly while children peer through the open smithy door at the unearthly scene within. He was closely allied to the gods, and his craft, indeed, was learned from a heavenly prototype. Not so the founder.

> The founder is always like a chimney sweep, covered with charcoal and distasteful sooty smoke, his clothing dusty and half burned by the fire, his hands and face all plastered with soft muddy earth. To this is added the fact that for this work a violent and continuous straining of all a man's strength is required, which brings great harm to his body and holds many definite dangers to his life. In addition, this art holds the mind of the artificer in suspense and fear regarding its outcome, and keeps his spirit disturbed and almost continually anxious. For this reason they are called fanatics and are despised as fools. But, with all this, it is a profitable and skilful art and in large part delightful.[16]

Lead-mines, like iron, had been worked by the Romans and had never been completely abandoned. In Derbyshire, in the Mendips, on Alston Moor lead was mined, and it was a staple export in Saxon times and through the Middle Ages. There were mines in Devonshire which were in production for the half-century before the Black Death, and prospectors were sent as far afield as Ireland in the search for more seams. Lead ores owed much of their importance, as they had in Roman times, to the fact that from them silver was refined. In the thirteenth century the Devon mines, in particular, were rich in silver, yielding over £4 000 worth between 1292 and 1297, compared with £360 worth of lead.[17]

After the lead had been broken up, washed and sieved for the removal of the cruder impurities—a process in which women assisted—it was brought to the furnace. The silver was refined from the lead by an open-hearth process in the course of which the lead rose to the surface and was skimmed off. This could be done several times. When the silver was fully refined it was cast into plates or ingots ready for the silversmith. The lead, meantime, having a low melting-point, was rapidly brought again to liquid form and then run into moulds. Silver was used for dishes, plates, cups, goblets, buckles, ornaments, jewellery of all kinds. The shrines of saints, the thrones of monarchs, the altars of churches, the regalia of kings and princes, of churchmen and queens were made or decorated with silver. Household silver demonstrated the wealth and standing of the occupant. At a time when investment in the modern sense was hardly known, all who were rich enough put their wealth into the precious metals. That London used her silversmiths to an unprecedented degree is evidenced by the astonished comment of the Venetian traveller in 1500, who found, in one single street, 'fifty-two goldsmiths' shops so rich and full of silver vessels, great and small, that in all the shops in Milan, Rome, Venice, and Florence put together, I do not think there would be found so many of the magnificence that are to be seen in London'.[18] The scale on which silver was ordered can be seen from the six serving dishes, twelve goblets and thirty saltcellars which were presented to the Black Prince in 1371 by the City of London, or the four dozen serving dishes and eight dozen other dishes of silver which were made for Henry V in 1416.

But lead was also valuable in itself, and had a variety of important and practical uses. In England in the Middle Ages, in contrast to the Continent where more stone, tiles and slate were employed, it was widely used for church roofing, being easily worked and at the same time resistant to climatic conditions. Not only were actual roofs made of lead but timber spires were enclosed in lead, like those of Hereford, Rochester and Canterbury Cathedrals and Old St Paul's in London, whose leaden spire was over two hundred feet high. Lead was used for baptismal fonts, often very beautifully worked and decorated. It was used for coffins and ossuaries, sometimes as a lining, sometimes by itself. It was used for garden figures, urns and pots; for water cisterns and for caskets; rather later—perhaps not until the fifteenth century—for gutters and rainwater pipes, often with ornamental heads; it was used for water-pipes underground and for drainage pipes. Weights, coins, cups, plates and other domestic ware were made of lead. And because lead is soft and malleable the medieval craftsman was able to use his skill and artistry in many decorative forms. He made charming amulets and tokens for the pilgrim to bring home from his pilgrimage, many of which have been found in the mud of the river Thames. 'Thou art . . . laden on every side with images of tin and lead!' exclaimed a traveller to a pilgrim, and indeed the custodian of the shrine did a brisk trade in these mementoes. They were virtually mass-produced by casting, and some of the little stone moulds which were used still exist. They were round, oval, square, or lozenge-shaped, and the finished token had either a loop for sewing to the dress or a pin so that it could be used as a brooch. There were also little leaden ampullae or bottles, usually made to hang round the neck and generally containing some specific. One, for example, from Canterbury is about $3\frac{1}{4}$ inches high, has on one side a bishop in robes with mitre and staff and on the other the inscription: *Optimus egrorum medicus fit Toma bonorum* (The best physician for the good invalid is Thomas). It probably purported to contain St Thomas's blood or dust from his shrine.[19]

The lead-miners, particularly those of Derbyshire and the Mendips, were even more highly organized than the iron-miners of Dean. A lead-miner in either of these areas had the right to prospect anywhere except in churchyards, gardens, orchards or highways. If he struck a likely vein he marked the spot with a cross, and was bound to set up his mining machinery within a certain time. Like the iron-miner, he had the right of access to the nearest high road in such a way, it was laid down, that three men walking abreast with arms outstretched would mark the direct way from the mine to the road, even through standing corn. The immutable customs governing the lead-miner's work were laid down and enforced by a special mine court, which met every three weeks. The court defended the miners against outsiders and it defended them against each other, it enforced their privileges during life, it took responsibility for them after death, it laid down and enforced the strict code under which they dug the ore and the various regulations that governed its sale. It was all expounded in a rhymed chronicle which one of the stewards of the miners' court wrote in 1653.[20] But, although in Derbyshire and over a large part of Mendip the miners were independent producers, the hope of refining silver brought many speculators into the lead-mining business. The king himself owned many mines, particularly in Devonshire, the Bishop of Wells owned mines in Mendip. In cases like these the miners were wage labourers, and the organization was capitalist.

But in the fourteenth century, as in ancient times, the tin-mines of Devonshire and Cornwall took pride of place. English tin had been known throughout the ancient world; in the Middle Ages it was exported to Europe and beyond, including Cyprus and the countries of the Eastern Mediterranean. Efforts were made to establish a staple, as for wool, but these did not endure. For a short while between 1376 and 1492 Calais, for a short time after 1492 Southampton, acted as partial staples, but they never had a complete monopoly, and much tin was exported through other ports. A great deal made its way from Devon and Cornwall by pack-horse to London and, as with wool, there was much smuggling. Foreign merchants for long did much of the shipping, as they did with wool. In the middle of the fifteenth century Italian merchants, buying wool, were said to get tin cheaply by offering ready money.[21] Tin-miners themselves often took goods in direct exchange for their tin, exchanging with foreign traders or English middlemen. Jews, before their expulsion in 1290, were said to be dealers in tin.

For a long while the main importance of tin was in its hardening effect upon copper. Copper is a relatively soft metal, but an admixture of up to 10 per cent of tin makes it sufficiently hard to be sharpened to a fine point. The mixture also becomes more fluid than copper alone, and is therefore more easily cast. The copper-tin combination, known as bronze, was very important to the ancient world, giving its name to the period between the Stone Age and the Iron Age. Weapons, even in early times entire suits of armour, were made of bronze. Its value continued through the Middle Ages when it was used for coins, for cooking utensils, for a variety of domestic articles. Some very fine statuary was cast in bronze, though its expense compared with stone was a limiting factor. There is, for example, in Westminster Abbey a bronze effigy of Queen Eleanor, cast at the end of the thirteenth century, and, above all, the effigy of Richard Beauchamp, Earl of Warwick, which was cast in bronze about 1450 and still lies in the Beauchamp chapel at St Mary's church, Warwick. It is magnificent in every way, the veined hands raised in a gesture of welcome, the eyes greeting the Virgin carved in a corbel above the east window.

Cannon were sometimes cast in bronze before iron was used, but perhaps the widest use of bronze in England in the Middle Ages was in the making of bells. The bellcaster's task was highly skilled, in that he had to adjust his bell in size and shape, and in the exact turn of the rim to the peal he required. A 'core', which was an exact model of the inside of the bell to be cast, was made of successive layers of clay which were rotated on a wooden bar or lathe until the precise shape was achieved. An iron staple, upon which the clapper would hang, was then inserted at the top, and the clay mould was baked. A 'thickness', corresponding exactly to the required thickness of the bell, was then built up round the clay core. As this 'thickness' had to be dispersed before the actual bell was cast, it generally consisted of clay or earth or, in early times, of some kind of fat or oil which would melt away in the furnace. On top of the 'thickness' would then be moulded a thick clay 'cope'. This done, the 'thickness' would be destroyed, leaving a hollow between the 'core' and the 'cope' into which the molten copper and tin was poured—this last being an operation of skill.

A second important use for tin was in the making of solder, an alloy of tin and lead which makes simple and easy contact with surfaces to be joined and retains them in position. Solder was required in metal-work, in building, in woodwork and had countless other uses. But in the Middle Ages the most important use of tin in Britain, in which the metal was employed in its purest form, was in the making of pewter. Pewter is essentially tin with varying additions, perhaps 20 per cent in inferior pewter, less in the best, of copper or lead. The best pewter was tin with a little copper, sometimes called 'fine pewter'; 'common pewter' was tin and lead, and the Pewterers' Gild in 1348 drew up Ordinances to control the substance and the proportions used in various articles. By the fourteenth century both fine and common pewter were beginning to replace other forms of material for table and household purposes. Pewter mugs, plates and dishes of all kinds were attractive to look at, easily cleaned, unbreakable, light in weight, and cheaper than silver. The Italian visitor who so marvelled at the Londoner's display of silver also remarked, referring to their pewter plates, that 'they eat off that fine tin, which is little inferior to silver'. Their pewter vessels, he said, were 'of the purest quality' and 'as brilliant as if they were of fine silver'.[22] Indeed, so excellent and so highly esteemed was English pewter that early in the reign of Elizabeth I it was asserted that 'beyond the sea a garnish of good flat English pewter . . . is esteemed almost so precious as the like number of vessels that are made of fine silver'.[23]

Pewter was also used for jewellery, sometimes for religious chalices, croziers and other objects, particularly when these were buried with the dead. Pewter boxes and caskets were common, while the heart of Richard Cœur-de-Lion was preserved in a casket of pure tin.

In Cornwall and Devonshire, the areas of most extensive tin-mining, production was similar to, but even more highly organized, than that of lead. It was based on immemorial custom, and had been ratified in a charter of 1201 which gave the tin-miners the right of 'digging tin and turfs for smelting it at all times, freely and peaceably and without hindrance from any man'. A man might prospect single-handed, or several might join together in partnership. Mines might be worked by a man who himself hired labour for the purpose. Such a one was 'Abraham the Tinner', who in the middle of the fourteenth century employed over three hundred men, women and children. A lord of the manor might try to work the tin directly or through his agents. In Cornwall, where most of Britain's tin was mined from the thirteenth century onwards, the land belonged to the Duchy of Cornwall, which was (and is) in the ownership of the Prince of Wales. The Crown therefore was intimately connected with tin-mining, and had a pre-emptive right over all tin produced. But a villein was also free to 'bound' for tin. Staking out his claim entailed digging a small pit and making a small pile of turf at each of the four corners of the plot. When he had thus 'pitched his bounds' it was necessary for the tinner to register them with the Stannary Court, and the bounding had to be repeated each year. Each tinner needed, also, to register his own private mark. He received not only the right to running water to wash his ore, but the right to divert streams to his own use, and the landlord was obliged to sell him fuel for his fire. He himself was bound by certain restrictions and obligations: digging in highways, gardens or churchyards was prohibited; so was 'bounding upon bounds'; the washing of ore must be in public; the buying or selling of ore could legally take place only at the tin-works or at the washes; no rubbish could be dumped on other men's works; the wearing of arms at any tin-works or washes was prohibited. The landlord for his share in the enterprise normally received a fixed proportion of the ore.

By the fourteenth century there were four independent units, known as Stannaries (from *stannum*, the Latin word for tin) in Devonshire and five in Cornwall, each governed by its own court with, over all, a Tinners' Parliament which met periodically. This organization, by immemorial custom, effectively controlled the tin-mines and the lives of the tin-miners, protecting them with a hedge of privilege from many normal obligations. They were exempt from ordinary taxation, they were mustered for war by their own stannary representatives and not by the king's, they were, as expressed in the charter of 1201, removed from all pleas of serfs, they were freed from all jurisdiction save that of the Stannary Court. The tin-miners formed a state within a state. Their lives were governed by custom and ancient usage expressed through their own courts. But, unlike the open-field farmers, they were free, and their courts controlled their lives as free men and not as bound.

But, free miner or wage-earning miner, in coal or iron, lead or tin, it was no easy life, and full of danger. 'They venture lives full dear in dangers great', wrote Edward Manlove of the Derbyshire lead-miners.[24] The Somerset lead-miners had their own rules for dealing with accidents. If any man, they said, 'tack his deth and ys slayne by faulyng of the yerth upon hym, by drownyng, by styffyng with fyer or wother wyse, as in tymes past meny hath ben so murthryd' the miners shall take up his body—even if he be killed sixty fathoms down—and bury him at their own costs.[25] Piers le Graver was one such, killed by the collapse of the coal-pit in which he was working in 1290. Emma, daughter of William Culhare, was killed by choke damp in 1322. Old mine workings were a hazard to everyone, and there are many stories of broken limbs while water often accumulated in disused pits in which people and animals were drowned: at the end of the thirteenth century it was said to be dangerous to approach the town of Newcastle after dark for this reason. Mining and metal-working were already of considerable importance in Britain at the time of the Black Death, but although some of the miners were in a privileged position compared with other workers, the last word rests with the Somerset lead-miners who spoke of mining as 'thys doubtfull and daungerous occupasyon'.

CHAPTER VI

The Break-up of the Manor

While such activities as quarrying, mining and metalwork had their importance, the greater part of the country was concerned with the land and its attendant problems. The long and difficult transition from feudalism to modern contractual society had been apparent in various ways in the expansion of the twelfth and thirteenth centuries: the lord of the manor reached out not only to take in land from the forest and waste but also to farm for his own use some of the common land of the village; land-hunger caused both bond men and free to break in new land, for which they paid either a money rent or a lump-sum quit payment; freemen even took up land in villeinage, although this entailed taking over villein obligations and services—for these pertained not to the person but to the land. At the same time, feeling increasingly the disadvantages of having part of his land in strips scattered in the open fields, the manorial lord was beginning to consolidate them, exchanging with his tenants in such a way as to secure his land in a block and, wherever possible, contiguous with the area he already held round his manor house. The open-field farmers also benefited from consolidation, and made exchanges between themselves.

Another movement slowly proceeding during this period of high farming was a commutation of labour dues into money rents. For the lord this entailed freedom from the organization of villein labour. It meant a saving of money on harvest meals and other refreshment—for appetites were large, and the bills for estate workers' food and drink were high. It meant service, perhaps, more gladly performed—'customary tenants neglect their work and it is necessary to guard against their fraud', advised Walter of Henley. It gave greater scope for innovation. It meant a welcome money receipt at a time when profit in ready cash counted for much. But, on the other hand, it meant finding, and paying, other labour to work his lands; if labour were going to be scarce he would do better to make sure of it by taking his dues in service. Many an illiterate but profit-seeking lord must have scratched his head before making his decision: where he was rapidly enlarging his demesne he was most likely to press for all the feudal 'works' he could get; where *famuli* worked his estates, as in the Midlands, commutation was the better way; he sometimes changed from one to the other.

In so far as labour services were a mark of servitude the villeins welcomed commutation; they welcomed also an end to the uncertainty of working for others when their own land needed attention—this was particularly the case where they themselves had acquired new land, and needed all the family labour they could muster. At the same time, to them as to their lords, money was becoming something to be saved, to be preserved, and they were reluctant to part with it; they also were reluctant to forgo such perquisites as the abundant harvest meals. Whether they were asked to continue or to revert to labour services, or were asked instead for a rent which they considered too high, there was dissatisfaction.

The whole situation was extremely fluid by the time of the Black Death. The scramble for land, together with commutation, had somewhat blurred social status, villein and freeman often working side by side on land for which they paid a money rent. The lord, on the one hand adopting the role of employer farming for profit, on the other reasserting his feudal rights, had demonstrated the mutability of what had seemed unchangeable. It was a time when the industrious, the lucky, the speculator, was able to add acre to acre and become richer than his fellows. It was a state of affairs in which the servile might be economically better off than the free, and in which the peasant who acquired land, helped by the reserve of family labour, was occasionally in a better position than the lord. That his holding might be of considerable size is illustrated by the villein with a hundred acres of land and fifty sheep who was the subject of discussion by the thirteenth-century lawyer Bracton. It followed that the manor court, charging a man with the non-performance of some servile obligation, might well find itself faced, not with a humble villein, but with an affluent land-holder. At the same time the villein was becoming not always so humble.

Freemen with villein holdings, economically prosperous villeins, had their problems as well as the poor villein, and the need to reconcile the legal with the actual situation caused much friction. It sometimes happened that a man's status was in question, whether he were villein or free. Such cases were for the royal courts, for to summon him to be heard in the manorial court was a prejudging of the issue. One hears, for example, of William, son of Andrew, a tenant in the village of Crowmarsh, who claimed before the royal justices at Oxford that he was a freeman and no villein. The case went against him on the grounds that he had relatives who were villeins. But he had, for that brief space, been accorded the rights of a free man.

Apart from status, the holder of unfree land was troubled by the fact that legally he could not assign it without the lord's consent. This gave the lord the power to break up accumulated holdings, and to prevent their sale or bequest. These were but a few of the factors that were leading to a questioning of the very concept of feudalism itself: the withholding of labour services, bad work, refusals to come to the ploughing, absence from the autumn boon work, non-performance of carrying services were repeated all over the country. Tenants manhandled those who tried to coerce them, and the reeve was known to throw in his lot with the peasants.

On this expanding, restless, and trouble-fraught economy a recession fell in the second decade of the fourteenth century, swiftly followed by the plague. The reduction of population caused by the Black Death was so severe that it outstripped the recession and sent wages soaring upward. So profitable did wage labour become that villeins abandoned their land and offered themselves as wage labourers, sometimes leaving their manors and going elsewhere to get a better rate. Employers not only overbid each other in their efforts to get labour but openly enticed other people's workers by offers of livery and food as well as higher wages. Cases of the abduction of serfs by desperate landlords were not unknown. At the same time, with plague and flight sharply increasing the quantity of land available, many plots were bought up cheaply in a way that accentuated the changing relationships of the previous couple of centuries.

While the peasant found further opportunities for bettering himself in the years following the Black Death, the lord of the manor was less adaptable. He gained initially from the entry fines of new tenants, but, with more land than the available labour could work, land values fell; the manor was overstocked with beasts coming in as heriots, for whom there was insufficient grazing and too little money for food. As they were sold off in manor after manor their value fell. The price of corn and other crops in short supply through shortage of labour did rise, it is true, but with insufficient labour to sow or reap, this was little compensation. The situation was such that the lord, particularly the lord of an arable manor, found himself burdened with too much land. The big pasture farmers, where comparatively little labour was needed, were in a better position, and there was indeed some change from arable to pasture farming. But more often the owner of an arable manor was compelled to lease some of the demesne land so recently and so profitably enlarged. It was taken up not only by people already working on the land, who could supply their own labour, but by professional people of many kinds who were prepared to take a risk. The leasing of the demesne began on a considerable scale after the Black Death, and remained a permanent feature of the English system of landholding. Among artisans, meanwhile, a similar story of higher wages and betterment followed the plague and within a few years wages and prices in general had risen by an estimated 50 per cent.

In face of these rising prices, of the decay of agriculture and a weakening of the bonds of society as villeins left their manors and bands of unattached labourers wandered over a country fearful and appalled at the ravishes of the plague, the King's Council proclaimed the Ordinance of Labourers of 18th June 1349. It laid down that all able-bodied men and women under the age of sixty years, free or servile, having no means of support, should work when required; that all labourers should accept the wages paid in 1346 or in the five or six years before; that none should break an agreement made on these terms; that none should offer or demand higher wages. Retailers of food and innkeepers were to charge prices that gave 'a moderate profit and not excessive'. But there was no improvement in the situation and the seriousness of the labour problem was one of the reasons for summoning Parliament, which supplemented the Ordinance by the Statute of Labourers of 9th February 1351. This made the law more precise, and fixed many wages at definite levels. The Statute was reissued from time to time, and the penalties made more severe. It was operated by justices of labourers specially appointed by and responsible to the Crown, and labourers were required to swear obedience to it. This was the first serious effort of the central authority to legislate in labour matters for the country as a whole, and meant overriding the authority of the manorial court and of the gild. It was also the first time there had been a restriction on the movement of free labour.

But the very confusion of the complicated penalties aroused anger and hindered the operation of the laws. Labourers refused to take the prescribed oath that they would keep to their contracts, or broke the oath if they took it. Constables reported long lists of rebellious labourers, and often they themselves, kept over-busy, were bound over for not having their cases ready. Frequently even the constables were under indictment for concealing their knowledge of guilty labourers—fairly good evidence that the whole area was united against the Acts.

It is a measure of the success of the opposition that wages were not kept down to the level prescribed. It is a measure of the success of the Statutes that wages were probably for some ten years held at a lower level than they would have been without legislation. In either case the influence on labour revolt was considerable: in so far as the workmen successfully flouted the Statutes they were encouraged to further action; in so far as the Statutes continued to operate against them they were determined on further resistance. That that Statutes of Labourers accelerated the flights of villeins was pointed out by the Government itself:

> If their masters reprove them for bad service, or offer to pay them for the said service according to the form of the said statutes, they fly and run suddenly away out of their services and out of their own country, from County to County and town to town, in strange places unknown to their said masters. And many of them become staff-strikers and live also wicked lives, and rob the poor in simple villages, in bodies of two or three together.

The stories, well known at the time, of outlaws like Robin Hood gave encouragement to such conduct, and the Government itself drove many a villein to the forests by its pronouncement that if the sheriff failed to catch a workman condemned under the Statute of Labourers he should declare him an outlaw whom any man might slay at sight. These men, together with the artisans, bailiffs, schoolteachers, chaplains and others who were on the move were all good combustible material in an inflammatory situation. They were natural messengers, bearers of news, organizers. When the Government complained that the peasants conspired, that they gathered by night, that they had a common purse, and that agitators led them they were not far from the mark in attributing organization to these people.

Equally significant was the role of the clergy. To the people of the fourteenth century the pulpit was the book, the newspaper, the theatre; the influence of the preacher, whether regular incumbent or wandering priest, was widespread. Denunciation of the rich, the covetous, the oppressor, the unscrupulous, the dishonest, poured from the pulpit in lurid phrases. The range of invective was wide—the thieving miller, the dishonest baker, the deceiving chapman, the rascally brewer, no less than the incontinent priest, the worldly incumbent, the avaricious merchant, the hard-hearted master, the selfish or brutal lord. Judgment Day was never far from their minds as they forecast the reversal in fortune:

> Instead of riches, poverty; instead of delights, punishment; instead of honour, misery and contempt; instead of laughter, weeping; instead of gluttony and drunkenness, hunger and thirst without end; instead of excessive gaming with dice and the like, grief; and in place of the torment which for a time they inflicted on others, they shall have eternal torment

thundered John Bromyard.

It was natural that the pulpit should concern itself also with first principles, and of these none was more compelling or more basic to the Christian religion than the principle of equality. 'All are descended from the same parents, and all come of the same mud', said Bromyard. 'All Christians', said Bishop Brunton, 'rich and poor alike, without distinction of persons, are from one father Adam . . . In these and many other things the rich and the poor are alike and equal'.[1] It was in line with these well-known sentiments that John Ball, in his turn, asked:

When Adam delved and Eve span
Who was then the gentleman?

John Ball, a simple itinerant priest who practised the true evangelical poverty of the Franciscans, had for twenty years before the Peasants' Revolt been preaching his message. There is no doubt that he and others like him were also planning a concerted rising, that they acted as messengers and carried instructions in code from one part of the country to another. But the spark that lit the inflammable material was the poll-tax imposed to finance the long and disastrous war with France. Peasants of Essex and Kent rounded on the tax commissioners, beheaded some of the officials, burned local manor-houses and then set off to march to London. In days the Kentish men were a few miles south of London at Blackheath, while the Essex men lay at Mile End to the north-east. The Government was paralysed with amazement and fear. The peasants, for their part, although they had sent out letters and emissaries to other parts of the country, received no reinforcements. They had burned many charters and legal documents on their way to London, and now appeared at a loss. The following day they swarmed into the City over bridges unaccountably left open for them. They destroyed more charters, records and muniments. The great houses of their chief enemies were set ablaze. The Fleet and Newgate were made to disgorge their prisoners. The young King Richard II agreed to parley the following morning at Mile End. Here Wat Tyler, the peasants' leader, with the whole congregation of peasants in orderly array behind him, put forward their demands. They were simple enough. They asked that serfdom be abolished all over the kingdom; that all feudal service should disappear; that all holders in villeinage should become free peasants paying 4*d*. an acre each year to their lord; that all restrictions on free buying and selling be removed; that market monopolies be abolished; and, finally, that a general amnesty be proclaimed for all offences committed during the rising. The King promised charters to embody these demands and banners which the peasants could take home as a sign of his goodwill.

Only great naïveté could believe that feudal obligation could be abolished by the King without the sanction of Parliament, but many of the peasants appeared satisfied and returned home. But others who had joined the revolt were now turning to riot, destruction and murder within the City. The final episode occurred on the morning of the 15th June at Smithfield, when the King's followers at last rallied and Wat Tyler was killed before the eyes of his followers. This was the end of the Peasants' Revolt. The men of St Albans, where the Abbey kept a tight feudal rein on peasantry and townsfolk alike, had won a temporary victory, but surrendered when it was clear that the revolt in London was crushed. A violent revolt in East Anglia, though it had started before the climax in London, came to a head too long after to be of real use, and the rebels were routed without mercy by the Bishop of Norwich and an armed retinue. There was a great deal more activity in various parts of the country but it was all spasmodic, and all the outbreaks suffered because of the news from London. When the ruling classes recovered from their fear and shock they were still in time to prevent any wide union of the peasants and were able to crush each outbreak individually.

The particular form of poll-tax which sparked off the revolt was never reimposed. Many peasants continued to tender 4*d*. an acre for their holdings in accordance with the demand made at Mile End and copied into their charters. These charters themselves were copied and recopied in spite of their abrogation by King and Parliament. Spasmodic local outbreaks and refusals of service continued as they had done before 1381; documents relating to servile tenure or the break-up of peasant land were frequently burnt. In short, that process of decay of manorial organization which was perceptible a couple of centuries earlier and which had been accelerated by the Black Death, was given a further impetus by the Peasants' Revolt. But economic factors were continuing to work for change in a manner more decisive than that of the Revolt of 1381: the pattern of landholding continued to change, and social relationships were becoming more fluid as towns grew and trade expanded.

CHAPTER VII

Towns and Internal Trade

Towns had developed in various ways connected with geography, trade, defence, the specialization of function, the need for protection. They had grown round a king's court, a monastery, an abbey, a fair. They had been deliberately planted or they had grown naturally. Their inhabitants varied. There were men who concentrated on a craft rather than upon agriculture; there were merchants and traders of all kinds; the liege-men of kings and feudal lords whose job was to provide a refuge for their lord, to fight for him when need arose, to keep the town wall in repair. There were the little shopkeepers and others who gathered round any centre of population to meet the needs of those already there. There were villeins who had come in from the villages, with or without their lord's consent, to try their hand at whatever occupation the town might offer. Many of these were encouraged to settle by offers of a fixed money rent for their houses and workshops; villeins were promised, in addition, their personal freedom.

But while the English town was enriched by a variety of people with different skills, social outlook, wealth and way of life, it was disrupted by divided allegiance and continuing feudal obligation. A town could be part of a manor or even be divided between several manors. The citizen could be subject to feudal taxation, feudal property laws and feudal service, many now prosperous burghers being liable to muster arms at their lord's command as well as being subject to the obligation of boon days and harvest, suit of court and suit of mill. Yet, though the unity of the manor was absent from the town, the town had a unity of purpose that enabled it to bargain with its overlords, to become wealthy, and to turn wealth to the best advantage. A great historian found this unity enshrined in the market and the moot—in trade and commerce and in law and justice[1]—and the interaction of the two is apparent throughout the history of any prosperous town. Townsmen sought by law to protect and enlarge their commercial interests and to give them permanence in a legal document known as a charter. They paid handsomely for the charter, their growing wealth put them in a strong bargaining position, the concessions they won increased their wealth and so trade and the law, wealth and privilege, developed side by side, each assisting the other.

Of all the privileges which townsmen sought, none was more highly prized burgage tenure. This valuable form of landholding—the word derives from Old English *burh*, a town—freed them from all servile dues and services. Their property was their own to sell, let, divide, bequeath, as they wished. For their land they paid a money rent, and a money rent only. They were justiciable in a court in which their fellow-burgesses were the jurors, and they were generally exempted from attendance at the Shire and Hundred Courts. It became customary to call these free townsmen burgesses. The control of taxation was also of the utmost importance. Taxes of varying amount and extent, a combination of all that had grown up through the Middle Ages, probably variable at the will of the overlord, were crippling and disorganizing. To compound for a fixed sum was one of the first aims of a developing town. Sometimes this *firma burgi* (literally, the farm of the borough) was given in fee ferm (in perpetuity), sometimes for a prescribed period; it was not unusual for it to be withdrawn, and it could be the subject of bribe and bargain. But gradually by the fourteenth century the *firma burgi* had become recognized as advantageous to both sides of the bargain. To the overlord it gave the certainty of a fixed tax without the trouble of organizing its collection; to the burgesses it gave freedom from arbitrary taxation and freedom from an outside tax-collector. If the amount collected was in excess of that due the town gained. In bad times, on the other hand, a town could find itself saddled with a tax it was unable to support, and it had to beg for the reduction of the *firma burgi*, as did Southampton in 1376, and Winchester in 1440.

Legal rights were at the same time most tenaciously sought. To plead and be responsible only to a town court and not to a manorial court was an obvious measure of freedom. Their right not to be impleaded beyond the walls of the town gave to the burgesses the advantage of avoiding journeys, of keeping the profits of justice in their own hands, of pleading before their fellow-citizens rather than strangers, while the right to appoint their own magistrates kept out unwelcome officers of the Crown or of a feudal lord, like that much-hated representative of the monarch, the sheriff. At the same time there developed the right of making their own bylaws and of electing their own mayor. The towns also sought the protection which comes from being able to act as one body—a corporate body. Incorporation enabled them to hold property in common, and by mortmain to secure perpetual succession; to sue and be sued in the name of the corporation, and to crown all with the creation of a common seal. Practice frequently came before actual incorporation, many towns making corporate contracts, owning corporate property, even using a common seal before being legally registered as corporate bodies. Oxford, for instance, did this for four hundred years before its charter of incorporation was given by James I in 1605. What later came to be considered a town's finest privilege—the sending of a Member of Parliament—was not always considered so, and it is probable that fewer towns were being summoned to send burgesses to Parliament at the end of the Middle Ages than there had been in 1300, while charters even contained clauses exempting towns from so doing[2].

The towns at the time of the Black Death, and for long after, present no unified picture. Their origins were different, the persistence of feudal connections and feudal obligations varied in extent and duration, they won varying privileges at different times. The very privileges won by some interfered with those won by others. Their quarrels and feuds were as bitter as those between feudal lords or nation-states, the difference being that increasingly they resorted to law rather than to arms. The development of English central government, however, which proceeded more quickly than in many European countries like Italy and Germany, prevented the towns from reaching the pinnacles of bellicose independence they attained in those lands. Before they had the opportunity to do so they had been contained within the framework of a nation-state.

Since much of the borough's wealth was founded upon trade, and since it was this wealth that enabled the burghers to pay for their privileges, trading rights necessarily played a large part in the concessions they won, and the right to markets and fairs was embodied in most charters. Often there was included a virtual monopoly of trade within the borough and far-reaching powers of regulation. A stranger could be prevented from opening a shop or buying or selling or otherwise engaging in trade unless he paid for the privilege. Toll could be levied upon the goods of alien merchants, while those of the burghers were free. A burgess could be given the right to make a bargain in advance of other people—though he could also be compelled to share the benefit that accrued with his fellow traders. Conversely, burgesses could be given the right to share in any bargain others made. It was paradoxical that the very privileges thus won by various towns operated against each other, and hampered the trade they were trying to increase: there are two sides to a tax or toll, and two sides to a trading privilege. From an early date merchants sought both to protect themselves from such exactions and to enlarge their trade through an organization known as the gild merchant or merchant gild, which was generally sanctioned by charter. The earliest known reference to a gild merchant is in the charter to the town of Burford, in Oxfordshire, at the end of the eleventh century, and for more than two hundred years thereafter the gild merchant was an accepted part of commercial life.

Although the merchant gild was associated with a particular town, and there were as many merchant gilds as there were prosperous towns, functionally town and gild differed. While the borough's chief concerns were the administration and defence of the town, merchant functions were concerned with trade and with the questions involved therein of monopoly, price, tax, toll and protection. In particular, there was a clear distinction between the merchant court and the borough court. All questions concerning the gild merchant were heard in its own merchant court and not in the borough court, and in this way there grew up a body of merchant law—a *lex mercatoria*—which sharply distinguished the merchant from the non-merchant. At the same time, because of the preponderance of commercial business, the merchant court became busier and in some ways more important than the borough court. It was, for example, the court whose power was absolute at all fairs and markets. Yet, in spite of differences in qualification for membership and in function there can be little doubt of the close connection between merchant gildsman and burgher, and it is likely that burgage tenure and gild membership belonged to the same group of people, who thus formed a close and powerful ruling class.

In its simplest form, the establishment of a gild merchant conferred the right to exclusive trading within a borough.[3] Exclusiveness was later combined with privilege and protection. Within their own territory the merchant gilds were monopolists; outside they were protected against other monopolists or any sharp practice. But monopoly needed to be tempered by concession in view of the large number of other merchant gilds; exclusiveness could be maintained only at the cost of their own exclusion from other markets. Moreover, that it was not always easy to uphold a monopoly is indicated by the case of the merchant of Stafford who in 1280 successfully claimed against the town of Newcastle-under-Lyme the right to cut and sell cloth in their town. So a great deal of bargaining and concession was necessary, exclusiveness was dropped and merchants from other towns were allowed to trade provided they paid toll. As tolls multiplied over the country the travelling merchant found himself badly hampered, and the institution of toll became a two-edged weapon. To preserve it on home territory and gain exemption elsewhere was the ideal sought by all merchants. The position was confusing in the extreme, the only gainers being those in whose hands lay the right to grant or exempt. To these monarchs and mesne lords the merchants' needs were a source of financial profit, and out of the contradictions of grants, exemptions and privileges they did well. A different twist could, however, be put on the situation by the practice of reprisal, or 'withernam', the right to which was frequently embodied in charters: if a community unrightfully exacted toll from merchants of another community, its own merchants could be likewise taxed. This seemed fair enough, but the practice often developed into a kind of competitive blackmail, entailing the seizure of merchants' goods in any place were they could be found.

But, on the whole, the trader from another town did not win, and he was beset with nearly as many restrictions as the merchant from overseas. In particular, he was compelled to sell wholesale, which meant that he could not set up in the market-place and offer his wares to all who came but was bound to sell to middlemen who would almost certainly be gildsmen. He was further hampered by the extension of the principle of withernam to defaulting debtors. This meant that any trader of the community to which the debtor belonged might be seized when he entered a town to which the creditor belonged. This added to the hazards of travel and trade: wrongful seizure was easy, and so much disorganization resulted that all the burgesses of a town sometimes combined to pay a debt in order to wipe the slate clean. Gradually it was sought by law to end this state of affairs, and it was repeatedly prescribed, with somewhat doubtful effectiveness, that no merchant, alien or native, was to be distrained for debt unless he were himself the debtor or a surety of the debtor.[4]

Within the merchant gild fairness and equality were the governing principles. Its organization seems to have been directed primarily to business affairs, and, although organized help was given to gildsmen who fell ill or on hard times, there is less philanthropic activity than there is in the craft gilds.[5] But if any member of the gild suffered imprisonment or attack or unfair treatment, or had any cause for complaint against any person or institution, his case was straightway taken up by the officers of the gild: it was not to borough or to central government that he turned, it was to his gild that he looked for protection and redress. If the wrongdoer were within the gild he could be punished severely. It was decreed by his fellow-gildsmen against a malefactor at Andover, for example, 'that no one receive him, nor buy and sell with him, nor give him fire or water, nor hold communication with him' under penalty of the loss of gild membership.[6]

Members of the gild merchant could be appointed for life, with sometimes the right of hereditary succession. In the election of new members preference was sometimes given to relatives of gildsmen, and women were not excluded. Rules and Ordinances were made governing admissions, the conduct of members, and the aims and objects of the gild. Fees were probably variable, proportionate to a man's income or to the extent he was likely to use the privileges of the gild. Meetings were held annually, twice a year or even quarterly, and were known as 'gilds' or 'morning talks'. Here business was discussed, complaints heard, fines levied, punishments prescribed, suggestions made and new members admitted. On special days it was the custom 'to drink the Gild Merchant' when, as in the craft gilds, great feasting and merriment prevailed with 'drynkyngs with spiced cakebrede and sondry wynes, the cuppes merilly servyng about the house'.[7] At Yarmouth four of the merchant brotherhood successively bore the cost of a feast on Trinity Sunday which must have been a considerable expense: 'frometye, rost byffe, grene gese, weale, spyce cake, good bere, and ale', and 'not sparing any dainty fare which might be had for money'. The feast took place in a hall 'richly hanged and adorned with cloth of Arras Tapestry and other costly furniture'.[8]

The merchant gild, closely allied with town or borough, remained a dominant feature of English town life until the fourteenth century, when its break-up was obvious. The reasons for its decline are obscure, but they are bound up with the increasing specialization of function which developed as society became more complex. Many original members of the gild merchant were part merchant, part craftsman, the line between the two being as thin as that between merchant and burgher. The saddler and the goldsmith, for example, bought their raw materials and sold their finished products as merchants, while at the same time practising their trades as craftsmen. The crystallization of the craft gilds from within the merchant organization and their breaking away to form their own organizations undoubtedly weakened the parent body. At the same time some trades—in particular, the wool trade—grew increasingly important, and developed their own organization of buying and selling. It was particularly simple to do this when the trade—and the wool trade is again the chief example—developed outside the restrictions imposed by the gild merchant. For the gild merchant remained an urban organization too closely linked by membership and by regulation to flourish without reference to its parent town. Its base remained too narrow to support the rapidly expanding markets which by the fourteenth century were opening overseas as well as at home.

The trade which was the life-blood of the towns and the *raison d'être* of the merchant gild had by the time of the Black Death spread far beyond the boundaries of manor or of town. The output of quarry and mine, wool, food of all kinds, specialized handicrafts, were travelling from their district of production to centres of sale and consumption all over the country. Much of the exchange took place at the weekly market, more at the periodic fair.

The market was probably held weekly, and was for the most part a local affair, satisfying immediate demand. It was even so subject to tax and toll, was governed by regulations, and its existence depended upon permission of the king or feudal lord. Edward I, for example, in 1293 granted the right of a market at St Ives to the Abbey and Convent of Ramsey, 'that they and their successors for ever have a market every week on Monday at their manor of St Ives . . . with all the liberties and free customs to such market pertaining'.[9] The market, while being granted 'liberties and free customs', was at the same time bound by the national regulations then in force governing purchase and sale. It had to conform, for example, to the stipulation of Magna Carta that every market should have a pair of scales, and to Parliament's regulation of 1340 that 'one measure and one weight shall be throughout the realm of England'. Weights and measures were tested from time to time, and in the fourteenth century an effort was made to send standard balances and weights to all parts of the kingdom. The market, in short, had to conform to all the regulations by means of which authority was trying to protect the consumer, and it was obliged to have at hand the means of punishing offenders—the pillory, the tumbril and the cucking stool.

The fair was much larger than the market, the range of its products was greater, and it supplied a wider area, the more important fairs being truly international in scope and reputation. The fair was normally an annual event, preceded by much preparation and planning; it lasted for days, a week, even as long as two weeks. It may have had its origin in religious festivals: people coming together from distant parts for the purpose of religion would need to buy refreshment, would bring with them a means of exchange, would take home with them a souvenir or some speciality of the district. Numbers and regularity encouraged trade; at a recognized place it was easier to guard against fraud, to find witnesses to a transaction, to appeal to a recognized custom or law, to collect taxes and tolls, to arrange mutual protection. There is little evidence of the formal fair before the Conquest, although there were religious gatherings like those of the Feast of St Cuthbert in Durham, and of St Ives in Huntingdonshire. The first big foundation was the fair of St Giles, Winchester, which was established in 1096 by William II; its geographical position gave it importance for foreign trade and it served, in particular, as an exchange for English woollen goods. The fair of St Ives, near Huntingdon, was established in 1110 by Henry I; again, it was geographically well placed for foreign interchange, and traded English wool, cloth and hides to foreigners as well as natives. The fair of St Bartholomew in Smithfield, London, was founded in 1133 by Henry I on the site of an already famous market and it became the greatest cloth fair in England. Stourbridge (or Sturbridge) fair, held at Barnwell, Cambridge, was given its charter by King John about 1211 and came to be the most famous of all English fairs, with exotic velvets and cloth-of-gold rubbing shoulders with famous cheeses and the salted herrings widely sought for winter food.

These fairs, and many more, were at the height of their prosperity by the fourteenth century, and continued to prosper for several centuries more. The right to hold the fair generally rested upon the king, who conveyed it either as part of a town charter or by means of a special charter. He could make the grant to a community, such as a town or abbey, or to an individual, such as a feudal lord or prelate: Stourbridge fair was granted to the local Hospital of Lepers, Bartholomew's to a monk who also founded a hospital on the site. The right to a fair was prized, and was paid for handsomely. There was generally a stipulation that markets or fairs should not be held within a certain distance of one another, so the grant constituted a monopoly, and generally paid for itself over and over again. It paid the merchant to the extent that he profited from trading; the authority to whom the fair was granted reaped profit from taxes and tolls; all who supplied the fair with its food and drink and fairings did a brisk trade; the whole community gained in the variety of merchandise at its disposal.

For its duration the authority of the fair superseded that of the town, the period of the fair being marked by an elaborate opening ceremony in which the Peace of the Fair was proclaimed and the town surrendered its keys into the keeping of the Lord of the Fair. Since shops were little more than wooden booths, it was possible to erect whole streets of them in the meadow or on the hillside outside the town where the fair was held, so creating a miniature new town, each street devoted to a particular commodity, as in the town itself. Thus there would be the hop fair, where a great beam was erected for weighing the hops, the cheese fair, the wool fair, the goldsmith's row, and so on. Special days were set aside for the really big sales, like the horse fair, which customarily drew large crowds. On each Sunday of the fair there were morning and evening services and a sermon, all in the open air. There were opportunities for merry-making, and the tall maypole was a prominent feature. So were the booths devoted to supplying food and drink—hot and cold roast goose, roast or boiled pork, oysters, herrings and ale. The mummers, the tumblers, the strolling players, the musicians were all there, making their way round the fairs and markets of the land. Men tried their strength at wrestling and the cross-bow. They danced with their girls in the evening. The healers, the patent-medicine sellers made money out of the credulity of the sick; the barber pushed his cure for baldness; all these were sure to be miles away before their fraud could be proved. John, son of John of Eltisley, did, however, catch Roger the Barber at the Fair of St Ives and was able to get him convicted of falsely obtaining 9*d.* on an undertaking to cure baldness. All Roger had done was to put John's head in plaster for two days running and then abscond.[10] John grew no more hair, and the Court of the Fair of St Ives fined Roger the Barber and ordered him to return John's 9*d.*

At the heart of the fair were the native and stranger merchants conducting their business, and much money and many promises as well as quantities of goods changed hands, tradition and precedent developing into a special law governing the conduct of business at the fair. Whenever a judgement needed to be given it needed to be given speedily, and the fair developed also its own court—the court of *pied poudre*, or dusty feet, typical of those who attended the fair. To this court, which was always open, all questions of debt and obligation, all quarrels over bargaining, disputes over tolls and taxes, personal feuds and other quarrels had to be submitted and were resolved, if not immediately, then within the day. Moreover, since the Peace of the Fair reigned for its duration, any breach had to be dealt with summarily. Nor could any outside feud be allowed to disturb the peace of the fair. 'I will and ordain', said the king in a typical pronouncement, 'that all who come to the fair, remain at it, and return from it, have my firm peace'. This was sometimes interpreted to mean that even the fugitive villein could not be apprehended while the peace of the fair lasted.

Much of the trade of the big fairs was specialized, like the cloth fair at Leeds, the fair of Weyhill for cheese, or the herring fair at Yarmouth. The importance of the trade in fish, particularly herring, can hardly be overestimated.

Throughout the Middle Ages fish, with bread, was the basic and universal diet, and any variant remained a supplement and not an alternative. Britain, being an island and well watered by rivers, streams and lakes, was fortunate in this respect. The fish-pond, well stocked with eels, with tench and trout, was a common adjunct of manor-house and monastery. In the rivers and river estuaries of the North salmon was supreme; trout and mullet, pike, roach, lampreys and lamperns could be caught in various rivers up and down the country; a coastal manor or one traversed by river or stream reaped the harvest of the waters as it did of the land —often with less trouble and greater certainty. All round the coasts of Britain fishermen/farmers combined the two occupations in varying proportions, sometimes merely making a living for themselves and their families, sometimes selling fish to those less well placed. There was cod to the north, haddock to the east, plaice and sole to the south, mackerel to the south-west, shrimps and prawns, cockles and whelks everywhere, oysters in a few places, notably Colchester in Essex. Sturgeon, porpoise and whale were a less frequent, and less profitable, catch for these were 'royal fish', to be surrendered in part or in whole to the sovereign.

Above all, it was the herring that reigned supreme in the sea and upon the tables of rich and poor alike: 'a red Herring, such a hot stirring meate', wrote Thomas Nashe in his poem *The Prayse of the Red Herring*, the *red* referring to the smoked herring. 'On no coast like ours is it caught in such abundance', he wrote,

> 'hosted, rosted, and tosted, heere alone it is every man's money, from the King to the Courtier; every householder . . . that keepes a family in pay, casts for it as one of his standing provisions. The poorer sort make it three parts of there sustenance; with it, for his dinner, the patchedest . . . may dine like a Spanish Duke.[11]

While Hull, Scarborough and Grimsby dealt particularly in cod, Rye and Winchelsea in whiting and plaice, and most towns had their specialities, Yarmouth was the acknowledged port and market for English herrings. She commanded the herring belt off her shores, and her Herring Fair was famous. 'Saint George for England, and the Red Herring for Yarmouth!' exclaimed Nashe.[12] The herring harvest was so rich that, although part of the catch was eaten fresh, hundreds of thousands of the fish were salted or smoked for future consumption far from the sea.

The curing of herrings was a specialized occupation. Packed generally in barrels, the preserved fish were sent long distances at home and overseas—for such was the popularity of the herring that even countries like Holland and the Baltic lands, which fished their own, had need of more. At home merchants travelled from miles away to negotiate their purchases at Yarmouth and other herring towns. Yarmouth profited in many ways. The herring-fishers paid for rights to spread their nets and to land their fish on her shores. Alien fleets, like those which came annually from the south-coast Cinque Ports, had to negotiate their rights; the sellers of fish paid toll; stall-holders at the Herring Fair, at the market, or in the streets paid for the privilege; so even did the fish-hawker. Yarmouth's supremacy was so complete that she obtained a statutory monopoly of selling and curing herrings.

Other coastal towns likewise did well from the fishing industry. Dunwich laid an annual charge on every fishing-boat of twelve or more oars. Scarborough took one herring in every hundred of those that were landed on her shores. Lynn claimed two salmon from each ship carrying thirty-two or more, as well as a herring toll. London put a toll on all fishing boats coming into her port. The Crown took 'herring rents' in the form of thousands of herrings from various places; it received annually from the City of Norwich twenty-four pies of the first fresh herrings of the season, each pie containing five herrings, flavoured with ginger, pepper, cinnamon, cloves and other spices. The king also frequently had the right of a first selection of fish from any catch.[13]

While seaside towns exercised control over fishing off their shores, the right to fish in rivers and estuaries and off the shores of coastal manors usually vested in the riparian owners, who would frequently lease the right to set up kiddles or other form of fish-trap.[14] The open-sea fisherman generally escaped such exactions: in any case, he used fishing-nets and sometimes line and hook, which were not easy to control. But he, and all fishermen, were subject to a further series of extortions when they landed their catch. Buyers and sellers of fish, who were middlemen and not fishermen, early emerged to make profit on the sale of fish by buying cheap and selling dear. That these practices could develop into a price ring was shown in 1397, when a herring merchant of Scarborough was beaten up by fish-dealers for selling at a lower price than the others.[15] By this time the London Fishmongers Company had emerged as the biggest and most powerful of such merchant monopolists. The London Fishmongers was one of the earliest, one of the largest, one of the most prominent, and one of the most prosperous of the London Companies. Its representatives travelled to the herring belts and the fishing-ports. It bought whole catches cheaply and controlled their sale; it owned fishing-boats and even stretches of river. The London trade in fish was entirely in their hands. Their monopoly, and the evidence of 'rings' in various ports, could indicate that many fishermen were virtually in the position of wage-earners, owning little but their nets—if those. But others, away from such intrusions, merely continued their healthy, if at times dangerous, existence, for the benefit of their own families, the local population and perhaps some nearby manor.

Indirect encouragement was throughout the Middle Ages given to fishermen by the compulsory eating of fish which the Catholic Church prescribed on Fridays, Saturdays, Ember Days and Lent. With the Reformation the religious significance of refraining from meat was lost, and the Fish Days lapsed, but by the middle of the Tudor period it was being asked whether the trade of fishing might not thereby decay, to the detriment of the Fleet, and of coastal defence. Henry VIII took no action, but Edward VI in the interests of English policy—not of religion—revived the Fish Days by Statute in 1548. As it was said in 1559, the 'old course of fishing' must be preserved 'by the straitest observation of Fish Days, for policy sake; so that sea-coasts shall be strong with men and habitations and the fleet flourish more than ever'.[16] The Act of 1564 added Wednesdays to the Fish Days and exempted the ships of English subjects, as well as their fish, from tax or toll.

The red herring of Nashe's eulogy was the smoked fish, but the more usual means of preservation was by salting. There is no evidence that this was done at sea, it being likely that the Roman practice was followed of keeping the fish in water in the ships' holds and landing them alive. But salt thereafter played an important part in their saga. Transported fresh they were packed in salt as a preservative; smoked they were treated to a preliminary salting before being toasted over a wood fire and impregnated with the wood-smoke for some days; salted they were subjected, after the preliminary salt treatment, to the full salt cure, which consumed large quantities of salt and had to be undertaken within twenty-four hours of the catch. Salt was also used in the preservation of the carcases of animals which normally had to be slaughtered at Martinmas (November) because there was no winter feed for them. It was used partly as a preservative, partly as a flavour, in butter and cheese and in spicing other food. In the Middle Ages, as now, salt was added to bread when it was baked. Its place on the board was one of honour, being placed 'above the salt' indicating priority. It was used in the soldering of pipes and gutters and in the preparation of leather. It was prescribed, as sometimes now, for the relief of toothache and for acidity.

Until the middle of the fourteenth century Britain and most of Northern Europe obtained salt from indigenous sources. Britain could rely upon brine springs in Worcestershire and Cheshire, where salt was obtained by boiling the brine. On the south coast, in Sussex and Kent, sea-water was evaporated by the sun as far as possible and then boiled, but the product was not so good as the brine salt. On the east coast, where the big herring catches required an immediately available supply of salt, sea-water was also evaporated and then boiled, and the salt-impregnated marshes and bogs were made to yield their salt by a similar process which produced a high-quality, though expensive, product. In Lincolnshire and Norfolk salt-making was frequently combined with farming, and early in the fourteenth century Lincoln in particular had achieved some eminence in the production of salt. It was even exported from Boston and some other east-coast ports. Everywhere in Britain—unlike warmer countries, where the heat of the sun was sufficient—boiling was necessary to evaporate the salt, so it was intrinsically more expensive in Britain than in central and southern Europe. By the time of the Black Death most of Britain's salt was imported, only a few salt-burners, producing for a small local market, continuing to operate.

CHAPTER VIII

The Development of Foreign Trade

By the fourteenth century the agricultural produce of a large manor was finding its market not only in other parts of the country but overseas, and English wool, corn, meat, cheese, butter and honey were known and prized in many parts of Europe. So also were the herrings caught round her coasts, and the salmon from her rivers. English tin from Devonshire and Cornwall, lead from Cumberland, Derbyshire and Mendip, iron ore and coal from the Forest of Dean were important exports. Coal from Newcastle was more highly prized abroad than at home. There was a popular export market for her manufactured goods, such as pewter tankards, plates, bowls and buckets; agricultural tools and daggers made partly from iron; leather goods such as shoes, bottles and bellows. But supreme throughout the Middle Ages was English wool—the Goddess of Merchants—and the decline of the export of raw wool at the end of the fourteenth century was merely that the fleece might be used at home to make woollen cloth for even more profitable export.

Britain's chief import was wine from Gascony. Salt and the famous Caen stone for building came from France. Woad for dyeing came from both France and Italy. From an early date manufacturers would pay dearly to import this dye, which could produce a range of colours but particularly the varying shades of blue so popular in the Middle Ages. So important was woad that towns who were normally suspicious of foreigners welcomed traders who came with the blue dye, waiving restrictions and granting them residence for as long as they pleased. From the Netherlands England imported the popular salted herrings, linen cloth and 'Flanders tiles';[1] from Spain the fine white, curly merino wool (considered inferior to the English wool, and not allowed to be mixed with it), oil, leather and iron. From the north and north-east of Europe the Hansards[2] brought to her corn, amber, flax, wax, iron and important shipbuilding materials like pitch and tar, as well as timbers of fir and spruce which were not grown at home. They also brought the highly prized furs which were used for lining and trimming the garments of the rich, and more salted herrings. That herrings should be both imported and exported was due partly to fluctuations of the weather, the size of the catch, the extent of demand, and also upon geographical location: London, for example, might find it easier to import from the Hansards than to ship from Yarmouth. From the south the Venetian galleys came into London and Southampton with their spices and sweet wines, silks and velvets and brocades and all the luxuries of the East. The Portuguese carracks brought pepper, silk, cotton and cloth of gold.

Because of her island position, England's foreign trade depended upon water. The Baltic Sea connected her with Scandinavia and north-east Europe. The Channel by two short sea routes, one to Calais and one to Flanders and the Netherlands, opened the doors to central and southern Europe: Calais was the great vent for English wool, Flanders and the Netherlands were the distributing centres for the whole Continent. Navigable rivers necessarily played a large part in this inland trade, and coastal shipping, in Europe as in England, was everywhere important. The third sea route connected England with western and southern Europe and, through Genoa and Venice, with the Near and Far East. After 1381, when she emerged victorious over Genoa, Venice had no rival and, though Portuguese carracks still traded with the north and west of Europe, it was Venice upon which the trade routes of the East converged, and Venice who distributed their cargoes to the rest of Europe by land, and by sea. To England came the 'Flanders Galleys', so called because they touched Flanders before putting in to Southampton with their precious cargoes. For her services in ships and as merchant, banker and middleman, it was natural that Venice should be paid handsomely. It was also natural that in time England should come to resent such payment, and

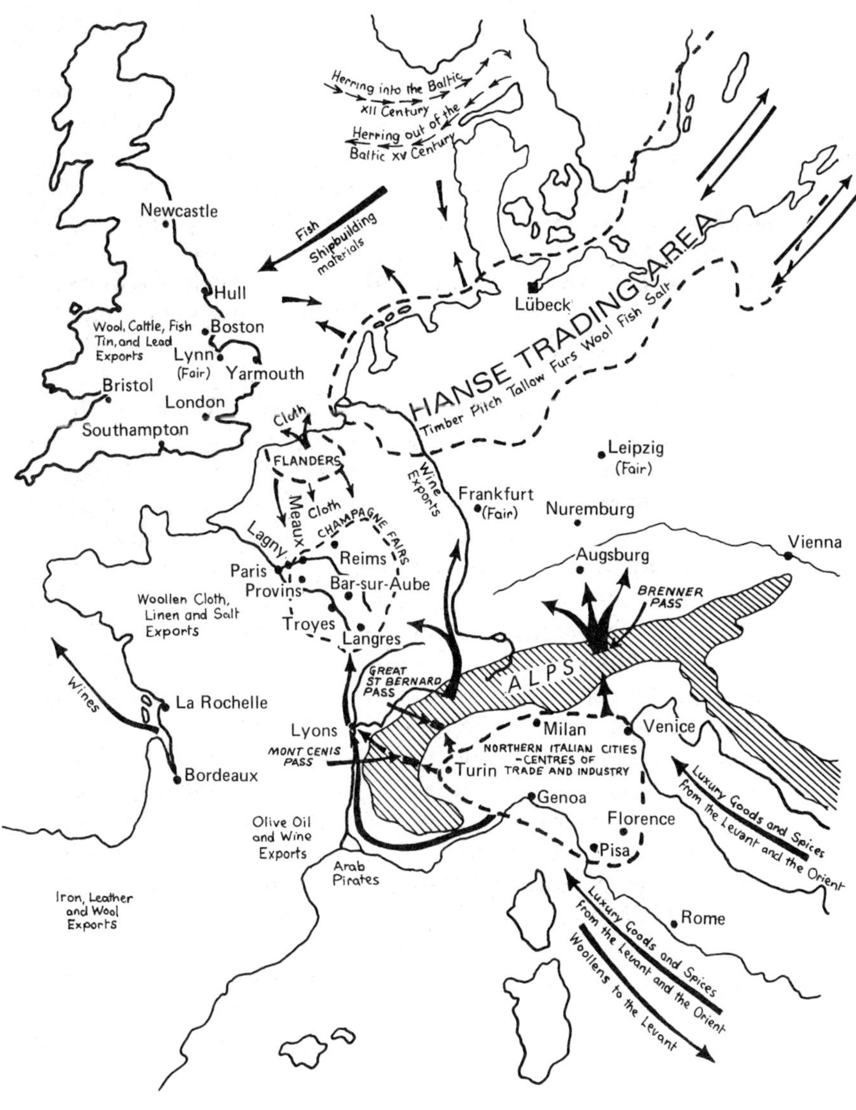

Fig. 3 European Trade in the Early Middle Ages

seek to use her own ships. It was indeed surprising that with such dependence upon the oceans for her trade she took so long to achieve maritime independence. Not that this was easily done.

The hazards of the ocean were considerable. With seas uncharted and coasts for long stretches unknown, shipwreck and storm and total loss had to be reckoned with on every voyage. For the most part the sailor steered by the stars at night, while by day he made his way from visible point to visible point. When he was in mid-ocean he used the astrolabe, a device which had been known in the ancient world, for marking the positions and movements of the heavenly bodies, and for computing latitude. By the sixteenth century, and occasionally earlier, he might have used a rudimentary form of compass, consisting of little more than a piece of iron touched with the lodestone (the magnet) floating in a bowl of oil.

Britain's home waters were little better. Here also there was risk of perishing on uncharted coasts, of wreck on unmarked headlands, of grounding on shoals or sandbanks, of sticking fast in silted-up harbours, of floundering where no pier or jetty existed for unloading goods. Hythe and Dunwich reported blockage, Yarmouth harbour was so choked with sand that ships could barely enter, Melcombe and Lyme Regis, Dover—chief passenger port to the Continent—were among countless other harbours where the necessary continuous attention was never given. The count of wreckage was considerable: Dungeness, the Goodwins, the Isle of Sheppey, the Humber mouth, all claimed their victims. In 1363 four great ships carrying wool, cloth and tin were wrecked off Plymouth; a century later four ships carrying nearly 1 000 tons of wine and other goods were wrecked in Mounts Bay, Cornwall.[3] In October 1587 the last of the Venetian galleys to come to England, a ship of 1 100 tons, met her end off the Needles.[4] In case of wreck the cargo could be jettisoned by the master of the ship, but if merchants were aboard he was obliged to consult them. Compensation would be later paid to the merchants by the shipowners at market price.[5]

There is little evidence of buoys, lighthouses or harbour lights until Tudor times, and to Henry VIII falls the distinction of envisaging some continuous overall protection for mariners and their ships. In 1514 he incorporated the Fraternity of the Holy Trinity at Deptford, based upon an older organization of

Thames Pilots. Trinity House, to give it its later name, was empowered to frame articles 'concerning the science or art of mariners' and 'the relief, increase, and augmentation of the shipping of the realm'.[6] Elizabeth I, renewing their charter, empowered them to erect beacons and sea marks, and gave them all rights connected therewith, specifically including the general oversight of coasts and harbours. Money was also spent on piers at Dover, Scarborough and other ports, and when in 1532 Parliament was asked to take action about the silting-up of the harbours of the south-west because the tin-workers 'more regarding their own private lucre than the commonwelthe and suertie of this Realme' were so blocking them with refuse that a ship of a hundred tons could hardly enter at half-flood it responded by commanding the tinners to have 'sufficient hatches and ties in the end of their buddels' to keep the sand from being washed away down the streams into the harbours.

As though there were insufficient natural hazards, man added his own. The wealth entrusted to vulnerable craft on dangerous seas gave scope for piracy of various kinds. In the Mediterranean the pirates of Algiers and Morocco struck dread into any trading vessel. To protect themselves the great galleys of Venice and Genoa not only sailed in fleets but they recruited their crews from fighting men as well as from sailors. Bartholomew, brother of Christopher Columbus, met disaster coming up from Spain to the English court, when he was set on by pirates and robbed of all his possessions. The North Sea and the Baltic were infested by such organized piratical groups as the Rovers of the Sea and the Victual Brothers. The English Channel was seething with pirate ships which hid in creeks on both shores. The Isle of Wight was at one time the lair of the piratical John of Newport, who sallied out to rob vessels coming into Southampton. On Lundy Island the notorious pirate William de Mareis had his headquarters. Even the mouth of the Thames was unsafe, as Henry IV realized when he was set upon while crossing the river. He escaped, but the pirate gang made off with all his baggage. A London merchant, Bartholomew Couper, in 1477 took merchandise in the *Mary London* to Ireland, there took on board 400 pilgrims for Santiago de Compostella, and on the way back was captured by Irish pirates. To add to the terrors of coastal villages, kidnapping by pirates was not unknown. The effect upon the lives of ordinary people, not only upon those whose livelihood was the sea, needs little imagination. Seamen banded themselves together in such associations as the Thames Pilots, and most coastal and riverside settlements organized a rota of inhabitants to sound the warning and lead the attack against pirates and other enemies: it is noteworthy that at the time of the Peasants' Revolt enough people were left in the Thames-side villages to guard against marauders.

It was not always easy, however, to distinguish friend from foe, for a temporary alliance with a pirate to destroy a trade rival was not unknown. The actions of the traders themselves, indeed, frequently verged on the piratical, the ships in control of the regular trade routes stopping at nothing to keep out an interloper, as Robert Sturmey, an enterprising merchant of Bristol, found to his cost in the middle of the fifteenth century, when he sent the *Katherine Sturmey* to the Mediterranean with a cargo of cloth, lead and tin. This so affronted the Genoese that they waited for the *Katherine Sturmey* near Malta, set on her and plundered her in an act of virtual piracy.

Nor were the English themselves averse from the profits of piracy. In the English Channel any shipwreck, any ship that drove towards the shore, was a signal to the pirate ships that lay in wait around the coast. It was even known for local inhabitants themselves to cut a ship's cable, as Cornishmen did in 1454 to a Genoese carrack that was anchored off the coast. Since the pirate ships were often owned by men of local eminence and good repute their activities were not always inquired into. Indeed, it was demonstrated time and time again that in the West Country the pirate was a man of influence and standing, that no moral slur attached to piracy, and that whole sections of the coast and hinterland not only thrived on the spoils of wreck but worked hand-in-glove with the pirates.[7]

Ships frequently sailed in convoy, and kings gave letters of safe-conduct to merchants which, if not protecting them from out-and-out piracy, might save them from the attention of rivals who would fear reprisals. The operation of reprisals, however, on sea as on land, could be double-edged, as when Bordeaux merchants had wine taken from them by Flemish pirates, and procured letters of reprisal against Flemish merchants in England. A court of Admiralty took shape to deal with the claims and counter-claims which resulted. But, in spite of all efforts, at the beginning of the seventeenth century 'misadventure of Pyrates' was included with shipwreck, confiscation of goods by foreign countries and fire as the chief perils to which London merchants were exposed.

Political uncertainties, the political and military ambitions of rulers, added further hazard to merchant shipping. Any English merchant ship was liable to be impressed for wartime service at short notice at any time. When Edward III needed ships to carry his armies across the Channel in the course of the Hundred Years' War he conscripted merchant and fishing vessels time and time again. It was not only that they were commandeered but that the requisition order was put on them long before they were needed. They were thus put out of commission for a long period, during which the owners received no compensation, the sailors no wages, and the merchandise decayed.

English dependence upon the sea would suggest that her ships and shipbuilding would be as powerful as any in the world, yet her wooden sailing-ships changed little between the Conquest and the Black Death. They kept to the same design—broad in the beam, high in the water at bow and stern, with a single mast and square sail—and were rarely more than 300 tons,[8] even by the end of the fifteenth century. Sizes of merchant crews are indicated only occasionally—a master and twelve men; crews of twenty or thirty. The larger ships had some form of cabin accommodation for more important passengers such as commanders travelling with their armies or merchants travelling with their goods. For the rest there was merely a protective covering spread over wooden hoops on the deck, and the passengers sat on wooden benches. This is the way that pilgrims travelled, and conditions could be very grim indeed. Choose the highest part of the galley, counselled one writer in 1458 in a guidebook for pilgrims to the Holy Land, 'for in the lowest under it is right smouldering hot and stinking'.[9] It is hardly surprising that sea-sickness was added to the perils of the sea. How bad it could be was emphasized by the order that contracts made before a ship moored were not valid 'because at times merchants or honest men and many others, whom the sea makes sick . . . go on board ships, and if they had a thousand marks of silver they would promise it all to anyone who would ask it and put them ashore'.[10] Cargo in the smaller ships was simply covered and left on deck. In other cases it was also stored between decks or in the hold. Descriptions of wool cargoes give a vivid picture of the ingenuity employed in stowing away as much as possible in the limited space of a single ship.[11] When, as sometimes happened, ten or fifteen horses were included with a mixed cargo the captain's task was probably very difficult. Journeys could be long. In the fourteenth century it took thirty days for a cargo of grain and flour to reach London from Grimsby. It took two months in 1307 for a cargo of wine to come from Dalkey, near Dublin, to Cumberland. The journey from Venice to the Holy Land normally took about two months, but in 1506 one ship took four months to make the voyage. The Venetian galleys normally took about a year before they touched down in Flanders.

Both Henry VII and Henry VIII were acutely conscious of the needs of defence, and less willing than their predecessors to rely upon such merchant vessels as existed. Under their encouragement, and particularly with the help of bounties for shipbuilding, a royal navy began to emerge. But shipbuilding lapsed under their successors, and there was no revival until the reign of Elizabeth I, when more ships and new types of ship, longer in proportion to their height, lower in the water and more manoeuvrable, were produced. These vessels served the sea-dogs in the Spanish Main, and were largely responsible for defeating the Armada. They were also frequently hired by merchants, and it was not unusual for freight to be carried by men-of-war until, in the general expansion of trade and commerce, a shipbuilding industry developed which catered both for the navy and for the merchant marine. This expansion was encouraged by various navigational aids, in particular by the development of astronomy and navigational mathematics, and above all by the mariner's compass. Even so, it is unlikely that the total of English-owned merchant shipping amounted to more than 50 000 tons in 1572.[12]

The paucity and unreliability of England's shipping services meant, inevitably, that much of her foreign trade remained in the hands of foreign merchants who were able to bring overseas produce in foreign ships, sell it in England and with the proceeds purchase and export native goods in their own vessels, or even take the proceeds of sales out of the country in the form of English money. The whole procedure from start to finish could be in their hands. There was naturally much resistance, and local and national authorities made repeated efforts to restrain and restrict the merchant stranger long before it was possible to do without him altogether: the length of his sojourn was limited; he was not allowed to sell by retail; he was to sell in gross within forty days of his arrival, and to sell all before he left; he was to spend the proceeds of sales on native goods, and could not export coin of the realm. Foreign merchants were not allowed to trade with each other, they were not permitted to use their own weights and measures, and they were bound by any particular rules and regulations operative in the towns in which they were trading. From at least as early as the twelfth century repeated attempts were made to enforce these regulations, of their nature very difficult to control, by providing alien merchants with native hosts with whom they were compelled to reside, and who swore on oath to be personally responsible for the length of their stay and their observance of the law. Not unnaturally, the hosting of aliens could prove a difficult matter.

At the same time, just as trade between towns provided a lucrative source of tax and toll, so the alien merchant could be a milch cow for the Exchequer or the royal purse. Customs duties, taxes of various kinds, the raising of loans in return for privileges, the removal of restrictions for a consideration, became regular features of commercial policy. Nor were the king and the nobility always averse to trading direct with the purveyors of coveted luxuries. Edward I summed it all up by saying that he found foreign merchants 'convenient and useful', and the long struggle between successive kings and their landowning Parliaments on the one hand and the growing power of the merchants of London on the other indicates the difficulties of the conflict. It was punctuated by demonstrations against aliens, like those of 1359 when Lombards were badly beaten up in London, or the London riots of 1374 against aliens generally. Aliens were a target during the Peasants' Revolt, while a more sober petition of 1514 from traders and artisans complained to the monarch that the realm was

> so inhabited with a great multitude of needy people, strangers of divers nations . . . that your liege people Englishmen cannot imagine nor tell where to nor to what occupation that they shall use or put their children.

The aliens who held their privileges longest, and who occupied a unique position in Britain, were the Merchants of the Hanse and the Venetians. The Hanseatic merchants dealt in important essentials from the northern countries. Their headquarters were in Lübeck, Hamburg and Danzig, and from their beginnings as a trading alliance they had become strong politically as well as economically. They won concessions, trading privileges and even their own residence in most of the countries of northern Europe, including the towns of Bergen in Norway, Bruges in the Low Countries, and Novgorod in Russia. In England German merchants had been settled from Anglo-Saxon times, their privileges being set down in the laws of King Ethelred. By the early thirteenth century they had their own London house called the Steelyard, which, it is recorded, was enlarged in 1260 by the purchase of an adjoining house and garden. By the end of the century they also had local organizations in Boston and Lynn and Hull. In the sixties of the fourteenth century the Hanseatic League was formally established. The Steelyard—the name deriving, possibly, from the German *Stapelhof* or merchandise yard, or from *Stahlhof*, sample house—which remained the headquarters of the League in London, was a walled community with residential quarters as well as warehouses, and large wharves on the Thames. The community was governed by merchant law, and it was allowed to elect its own officers. The Hansards enjoyed considerable privileges: they paid lower taxes on English cloth for export than did the natives; they had the right of selling their imported wares retail; they were allowed to reside where they chose for as long as they pleased.[13]

The Venetians had no territorial settlement in England, but from 1319 they maintained an Ambassador in London, and their privileges were at least equal to those of the Hansa merchants. Others who long retained the privilege of making their own purchases were the Italian wool merchants who bought their clip and arranged for its shipment to Italy in Italian ships even when the native organization was at its height.

In spite of the tenacity of foreign merchant organizations, the role played by the small native ships who took wool and other goods across the Channel, who traded with the Baltic and the North Sea, who pushed their way down the coast of Europe to Gascony and into the Mediterranean was far from negligible, and it was inevitable that trade should pass increasingly into native hands as experience grew, shipping and navigational aids improved, and capital accumulated. The power of the Hansards was beginning to decline by the fifteenth century, and their privileges were ended in the reign of Elizabeth I. The Venetian power in England waned as their strength at home was sapped by the new trade alignments following the geographical discoveries, and by the growing enterprise of newly emerging nation-states. England also was affected by both these factors: in the new geography she was more squarely on the trade routes than before, and she shared in the developing European nationalism. It is likely that the total tonnage of English shipping increased sevenfold between 1560 and 1689.[14] At the same time her resources in wool and her superiority in the production of woollen cloth were a continuing impetus to mercantile self-sufficiency, while their profitability helped the capital accumulation essential to large-scale trading enterprises.

CHAPTER IX

The Wool Trade

Of all England's trade none was more picturesque, nor more profitable, than the export of her wool, its marketing creating a busy, bustling scene from start to finish. The trade suffered in the Black Death, but recovery was rapid, the 30 000 sacks of wool sent abroad each year at the beginning of the fourteenth century being 40 000 by the middle years. In early times it was general for the buyer to be in direct contact with the grower, and many foreign merchants came to England to make their purchases and arrange for shipment. By the end of the thirteenth century, however, English merchants were playing an increasing part in this export, and from 1378 onward the only foreign merchants who were allowed by law to ship wool were the Italians and the Catalonians—provided they did not land the wool anywhere within the staple market of Western Europe. The Italians were by far the more important of the two, using mainly the bigger ports of Southampton, London and Sandwich for their large carracks and galleys, which were in sharp contrast to the assortment of ships, often very small, used by the English exporters. There can be little doubt that this superiority in shipping was one of the chief reasons for their continuing privilege: it would have been impossible for English merchants to deal with all the wool exports in their own little ships.

Many merchants rode direct to the big sheep-farms and, upon examination of a sample of wool, or upon knowledge of previous clips, would purchase the whole clip in advance. In districts of small sheep-farms wool would be collected, possibly by one of the bigger graziers, into the barns of the more substantial farmers or into the big stone wool markets of the wool towns which still stand in Yorkshire, in East Anglia, but above all in the Cotswold towns of Chipping Campden, Northleach, Fairford, Burford, Stow-on-the-Wold—monuments of the time when 'Alle Naciouns afferme up to the fulle/In all the world ther is no bettir woole'.[1] The prospective buyer would assess the quality of the wool and strike his bargain. A time for delivery at the port would be agreed upon, possibly a down-payment made, and arrangements concluded for the rest of the payment, most likely by bills payable six months ahead.

Wool was sold either shorn and wound from the clip and packed into canvas sacks (known as sarplers), each containing about 364 pounds, or as unshorn wool fells—sheepskins with the wool on them. One sack of shorn wool was normally taken as the equivalent of 240 wool fells for the purposes of taxation. After the shearing the packers would grade and pack the wool into the sarplers. Each was marked with its place of origin and its grade or quality. This had to be done on the spot, for it was required by law that wool be packed in the shire where it was grown. The packers worked under the supervision of collectors sworn in before the Exchequer, and it was they who actually fixed the seals to the fastened sarplers.

Then came the long journey by pack-horse to the port. Sometimes the wool was stored for a while at a central depot, such as Leadenhall in London. Then on to the quays it went at London or at some Medway port, or even at some small South Coast port. Here collectors of customs would enter the names of merchants making shipments, with the quantity and description of their cargoes, and the sarplers were weighed, marked and assessed for taxation. It was rare for a complete purchase to be consigned to one ship. Normally each purchase was spread over a number of vessels to minimize the danger of loss to one person; perhaps a dozen merchants might have consignments on one ship, and each merchant spread his purchases over as many ships. The Celys, important wool merchants, used twenty-one different ships in the summer of 1478. A large wool fleet could consist of thirty-eight ships, like those which left London on 20th July 1478. They carried between them more than 1 160 sacks of wool and over 268 000 wool fells. The next big fleet to sail from London was on 27th

March 1479. It consisted of twenty-four ships carrying 945 sacks of wool and nearly 112 000 wool fells. Fleets from other ports were generally smaller, and even from London they were not always as large as this, but might number no more than three ships. Shipping went on throughout the year till Christmas, but during the winter months it was usually the wool fells or sheepskins which were sent after the winter slaughter of the animals. Sometimes very small ships, not much bigger than barges, took the valuable cargoes.[2]

As well as the official customs lists, some of the letters of the wool merchants give vivid pictures of the wool sailings. In October 1481, for example, the Celys heard from their factor of the disposition of their fells: the simple, somewhat haphazard methods by which the merchants kept their various consignments apart, and by which they identified them, is in strange contrast to the scale upon which buying and selling was taking place. Some, for example, were dispatched 'by the grace of God'

> in the 'Mary' of London, William Sordyvale master, 7 packs, sum 2800, lying be aft the mast, one pack lieth up rest and some of that pack is summer fells marked with an O, and then lieth 3 packs fells of William Daltons and under them lieth the other 6 packs of my masters.[3]

When English wool was sought by the whole world, and before she herself had a large cloth trade, the object of English rulers was to make money out of its export. Hence the taxes on wool exports. As the advantages of keeping the wool at home for home manufacture became apparent these taxes were used not only for revenue but as a means of restricting export. There was always a conflict of interest between the wool-growers and the exporters on the one hand (who wanted the widest possible market without restriction of any kind) and those who, for whatever reason, wanted to impose taxes or other checks on export. The taxes on wool figured in the struggles between medieval kings and their governments, each concession of a tax for the king being accompanied by a 'right' for his government: it has been said that the development of Parliament and of the wool taxes proceeded together.[4] At the same time, with the European demand for English wool so high the wool tax was a political weapon of first-class importance.

There were broadly two export taxes—the wool custom and

the wool subsidy, both firmly established by the beginning of the fourteenth century. They were both graded taxes, embodying the principle that aliens paid more than natives. Both taxes had to be paid on every sack of wool, and every batch of wool fells. By the early fifteenth century the wool custom stood at 6*s*. 8*d*. a sack for denizens and 10*s*. a sack for aliens. The subsidy

Some Index Numbers of English Wool Prices, 1450–1635, taking an average of the Years 1450–99 as 100[1]

Year	*Index Number*
1450	91
1481	107
1482	122
1483	128
1484	132
1485	117
1486–1513 a fluctuating fall. Prices do not again reach the 1485 figure until	
1514	119
Then the rise is resumed, with fluctuations, the peak years being	
1515	135
1517	141
1533	146
1550	281
1594	346
1603	412
1618	428
1635	428

[1]From P. J. Bowden, *The Wool Trade in Tudor and Stuart England*, Appendix, pp. 219–20.

varied, but was about 33*s*. 4*d*. for denizens and anything between 43*s*. 4*d*. and 110*s*. for aliens. An Englishman's total tax would therefore be about £2 for every sack of wool or corresponding quantity of wool fells he exported, while the alien might pay as much as £5 10s. The king might also in emergency take wool as a loan in kind, or as a non-repayable tax, disposing of the wool himself for ready money; but this was exceptional.

It was found convenient for collecting the taxes on wool and for the necessary weighing and checking to canalize its export through a definite town, or staple, where collectors would reside. The wool staple was moved from place to place, at home and abroad, in response to conflicting interests. In 1294 it was at Dordrecht, but it may have been established there or elsewhere even earlier. It subsequently vacillated between various towns, including Antwerp, Bruges, Saint-Omer and Calais, finally coming to rest in Calais in 1392, where its position was confirmed by statute in 1423 and subsequently. In the fifteenth century its monopoly was reinforced by an additional tax (known as the 'Calais penny') on wool sent anywhere but to the staple town. The wool staple remained at Calais until 1558, when the town ceased to be in English hands.[5]

Once the Crown had established the staple as a means of collecting its taxes regularly and with the minimum of evasion it was typical of royal policy that it should then proceed to make a handsome additional income by selling licences to individuals to export wool to places other than the staple. It was a practice much in favour with Henry VI and Edward IV. But more profitable still was the ability, given by a stable and regular system of taxation, to raise loans on the security of the wool custom. Calais as a staple town had many advantages. It was of easy access from London and Southampton and other south-coast towns which were used for export, such as Sandwich, Poole and Chichester. It was also as easy of access as any Continental port from east-coast wool towns like Boston, Ipswich, Hull and Yarmouth. At the same time, it was a good centre for the cloth-making areas that wanted English wool—the towns of Flanders, Brabant, and Holland. From Calais the wool could easily be taken to the big international fairs of Bruges and Antwerp and Bergen-op-Zoom, for further distribution over Europe. Besides this, the town was fairly easily defensible by a strong garrison.

English wool merchants, concerned in the country's biggest export, were naturally among the earliest to follow their trade into Europe. They were foremost among the English merchants who began to frequent the fairs of Northern Europe, and to feel their way into the exchange marts where English wool was sold. It followed that the wool staple became their residence, and they became known as Merchants of the Staple, or Staplers. At Calais the Merchants of the Staple were in complete command. Not only was the bulk of English wool shipped there, but they shipped the bulk of the wool; any that was shipped by merchants not of their Company had to be sold at Calais under the Company's regulations. In the middle of the fifteenth century about four-fifths of the English wool trade was in the hands of Staplers using for the most part English, though occasionally foreign, ships. There were many advantages in this canalization of the wool trade: safer shipment, easier business relationships and, for the Crown, a better-regulated and more assured system of taxation. The Staplers became entirely responsible for the collection of the wool taxes and for checking weights and measurements and making spot-checks for quality. They were incorporated under a mayor in 1354. By the Act of Retainer of 1466 they took the entire custom and subsidy on wool, in return for which they paid the garrison at Calais and certain other fixed charges, they repaid themselves for loans already made to the king, and any surplus over and above an agreed fixed sum they paid to him. Not only were they thus able to pay the garrison without transporting cash from England, but they also ran a mint at Calais into which foreign merchants were obliged to pay a certain proportion of the gold and silver received from their sales to Englishmen. The Crown was also able more easily to anticipate its revenue from the wool duties by means of loans raised on the security of the Merchants of the Staple.

The Staplers gained by having their quasi-monopoly of the wool trade virtually confirmed, and the recognition of themselves as a corporate company with their own mayor and officers. No complete list of Staplers has been discovered, and their own estimate of a membership of 400 in the fifteenth century may well be too high.[6] But it is clear that in the fourteenth and fifteenth centuries it was mainly Staplers who bought the wool in England, transported it to Calais and there sold it to foreign merchants. It is also clear that the Stapler was often himself the sheep-farmer who had reached forward to control the sale of his product at all stages, or that the two were at least closely connected by marriage or other ties. The Stonors, for example, were sheep-farmers with estates in the Chilterns and the Cotswolds. In 1475 William Stonor married Elizabeth Riche, of a wealthy merchant family interested in the wool trade, and went into partnership with Thomas Betson, the Stapler. Whether Stonor became a Stapler himself is not clear, but the marriage and the partnership illustrate the closeness of the trading and the wool-producing interests. The Staplers clung to their monopoly at every stage. English wool-packers, for example, would sometimes deal in the wool as well as pack it. But in 1473 the Staplers procured an Act of Parliament forbidding any packer of wools to buy or sell wool or wool fells within the realm for himself or for any other person.

All was not plain sailing, even with the establishment of the staple. There were still pirates in the Channel, still storms and shipwreck to be reckoned with, and there was always smuggling. From innumerable creeks and little harbours round the English coast it was easy to send a small ship or two laden with wool from a nearby pasture to some little-known Continental port, probably in the Low Countries, where willing hands would quickly disperse it and no one be the wiser. Or what was to prevent a bale of wool from being hidden in some miscellaneous cargo? In an effort to guard against this the Staplers were given the right to search ships at sea, and customs officials were authorized to search cargoes on land. But they could not always be in the right place at the right time, nor could connivance be ruled out. At all events, the Abbot of Furness is said for five years to have been repeatedly loading a ship with 200 tons of wool from a Lancashire creek and sending it off without detection.[7]

Merchants came from all over Europe to the Staple at Calais to buy English wool. They bought partly for cash—a miscellaneous collection of foreign money, often clipped and debased, whose value in Engish pounds was uncertain—partly in Bills of Exchange, provided generally by Italian or Spanish merchants, or possibly by English merchants who were beginning to speculate. The dates for repayment, whether near or far away, constituted a bargaining factor which was equivalent to a variation in price or to a rate of interest. The rate of exchange was also made to vary to constitute a better or worse bargain. Bills were often 'assigned' or 'transferred' to others before they fell due, and in this way they came to constitute a means of exchange. Other practices were not so commendable. Lombards were accused of buying wool on credit in Calais, selling it for ready money, and with that money making loans at high rates of interest to English merchants:

> And thus they wolde, if ye will so beleve
> Wypen our nose with our owne sleve[8]

By the fifteenth century no wool was more highly prized than

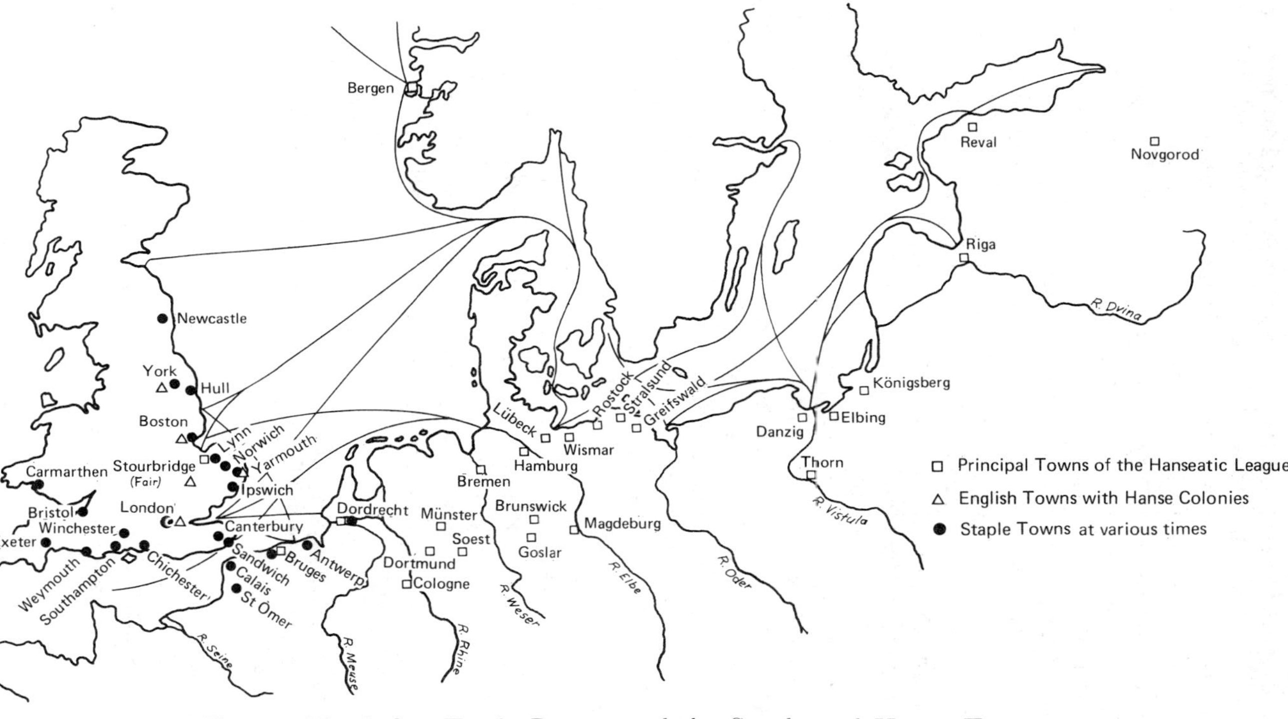

Fig. 4 North Sea Trade Routes and the Staple and Hanse Towns

that of the Cotswold sheep, and no men achieved greater fame and fortune than the woolmen of the Cotswold towns. They commemorated their fortune in charitable bequests, in schools and almshouses, in churches and in their own houses, many of which still stand in grey Cotswold stone towns from Chipping Norton and Broadway to Fairford and Northleach, from Stow-in-the-Wold to Burford in the valley of the Windrush. The whole area is a memorial to the men who rose to fortune and to a fame which was sometimes more than local if not on the backs, at least upon the fleeces, of the black-faced Cotswold sheep. William Grevel, who lies with his wife in Chipping Campden church, is described as the 'flower of the wool merchants of all England'. Thomas Fortey in Northleach church is described as a 'woolman' and lies with one foot on a sheep and the other on a woolpack. In this church, at the centre of the Cotswold wool trade, are no fewer than seven brasses to woolmen, all of them associating themselves in this way with the source of their prosperity. Sometimes the merchant mark, sometimes the mark of the Staplers, are associated also with the dead man and displayed as proudly as any coat of arms. John Field, Alderman of London, Merchant of the Staple, Commissioner appointed to regulate the wool trade to the staple town, was clearly a man of wealth and importance. His brass in his native church of Standon in Hertfordshire bears three shields—that of the City of London, that of the Merchants of the Staple, and his own personal merchant mark. His son, whose brass lies beside his father's, has discarded the woolman's tunic for the foppish clothes of the Court, looking somewhat like Chaucer's Squire, and displays the emblems of landed estate and a family coat of arms in place of the trademark. But there were many second-generation woolmen, happy enough to be commemorated by their woolmark, whose feet rested still upon the woolpack and the sheep, much as the Lord Chancellor in the House of Lords took his seat, and still does, upon a woolsack. It was a Merchant of the Staple, John Barton, who, in Holme beside Newark, inscribed in the stained-glass window of his house the most famous of all epitaphs upon the sheep: 'I thank God, and ever shall/It is the shepe hath paid for all!

Raw wool held the field as England's dominant export until the middle of the fifteenth century. The decline which thereafter set in, reducing the quantity of wool exported to some eight thousand sacks in the middle of the century, continued until the complete embargo repeatedly placed upon its export in the seventeenth century.[9] This decline was in no wise due to the eclipse of wool nor of the sheep, but to the diversion of raw wool to the manufacture of cloth at home. It is less surprising that woollen cloth should supplant wool as England's chief export in the sixteenth century than that it took so long to do so; but the landed interest was strong, the foreign demand high, the procedure of export well established, the profit substantial, rulers relied heavily upon the wool taxes and any change might well be for the worse. The revolutionary change in which the cloth industry supplanted raw wool as the basis of England's prosperity is another story.[10] It still left the sheep supreme, and gave no reason to qualify John Barton's prayer of thanks.

CHAPTER X

The Gilds

'The gild has lasted, and its beginning was, from time whereunto the memory of man reacheth not.' Eight years after the Peasants' Revolt it was felt necessary to inquire into these organizations, which existed all over the country, and which had been referred to in the course of the Revolt. The Parliament of 1388 accordingly sent out questionnaires to the farthest corners of the kingdom instructing all gilds and brotherhoods, misteries and crafts, to send up to the King's Council details of their foundation, property, and legalizing documents.

The returns came in during the winter of 1388–9, forty years after the Black Death and many of them dating their replies by that catastrophe. Some returns are lost, but more than five hundred remain from all parts of the country. The big, wealthy gilds sent formal returns—the Fishmongers, the Vintners, the Goldsmiths, the Mercers—but many replies came in the words of the members themselves, in their own handwriting, in a mixture of languages—Latin, English and French—which had not yet been integrated. These simple, often poignant documents show how widely the idea of the gild had taken root, what strength and comfort it gave the brethren. They show too that gild organization was not confined to any one class or group of wealth or occupation, that it was not necessarily the bond of trade or craft that drew people together, but that it was in the first place the kinship of like with like that formed the basis of a gild. This is emphasized by the names they generally gave themselves—not gilds, but fraternities or brotherhoods.[1]

Perhaps the first gilds were for mutual protection, affording the comfort of unity and sworn brotherhood at a time of war and uncertainty. In Christian times the brotherhood was frequently religious, growing out of common worship, like Corpus Christi, York, or the Gild of the Trinity, Coventry. Sometimes a permanent association grew from a common function—the Shephirdes Gild of Holbech, the Young Scholars of Lynn. A common disability might draw people together, as it did the Poor Men of Norwich; or a common experience, like a gild at Burgh, in Lincolnshire, founded by some pilgrims in fulfilment of a vow they made when tempest-tossed at sea. Organized fraternity might come simply from the attraction of like with like, as when bellringers founded societies. In the same way those engaged in similar work naturally drew together from interest in a common calling, and to strengthen their position in relation to the rest of society. The Merchant Gilds and Craft Gilds were of this kind.

All the societies had at least some things in common: they subscribed to a common fund, elected officers, made their own rules, and normally admitted women to their company on equal terms with men. Whether actually religious foundations or not, they all paid attention to religious rites, went to church as a body, frequently had their own chaplain, lit candles to the saints and to the Virgin. They made provision by subscription for the sickness, death and burial of their members, they gave alms to the poor. The more wealthy founded, or made donations to, educational establishments and hospitals, they gave money to public works like bridge-building or road-repair. One other thing they had in common. Whatever the interest that brought them together, they were organizations of a place—of London, of Norwich, of York; the emphasis was equally upon the function and the place.

Membership subscription varied considerably. It was normally in money but payment could be in kind, as at a gild of Ely where two pounds of wax for candles and one bushel of barley was required. There could, in addition, be an entrance fee. Each member took an oath of obedience, and was received with the kiss of peace. Thereafter he would join the meetings which took place once, twice, or most commonly four times a year. Generally a meeting was preceded by worship at the church of the saint with which the fraternity was associated, and members would march in procession in their best clothes or in the vestment of their gild from one to the other. At the meetings officers would be elected, to serve generally for a year. There was usually a Master, several Wardens and perhaps a paid officer like a Dean or Clerk. Feasting together for 'the nourishing of brotherly love' was normally an important part of their ritual, some of their officers having a special allowance in order to provide the banquet. Sometimes admission to the fraternity was dependent upon giving a feast, the Company of Saint Stephen's Ringers of Bristol, for example, having a rule that 'there shall be none made free of the said Company, unless he give the Company a breakfast, or pay the sum of three shillings and four pence in money'.

These societies expected a high standard of conduct from their members, and there were fines for disobedience or for disclosing the affairs of the gild. Perhaps the Bell Ringers had particular reason for placating their neighbours. At all events the Ringers of Bristol required members to be 'honest, peaceable, and of good conversation'. If anyone should 'curse or swear, or make any noise or disturbance, either in scoffing or unseemly jesting' or if he was quarrelsome, or made a mistake in ringing, he was fined. Even more serious was it if over-exuberance caused any one to 'be so rude as to run into the Belfry before he do kneel down and pray'. He would be fined 6*d.* the first time and cast out of the Company the second time.

The Bell Ringers strike a happy note of keenness and enthusiasm. The Gild of Young Scholars of Lynne, on the other hand, have got themselves into difficulties, and they appeal to their elders: all the goods of the gild have been spent, 'wherefore, as children in young age, hoping in time coming to have been increased by help and counsel of wise men . . . trusting as children, with gifts to been amended'. Village societies were small, but in towns a big fraternity like Corpus Christi at York could muster a membership of nearly 15 000; even kings could be included, both Henry IV and Henry VI being enrolled in the Gild of the Trinity, Coventry. But economically two types of gild stand out—the Merchant Gild[2] and the Craft Gild. Both played an important part in Britain's industrial development, the Merchant Gild being probably half a century earlier.

Craft gilds were first mentioned in England in the twelfth century when there were weavers' gilds in London and Lincoln and bakers' and goldsmiths' gilds in London. As with other fraternities, there was the crystallization of like workers into a recognizable group, the drawing up of rules and the licensing of the gild by some authority which might be the town, the lord of the manor, or even the king. In this form many gilds flourished for centuries. But powerful craft organizations needed a more secure background for their activities, while cities and monarchs found it desirable to exercise stricter control over them. Hence it became customary for the craft gilds, in the same way as the merchant gilds and the towns themselves, to obtain recognition in the form of a charter. Some gilds, nevertheless, continued to exist without any official recognition at all; they were referred to as 'adulterine' gilds, and from time to time action was taken by the Crown to penalize them.

Whether licensed, chartered or adulterine, craft gilds multiplied in the century between 1350 and 1450. They differed widely in size, in wealth and in function. There were purely craft gilds like weavers and tailors and saddlers who worked to specific orders and at the same time laid up stock for general sale; there were blacksmiths and tylers, whose work was largely personal and immediate; bakers, mostly small men who made the daily bread in constant and repetitive demand; fishmongers, who early became wealthy and powerful and were merchants rather than craftsmen. Yet they all had this in common: they belonged essentially to the town, where industry and a division of labour early developed; they were monopolists who sought to protect their monopoly by excluding interlopers and by obliging all of the same craft and city to join their gild; they controlled their crafts by roughly similar organizations; they had on the whole high standards of workmanship and service; they exercised exclusive jurisdiction over all workers in their craft, modified to greater or less degree by the competence of the town in which they flourished.

Like other gilds, the craft gilds played their parts in a local context,[3] being bakers of London, tailors of Wisbech, weavers of Lincoln, barbers of Norwich. By the fourteenth century, when a rigid and fairly formal organization had crystallized, a craft gild consisted of masters, journeymen and apprentices. Each master, while bound by the rules of his gild, worked independently with his journeymen and apprentices, serving his own customers, owning the raw materials and the tools of his trade, and free to dispose as he wished of the finished articles.

The journeyman had served his apprenticeship but was not yet ready to set up as master. The apprentice was helping the master, while at the same time learning the skills of the trade. A good master–apprentice relationship was far from being one of master and servant, and was more often that of father and son. It was normal for journeymen and apprentices to live in the same house as the master, virtually as part of his family, for there was as a rule no class-distinction between them, but only one of age and skill. Generally the master had in his time served just such an apprenticeship, and been just such a journeyman.

Fundamentally apprenticeship was the same all over the country. The master's obligations were first and foremost to teach the apprentice his craft 'and nothing hid from him thereof'.[4] The master was to find the apprentice meat and drink and lodging, usually apparel, and sometimes a small wage as well. He was responsible for the dress, appearance and conduct of his apprentice. Sometimes he was required to send the young man off into the world at the end of his term well clothed, armed with the tools of his trade, and with a sum of money to set him up. Various other obligations could be written into the indenture. They might concern schooling, as when a master haberdasher provided two years at grammar school for an apprentice of fourteen. Sometimes instruction in languages was required, apparently being thought necessary to a good businessman. A mercer's apprentice of Norwich was to be sent to France for a year to learn the language, a grocer's apprentice was to go to Flanders to 'be sufficiently taught to speak Dutch', a weaver's apprentice was to receive 'instruction in the language of Britanny'.[5] The master was allowed the often very necessary powers of chastisement and correction. But the apprentices for their part were apt to appeal to their gild against what they considered any 'undue' punishment. The redoubtable John Lilburne in the seventeenth century even appealed successfully to the Lord Chamberlain of London against alleged ill-treatment by his clothier master.

The apprentice's obligation was to be diligent, to learn well, to be a credit to his master, to his craft, and to his city. In particular, he must be honest, protect his master's goods and his master's interest in every way, do any menial offices about the house which might be required, and be obedient to his master's wishes. He was not to frequent inns or gaming-houses, not to stay away from his master's house without permission, he must not marry without his master's consent. The craft officers, as their part of the obligation, would protect an apprentice from ill-treatment and see that the master was not failing in his duty in other respects. At Coventry, for example, not only would the coopers hear complaints from apprentices, but once a year they made the rounds of their members, calling every apprentice before them to learn how he fared.

But before his apprenticeship could even begin the young man had to be formally admitted to the trade of his choice. The Ordinances of the Cordwainers (shoemakers) of London are typical in stipulating that an apprentice must be admitted before the mayor, that he must be shown to be of good character, and that, besides the premium payable to his gild, he must subscribe to his city and to the poor-box of his craft. Indenture was generally for seven years, though until the Statute of Apprentices of 1563 prescribed this period of time, as few as four or as many as sixteen years were known. A boy might be apprenticed as young as eleven years old, but fourteen was a normal age, and as old as eighteen not unknown. As a result the apprentice was frequently well into his twenties when he emerged as a journeyman. But this was accepted in both medieval and Tudor society: the Common Council of London in 1555 sanctioned a rule that no apprentice was to be admitted as a freeman of the city or allowed to set up house until he was at least twenty-four years old, while 'until a man grow into the age of twenty four years', it was said in the Statute of Apprentices,[6] he was not 'grown unto the full knowledge of the art that he professeth'. The number of apprentices which a master might take was also regulated from time to time by the Government and by the gilds themselves. A master who wanted cheap labour and the indenture money might take too many apprentices too young, but the whole craft then in course of time would find itself with too many ill-trained workers.

The apprentice learned a craft, he won the company of others like himself in a close community, and if he was lucky he won an accepted place in a happy family. He would expect to attain the freedom of his craft and the freedom of his city, and ultimately to set up for himself as a respected master. But he paid for this by leaving his own family at an early age, and probably never again came close to them, for he might be indentured far away from his home. This aspect of English employment struck an Italian observer in the fifteenth century very forcibly. 'The want of affection in the English is strongly manifested towards their children', he wrote,

> for having kept them at home till they arrive at the age of seven or nine years at the utmost, they put them out, both males and females, to hard service in the houses of other people, binding them generally for another seven or nine years . . . if the English sent their children away from home to learn virtue and good manners, and took them back again when their apprenticeship was over, they might, perhaps be excused; but they never return, for the girls are settled by their patrons, and the boys make the best marriages they can, and, assisted by their patrons, not by their fathers, they also open a house and strive diligently by this means to make some fortune for themselves.[7]

When he finished his apprenticeship the young man emerged as a journeyman. His object then was to work for a good master until he had saved sufficient money to set up on his own, and regulations of craft, borough, and state directed masters to take at least one journeyman. But the path to mastership was obstructed by payments to be free of his gild, payments to be free of his town, and by the production of a proof piece, or masterpiece, to attest to his skill. By the seventeenth century most trades required the masterpiece and, according to the standard desired, the barrier to mastership could be raised or lowered.

The craft gild was held together by its organization of master, wardens and other officers. It held its Feast and Saint Days, and adhered to regulations enforced by either its gild court or the city authorities, or both. In the rules and ordinances of the craft gilds the breadth of their purpose is revealed, covering every aspect of life, industrial, religious and social. At the forefront of gild policy was always the quality of their product, which they set about achieving in a variety of ways. The Weavers of Bristol fixed the width of the woven cloth, and decreed not only that cloth whose threads were deficient, or too far apart, should be burnt, but that the instrument upon which it was worked should be burnt also. Cloth that was worse at the middle than at the sides—a common fault or deceit—was to be similarly dealt with. The Dyers of Bristol were keen to make amends in case of faulty work: 'If any damage is done to any person through defect of dyeing by any man or woman of the said craft, that then he shall pay sufficient amends to the parties damaged'.[8] The Fullers of Bristol were in 1406 given permission by the City to search for bad work twice a week, penalties involving a fine to the town, a fine to the gild, and recompense to the customer.[9] Searchers of the White Tawyers of London had to search 'without sparing any one for friendship or for hate'. They must not be 'lax and negligent about their duty, or partial to any person, for gift or for friendship'. To make assurance doubly sure, it was also agreed that the searchers should be fined if they did not do their work well.[10]

The rare cases of resistance to search incurred severe penalties, a Norwich tailor, for example, being made to pay sixteen pence and donate a pound of candle wax to his craft for hindering search of his premises. Faults or bad workmanship were not only punished by fine but with the pillory and, in the case of persistent fault, with expulsion from the craft. The London Blacksmiths, in a telling phrase, decreed that any one found 'false of his hands' should be immediately expelled.[11] The London Pewterers were allowed three chances—the first time faulty ware was discovered the workman lost it, the second time he was fined in addition, the third time he was expelled from his gild.[12] As industry expanded and crafts grew in size and number, house-to-house inspection became increasingly difficult, and it sometimes then became the custom, as at Coventry, to provide a central depot where work was brought on certain days of the week for inspection.

But the assurance of good work being better than the detection of bad, many craft ordinances were directed to keeping up the quality of the product. The use of good materials was enjoined, and satisfactory conditions of production were insisted upon. Night work was prohibited—in the uncertain light of candles faults would escape notice and bad work pass for good; nor was holiday work permitted, perhaps on the grounds that the disgruntled or tired worker would not produce his best, perhaps to prevent the over-industrious stealing a march on his more pleasure-loving competitors, perhaps for religious observance, or perhaps merely to protect the rights of the apprentice. The Fullers of Lincoln demanded of their members that 'none of them shall work after dinner on Saturdays nor on any days which they ought to keep as festivals according to the law of the Church'. The London Goldsmiths, in an Ordinance of 1370, decreed that no men should work at night, nor in alleys, but that all should be in the High Street where their work would be seen. This introduces another aspect of medieval craft regulation—that all should be done above board—and is a reason for the practice of the workman sitting outside his shop, working in public upon the board or table before him.

Deceit or fraud in other ways was guarded against by a periodic inspection of weights and measures. The Goldsmiths particularly, as dealers in precious metals, kept their weights carefully checked, and many of their Ordinances were intended to guard against adulteration. Quite early they instituted the sign of the leopard's head as a mark of quality in both gold and silver work. In addition, to ensure that each piece of work could be assigned, an Act of 1363 ordained that ever master goldsmith should have his own particular mark. Quality was rigidly maintained by reference to what was known as the Paris touch, which consisted of rubbing gold or silver on a touchstone to test its quality. The Ordinances were quite explicit that if gold found in buckles, rings or other articles was not worth the assay they should be broken up and the metal forfeited. 'False stones' should be ground to dust in a mortar. There are also records of fines for putting glass into gold, or making buckles of 'feeble gold'. Instructions about workmanship were equally clear: certain articles, such as girdles, should be riveted and not soldered, others must be solid and not hollow.

With a less valuable product than the Goldsmiths', but with a product often more important, the Founders also maintained a very high standard, and their Ordinances insist upon the highest quality of workmanship and material. In 1365 they sought the co-operation of the City of London, complaining that

> some of the said Mystery do work and make their works of false metal and false solder, so that their said work, to wit, Candlesticks, Buckles, Straps and other such like articles, when exposed to fire or great strain, crack, break, and dissolve, to the peril and damage of those who purchase them, and to the great Slander of the City and the whole Mystery . . .

They asked the City to ordain 'that no one shall make any Stirrups, Buckles, or Spurs, unless of the best and finest Metal that can be found or obtained, and of Metal that will not break, and no other'. A very different craft, but one of paramount importance, made use of a device similar to that of the leopard's head to protect its standards: the Bakers required each baker to mark his bread with his own seal so that it could be traced to him. The Gild Brethren elected a jury for the purpose of inspection, to which every baker had to bring his seals for examination. If one were broken or worn it had to be replaced, and the baker was charged a fee.[13]

The crafts sometimes tried also to control the prices at which their products were sold, and to prevent manipulation of the market. In London shearmen, coopers, weavers, founders laid down quite clearly the rates which should be taken by master craftsmen for their work. The crafts of Leicester did likewise. There were also questions of what wages should be paid to the 'servants and workmen' who were not apprenticed to the craft but whose work was necessary for such routine tasks as sweeping and cleaning, packing and rolling of barrels. Both gilds and cities concerned themselves in this, the Fullers of Bristol, for example, being given authority by the City to fix wages, with power to take before the Mayor any who proved 'rebels or contrarious', there to be dealt with 'according to law and reason'.[14]

Besides regulations covering entry into their craft, most gilds had a list of exemptions. Some gilds excluded bondmen, though others admitted villeins and unfree persons so long as they fulfilled the requirements of apprenticeship. Aliens were normally excluded, and one gild included 'rebels of Ireland' among those it banned. Women were not excluded. The female silk-weavers were well known. There were women brewers, who in some towns had a virtual monopoly, women barber-surgeons, women bakers, many women in all branches of the woollen and cloth industries, and the gild of wool-packers of Southampton was an entirely female organization with the rule that members were 'not to bawle nor scold oon with anither'.[15] When women were excluded from a craft it seems to have been largely on economic grounds. At Bristol in 1461 it was made clear, for example, that a prohibition against women weavers was because many men were unemployed. Some crafts permitted only the wives and daughters of their members to work, and it was accepted practice for a widow to carry on her husband's craft after his death, as many stories testify.

There developed, also, a form of labour exchange within some crafts. The Carpenters of York appointed an officer to bring together those seeking work and those requiring labour. In other cases workmen for hire would gather at a recognized spot—in Coventry at 5 a.m. at the Broad Gate 'with their tools in their hands', at Norwich between 5 and 6 a.m. at the market cross.[16] Sometimes, when labour was short, a master would try to win the services of a servant or apprentice away from another man. Craft Ordinances, like that of the tailors of London, repeatedly forbade the practice in no uncertain terms: 'If any master of the craft keeps any lad or sewer of another master for one day after he has well known that the lad wrongly left his master and that they had not parted in a friendly and reasonable manner . . . he shall pay a stone of wax'.[17]

Throughout the Ordinances of the craft gilds runs the thread of religious worship. The very number of candles to be kept burning to the Virgin or to a saint were prescribed, and entrance fees and fines to the Gild were frequently in wax. The Barbers of Norwich offered candles and torches on Midsummer Day to the Virgin and St John the Baptist. The Gild of Peltyers (Furriers) of Norwich would offer candles and flowers at St William's tomb, and hear mass before going in to audit their accounts and choose officers. Gilds not only organized religious services for members who died but made detailed rules about following the coffin. Many also made provision for holding services for those dying abroad. The Tailors of Lincoln encouraged their members to go on pilgrimage by raising a subscription for them:

> If any one wishes to make pilgrimage to the Holy Land of Jerusalem, each brother and sister shall give him a penny; and if to St. James's, or Rome a halfpenny; and they shall go with him outside the gates of the city of Lincoln; and, on his return, they shall meet him and go with him to his mother church.[18]

The philanthropic side of the trade gilds was highly developed. Schools, almshouses and hospitals were founded and maintained, alms were given to the poor, within their own ranks a system of mutual self-help on a friendly-society basis covered old age, sickness, burial and general misfortune. Some trades had their own particular hazards, for which they made provision. The Goldsmiths reported that 'many persons of that trade by fire and the smoke of quicksilver had lost their sight and that others of them by working in that trade became so crazed and infirm that they were disabled to subsist but of relief from others'.[19]

The gilds gave help also to apprentices coming out of their time, often assisting them to pay for their freedoms. Journeymen were assisted to set up on their own; parents were given help to pay a child's indenture. The Fraternity of St Mary in All Hallows, London Wall, offered to give legal or charitable assistance to any member whose son or daughter had been unjustly treated by the master to whom he had been apprenticed.

In reports of gild meetings and of the gild courts not only the larger issues but frequently the every-day incidents of life are revealed in illuminating detail. Here an apprentice is admonished, a master brought to book for not paying a journeyman his wages, for ill-treating his apprentice, for turning out faulty work; it is agreed that an apprentice should be 'whole of limbs' and of good physique as well as of good character. Petty crime was dealt with summarily; the Fullers of Lincoln found a member guilty of theft of a penny and expelled him from the gild.

Firmly associated with the craft gilds was the annual pageant or miracle play or mystery play, often performed on the festival of Corpus Christi. 'Once on a time', as they said, the simple pageants began, and doubtless took many forms. But by the thirteenth century it was usual for at least the bigger productions to be organized by the various craft gilds. The very term 'mystery play' by which they were known indicates their craft connection, and it became the practice for crafts to contribute to part of an annual cycle of plays according to their occupations: the carpenters or the shipwrights would present *Noah's Ark*, the mariners *The Flood*, the smiths would play *The Fight of David and Goliath*, the goldsmiths *The Three Kings* and *The Adoration*, the vintners *The Marriage of Cana*. And even where the incident portrayed did not resemble their craft, it was still customary to assign traditional parts. The mercers, drapers and haberdashers at Norwich would present *The Creation*, the grocers were chosen to present *Paradise*. At York *The Creation* and *The Fall of Lucifer* fell to the barkers, and the fullers portrayed *Adam and Eve* and *The Garden of Eden*.

The plays were often performed many times, and the authorities of the town, as well as the gilds themselves, took a great interest in ensuring a production of high quality. The crafts were to provide 'good players, well arrayed, and openly speaking'. In York four of the most 'cunning, discreet and able players' within the city were 'to search, hear and examine' the players of the various trades, and only those 'sufficient in person and cunning' were to be chosen for the big day.

The mystery play was performed on a movable stage resembling a large cart, horse-drawn, with curtains at the back which could be lowered for preparations between scenes and drawn back while the action was in progress; it was played frequently on two levels, or on the stage and on the street. The play could be performed as many as sixteen times in different parts of the city. As there could be as many as thirty-eight scenes, and all performances had to be got through in the same day, considerable stamina was required, and the performers were required to rise at 4.30 in the morning. The costumes were elaborate, music played a large part in the performance, the enthusiasm of the audience was no less than that of the players, scenes portraying the devil being the most popular, like the opening sequence of the York Mystery where Lucifer and his followers are relegated to hell. There was clearly much expense involved: each craft paid for its own production and often 'pageant silver' was collected throughout the year.[20]

The idealized picture of the gild is a happy one. But gilds were not developing in isolation, and their history is part of the wider history of the country. They began to change in response to the demands of a complex society for which the apprentice-journeyman-master progression was at once too restrictive and too simple. Some industries, notably the woollen-cloth industry, moved out to country districts where they escaped the net of gild organization; newer industries deliberately established themselves outside the towns. For the gilds themselves the role of the town, the requirements of the market, the evolution of capitalist production, the beginnings of industrial mechanization made demands which the gild system could not meet. Moreover, the whole concept of the ordered hierarchy of the gild was based upon status, and status is a medieval concept which operated throughout feudal society but was alien to the new society which developed as feudalism broke up and the idea of contract emerged.

Inside the gilds the change was apparent in a sharp division in wealth and power between the gildsmen. It was inevitable that some masters should grow richer than others, and the growth of a wealthy oligarchy within the gilds became increasingly noticeable as trade expanded. At the same time the identity of interest between wealthy gildsmen and wealthy burghers became more pronounced, frequently merging in the same person. As he became richer, the bigger master became more of an employer of labour, less of a worker himself, tending to concentrate upon management and sale rather than actual production, and the craftsman proper was differentiated from the merchant.

The growth of a wealthy oligarchy within the gild was encouraged by raising indenture fees and insisting upon the wearing of an expensive livery. The Gilds began to call themselves Companies and came to be known as Livery Companies because of the wearing of the livery. They also reached out to the more complete independence of incorporation. The Grocers, for example, became an incorporated Company in 1428, the Fishmongers in 1433, the Vintners in 1436, the Brewers in 1437, the Drapers in 1438, the Haberdashers in 1447, the Leathersellers in 1444, the Bakers in 1496 and others followed. By this time they differed from the original trade gilds not only in having a wealthy ruling class (the wearers of the livery) but a subordinate class of workers who might be small masters, journeymen or apprentices. Their governing bodies came from the Livery, who retained control by a number of devices, and were frequently self-perpetuating. This oligarchy began to enrol rich or influential members from outside the ranks of the gilds, so strengthening their position against the brethren. They organized pageants on a far more lavish scale than the miracle plays, they welcomed and escorted kings and queens and potentates. The London Companies particularly were famous for their elaborate water pageants. They acquired magnificent premises, they collected costly plate of gold and silver, they acquired landed property. Their divorce from the humbler craftsmen of their gilds reached its apogee in the pronouncement of the Court of the Livery Companies of 27th July 1697 that 'no person shall be allowed to take upon himself the clothing of any of the twelve Companies unless he have an estate of £1,000; of the inferior Companies, unless he have an estate of £500'.[21]

CHAPTER XI

The Woollen-cloth Industry

The obverse of the decline in the export of raw wool was the expansion of the English woollen cloth industry for both home and overseas consumption. Though the total production of woollen cloth—coming as it did from a variety of sources, all small by modern standards and mostly in various forms of domestic enterprise—can only be guessed at, the export duties imposed on both native and alien exporters in 1347 necessitated a careful accounting, and the enrolled Customs accounts supply figures of exports from 1347 to 1547 which give a reasonable guide to the size of the woollen-cloth export.[1] They show that exports of woollen cloth grew from some 4 000 broadcloths[2] at the time of the Black Death to some 13 000 at the time of the Peasants' Revolt, and to over 122 000 in the middle of the sixteenth century. A century later woollen cloth constituted 80 to 90 per cent of British exports. Of the total wool exports, raw wool accounted at this time for less than 8 per cent, cloth for over 92 per cent.

The cloth industry thus became the goose that laid the golden egg. It was protected by taxes and embargoes on the export of native wool, and by restrictions on the import of foreign cloth; it was encouraged by sumptuary legislation which prescribed the wearing of English cloth and forbade the use of foreign; it was improved by the bringing in of aliens to teach their craft to the English. Thus cared for, it reigned supreme and unchallenged until King Cotton at the end of the eighteenth century usurped the throne it had occupied for over three hundred years.

There was nothing essentially new in the manufacture of cloth from England's excellent wool: it is, rather, surprising that it took so long to achieve an eminence in cloth-production comparable to the quality of the raw material. The Romans had manufactured a fine cloth at Winchester, and they left evidence of dyeing and fulling. In Anglo-Saxon times cloth was even exported to the Continent. The strong rule of the Normans gave a measure of security to the industry, while Flemish artisans who settled in England in the wake of the Conquest imparted their skills to the English. In the course of the eleventh century a woollen-cloth industry, producing for both an overseas and a home market, grew in the settled south and east of the country, and by the twelfth century the fame of the cloths of Stamford and of Leicester, of York and of Beverley, and in particular of the Lincoln Scarletts, was widespread. Weavers' gilds were early formed in the cloth towns, and gilds of dyers and fullers followed. Spinning, however, remained a dispersed and unorganized occupation, generally, through its very nature, performed by women and girls as a part-time task. The Government early appreciated the value of the cloth industry, and the need to keep up the standard of production. The Assize of Measures of 1197 confined the production of dyed cloth for the market to the towns, where control was possible, it stipulated that cloth should be two ells wide and, to prevent fraud, that it should be of the same quality in the middle as at the sides. Magna Carta in 1215 included similar provisions: 'One width of cloth, whether dyed, russet or halberget, to wit, two ells within the lists'. But the early woollen-cloth industry, based upon the towns of the settled and more populous parts of the country, was in decline by the time of the Great Charter, largely because of the superior skills of Flemish and Italian clothmakers and their high demand for English wool: graziers made more profit, and the Crown raised more revenue in taxes from the export of raw wool than from the production of cloth at home.

Nevertheless, the case for rebuilding a profitable cloth industry was never completely lost sight of, and it was realized that the very taxes on the export of wool, which were so fruitful a source of royal income, could serve this end. Thus, while the export duties on wool increased throughout the thirteenth century there were no export duties on cloth until 1303, and then on alien exporters only. Nearly half a century later, thinking it might be letting slip an opportunity, the Government announced that there was 'good reason that such a profit be taken of cloth wrought within this realm and carried forth out of the land, as a profit is taken of wools that are carried forth'. Accordingly, in 1347, the native cloth-exporter, as well as the alien, became liable to duty, although he paid only a 2 per cent tax, compared with a 33 per cent tax on the export of wool. A century later the export duties on wool and cloth together amounted to some 74 per cent of the entire Customs revenue, and there was also a duty on home sales. The State did very well out of the sheep. To facilitate the collection of the cloth taxes and to avoid deceit, regulation was made that the finished cloth should be sold at specified times at specified places, Blackwell Hall in London, which was established at the end of the fourteenth century being one of the most famous. The aulnager was the key man in the collection of the woollen-cloth taxes. His office was in existence as early as the thirteenth century with the task of testing the quality and dimensions of the cloth for sale, sealing that which was up to standard, confiscating faulty material.

If the English cloth industry was to be encouraged it was necessary to produce cloth of as high a standard as the quality of the wool warranted. The settlement of skilled foreign weavers which began in the wake of the Conquest was encouraged, weavers from the Low Countries in particular being welcomed by promises of protection and freedom from taxation. The first big wave came in the last quarter of the thirteenth century. In 1326 inducements were again offered to all cloth-workers from abroad who would come and practise their craft in England. In 1331 the offer became more specific, when Edward III gave to the Flemish weaver John Kempe, with his men, servants and apprentices, letters of protection while they practised their craft in England. Six years later an Act of Parliament extended the offer to all immigrant cloth-weavers. The fourteenth-century immigrants settled widely in various parts of the country, including London, Oxford and Winchester, Northampton and Leicester, Ipswich and Colchester, Bristol, York and Leeds. The Flemings in particular found the prospect of working in England attractive: they escaped the political discrimination to which they were subject at home; they would have abundant raw material to work upon; they were promised they would feed on beef and mutton 'till nothing but their fatness should stint their stomachs', and they were reminded of the English tradition that such 'who came in strangers within doors soon after went out bridegrooms . . . having married the daughters of their landlords'. At the same time, the customs of the foreigners, their speech, their very skills, their segregation in their own weavers' gilds, made for resentment. At times of unrest this antipathy flared up, as, for example, during the Peasants' Revolt. Yet many immigrants were happy enough to send for their friends and families, the formation of 'one entire fellowship of the gild of weavers' strengthened their craft affinity, and by the fifteenth century little animosity was left.

Less effective as an aid to the woollen-cloth industry was the effort to make English people wear English cloth, and to exclude foreign cloth from the country. Like the encouragement of foreign weavers, the long line of sumptuary Acts began in the Middle Ages. In 1326 the Government of Edward II laid down that no cloth not made in England, Wales or Ireland should be bought in these countries except by the 'king, queen, earls, barons, knights and ladies, and their children born in wedlock, archbishops, bishops, and other persons and people of Holy Church, and seculars who can spend forty pounds sterling a year of their rents'. The number of exceptions makes it clear that no one with money to spend was prepared to be inconvenienced by the prohibition. But the Act of 1337, when England was at war with France, instructed *all* subjects to wear English cloth, while forbidding the export of English wool or the import of foreign cloth. During the following century the import of foreign cloth was several times again forbidden, and there were many injunctions that everyone should use woollen cloth made within the country. Sumptuary legislation is, of its nature, difficult to enforce, and there is no evidence that the repetitive injunctions had more than a passing effect.

Indeed, the expansion of the cloth industry owed more to technical factors than to any Government action. Fulling was essential to the making of cloth from the shorter-stapled wool which made the best broadcloth. Originally it consisted of trampling or beating the woven cloth in water until it was shrunk and thickened so that the fibres of weft and woof were virtually indistinguishable. When someone, somewhere, devised a mechanized process of fulling, in which wooden hammers attached to a wheel were driven round by the force of water an entirely new situation developed. Very little is known about the origins of this earliest mechanical invention in the textile industry. It appears to have been in use in Western Europe in the twelfth century, and references indicate that it was known by the end of the century in Yorkshire and the Cotswolds, though its use was not then general. The use of the fulling mill implied better cloth more easily made, but, on the same principle as the mill-wheel, it required not only water but water running with some force to drive the wheel round. This meant that fulling moved from the town to the country, and from the home to the stream. It meant that the revival of the cloth industry was not in the settled plains of the south-east but in hilly country, where rapid streams of water drove the fulling wheel. It was a process similar to that which in the eighteenth century would cause the textile industries to move from the streams to the coalfields.

The second effect to flow from the invention of the fulling mill was the need for capital. The family who had fulled cloth by their own manual power could rarely afford to erect a fulling mill, and became partly dependent upon the richer man who could, either paying him a fee for the use of his mill or working for him. Manorial lords found it profitable to build fulling mills on their streams, and to repay themselves by instituting suit of mill for fulling cloth as for grinding corn. Fulling mills were not established without opposition, and their introduction was neither rapid nor uniform. City fullers in particular resisted the bypassing of their gild regulations, and London in 1298 prohibited fulling at the mills instead of 'by might and strength of man and that is with hand and foot'—a prohibition which was not removed until 1417, and was then revived twenty years later. Opposition from tenants on manorial estates could be long and severe. Resistance to the use of the monastic fulling mill, for example, was part of the centuries-long struggle that brought both the men of St Albans and the men of Bury St Edmunds into the Peasants' Revolt against their monastic overlords.[3] These men were not fighting mechanical fulling but were claiming the right to use their own fulling mills without payment to a feudal lord. But there were many poor men whose equally long struggle was directed to the destruction of the mill itself. As late as 1485, for example, the owner of a mill in the

Stroud valley was attacked by workpeople. But mechanical fulling was well established in this area by this time, and the attack was in the nature of a last-ditch stand.

The move from the towns brought about by the fulling mill had other reasons also to commend it. It removed the industry from the restrictions of the town-based gilds to country areas where regulation was less onerous and employment was unfettered. Labour was required not only for fulling but for all the processes of cloth-production, and there were many in country districts anxious to take up new work: a cottar with too little land, younger sons of villeins not needed full-time on the family holding; younger sons and others who, rather than assart or rent land, would turn to industry. At the same time cheaper food and a lower cost of living generally meant lower wages than in the towns. It also frequently happened that supplies of fuller's earth required for fulling were found in the same hills where the swift streams ran and the best sheep grazed and the water was soft and suitable for dyeing. One of the most favoured areas was in the Stroud Valley of the Gloucestershire Cotswolds—the best wool, fuller's earth, water-power and, for dyeing, what Fuller described in the seventeenth century as the 'sweet rivulet of Stroud'. While the fulling mill thus changed the geographical pattern of production in England, and gave the capitalist entrepreneur his first chance in the woollen-cloth industry, it also gave to England supremacy over the cloth-producers of Flanders and Italy. The flat plains of Flanders could produce no swift streams to drive the mill-wheel, and even North Italy lacked the combination of stream and pasture and fuller's earth, as well as the best wool, which England possessed. It was mechanical fulling which enabled England to bring all these advantages together, to catch up, to surpass and then to maintain her lead over other nations.[4]

The rise of the woollen-cloth industry to its greatest heights coincided with the rule of the Tudors. Civil war was for the time being ended, firm domestic government, treaties with foreign princes like the Magnus Intercursus of 1496, encouraged trade at home and overseas. Population expanded, towns grew, new industries developed, the very world itself expanded—in line, it would seem, with Tudor exuberance at home. Even the great price-rise that confounded contemporaries and still confounds their descendants[5] seemed to reflect the enormous gusto of the age, while in dress, building, intellectual attainments, the bragadocio of Tudor times left its mark. At the same time, the ruling class was well aware that much of the glitter and excitement of Tudor life rested still, as the more restricted life of medieval England had done, not upon her explorers nor her sea-dogs, her courtiers nor her poets, but upon the sheep. It was one of the contradictions of the age that while so much Tudor discussion and legislation was directed against enclosure for sheep[6] voyages of discovery were planned to find new markets for woollen cloth in the colder lands of the North-West Passage.

There were certain areas where the cloth produced was of outstanding quality, particularly the Cotswolds, parts of the Mendips, and the valleys of the Wiltshire and Berkshire Downs. By the Tudor period the best wool of all came from the Wiltshire flocks, and those of parts of Gloucestershire and Somerset, and here was produced the bulk of the famous broadcloth. This cloth was generally exported undyed, but in the valley of the Stroud could be dyed scarlet, the water of the river being particularly conducive to the colour. In the West Riding of Yorkshire a rougher cloth, of inferior quality, was produced, in parts of the Lake District and in Devon and Cornwall the coarser wool of the local sheep was woven into the serge which, around Exeter particularly, became very popular, and the source of a large export trade.

While all these were entirely, or partly, made from short-fleeced wool, in Lincolnshire, Northamptonshire and East Anglia the longer-haired sheep were bred. Their fleece produced a different kind of cloth, made, both warp and weft, from the longer, combed wool. This was known as worsted, the name deriving from the small village near Norwich where much of it was produced. It was not fulled, and was not subject, therefore, to the pressures which moved the broadcloth industry into the areas of water-power. Worsted was a strong and warm cloth but it was not thickened by fulling, and was consequently not so heavy as broadcloth. One of its attractions was that it was patterned in the weave. This process, introduced by Flemish immigrants, required considerable skill, and gave the East Anglian worsted industry an unrivalled monopoly for two hundred years. Among other uses it was popular for church vestments, for church hangings, for bed-coverings. By the time of Elizabeth, however, it was somewhat out of fashion, and Norwich in particular was suffering a severe depression.

At this period, however, there was a further influx of foreign weavers, again mostly from the Low Countries, this time fleeing the religious persecution which the Duke of Alva was perpetrating in the name of Spain. These immigrants, like their forebears, settled in Norfolk, Suffolk and Essex, particularly in Norwich and Colchester. They were the more welcome since they taught the English how to make the finer fabrics known collectively as the 'new draperies'. These included bays, a fine lightweight cloth; arras, a rich tapestry fabric; says, another fine cloth resembling serge; and kerseys, a coarse but still lightweight material. They were all eminently suited to export to the Mediterranean and other warmer countries where the heavier worsted and still heavier broadcloth were becoming less popular. The art of making the new draperies was a welcome adaptation of skills and resources to meet the needs of the market. The product was varied and flexible. Like worsted, it generally called for some long, combed wool, but this was generally used in conjunction with short, carded wool. The popularity of the new draperies caused them to spread to other manufacturing areas, kerseys in particular even being found in Berkshire, close to traditional broadcloth country.

The Tudors and Stuarts, like their predecessors, were fully aware of the value of the woollen-cloth industry. Not only did they welcome immigrants, but they continued the sumptuary legislation of the Middle Ages, as when Parliament in 1571 ordered everyone above six years old to wear a cap of wool on Sundays and holidays. When in 1621 a Bill was proposed in Parliament 'for the better venting of the cloth of this Kingdom' a suggestion was made to include a clause 'that none under the degree of a baron should mourn in anything but cloth'. But one Member objected: 'It is hard to make a law whereby we shall not know our wives from our chambermaids', and the Bill was dropped. The following year, nevertheless, Proclamation was made for English cloth to be worn at funerals. In the same year, 1622, a Commission was trying to find causes for the prevailing depression in trade; it recommended, among other things, that the 'nobility and gentry' should set the example of wearing English woollen cloth in winter. Five years later the legislature turned to the dead and enacted the famous injunction that the dead must be buried in woollen shrouds, and not in linen as was customary: 'forcing the dead', as Arthur Young remarked later, 'to consume what the living were inadequate to purchase',[7]—'Since the Living would not bear it/They should, when dead, be forc'd to wear it', as a pamphleteer expressed it.[8] In 1688 Parliament resolved to set an example by wearing English wool, and urged the King and Queen to do likewise. Ten years later a resolution was approved in Parliament for 'all persons whatsoever to wear no garment, stockings, or other sort of apparel, but what is made of sheep's wool only, from the Feast of All Saints to the Feast of the Annunciation of Our Lady inclusive', leather only excepted. As in the Middle Ages, the repeated injunctions reflect both the concern of the Government for the cloth industry and its inability to enforce sumptuary legislation.

Such ineffectiveness was partly due to the many interests that were at work. While the producers of woollen cloth wanted abundance of raw material and no competition from foreign cloth, the breeders of sheep wanted the widest possible market for their raw wool. The monarch looked indifferently to one or the other for revenue. Parliament consisted largely of landowners, which meant many sheep-breeders, and was therefore in favour of supplying as much wool as possible everywhere, both at home and abroad, and was against any tax on wool that would reduce its sale. At the same time, as a Parliament, it was glad to see the monarch supplied with some form of revenue which would lessen the need to find him more. But there was still another side to the story: sheep-farmers began to complain that the attempt to ban exports was creating a glut in wool at home, and was bringing down prices to an unreasonable level. Indeed, as enclosure for sheep increased,[9] and the numbers of sheep multiplied, it could not be claimed that restrictions on the export of wool were to prevent a shortage; they became frankly protectionist. James I made no attempt to hide this when he made Proclamation for restraining the export of wool 'so that we may not be killed with arrows from our own quiver'. In 1617 not only was the export of wool again forbidden but, after four hundred years of existence, the foreign wool staple was formally abolished.

This marked, indeed, the end of an epoch. The institution of the staple had been a symbol of English prosperity in the Middle Ages, and the staple town was as real and as important to the wool merchant as his native wool-market. In its way it represented abroad what the woolsack did at home. That its passing in the early seventeenth century aroused so small a ripple is merely because the reality had long since outstripped the image. When Calais was won back by the French in 1558 the Staplers moved first to Middelburg and then to Bruges. That they never regained their earlier eminence is due more to the factors that were building up the trade in woollen cloth than to the loss of their mart. Many of them were astute enough to try to make their way into the lucrative cloth trade. But here they met the monopoly of the Merchant Adventurers and, although individual Staplers might become Adventurers, most of them were forced to look in other directions.

The Act that abolished the foreign staple in wool established in its place more than twenty home staples, and Merchants of the Staple were empowered to buy wool anywhere in England and sell it in any of these staple towns. The fact that they were often sheep-farmers as well as merchants encouraged many Staplers to do so, and they became middlemen, 'broggers' or 'factors' who forged a link between the sheep-breeders and the clothiers who made the cloth. Others preferred the manufacture of the cloth itself, and used their capital and experience to set up for themselves as clothiers. In the second case they rapidly lost their identity as Staplers. In the first case they remained of sufficient importance for a Committee of the Common Council of London, in the time of the Commonwealth, to inquire into their privileges. The Committee reported not only that Merchants of the Staple were no longer necessary but that their activities were positively harmful to the cloth trade, for they attempted to monopolize the trade in raw wool and so to enhance its price, at the same time mingling wool of different kinds and qualities to the detriment of the finished cloth.

The Report would have been damaging, indeed, to the pride of the Merchants of the Staple who still lay serenely delineated in their rich brasses in the churches they had helped to endow. But the end, in any case, was near as the remaining Staplers were absorbed, in one role or another, into the expanding economy. Soon the very name of Stapler faded out as the export of woollen cloth absorbed the material and the energy that formerly had gone into the export of wool. It was now only a question of time. The moment came when a Restoration Act of Parliament in 1660 laid the complete embargo on the export of wool which continued for a hundred and sixty-five years. Live sheep were from time to time added to the prohibition—an indication of the method by which it was sometimes attempted to circumvent the law. The wool embargo was naturally an invitation to smuggling, and the same creeks that saw the smuggling of wool to evade the wool taxes and the monopoly of the Staplers saw the smuggling of wool to evade the embargo: the second was equally profitable. How far English wool was by this time superior to any other was sometimes questioned. Enclosure and the breeding of fatter sheep had, it was said by some, lowered the quality of the fleece—'so long as Englishmen are fond of fat mutton they must not expect to grow fine wool'. The quality was nevertheless sufficiently high to maintain the supremacy of English cloth.

CHAPTER XII

Clothiers and Workpeople

By the time woollen cloth had ousted raw wool as England's chief export its production had passed through several stages, most of which still existed simultaneously. The first was the making of the 'homespun' common to early stages of society; this was still practised all over the country, and was the normal wear of poorer people everywhere. It was generally made from local wool spun and woven, fulled and dyed, by peasants using their own implements in their own homes.

The second stage was the expansion and refinement of the home market, met by making cloth of better quality; most people wore some garment of wool, even when expensive velvets and brocades were imported, and English cloth supplied this need at home and even abroad. Such production might be carried on by a single family, by an enlarged family group, by a small village organization. It was natural for the processes of production and sale to come under the supervision of a master workman, and so the domestic system of production emerged, becoming more carefully organized as it grew, though remaining of its nature small-scale and individual. The master workman would generally provide the raw wool, it was carded or combed, spun, woven, and finished under his supervision by his family and neighbours, with the help, possibly, of an errant journeyman. Finally the cloth was marketed by the master himself. The essence of this system was that either the workers or the small master owned the raw material and the implements of production and the finished product, that they worked in their own homes, and that the area involved, whether for collecting the fleeces or marketing the cloth, was no wider than the master himself could compass.

This, the domestic system proper, took deepest hold in the West Riding of Yorkshire. Many of the small masters had become affluent, and the scale of their enterprise had grown, but the essentials were there in 1724 when Daniel Defoe was touring Yorkshire on horseback. As he describes the scene there were a number of master-manufacturers' houses dispersed on the hills near Halifax, all supplied with running water from the numerous streams of the area. Some little distance from the clothiers' houses, where all the processes from weaving to fulling and finishing were carried on, were the houses of the work-people where their women and children were employed upon carding or combing and spinning. The master kept one or two horses which collected the raw wool and took the finished cloth to market. From the cloth fair at Leeds, 'prodigy of its kind', which was held twice a week, the bales of cloth were taken all over the country by travelling merchants with droves of pack-horses. In the sixteenth century the Yorkshire wool-towns of Leeds, Halifax, Wakefield, Huddersfield, Bradford were famous for broadcloth but by the eighteenth century the domestic workers whom Defoe describes were probably supplying the cloth market with the cheaper kersey. Both kinds of cloth were popular, and were in high demand abroad as well as at home, where they were sold in fairs and markets up and down the land.[1]

In other parts of the country the domestic system rapidly developed into an enterprise far larger in scale and far more dependent upon capital than the true domestic system. This was particularly so in the areas of best wool-production like Norfolk, Suffolk, Essex, the Cotswolds and Wiltshire. Expansion took place in many ways. There might be contract work for a bigger manufacturer; or a small master might enlarge his field of operations, collecting more wool, employing workpeople outside his immediate circle. Occasionally people employed in the later stages of cloth-production—the dyers or finishers perhaps—might find it worth-while to reach back to weaving, to spinning, finally to procuring the wool itself, and from small beginnings proceed to more ambitious projects. More often a middleman might be attracted into the area to collect the raw wool and take it to the spinners in their scattered homes. From this it was but a step to convey the spun yarn to the weavers, and then to collect the woven cloth for finishing and dyeing and finally to take it to market. A biggish clothier might employ in this way as many as a thousand outworkers. Some of these clothiers started by being already substantial men, perhaps graziers themselves, using their own wool and adding to it. Perhaps they were Staplers or other wool merchants turning to cloth as the demand changed. Perhaps they were merchants dealing in a variety of commodities but finding that the making of woollen cloth was the best investment. On the whole they were people who had sufficient money to bear the taking of a risk, or people who were of sufficient standing to get credit for a new venture.

The next stage came when the clothier owned the instruments of production as well as the raw material. This happened in the weaving industry before the spinning. Spindles were less expensive than looms, and spinning was a widely practised part-time occupation which it was difficult to control. The weavers' profession was different. It was more specialized, and was generally full-time work, sometimes employing a whole family. In spite of the comparatively high cost of looms, the weaver sometimes owned more than one, and frequently kept more than one master supplied with the fruit of his labour: the clothier's need to control the full output of the looms was one reason for buying them himself. Having done this, it was a natural sequence to gather these looms together into a shed or outhouse, possibly adjoining his own dwelling. The weaver then would need to leave his own home and gather with his fellows at the place of work, staying there for a specified period of time at an agreed wage. Here is the factory system in embryo: the employer owns the raw material, the instruments of production, the place of production; the worker owns neither raw material nor instrument, nor does he use his own home. Only his manual skill remains his own. The system depended upon a middleman who had the ability in time, resources and money to collect wool from a large area, to bring the raw wool to the workers, to make contact between stage and stage of the process of production, to market the finished product, to pay the workpeople, and wait for a return on his money for perhaps many months. Money had to be laid out on each enterprise, and larger amounts were tied up as the trade grew. The clothier also helped to iron out unevenness in production. The weavers especially were always getting ahead of the spinners, in spite of the large number of spinning women. A wealthy clothier, centralizing production, could make adjustments more easily than the workpeople. The weaver exchanged capital expenditure on his loom, irregular work, periods of near-destitution, perhaps, for a more regular, if small, wage. How far he was a free agent in making the choice depended upon many factors, tangible and intangible.

As the whole enterprise of cloth-production expanded it became still more specialized. Between the clothier and the supplies of raw wool there now appeared the wool broker, or middleman. Wool broggers had collected for the Staplers; they now collected for the clothiers, and the spinner was twice removed, instead of once removed, from the fleece. At the same time, a number of intermediaries appeared on the marketing side. The clothier did not send the finished cloth direct to market. It did not even go direct to the Merchant Adventurers, who were waiting to export it, with a monopoly as strong as the Staplers' monopoly had been with the raw wool. It went instead to another group of middlemen—the Drapers. The Drapers had been concerned for centuries in such cloth-export as existed. If the cloth was for the home market the Draper would take it to Blackwell Hall in London, or to the cloth hall of some other town. If for export, it would go into the Merchant Adventurers' wharves at one of the ports. But, as wool broggers collected wool for the clothiers, coming between them and their raw material, so now factors came between the clothier and the draper, collecting the finished bales of cloth from the clothier and transporting them to the towns. So the picture was now of a clothier standing on the shoulders of the workmen, on the one hand receiving the wool, twice removed, from the sheep, on the other hand marketing the finished cloth, three times removed from the process of production. The workman remained at the base of a pyramid of conflicting interests, none of them his own. This form of enterprise became most highly organized in Essex, East Anglia, and the south-west of the country, and it is in these areas that it earliest displayed all the signs of a capitalist system: the area from which the fleece was drawn was wide, the quantities of cloth dealt with were large, middlemen were well established, the employer owned the instruments of production but rarely worked at them himself, the people employed were in the relationship of workpeople and not of friends or family, and they frequently left their homes to work in an embryo factory.

The clothier, the co-ordinator, the capitalist entrepreneur, generally did well out of the enterprise. However they started, many became wealthy on the rapidly expanding market for cloth, and were able to work their way to prosperity if not to fortune. It was not unusual for a clothier to end his career with a fortune of £40 000 or even £100 000.[2] Many became 'gentry', bought estates, founded schools and hospitals and almshouses and left legacies to local people. They became famous men in their own districts, and some were known throughout the country. Their money went into elaborate Perpendicular churches, their spacious houses with beautiful gardens replaced the simpler Early English styles. The tombs and brasses of the clothiers lay beside those of the woolmen and the Staplers, often in the same churches to which they had added in their own style. Like the earlier woolmen, they gloried in the trade that had made them rich and respected, and their feet still rested upon the woolsack and upon the sheep. Such a one was Thomas Paycocke, of the village of Coggeshall in Essex, whose house still stands in the village street. He employed many spinners and weavers in their own homes, and he probably employed weavers in an embryo factory in the long, low shed at the back of his house.[3] Another was John Winchcombe—the famous Jack of Newbury[4]—who combined the virtues of the nineteenth-century Samuel Smiles with the traditional good fortune of the medieval apprentice. In *The Pleasant Historie of Jack of Newberie* he did indeed become the subject of an improving story after the fashion of Samuel Smiles. Jack, it was therein said, was 'a man of a merry disposition and honest conversation' who would 'spend his money with the best', yet never be found drunk or idle. After his master's death the widow gave to Jack the guiding of the clothier's business, which prospered 'wonderous well'. The upshot was that Jack married his master's widow in traditional style and built up the business until he employed under his roof well over a thousand men, women and children at various stages of cloth-production. When his first wife died he married a beautiful young girl. And so virtue had its reward all round.[5]

Another clothier whose career is illuminating was Benedict Webb, whose family were clothiers and whose education was intended to fit him for the family business. At the age of sixteen he was apprenticed to a linen draper in London for whom he travelled in both France and Italy. He introduced from the Continent a new form of loom, he turned his attention to new kinds of cloth—a thin, light material called perpetuanas and a medley or mixed colour cloth of Spanish origin which he worked upon and improved. He experimented with rape seed to replace the imported olive oil normally used in cloth-making and grew considerable quantities of the crop on his own land, as well as erecting a mill to process it, for which he was given a patent in 1624. Webb in due course took over the family clothing business at Kingswood in Wiltshire, he had a finger in commercial enterprises, he acquired farm-lands in the Vale of Berkeley and in the Forest of Dean, he had eighty acres of meadow and pasture at Alveston.[6]

The numerous people 'of the poorer sort' who worked for the clothiers were outside any gild organization and were removed by several generations from the proletarians of the future. No laws of gild or state controlled their working conditions, their wages or the number of hours they worked. In busy times they rose long before and worked until long after the hours of daylight by means of improvised lights; if they worked at home the machines they operated were crammed into their small cottages and raw material and finished work was piled up around and within their living space, while the labour of the youngest was put to use. Trade crisis and depression could result in near-famine. In 1623, for example, textile workers in Wiltshire complained

> of the distressed estate of most of the weavers, spinners and others that work on the making of woollen cloths, that are not able by their diligent labours to get their livings, by reason that the clothiers at their will have made their works extreme hard and abated wages what they please. And some of them made such their workfolks to do their household businesses, to trudge in their errands, spool their chains, twist their list, do every command, without giving them bread, drink or money for many days' labours.[7]

There is a growing feeling of class consciousness in the complaint of textile workers from the eastern counties, who in 1631 complained that

> the poor spinsters, weavers and combers of wool in Sudbury and the places near adjoining thereunto in the counties of Suffolk and Essex, are of late by the clothiers there (who are now grown rich by the

labours of the said poor people) so much abridged of their former and usual wages, that they (who in times past maintained their families in good sort) are now in such distress by the abatement of their wages in these times of scarcity and dearth, that they are constrained to sell their beds, wheels and working tools for want of bread.[8]

Contemporary literature took up their cause. 'The poor have the labour, the rich the winning' declared *England's Commercial Policy* in the fifteenth century. *The Clothier's Delight; Or, the Rich Men's Joy and the Poor Men's Sorrow* expressed the class war both in its title and in its verses:

> Of all sorts of calling that in England be,
> There is none that liveth so gallant as we;
> Our trading maintains us as brave as a knight,
> We live at our pleasure, and take our delight;
> We heapeth up riches and treasure great store,
> Which we get by griping and grinding the poor.
>   And this is a way for to fill up our purse
>   Although we do get it with many a curse.

Low wages, sweated labour, child labour, were not the inventions of the Industrial Revolution. What was left for that Revolution to do, which the earlier transformation of the cloth industry never accomplished, was to take from the worker the land with which he both supplemented his income and refreshed his spirit. It is difficult to determine how much land the clothing workers owned while they were being swept into the ambit of capitalist industry. If they had been successful landowners they would not have become domestic handicraftsmen. But the clothing areas were the districts of the old-established smallholder, and it is likely that many families had clung to their bits of land through various changes, whittled down and insufficient for a livelihood in themselves, perhaps, but a useful supplement to industrial earnings. It could well be that, with garden and fields, crops and animals, the clothing worker made the best of both worlds and was better off than a factory worker proper on the one hand, or a peasant on the other. In practice, it all depended upon the combination of the two. But so long as he kept some open space to call his own, there can be little doubt that the worker who lived within touching distance of his trees, his crops, his bees and his animals was far removed from the proletarian created by a later age.

It is, perhaps, surprising that although new types of cloth were produced there were no revolutionary improvements in methods of production. John Kay's flying shuttle, which made possible the weaving of wider cloth with fewer people at the loom, and doubled the amount of cloth a man could weave, came in 1733. But it was a mixed blessing, for the weaver was constantly waiting upon the spinner, and the need was rather for more yarn than for more rapid weaving. The scattered spinning women and girls, regarding their work as auxiliary to that in home or field, or at best working spasmodically, were erratic in the amount of yarn they produced. Different people had often been at work on the same hank, and there was wastage because of bad work and varying quality. For these reasons the flying shuttle was not widely adopted in the woollen industry. Even the introduction by Lewis Paul and John Wyatt of spinning by rollers, which came about four years after Kay's invention, and increased the output of yarn by both drawing out and twisting the thread at the same time, was not immediately adopted, possibly because it would turn auxiliary labour, easily combined with the normal work of house and farm, into something more demanding. Neither of these inventions came into general use before 1760.

Of other occupations which used wool, cap-making had long been practised, and in the sixteenth century, following the example of France and the Netherlands, the craft was extended to hat-making, of which Norwich became one of the chief centres. Ordinary hand knitting had been practised in the Middle Ages, and probably long before. In the second half of the sixteenth century William Lee invented a knitting frame which reproduced the knitter's action with much greater speed. It was one of the few inventions to achieve immediate success, and framework knitting spread rapidly over Nottinghamshire to Derbyshire and Leicestershire. The framework knitters were given charters in 1657 and 1663 which required all workers in the industry to join their Association, prescribed an apprenticeship of seven years, and called upon the members to see that all their products 'be workmanlike wrought, and if found badly made or of deceiptful stuff, to cut the same in pieces and to fine the parties making them'.[9] They thus followed the tradition of the craft gilds. A knitting frame might cost about £25, so it was not usual for a worker to own his own. Instead, he would rent his frame from an entrepreneur, but probably, since it was a small and simple machine, work in his own home; as time went on he would probably use his employer's yarn as well. He was then in the position of a domestic worker in the cloth industry. It had been intended to foster framework knitting as a native industry, but foreigners, being 'covetous and envious', managed to get frames out of the country, in spite of an Act of Parliament of 1696 which prohibited their export. By the third quarter of the eighteenth century, nevertheless, Leicester had become established as the centre for woollen hosiery and there were some 17 000 frames in use in the Midlands.[10]

Among other skills brought to the country from abroad was the art of the spinning and weaving of silk, introduced by French immigrants. Silk was in a different position from wool, since it required a foreign raw material—in spite of James I's activity in planting mulberry-trees. By the eighteenth century it was nevertheless established in Norwich, in Canterbury, but primarily in Spitalfields in London. When Thomas Lombe secured from Italy the secret of making a fine silk warp and in 1719 established a factory at Derby for the purpose, its future seemed established.[11] Silk was also used for silk hose, and framework knitting using silk was in addition established at Derby.

Linen was in a position similar to silk in requiring in hemp and flax a foreign raw material, or one not widely grown at home. There was not the luxury demand for linen that there was for silk, and the attempt to establish a linen industry in England was not very successful.

But the industry which, although using an imported raw material, took full advantage of the experience of the woollen-cloth industry, incorporating from the outset all that was most useful in organization and invention, was the manufacture of cotton cloth.

Cotton had been known as a 'fruit of the earth growing upon little shrubs or bushes, brought into this Kingdome by the Turkie Merchants, from Smyrna, Cyprus, Acra and Sydon, but commonly called Cotton Wooll'.[12] It also grew in the New World, for natives brought it, sometimes crudely woven into cloth, to the early explorers. Its weaving in England probably began with some of the Walloon and Dutch immigrants who settled in East Anglia in the second half of the sixteenth century, and by 1621 it seems to have been established in Lancashire. At first the raw material was imported from the Near East, but later the chief and best supplies came from the cotton plantations of the English colonies. Cotton textiles had an instant advantage over woollen in hot climates, by the opening of the eighteenth century the industry was well established on a capitalist basis, and by the middle of the century the amount of raw material imported and the value of the cotton goods exported had nearly doubled. A new industry, capitalist from its inception, it was hampered by none of the tradition of the woollen industry; its raw material, although imported, came from sources with whom trade was advantageous, and when world markets opened it was ready to take advantage of them.

CHAPTER XIII

'The Great Multitude of Shepe'

The substitution of the export of woollen cloth for the export of raw wool in no way discouraged sheep-breeding. On the contrary, in the course of the fifteenth century it became clear that a move to pasture was accelerating, and by the turn of the century sheep-farmers everywhere, from the big estates to the little one-man holdings, were increasing the number of their sheep. Farms were thrown together, for large pasture areas were more economical than small. Landlords called in land let at lease or raised the rent to the tenant. Tenants paid higher rents from the profit of the sheep. In the open-field village the lord of the manor contrived to increase his holdings and amalgamate his strips, to bring together small and scattered portions of demesne land, even to displace the strip farmers. Land was taken in from the waste for grazing. Even the commons, where the various animals of a whole community grazed, were taken over for sheep. The visible sign of these changes, apart from the sheep and the grass, was generally the enclosure of the pasture by hedge or fence or ditch. But actual enclosure, although sometimes taken as symbolic of the conversion of arable to pasture, was a mechanical device which could be used for arable farming as well as for sheep-farming, and for the protection of private parkland as well as for the appropriation of commons.

The immediate impetus to sheep-farming was the high price of wool, the comparatively low price of corn, a general price-rise which included wages, and a buoyancy of demand for woollen goods, resulting from a rising population both in Europe and at home. Even when the price of wool was not rising, its profitability lay in the fact that it needed little labour compared with arable farming. Little labour meant little housing, small victuals, low wage-bills—and the pasture farmer saved money; if the price of wool rose he made a substantial profit. Wool prices were rising from the middle of the fifteenth century, and a hundred years later had approximately doubled, with some exceptionally high years (for example, 1550, 1551, 1556, 1557) when they about trebled. Though there was some fluctuation in the second half of the century, generally attributable to depression in the overseas cloth market, wool prices were never back to the 1450 or the 1500 level. By the 1590s they were soaring again, and continued high, though with some aberration, until the end of the seventeenth century.[1]

The price of grain, meantime, was comparatively stable, showing no tendency to move until after 1520 when prices in general were rising. In such a situation Fitzherbert had no hesitation in asserting that there was 50 per cent more gain in enclosing for pasture than for arable. In an all-round rise in land rents a Commission of 1517, investigating enclosures for sheep in some of the Midland counties, produced figures to show that rents for pasture land were at least 40 per cent higher than for arable. They also showed, what was only to be expected, that 80 per cent of the 32 000 acres they investigated were enclosed for pasture.

The movement had already begun while the nobility were decimating each other in the Wars of the Roses, and by the time Henry VII came to the throne it was causing concern: John Rous, a local historian, named fifty-eight villages in Warwickshire alone which had been depopulated because of the increase in sheep-farming. The problem which the Tudors thus inherited was to continue throughout their dynasty and well into the Stuart period. With lessening emphasis, it continued through the rest of the seventeenth century and into the eighteenth, to reach a new crescendo in the nineteenth.

Concern was not, in the first place, because of an overproduction of wool or a cheapening of the price of wool: that was to come later. It was caused by fears for the corn-supply, and by what contemporaries described as 'depopulation'. The spectre of high corn prices and famine was more of a nightmare than a reality, and events were to prove that the threat to food was exaggerated. Depopulation, on the other hand, was a grim reality. It was caused basically by two things—the taking over for sheep-farming of common grazing-land which had formerly fed the animals of a whole community; and the substitution of pasture farming, which required little labour, for arable farming, which supported many families and entire villages. Its results were seen in an exodus of population from the areas affected, in the consequent decay of the villages they had occupied, and in a growth of unemployment and vagrancy.

Not that sheep-farming inevitably led to depopulation. Where a man converted, enlarged, or enclosed his own land little harm was done, except in so far as he had at times previously permitted common grazing, and in so far as he now required less hired labour than formerly. Nor did the turning of wasteland into sheep runs normally occasion distress, though hardship was caused by the appurtenances of the waste being denied to people who had used the firing, turf and rough grazing they provided. Greater harm was done where a landlord took over the common grazing-land of the village. It might have been overstocked, unhealthy and in need of rest, but it did nevertheless provide some feed for the animals which were vital to his way of life—for the plough, for carting, for leather, for food, for the dung which in most cases was the only manure available. If a man had no grazing his animals went too, for he had no knowledge of and certainly no ability to obtain any other form of animal fodder. The outcry against the loss of commons, the emphasis which Commissions of Enquiry put upon common grazing, attest its importance. The Commission of 1548, for example, was charged to report 'if any person hath taken from his tenants their commons, whereby they be not able to breed and keep their cattel, and maintain their husbandry', and their chairman, John Hales, advised them that the word enclosure was not taken to mean 'where a man doth enclose and hedge in his own proper ground, where no man hath commons . . . it is meant thereby, when any man hath taken away and enclosed any other mens commons'.[2]

But, apart from the commons, wherever a shepherd or two was substituted for a busy community of arable farmers, whole villages were depopulated, their inhabitants wandering away from the fields, which now were made over to the sheep. Their houses and farm buildings decayed, their household crops were untended, their domestic animals died through want of care, their churches fell into ruin through lack of worshippers, their villages were overgrown with the grass and weeds that no-one cared to subdue. A large-scale change in the nature of farming is disrupting, but it was particularly so in the rigid and complicated pattern of medieval life. The change was not only clear to the eye, not only apparent in the disrupted lives of small farmers and their families, but it left a very deep mark on society as a whole, from Parliament to pulpit, from literature to the law, from doggerel rhymesters to the peasants themselves, many of whom remembered only too clearly their forebears of 1381.

The area affected was not large by modern standards, amounting, perhaps, to little more than 750 000 acres in all.[3] However, it is not the actual acreage involved but its relation to the cultivated area which is important. Where so much of the country was still waste land the proportion of arable land converted to pasture was high. About two-thirds of it was in the Midland counties, particularly in Leicestershire, Lincolnshire, Bedfordshire, Northamptonshire, Warwickshire, Buckinghamshire, with Oxfordshire, Berkshire and Nottinghamshire possibly less affected, while Gloucestershire to the west and Norfolk to the east made up most of the rest of the area concerned. The northern sheep-runs, for long the home of the sheep, were unaffected; so too were the small farms of Devon and Cornwall, of Kent and Essex, most of which were already enclosed for mixed farming. Much of Suffolk and Hertfordshire, of Somerset, Worcestershire and Herefordshire, was probably also long since enclosed. So it was, in fact, the area of the open-field manor which was chiefly concerned in enclosure for sheep in the sixteenth century.

By this time the people who got their living from the land consisted of the landowner himself, who might own several thousand acres or who might be a small yeoman farmer, and those who paid rent. Of these latter there were a great variety, their position stemming—with innumerable modifications and ramifications—from the open-field system of the medieval manor.

The landlord might be the direct descendant of the manorial lord, he might be a freeholder who had prospered, he might be a 'new' man, a merchant, a city man, a wool man, who had bought land from the profit of his enterprise or married into the landowning class. He might well be a royal favourite or a royal creditor who had received monastic lands after the dissolution of the monasteries. He might have bought from one of these original recipients, or bought several times removed, in the orgy of speculation that followed the break-up of the monastic lands. It is likely that the 'new' men, at least, would bring a spirit of business enterprise to landowning, that they would farm for profit and introduce the business ethic of the higher return into relationships of which some at least had hitherto been guided by more personal considerations. Some of the older landowners had done this already, or were quick to learn. The small freeholder probably turned more sheep to graze than formerly, sometimes buying up neighbouring land, or perhaps taking in from the waste and enclosing, but he could generally do little harm to anyone else. Sometimes, indeed, he himself fell prey to unscrupulous enclosing landlords like Sir Giles Overreach, who explained his methods with unction:

> 'I'll make my men break ope his fences,
> Ride o'er his standing corn, and in the night
> Set fire on his barns, or break his cattle's legs,
> These trespasses draw on suits, and suits expenses
> Which I can spare, but will soon beggar him'.[4]

And so the man would be driven to sell at half the value of his property, or less. Sir Thomas More was already familiar with the unscrupulous harrying by which weaker men were 'so weried that they be compelled to sell all'.[5]

In spite of such cases, however, the small freeholders as a class were not badly affected by the movement to pasture. Greater sufferers were the open-field farmers known by the sixteenth century as customary tenants; they held their land at rent from the landowner, and were probably the largest group of people on the open fields. Though villeinage had virtually disappeared by this time, vestiges of the feudal system were incorporated still in the way the customary tenants held their land. The largest group were the copyholders, who held by copy of court roll, the assumption being, though it was rarely investigated, that there was in existence a document that laid down the terms upon which they held their land. A smaller group consisted of tenants at will—landholders who held still at the pleasure of the lord, and concerning the terms of whose holding no record was held. Within these classes there was no uniformity. As landowners could be large or small, 'new' or 'old', so could the copyholders. As a prosperous landowner might buy up more land, a prosperous copyholder, or even a tenant at will, could take on more land from his neighbours. Copyholders' property varied from a few acres to hundreds, and subletting was not unknown.

There were also the leaseholders. Areas of demesne land, areas assarted from the waste, strips from the open fields that had reverted to the lord of the manor after the Black Death—any piece of land, large or small, that for any reason a landlord had not wished to farm himself had been let at rent. The lease could be long or short, even at the lord's will; again, there could be new and old leaseholders, large and small, those who farmed land no bigger than a yeoman farmer's, and those who controlled estates of thousands of acres.

There was no real protection for any of these classes. The tenant at will was the most absolutely vulnerable, for nothing even pretended to stand between him and eviction from his holding if the landlord so desired. In dealing with the leaseholders the raising of rents, beyond the normal rise of the market, was easy. They were not protected by even a fictional copyhold, and their vulnerability was determined merely by the length of their lease—and this could be made to fall in early. Latimer in a famous sermon told his hearers how his father had paid rent of £3 or £4 a year which had become £16, and 'that which heretofore went for twenty or forty pounds by the year is now let for fifty or a hundred pounds by the year'. Generally speaking, landlords tried to follow the advice of Fitzherbert and other agricultural writers and convert copyhold to leasehold on short-term rent, easily raised. But it was not always so easy to dispossess the copyholder. A copyhold of inheritance was difficult to shake, rooted as it was in antiquity, and it would sometimes be upheld by common law. A copyhold for life was more difficult to uphold, and copyhold merely for a term of years was most vulnerable. But the security of any copyhold tenure depended upon tracing the original lease, and it was all too simple to record a court roll as 'lost'. Moreover, any land newly broken in or for any reason not in the original grant could be taken away or the conditions of tenure altered. If there was on the whole little open illegality a determined landlord could find many ways of dispossessing even a copyhold tenant. Sir Thomas More understood the sequence of events well enough:

For look in what parts of the realm doth grow the finest and dearest wool, there noblemen and gentlemen, yea and certain abbots ... leave no ground for tillage; they enclose all into pastures; they ... compass about and enclose many thousand acres of ground together within one pale or hedge, the husbandmen be thrust out of their own ... or by wrongs and injuries they be so wearied that they be compelled to sell all. By one means, therefore, or another, either by hook or crook, they must needs depart away ... Away they trudge, I say, out of their known and accustomed houses, finding no place to rest in.[6]

Dispossession meant not only taking a family's land, it meant depriving them of the use of waste and meadow and the other rights that pertained to landholding in the open fields. Even where a man had supplemented his farming by some handicraft he would lose that, for it too depended upon the open-field organization for its existence: why maintain and repair the plough for land that needed no furrow, or provide the hoe for land given over to grass, or mend the cart when there was nothing to carry? Those with special skills, like the blacksmith and the wheelwright, were wanted no longer. When there was no common pasture or other grazing the village animals went too, and with them their attendants; even the pinder no longer rounded up straying animals for the pound. It was not that the livelihood of one, or some, members of the family had gone. They *all* relied upon the open-field system for their living, at one stroke the livelihood of *all* had disappeared, and no question of compensation or alternative resources was ever raised. There was no question of re-employment for the vast majority, for pasturing sheep required only the shepherd and his boy, with a little auxiliary labour at the sheepcote and the shearing. So the displaced open-field farmer and his family wandered away from the village, their little homesteads decayed, their very garden tofts disappeared beneath the grass to provide more feed for the sheep. Where men and beasts and crops had lived and grown there was nothing but the sheep run and the shepherd. And so the deserted village became a reality, only the church remaining to fall into decay through disuse or to become a sheepcote for the sheep. A picture, like Goldsmith's picture of *The Deserted Village* nearly two centuries later, was painted in the late sixteenth century by the rhymester:

> The grasse grows greene where litle Troy did stand,
> The forlorne father hanging downe his head,

His outcast company drawne up and downe,
The pining labourer doth begge his bread,
The plowswayne seeks his dinner from the towne.[7]

The deserted village was often, indeed, a reality that remained so. For when the acreage of arable land grew again it was generally not by reconversion of the pasture but by ploughing up new land in the northern hills and heaths. Even when desertion was not complete and an emasculated village remained, 'depopulation' in the sense of a substantial reduction of population and a consequent diminution of village life was in sad contrast to what had existed before.[8]

The men who were responsible—the enclosing landlords, the rack renters, the engrossers of small farms—were meted out the fiercest denunciation the times could offer in innumerable pamphlets and sermons. They were 'insatiable cormorants', 'caterpillars of the commonwealth', 'unreasonable covitous persones', 'men without conscience', 'men utterly voide of Goddes feare'. Nor did the sheep themselves, innocent originators of the chain of misery, escape the blast. It was hard that a pamphlet should be headed 'The Decaye of England only by the Great Multitude of Shepe' but harder still that the gentle Sir Thomas More in his *Utopia* should castigate them: 'your sheep that were wont to be so myke and tame, and so smal eaters, as I heare saie, be become so greate devowerers, and so wylde, that they eate up and swallow down the very men themselves'. Nor did the enclosers of farmland for private parks escape obloquy, and John Hales specifically charged his Commissioners of 1548 to include enclosure for parks within their brief.

In attempting to deal with the various problems raised by the growth of sheep-farming the landowners who comprised a major part of the governments of Tudor and Stuart England had to consider many, often conflicting interests. On the one hand were their own interests as landowners, and probably sheep-breeders. Up to a point these coincided with the interests of the manufacturers of woollen cloth, but there was a point beyond which it was not in the breeders' interest to produce more wool because of a reduction in its price. There was, indeed, a sheepmasters' lobby: when an attempt was made at the end of the reign of Elizabeth to repeal the depopulation Acts 'the ears of our great sheepmasters', it was said, 'do hang at the doors of this house'. But these interests were peripheral to the Government's basic problems, as legislation made clear. They passed *tillage* Acts, depopulation Acts, and their concern was not only with the profits of woolmen and the development of the cloth trade, with matters of ancient usage and social justice, but with the corn supply, with internal security, and, above all, with the defence of the realm. With this as a measuring rod a country given over to sheep could not compare with one which relied upon arable farming: 'shepherds be but ill archers', it was said, while the husbandman was 'the body and the stay' of the kingdom; a country 'furnished only with sheep and shepherds instead of good men' would become 'a prey to our enemies that first would set upon it'.[9] And Lord Salisbury wanted to know in 1597 what was 'a trifling abridgement to gentlemen' set against 'the misery of the people and the decay of the nation's strength'.[10] The issue, wrote Francis Bacon,

> did wonderfully concern the might and mannerhood of the Kingdom, to have farms . . . unto the hold and occupation of the yeomanry or middle people, of a condition between gentlemen and cottagers or peasants . . . For the principal strength of an army consisteth in the infantry or foot. And to make good infantry, it requireth men bred not in a servile or indigent fashion, but in some free and plentiful manner . . . if a state run most to noblemen and gentlemen and that the husbandmen and ploughmen be but as their workfolks or labourers . . . you may have a good cavalry, but never good stable bands of foot.[11]

It 'stands not with the policy of the State', he urged once more in Parliament in 1601, 'that the wealth of the kingdom should be ingrossed into a few Graziers hands. . . . The Husbandman is a strong and hardy man, the good footman, which is a chief observation of good Warriers'.[12] 'I think', said Robert Cecil in the course of the same debates,

> that whosoever doth not maintain the Plough destroys this Kingdom . . . I am sure when Warrants go from the Council for levying of men in the Countries, and the Certificates be returned unto us again, we find the greatest part of them to be Ploughmen.[13]

These were the considerations, if not yet expressed so pertinently, that in 1489 prompted the first Tudor Act concerning the land problem. It arose directly from the depopulation of the Isle of Wight through the amalgamation of farms and the fear that the defence of the realm would thereby suffer: 'If hasty remedy be not provided that Isle cannot be long kept and defended, but open and ready to the hands of the king's enemies'. Nearly a century later, in 1574, the same principle was moving the Government of Elizabeth to instruct the Wardens of the Marches 'not to allow towns, villages or houses to be wasted, or lands turned to pasture, lest the tenants be unable to keep horses for service and the Borders be depopulated'.

A second Act of 1489, Agaynst Pullying Down of Townes, reflects the fear of disorder: 'great inconvenyences', it said, 'daily doth encrease by desolacion and pulling down and wilfull waste of houses and Townes within this . . . realme, and leyeng to pasture londes which custumeably have ben used in tilthe, whereby ydilnes grounde and begynnyng of all myschefes daily doo encrease'. Such arguments remained fairly constant and were reinforced by the fact that most political and religious disturbances in Tudor England were accompanied by some form of agrarian discontent.

Where the motive of legislation was to keep up the supply of corn and thereby keep down its price the argument could cut both ways, as when the repeal of the tillage laws was urged at the end of Elizabeth's reign on the ground that 'now corn is cheap; if too cheap the Husbandman is undone, whom we must provide for for he is the Staple man of the Kingdom'.[14] On this occasion Cecil replied that the country could deal with a glut of corn by export—it was still wise to maintain tillage on other grounds.[15] But there had been an occasion in 1593 when a tillage Act was repealed, partly because it was obscure but also because the price of corn at that time was very low. Generally speaking, bad harvests or shortage of grain were followed by the strict enforcement of the tillage Acts or, as in 1607, by another Enclosure Commission or, as in 1630, by an investigation by the Privy Council.

Taken as a whole, the intervention of the State was impressive if not always effective. By 1597 a dozen Acts had been passed, all aimed at preventing the conversion of arable land to pasture, ordering the reconversion of pasture to arable, directing that enclosures for sheep-farming be thrown open, ruined buildings restored and, as in the Act of 1534, actually prescribing that no man should keep more than 2 000 sheep, an intention whose barb was partially drawn by the exception of 'spiritual persons' (who were among the largest sheep-breeders) from the provisions of the Act.

The Acts were based largely upon the work of Commissions, beginning with the Commission appointed by Wolsey in 1517, of which Sir Thomas More was a member. This consisted of seventeen Committees covering thirty-five counties, and was typical in inquiring into all cases where farmhouses, villages or hamlets had been destroyed since 1488—i.e., since the first depopulation Act—or where ploughs had been put down by the increase in pasture farming. The Commission of 1548 was appointed by Protector Somerset, John Hales the lawyer being chairman. Somerset, himself a great landowner, yet pledged himself to the undoing of enclosure for sheep that hit the poor: 'Maugre the devil, private profit, self-love, money, and such like the devil's instruments, it shall go forward!', he swore. The instructions to the Enclosure Commissioners were detailed, and Hales solemnly charged the Commissioners that not only the letter but the spirit of the law be observed:

> For as there be many good men that take great pains to study to devise good laws for the commonwealth; so be there a great many, that do with as great pains and study, labour to defeat them, and as the common saying is, to find gapps and starting holes.[16]

There were similar Enquiries in 1566, 1607, 1632, 1635 and 1636. If they did little to stem enclosure they at least ventilated the issues at stake and publicized the various methods by which landlords tried to by-pass legislation. If an Act forbade the pulling down of houses a landlord would keep one or two standing, inhabited by a shepherd and a milkmaid, and still turn the land to pasture; some would meet the requirements of the law by ploughing a single furrow and putting the rest of the estate to grass; it was easy to override the law that prohibited a man from having more than 2 000 sheep by fathering other flocks on relations or servants.

The execution of the laws was indeed more difficult than their enactment. Penalties and forfeitures could go to the lord of the manor, the Crown, the informer or a combination of any of these. To rely upon feudal overlords to control their mesne lords was to expect the pot to clean up the kettle, while the Justices of the Peace, the very people who should have operated the laws, were frequently themselves those who should have been brought to justice. In practice much detection depended upon the common informer, with a subsequent trail of bribe and fine and purchase of exemption. After 1552 the Statutes accepted the realities of the situation by appointing a permanent body of Commissioners to enforce the tillage laws. But it is likely that the greatest effect resulted not from these but from the interest of that permanent Tudor and Stuart court, the Privy Council with its organs, the Courts of Star Chamber and Requests and the Councils of the North and of Wales. On all social matters, including agrarian problems, the Council was indefatigable in sending out and receiving a stream of instructions, exhortations, reports and assessments. Henry VIII, for example, instructed the Council of the North to 'make diligent inquisition who hath taken and enclosed commons, called intakes; who be extreme in taking of gressoms [entry fines] and onering [increasing] of rents'. Yet it was difficult to control powerful landowners on their own territories, and the effect of the Privy Council's intervention is not easy to assess. With the purchase of exemption to a law not only not unusual but rarely considered culpable, and punishment by fine not always so much of a deterrent as a means of channelling money into royal and other official pockets, with a large and powerful section of the population vitally interested in a policy opposite to that which the Government was trying to impose, Latimer's despairing cry is understandable: 'Let the preacher preach till his tongue be worn to the stump, nothing is amended. We have good statutes made for the commonwealth as touching commoners and enclosers, but in the end of the matter there cometh nothing forth.' It gave point to Sir Thomas More's description of effective government as 'a conspirary of rich men seeking their own commodities'.

At the same time there were other considerations which gradually won acceptance, tempering the attitude of the Government and resulting in a policy less rigid and more accommodating to enclosers. In 1556, in face of the low price of corn, it was admitted that the tillage Acts need not be fully executed. In 1593 the Act of 1563 was actually repealed, partly because it was obscure but also 'by reason of the great plenty and cheapness of grain at that time'. The Depopulation Act of 1597 contained a clause that permitted the conversion of tillage to grass along a strip two miles wide between Dunstable and Chester, so allowing the feeding of herds on their way south.

The debates on tillage in that year introduced a breath of reality by drawing the distinction between different soils and climates: Shropshire was fit for grass and could be the 'Dayrie house to the whole Realme', while Herefordshire could be 'the Barne'.[17] A special exemption from the Act of that year was granted to a landlord who got letters patent authorizing him to enclose 300 acres 'too moist and soft and altogether unapt for Tillage'.[18] Sir Thomas Burton was making the same point when commanded to sow corn on enclosed grass in Lincolnshire: 'the soile is a cold claie and not so fitt for Corne as Grasse'. The argument went back and forth: should 'land having once been tilled be put into a perpetual bondage and servitude of being for ever tilled?' was being asked, while Sir Walter Raleigh asserted, in a remarkable foretaste of the doctrine of free enterprise: 'I do not like the constraining of them to use their Grounds at our wills but rather let every man use his Grounds to that which it is most fit for, and therein use his Own Discretion'. The fact that land reconverted to arable from pasture had obviously benefited from the rest was a further inducement both to reconvert to arable and to lay down 'tired' land to pasture for a period. In 1618 a Commission was appointed to grant exemptions to the tillage Acts. The severe trade crisis of 1622 brought wool prices to their lowest ebb, the cloth industry languished, flocks of sheep were reduced. In 1624 the tillage and depopulation Acts were all repealed. According to the lawyer Edward Coke, it made little difference whether they were on the Statute Book or not, for 'they were labyrinthes, with such intricate windings or turnings as little or no fruit proceeded from them'.

But even before repeal landlords had been slowly pursuing their own advantage, in spite of the tillage Acts, by amalgamating and enclosing tracts of land by agreement with each other: 'within these forty fifty and sixty years past', it was claimed in the House of Commons in 1666, 'there have beene within this Kingdom multitudes of Enclosures of Commonable Grounds Wastes, Heaths fermgrounds and Marishes by consent'. Less obtrusively than before, watered down by the activities of Parliament and Privy Council, the enclosure movement continued in the form of these agreements which, by the 1630s—i.e., after repeal of the tillage Acts—were given permanency by being registered in the courts of Chancery or of Exchequer. The Privy Council in March 1631, referring to Leicestershire, pronounced such enclosures by agreement to be 'very hurtfull to the Commonwealth although they beare a fayre share of satisfaction to all Parties . . . but we well know what the consequences will be and in conclusion all turne to Depopulation'.[19] These were the years when Charles I was ruling without a Parliament and the Privy Council was under the control of Archbishop Laud. In 1630, after a rise in corn prices, it sent to the Justices of five Midland counties, commanding them to remove all enclosures which had been made in the previous two years. In 1632, 1635 and 1636 Commissioners were at work. Fines were levied for depopulation, and there was some ploughing back of pasture to arable. So energetic was the Privy Council in these years and so hurtful to the great landowners that when a later assessment of the causes of the civil wars was made it was one of the criticisms levied against Archbishop Laud that 'he did a little too much countenance the Commission for Depopulation'. Certainly the levying of fines was important to the impoverished King, and the mixture of motives needs no emphasis, but it remains true that in the years before the meeting of the Long Parliament the Privy Council was at its most active, and that one of its aims was the protection of the peasant. That the greater landlords disliked its activities intensely is evidence of some success.

CHAPTER XIV

Enclosure versus Open Fields

There was another aspect of the agrarian problem which had been exercising the minds of landowners and agricultural writers since at least the beginning of the sixteenth century. Enclosure, although associated with newly converted pasture land, both to mark ownership and to prevent animals from straying, was not applicable to pasture land alone. Some arable land was already enclosed, and agriculturists were beginning to urge its extension to all types of land on purely economic grounds. On the open fields, in particular, it was clear that yields were declining and farming was deteriorating, that strip farming with multiple ownership precluded change, that crops were becoming smaller, methods of husbandry more slovenly, that there was little or no manure, that many of the better agricultural practices were dying out. There was no gainsaying the fact that enclosed, better-cared-for land produced bigger yields and higher rents. 'The poor man', wrote Thomas Fuller, 'who is monarch of but one enclosed acre will receive more profit from it than from his share of many acres in common with others'. Fitzherbert was so convinced of the merits of enclosure in general that in 1523 he advocated giving each open-field farmer a compact plot of land near his house whose size depended upon his scattered holdings in the open fields together with his share of the common pasture and the waste.[1]

It was a similar story with the commons of the open-field villages: could the common lands be turned into better grazing for cattle or sheep when there wandered over them, by immemorial right, the animals of the whole settlement, many of whom infected the rest with the scab and other diseases? Could the overstocking of these commons, often at the instance of a few powerful landowners, sometimes by the inhabitants of neighbouring manors, be prevented while they were unenclosed and open to all? Fitzherbert was emphatic that livestock thrive best and cost least on enclosed ground.[2]

There were also many people who urged that if in one way enclosure of any land caused depopulation, yet in others it provided employment. After enclosure 'there be as many newe occupations that were not used before', said Fitzherbert, 'as getting of quicke settes, diching, hedging, and plashing, the which the same men may use and occupye'[3] and a second-generation encloser of the sixteenth century even claimed that he had improved the whole area in a number of ways, not only supplying the district with much-needed wood by the planting of trees and hedges for his enclosure, but restoring church and village buildings which were in decay.[4] A practical example of unopposed enclosure was when the Greenwich, Plumstead and Wapping marshes were drained and enclosed in the time of Henry VIII for profitable cattle-grazing for the London market, while royal munificence in 1545 enclosed and divided up the wastes of Hounslow Heath and let them on lease or copyhold. That new enclosure was not always for sheep was demonstrated by many private acts of enclosure for cattle or for arable: in Berkshire, for example, the Commissioners of 1517 found that less than 40 per cent of newly enclosed land was for pasture.

When, after the civil wars, enclosure for all purposes was resumed, it was reinforced by a new batch of pro-enclosing pamphleteers who not only argued that enclosure improved arable farming and produced better livestock but maintained, even more forcibly than before, that it did not necessarily lead to depopulation. Walter Blith, for example, was concerned to disprove the argument 'that because men did depopulate by Enclosure, therefore it is now impossible to enclose without Depopulation'[5]. Adam Moore and S. Taylor promised that wastes and commons could be improved immeasurably by enclosure to provide bread for the poor and contribute to the common good.[6] In particular, an argument which had been broached before was given more prominence: that the wool which sheep-farming produced went into the clothing industry which employed many hands, and any unemployment caused by sheep-farming was more than compensated for by employment in the clothing industry. Many of the leading economic writers of the time lent their weight to this aspect of the case—Hartlib, Yarranton, Houghton, Fortrey—and the argument gained ground that a division of labour resulting from the working of private interest led to the general good. The feeling grew that a man might do what he liked with his own, and that his best guide would be the dictates of the market. Following Raleigh,[7] Lee in 1656 asked: 'Have not landholders as much reason, and may they not with as good conscience put their lands to the best advantage?' 'It's an undeniable maxim that everyone', he asserted, in a foretaste of Adam Smith, 'will do that which makes for his greatest advantage',[8] while Fortrey in 1663 declared that 'liberty for every man to enjoy his lands in severalty and enclosure' would be 'one of the greatest improvements this nation is capable of'.[9]

By the end of the seventeenth century enclosure for sheep had spent its force. There were fewer smaller graziers but more great sheepmasters than there had been at the opening of the Tudor period. There was also a change in the type of sheep that grazed. It was no longer simply a matter of the fleece. Mutton was becoming the Englishman's national dish, and mutton required fatter sheep. Fatter sheep were becoming possible with better grazing and more winter feed, but fat sheep produce poor wool and it is a comment upon the condition of the cloth industry that fat sheep were so often allowed to prevail. Though the land movements of the previous two centuries had left the country with a greater amount of pasture-land than before, and with thousands of deserted villages, new arable land had been broken in on the northern hills and moorland, so that the move to pasture had not, on balance, seriously reduced the amount of arable, and corn continued to be exported throughout most of the seventeenth century, though it is possible that other crops had suffered in the move to pasture. The consumer was protected by price maxima for corn until 1660, but after that the Corn Laws were in the interests of producers[10] and, under their stimulus, some land enclosed for sheep was even turned back to arable. It is an apt example of the land's inherent resistance to change that, after two and a half centuries of flux, after the activities of the great sheepmasters, the advocacy of agricultural writers and a big rise in population, some three-fifths of the cultivated land of England and Wales was still unenclosed by the middle of the eighteenth century, and that much of it, particularly in the Midlands, was still held on the strip system.

The growth of population, particularly in the towns, had meanwhile been exercising an increasingly strong pull over a widening radius. There was more breeding of pigs, cattle and poultry for food in the neighbourhood of larger towns, more corn and other cereals, more dairy farming, while, encouraged by Dutch and Flemish precept and example, market gardens and orchards spread up and down the Thames from London and round other large centres of population: 'gardening hath crept out of Holland to Sandwich, Kent, and thence to Surrey,' wrote Fuller in 1660. London, above all, was a magnet which drew food supplies, and therefore influenced land usage, over a large area.[11] York, Bristol and other towns similarly dominated the agriculture of their immediate neighbourhood as well as drawing supplies from further afield, while any local demand or specialization might dictate the nature of farming in a particular area. In all, there was a slow turning to mixed farming and a lessening emphasis upon sheep-breeding.

Yet the improvement that enclosure had promised had not materialized. Few new crops were introduced: hops, brought over at the end of the fifteenth century by Flemish immigrants into the eastern counties, spread slowly; potatoes, introduced from the New World about 1585 by Sir Walter Raleigh, were grown as a luxury crop towards the end of the sixteenth century, but met with little favour, except in Ireland, and had to wait for a couple of centuries before they became a staple; flax, clover and root crops like turnips were introduced by Sir Richard Weston from Flanders in the seventeenth century, but were not in use until the end of the eighteenth century. When in 1669 John Worlidge in his *Systema Agriculturae* summarized the improvements which had been recently made there were not many: drainage had improved, meadows were irrigated, there was a more enterprising use of natural substances for manures such as chalk, seaweed, sea sand and the deposits of rivers and ditches; but ploughs were still heavy and cumbrous; and although some farm implements had better cutting edges of metal many were basically the same wooden articles that had been in use for centuries, while oxen were still preferred to horses for ploughing in most parts of the country. It is possible that the Civil Wars had stifled what might have been the beginnings of a real agricultural revolution, but a general lethargy coupled with difficulties in communication played its part in retarding progress. Above all, the legal position of the tenant farmer was against change, for it made no provision for compensating a tenant for improvements to his holding. With an insecure tenure, what was the point of 'improving', either by new crops or by more efficient farming or by repairs to farm buildings? Such improvements would merely make his holding more attractive to the landowner's net: 'He that havocs may sit/He that improves must flit'.

The biggest and most important development was in the draining of the Great Level of the Fens, an area of wet, marshy land intersected by waterways and interspersed with 'islands' where the inhabitants travelled by punt and walked on stilts. The Great Fen was some seventy to eighty miles long, stretching roughly from Lincoln in the north to Cambridge in the south, and it varied from ten to thirty miles in width. The enterprise of drainage, under the supervision of Dutch engineers, was begun before the Civil Wars, interrupted by the fighting, and completed during the Commonwealth, when the reclaimed area was enclosed. The inhabitants of the Fens clung to the life of watery freedom, with its open spaces, wildfowl and fish in plenty, and riots against the enclosing of the fenlands continued for nearly a century.

The three men who created the true agricultural revolution were not at work until early in the eighteenth century, but, even so, another half-century passed before their methods gained wide acceptance. Jethro Tull, farming on the borders of Berkshire and Wiltshire, taught the economy of sowing seeds in lines instead of scattering broadcast, the drilling of roots, the use of sainfoin and turnips; Lord Townshend demonstrated upon his Norfolk estates the value of marling, and of clover and turnips as field crops; Robert Bakewell, the Leicestershire farmer who improved the stock of cattle, made use of Townshend's turnips for their winter feed. But the practice of the new husbandry, and the new enclosure movement it precipitated, is the story of the Agricultural Revolution whose main force was felt after 1760.

As the story and the argument slips almost imperceptibly

into modern terms, a backward look at the Tudor or Stuart farmer must be permitted. Discussion of the merits of open-field or enclosed farming, of new crops or new methods, would for the most part have been far over the head of the destitute peasant whose home and whose livelihood had been taken away. All he knew was that, though farming might be poor and improvement slow, his fields had served to give him a living, and to give him the self-respect of equality with his fellows. In good seasons they all did well; in bad seasons they suffered together. So he replied to those who would take away and enclose his land in the only way he knew.

There were political rebellions in Tudor and Stuart England, risings against taxation and risings occasioned by religious grievances. Nearly all were accompanied by some form of agrarian discontent. The Pilgrimage of Grace of 1536, which was put down with many executions the following year, concerned itself with the rights and duties of customary tenants as well as with religious matters, asking, for example, that entry fines be limited to two years' rent. In addition there were innumerable skirmishes all over the country in the sixteenth century, important in the areas where they occurred and in total dangerous and significant to the landlord class as a whole, in which hedges were thrown down, ditches filled in, enclosures opened, and sheep driven from the pastures where they were thought to have no right. Many of the bands were armed, and threatened death to any who interfered with them. The picture is by no means only one of apathetic peasants driven away from their land to death or the poorhouse. It is also of militant farmers touched, but not always ruined, by enclosure, defending their land, claiming back their own property, and asserting their ancient rights. They also fought for their land in the law courts, they raised money for their cause as they had done three centuries earlier. There was no question of communism or equality or innovation, but merely the restoration of what had been taken away by enclosure. Though they frequently used romantic language, they were not revolutionaries, not destructive of the existing order, and their leaders were frequently men of some substance.

In 1536 peasants in Lincolnshire marched under a banner embroidered with a ploughshare 'for the encouraging of the husbandman' and were taunted by Ralph Green when they were half inclined to abandon their enterprise and go home:

'God's blood, Sirs, what will ye now do? Shall we go home and keep sheep?' In Yorkshire in the same year there was agrarian unrest, in 1549 in the south and east, in Devon and Somerset, in Hertfordshire and Hampshire, in Norfolk and Worcestershire, there was throwing down of hedges and driving of sheep. There were shadowy figures directing them like those of 1381.[12] But the best organized, the most compact, the longest and largest rebellion was that in Norfolk in 1549 led by the brothers Robert and William Ket.

Norfolk was a county of small farms which had been hit, though not as badly as the Midland counties, by enclosure for sheep. Robert Ket was himself a landowner, and also practised the trade of tanner. He was well off and well educated, and was supported throughout by his brother. Their cause may have received some impetus from the known fact that Protector Somerset felt strongly about enclosure, had appointed a Commission and issued a Proclamation against enclosers. Over 12 000 people joined the Kets, and they established their camp on Mousehold Heath, outside the city of Norwich on 12th July, 1549. They set up a government of their own, opened up some enclosures, kept good order, provisioned themselves and maintained a general good humour for four weeks.

The Articles that Ket and his followers drew up in 1549 asked for no more than that the tillage and depopulation Acts of the Tudors be honoured. Specifically they asked that it should be made illegal for a manorial lord to purchase land and let it out at enhanced rent; that the rent of all copyhold land and all meadowland should revert to that charged in 1485; that entry fines should be 'reasonable'; that all freeholders and copyholders should have their rights of common restored; and that no lord of the manor should be allowed to use the commons. The demands were not only not revolutionary but were for the most part in accord with Tudor agrarian legislation. Somerset is reported to have upheld them before the Privy Council, saying that the peasants' demands were fair and just, but there were many who thought otherwise. The Earl of Warwick (later Duke of Northumberland) with a force of English soldiers and foreign mercenaries dispersed the untrained peasants, the dead were estimated at 3 000, the brothers Ket were hanged, and the episode was counted against Somerset in his later impeachment and execution.

There were strands of feeling in the followers of Ket, which

Warwick and his friends may have discerned, that appear to have owed something to memories of the Peasants' Revolt of 1381. Their attitude to the rich, particularly, was sometimes reminiscent of John Ball. William Cowper of Norwich, for example, was alleged to have declared that 'as shepe or lambes are a praye to the woulfs or lyon so are the poore men to the Riche men or gentylmen'. And one of the demands of the rebels was: 'We pray that all bond men may be made free, for God made all free with his precious bloodshedding'. Though there was scarcely an unfree man left in England when this sentiment was uttered by Ket's followers, it breathes a spirit of equality whose affinity with the preaching of John Ball is unmistakable.[13]

Half a century later in Northamptonshire and the Midland counties the peasants were still violently cutting and breaking down hedges, filling up ditches, and laying open enclosures of commons and pasture land 'which of ancient time had been open and employed to tillage'. They called themselves Levellers and Diggers, being levellers of hedges and diggers of fields. They show a class-consciousness and a power of invective that is a foretaste of what was to come in the Leveller and Digger movements of the Civil Wars, protesting against the 'tirants' who would 'grind our flesh upon the whetstone of poverty . . . so that they may dwell by themselves in the midst of their herds of fat wethers'.[14] The Civil Wars themselves gave a further opportunity for throwing down enclosures, and there was anti-enclosure rioting in various parts of the country. But most significant of all was the agrarian programme which sprang to life under the hand of the group of religious fanatics who, like the earlier protesters, called themselves Diggers.

The Diggers' simple plan was announced by their leader, Gerrard Winstanley, in January 1649, when he instructed his followers that the Lord 'wil have us that are called common people, to manure and work upon the common lands'. 'No man', he said, 'shall have any more land than he can labour himself, or have others to labour with him in love'. He spoke directly to the people in words reminiscent of John Ball: If the rich, he said, 'hold fast this propriety of Mine and Thine, let them labour their own Land with their own hands. And let the common-People, that say the earth is ours, not mine, let them labour together, and eat bread together upon the Commons, Mountains, and Hils'.[15]

Accordingly, on 1st April 1649, two months after the execution of Charles I, when the country was ruled by a Council of State, a small group of half a dozen people began to dig on the commons of George's Hill, near Walton-on-Thames in Surrey. Though local landowners were alarmed, the Council of State found little to object to in the Diggers' activities. They were not opening enclosures and not trespassing upon private land but merely making barley sprout upon the commons, pasturing a cow or two, and living in crude huts which they built themselves. But in June the Diggers went a step further by announcing that if 'the Common Land belongs to us who are the poor oppressed, surely the woods that grow upon the Commons belong to us likewise'. They therefore would cut and sell the wood that grew upon the common.[16] This was a more specific threat than digging, and resulted in a near-riot as landlords, aided by small men to whom wood was an important family adjunct, tried to stop the Diggers. In the tumult that resulted the Diggers' crops were destroyed and their animals taken away but they preserved their policy of passive resistance, and in the autumn moved to common land on neighbouring Cobham manor, where they started again, building themselves four houses and planting winter grain. There followed tumults at Cobham as at Walton, and again it was the local people and not the Council of State who opposed the Diggers. In spite of the further destruction of houses and crops, the Diggers persisted, and by the spring of 1650 they had eleven acres under grain and six or seven houses.

But they were woefully short of funds, and in April issued an appeal for money which four emissaries carried on an extensive tour of the Home Counties and the Midlands. These men were taken in custody in Wellingborough, in Northamptonshire. But before that their example had been followed by some of the people in this town who in March 1650 had started digging and sowing corn upon the commons and wasteland called Bareshanke. They appeared to be practical men, taking the Digger line as the easiest way to solve their problems. 'We are in Wellingborough', they said,

> in one parish 1169 persons that receive Alms . . . we have spent all we have; our trading is decayed, our wives and children cry for bread, our lives are a burden to us, divers of us having 5, 6, 7, 8, 9 in Family, and we cannot get bread for one of them by our labor; rich men's hearts

are hardened; they will not give us if we beg at their doors; if we steal, the Law will end our lives, divers of the poor are starved to death already. . . . And now we consider that . . . the common and waste Grounds belong to the poor . . . and therefore we have begun to bestow our righteous labor upon it.[17]

People were also digging at Cox Hill in Kent. But, in both Northamptonshire and in Kent, in spite of some local support, the Digger houses were destroyed and animals trampled their growing corn.

The Diggers were simple agrarian communists, their claim to work the common land and live on its produce harking back to an idealized peasant society such as they believed existed before the Norman yoke was clamped upon the free people of England: they might have felt that their progenitors were to be found in the ranks of the peasants of 1381, although they never mention them. If, ultimately, they believed that all the land should be held in common, their claims reached at first only to the common land, and later to the Crown and Church lands which had been confiscated during the Civil Wars. It is doubtful whether, apart from their leaders, they ever thought beyond the most simple generalizations.

There had been dreams of an ideal society before the Diggers began to dig, some of which stressed the importance of the land. Sir Thomas More's *Utopia*, published in 1516, envisaged a society in which everyone worked for six hours a day and spent the rest of the time in social and intellectual pleasure, relying upon few luxuries, waging no war. The king would be chosen for life by all, and would live like an ordinary citizen; the priests of an undenominational religion would be similarly elected and chosen for their character. Peter Chamberlen in April 1649, just after the Diggers had started to dig, published *The Poore Mans Advocate*, a scheme for making land confiscated during the Civil Wars, and all common land that had been enclosed, into a joint stock for the benefit of the poor of the nation. Samuel Hartlib urged that 'England had many hundreds of acres of waste and barren lands, and many thousands of idle hands; if both these might be improved, England by God's blessing would grow to be a richer nation than it is now by far'. A Dutchman, Peter Cornelius, suggested (in English) a scheme for a series of communities, each on a joint-stock basis under an elected governor. John Bellers, at the end of the century when the turmoil of war had died down, elaborated a scheme for agricultural colonies of about three hundred persons each which would operate on a co-operative basis, the members being chosen so that all farming skills were represented. In these colonies the standard of value would be labour, and not money; Bellers thus anticipated Robert Owen's concept of labour time as a means of exchange.

The Diggers were the only ones to attempt to implement their beliefs, but they never won the support of more than a handful of people. This was largely because those among whom they might have won support were basically interested not in common ownership but in private ownership. They wanted land—not worked in common, but land for themselves—good peasant acres they could call their own. In this respect it was the Levellers and not the Diggers who won support. The Leveller movement, indeed, was in many ways the more attractive since it had a wider programme, which included agrarian reform, it was the more assertive and it had the more flamboyant leaders, thus attracting and keeping the discontent which might, in other circumstances, have turned to the Diggers.[18]

Both Levellers and Diggers believed that slavery, in the form of feudal landholding, had been riveted upon the free people of England by the Norman Conquest. They asked for the opening of the enclosure of fens and other common land for 'the free and common use and benefit of the poor' and for the abolition of any servile tenure that remained, particularly of copyhold tenure, 'the badge of slavery', whose uncertainties might at any time be used to penalize a tenant holding his land by copy of ancient court roll. It was, indeed, not the Diggers and Levellers alone who fiercely contested a tenure that appeared to epitomize all that was worst in feudal obligation. The eminent lawyer Edward Coke worked hard to bring all copyholders within the ambit of common law. How could a copyhold tenant, he asked, bring an action of trespass in the manor court against a lord who had ousted him, 'for it is against reason, that the Lord should be Judge . . . where he himself is party'.[19]

The basic importance of the land, to whatever use it was put, and whoever owned it, was undisputed and was acknowledged in a variety of ways. But before pursuing further the changing social, political and economic fortunes which were nourished by the land it is necessary to turn to those industrial developments which, like the production of woollen cloth, were adding to the country's wealth and changing the pattern of her life, and which frequently derived from, and often added to, the importance of the landowner and the very land itself.

CHAPTER XV

The Development of Industry

By the middle of the sixteenth century there was an all-round industrial expansion that matched the general exuberance of the age. Tudor stability, population-increase, geographical exploration, stimulated both industry and trade and engendered the confidence necessary for planning and investment. Apart from the woollen-cloth industry, the most spectacular industrial development was shown in coal-mining.

The prejudice against coal died hard. Queen Elizabeth was as annoyed at the taste and smell of smoke from the coal burned by the brewers of London as Queen Eleanor had been at the coal-smoke of Nottingham; but whereas Queen Eleanor moved her abode Elizabeth caused the brewers to abandon coal and burn only wood near her dwelling. John Evelyn in the seventeenth century wanted the premises of all who burnt coal removed beyond Greenwich because of 'columns and clouds of Smoake' which were 'belched forth from the sooty Throates' of coal-fires, causing the City to look like Troy sacked by the Greeks. Evelyn launched a crusade to stop the burning of coal, but as he was also crusading for the preservation of timber he was in a difficult position.

So far as domestic use was concerned, the antipathy to coal was partly overcome by the introduction of chimneys. These at least made the burning of coal attractive within doors, while outside, if the chimney were sufficiently high, the smoke and fumes would be carried away. John Leland noted as a novelty in the time of Henry VIII that there were chimneys in the hall at

Bolton in Yorkshire. They 'were conveyed by tunnells made on the syds of the wauls . . . and by this meanes . . . is the smoke of the harthe in the hawle wonder strangly convayed'.[1] In the reign of Elizabeth they were in general use in bigger houses. But more than anything else it was the shortage of timber which made the substitution of coal for wood or charcoal imperative for industrial as well as domestic use.

By the Tudor period the continuous strain upon the woodlands had taken effect, and they could no longer be regarded as expendable. The outward move of cultivation had in any case reduced the actual forest area, while centuries of uncritical felling and wasteful use with little replanting had reduced the forests to shadows of their former selves; not only was there a positive shortage of bigger trees but most woodlands were ill-kept and unhealthy. The lime-burners had preferred coal to charcoal at an early stage, and the smiths had used coal in their forges because it gave a continuous strong heat. But industries whose material came in direct contact with the fuel were slower to change, for the sulphur content of coal affected the quality of the product. The two industries most affected in this way were glass-making and iron-smelting. Their demands for timber were prodigious—even discounting the estimate that by 1629 thirty thousand oaks had been consumed by one ironmaster alone in the course of his lifetime[2]—and a glass-furnace could take even more trees than an iron-furnace. But since there were fewer glass-furnaces than iron-furnaces, it was the iron-smelters who made the greatest demand upon timber resources.

The situation was the more critical because the shipbuilding industry had now become one of the strongest competitors for timber. Boats of many kinds were being made in increasing numbers in every little haven round the coast in response to local trade and fishing demands, while a substantial shipbuilding industry for the Navy and for long-distance trade was developing round the Kentish coasts at Chatham, Deptford, Woolwich and Sheerness, as well as in Bristol, Newcastle and other bigger ports.[3] It was ironic that coal, the very material that could replace wood, was making its own demands in the form of pitprops and shaft linings. With increasing demand and dwindling supply timber prices soared, and home supplies were supplemented by imported wood. Now that they could no longer be taken for granted, the forests at last had their defenders. The villain of the piece was generally the iron-smelter:

> These iron times breed none that mind posterity . . .
> Jove's Oak, the warlike Ash, vein'd Elm, the softer Beech,
> Short Hazel, Maple plain, light Aspe, the bending Wych,
> Tough Holly, and smooth Birch, must altogether burn;
> What should the builder serve, supplies the forger's turn.[4]

A stream of proscription and legislation now attempted to halt the spoliation of the forests. The Tudors were particularly aware of the problem, and each sovereign after Henry VII added to the list of instruction and embargo. They sought to discourage early felling by exempting trees of twenty-two years' growth and over from the payment of tithe. An Act which classified willow and osier as weeds was repealed. Acts of 1559 and 1585 sought to preserve timber for shipbuilding by forbidding the use in iron-smelting of oak, beech or ash which was one foot square at the stub and grew within fourteen miles of the sea or a river. An Act of 1581, complaining of the scarcity of timber and its enhanced price, tried to protect an area of twenty-two miles round London and other populous places, both by forbidding established ironmasters to use timber there and by prohibiting the erection of new iron-mills in the area.

Statutory attention was also for the first time given to the general management and preservation of woodland. The Act of 1544 made compulsory what the best forestry practice had already evolved—the spacing of oak and elm to provide not only the long, straight lengths required for ships' masts but to allow sufficient lateral spread to their crowns to provide the curved timbers used for other shipbuilding purposes. The Act enjoined that in every acre of wood, besides coppice, there should be twelve standards,[5] if possible of oak, but otherwise of elm. Fellings should be immediately replaced, and the young trees protected from cattle by enclosure for fourteen years. The Stuarts showed a similar anxiety to preserve the forests, particularly from the encroachments of the ironmasters, Charles I creating the office of surveyor of ironworks expressly for the purpose, while at the same time enjoining that existing legislation be observed.

Government activity, coupled with the competition of shipbuilders, caused the ironmasters to depart from the Weald, leaving its depleted timber resources to the Kentish shipyards. They moved back to the Forest of Dean, to Wales and to other smaller forest areas. Even here they were not safe, for the Commonwealth Government pursued them to Dean itself, ordering the suppression of iron-mills there—with, however, little discernible effect. In Restoration England the preservation of the woodlands was still a vital issue when John Evelyn came to their defence in an address to the Royal Society, published in 1664 as *Sylva*. Legislation, it seemed, had barely halted the wasteful, extravagant, mercenary, careless and ill-informed practices that were destroying the woodland, and he propounded much practical advice based on personal experience of his family estates. He was bitter against the despoilers of the woodlands, comparing them to horse-stealers and demanding equally severe penalties for both: 'we might as well live without Mares, as without ships, which are our Wooden, but no less profitable horses'.

Relief came not so much through Government action or popular exhortation as through the substitution of coal for wood in smelting. The problem of using coal in glass-making was solved in 1615 by melting the potash and sand in a container that did not come into contact with the coal. But it was not until the early eighteenth century that iron was smelted with coal. After some years of experimenting at their ironworks at Coalbrookdale the Darby family succeeded in making a sulphur-free coke from coal with which it was possible to smelt iron. The iron they produced was at first most suitable for casting, but later adaptations made it equally good for wrought iron. Thereafter, although in remoter regions little ironworks still relied upon the local forests, the bigger ironworks were moving to the coalfields, and the association of coal and iron became an integral part of Britain's industrial development.

The use of coal had also been inhibited by difficulties in transporting so heavy and bulky a commodity. But the main coalfields were situated near rivers or the sea, and as the demand for coal increased this form of transport improved. At the beginning of the seventeenth century there had been 700 miles of navigable river; at the end of it there were 1 000 miles. Canals, however, were still to come. A link was cut between Exeter and Topsham in 1564–6, but the canal era did not begin until after 1760. Round the coasts, however, navigational aids and improvements to harbours and river mouths encouraged coastal shipping and London in particular took increasingly large shipments of coal by sea from Newcastle, her imports multiplying more than thirtyfold between 1563 and 1684.

Abroad, as the popularity of coal grew, ships which formerly had taken coal from Newcastle merely as ballast now came for the express purpose of buying it. Total shipments of coal from Newcastle grew at a phenomenal rate, being 35 000 tons a year in the 1560s and 400 000 tons in 1625.[6] And there were other coalfields, not so spectacular, perhaps, as those of the Tyne and Wear, but also important, in Wales, Yorkshire, Cumberland, the Midlands, in Somerset and in Dean. A coal-mine which might have been producing a few hundred tons of coal a year before the middle of the sixteenth century could well be producing 25 000 tons a century later, and continue the rate of expansion. Total coal output, which was about 160 000 tons annually in the middle of the sixteenth century, was over 2½ million tons at the end of the seventeenth century—before the Darby process of smelting with coal—and by the end of the eighteenth century had swept upward to 8½ million tons.[7]

The small enterprise run or let at lease by the lord of the manor, or the small working partnership of working miners, which had sufficed through the Middle Ages could not have produced such quantities of coal. Mines had to be dug at greater depth. This meant the digging and lining of adits or drainage tunnels, improved ventilation, more adequate timbering, haulage, winding. Between 1540 and 1640 depths of twenty or thirty or even fifty fathoms were reached, but the drainage problem remained intractable. Not until Thomas Savery and Thomas Newcomen, working independently, devised within a few years of each other 'an engine for raising water by fire' was the problem solved. These steam-engines with vertical motion for pumping were in use early in the eighteenth century, and led directly to Watt's steam-engine with a rotary motion, capable of driving wheels round: they were the first big mechanical inventions of the Industrial Revolution.[8] The transport of coal from the mine to the nearest water was also a problem whose solution was beginning to be found. In the reign of Elizabeth rails were first used to carry coal from the pits, the chief problem being not the mechanical one but the high price of the way-leaves over the land they needed to traverse. Roger North in 1676 described how 'rails of timber' were laid 'from the colliery down to the river, exactly straight and parallel; and bulky carts are made with four rowlets fitting these rails; whereby the carriage is so easy that one horse will draw down four or five chaldron of coals'.[9]

Capital to finance these developments was poured into the coal-mines from a variety of sources, and was encouraged by the granting of long leases on reasonable terms by the landowners on whose land the mine was situated. Labour was more difficult to obtain. Small-scale coal-mining had been, perhaps, a part-time occupation of an agricultural worker; sometimes it was imposed upon him as part of his feudal service, and as such it survived in the North of England long after villeinage had ended. It is not surprising that mining should attract few workers. At the deeper levels accidents were frequent and terrible. Flood, explosion and gaseous fumes gave rise to stories of evil spirits in the mines' depths. The miner himself, black and covered with mine dust, became an awesome figure to the rest of the population, particularly since he had the reputation of being noisy, insolent, quick-tempered and quarrelsome. It is likely that ordinary recruitment so lagged that mine-owners took into employ the rogues and vagabonds who tormented society, and that the Justices of the Peace directed the unemployed to mining either as part of their feudal obligation or, more likely, under the wide provisions of the Poor Law.[10] Women and children also were employed. The conditions of mining labour that were exposed in the Government Reports of the nineteenth century undoubtedly had their beginnings further back, though no searchlight of publicity ever penetrated to the mines' depths to make them known.

The extractive industries that the coal-mines were feeding developed similarly, if not in so spectacular a fashion. Iron, tin, and lead mines became deeper, and used more capital for drainage, ventilation and other purposes associated with larger-scale production. In the iron industry the most revolutionary innovation was not in mining but in the blast-furnace for smelting ore. The blast-furnace was brought into Britain from the Continent at the end of the fifteenth century, though it was probably not in wide use until half a century later, and it could produce about four to five times the amount of the old bloomery. Unlike the less spectacular capitalization of the mine itself, blast-furnaces were conspicuous over the surrounding countryside, being about thirty feet high, twenty feet square at the bottom, with walls five to six feet thick to preserve the heat, while a giant bellows some twenty feet long driven by a water-wheel stood nearly as high as the furnace itself. Such a furnace could produce a hundred to five hundred tons of iron annually,[11] and the total English production of bar-iron grew from some 10 000 tons in 1600 to 30 000 tons in 1760.[12] It is doubtful whether many of the free iron-miners were able to withstand the capitalization of the mines, and it is likely that they either became wage labourers or settled into some form of domestic industry. In the Midlands, particularly, there were many such independent masters producing a variety of small wares, such as nails, bolts, locks and keys.

Steel, which was known as a refined and hardened iron, was little used in the Middle Ages, but under the guidance of Dutch technicians it assumed some importance in the reign of Elizabeth. Though imperfectly produced, and not sufficiently hard for many specialized purposes, it became an important though small-scale industry, feeding innumerable small enterprises and domestic producers—again particularly in the Midlands, where cutlery, clocks, watches, pins and other small objects were made. Birmingham was said by Camden in the second half of the sixteenth century to be 'swarming with inhabitants and echoing with the noise of anvils'.[13]

Among those seeking a substance which was finer, harder and more suited to delicate work than the steel then in use was Benjamin Huntsman of Doncaster, a clockmaker and producer of fine springs and locks. Working in secret over many years, constantly purifying the raw steel as it then existed by melting it in fluxes at intense heat in enclosed earthenware crucibles, Huntsman at last about 1750 produced cast steel, the fine, hard substance he needed for his work. Strangely enough, the cutlers, who made knives and similar implements from the older form of steel, still preferred this to Huntsman's cast steel, but others were quick to take advantage of it and there was a large export demand. Huntsman supplied the cast steel but he did not publish his discovery, neither did he patent it. On the contrary, he endeavoured to keep his methods secret, working his furnaces at night with trusted workmen. He was a Quaker, of retiring disposition, with nothing of the capitalist entrepreneur about him, and his reticence seems to have sprung from a desire to shun publicity. Others, however, were not backward in seeking to wrest his secret from him, and it was apparently discovered by an ironmaster called Walker who, so the story goes, pretended one stormy evening to be a wanderer in need of warmth and rest. Huntsman's workmen took pity on him and let him lie by the furnaces all night, where, instead of sleeping, he took note of all that was done.

While iron and steel were serving the small-scale industries of the Midlands and other areas, and their producers were preparing themselves for the heavy load of bridges, ships, trains, machinery that would come in the nineteenth century, domestic and decorative uses of the metals continued in the hands of the successors to the early blacksmiths and founders. Wrought-iron gates and screens continued to be made for churches and cathedrals, but none rivalled for sheer exuberance the great screen wrought at the end of the seventeenth century by Jean Tijou for Hampton Court Palace, which consisted of twelve panels each six feet high and more than thirteen feet wide, the whole joined together by scrolls of elaborate ironwork. Bristol in the eighteenth century was noted for the quality of its smiths, as the gates of St Mary Redcliffe and the Temple church are sufficient to testify. Wrought iron was also being widely used for park and garden gates, for balustrades to staircases, inside as well as out, for balconies, for roof and other cresting.

Firebacks, fire-cheeks and other objects in cast iron proliferated. In the case of firebacks there was much competition from the Dutch, but the English founders copied them, learned from them and executed their own designs. Cauldrons and ovens of cast iron became popular, railings were often cast, particularly when a more massive and heavier railing was required than that provided by wrought iron. The iron railings round Wren's St Paul's, for example, were cast in the Weald and delivered by water between 1710 and 1714. They weighed over 200 tons, and cost more than £11 000.[14] Wren did not like them. Much of the later development of cast iron is associated with Victorian life—the 'functional design' of street plaques, notices, letter-boxes, lamp-posts, fenders, baths.

The story of the mining of tin is not dissimilar to that of coal and iron. The surface ores were running thinner, and this, coupled with increasing demand, called for deeper mines, and the capital expenditure that this required. The period of greatest technical advance lies between the middle of the seventeenth and the middle of the eighteenth centuries, by which time gunpowder had been used in blasting, and mines were often ninety fathoms deep. The engines first of Newcomen and, early in the eighteenth century, of Bolton and Watt, were used for pumping water from these depths, ventilation and fire precautions were improved. The tin-smelter, meantime, changed to coal in response to the pressure on wood and improved his final product with the aid of technical advances such as calcining—giving a preliminary burning to the tin before smelting—and the use of the hydraulic stamp. Output responded by rising from some 500–700 tons a year in the first half of the seventeenth century to about 1 500 tons at the end, and well over 2 000 tons by the middle of the eighteenth century. Thereafter production fluctuated. Tin remained a staple export, although in one way its use was curtailed: English pewter became less popular as cheaper pottery came into general use. Perhaps the opening of Josiah Wedgwood's works at Burslem in 1759, where comparatively cheap but still attractive household ware was produced, was an influence upon the fortunes of tin. The last Stannary Parliament was dissolved in 1750, but it had become little more than a quarrelling ground for rival entrepreneurs and was of little use to the tin-miners, whose position had deteriorated from the proud independence they had known to one of acute poverty dependent upon the capitalist mine-owner or the entrepreneur.

The story of lead is rather different. The Mendip mines, having reached their maximum development between 1600 and 1670, began to run down by the end of the seventeenth century, and declined in the eighteenth. Though the better-quality Derbyshire mines held their position longer by means of deeper mines and better drainage and ventilation, they too were in decline by the middle of the eighteenth century. Both areas faced the same basic problem: the easier-worked surface deposits had been used up, and the greater expense of mining at depth was worth while only if the market was sufficiently buoyant. There was, indeed, still a market for lead in church roofing and in statuary, in urns and fountains that adorned gardens and villas, in the utilitarian pipes and water cisterns that the plumber still embellished according to his fancy. But, although the Levant Company still exported lead to the Mediterranean, and the Methuen Treaty with Portugal of 1703 specified lead as an export, in other directions lead was rejected. The East India Company tried to export it to India, but Sir Thomas Roe, the

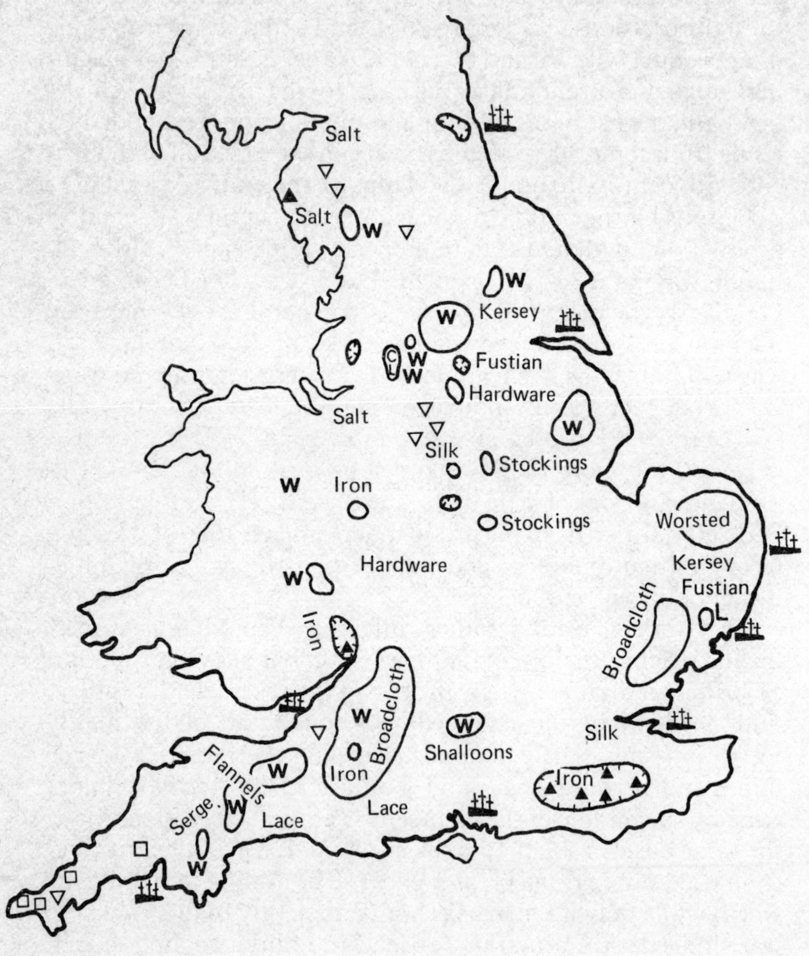

Fig. 5a Chief Industries and Manufactured Goods of Early Modern England

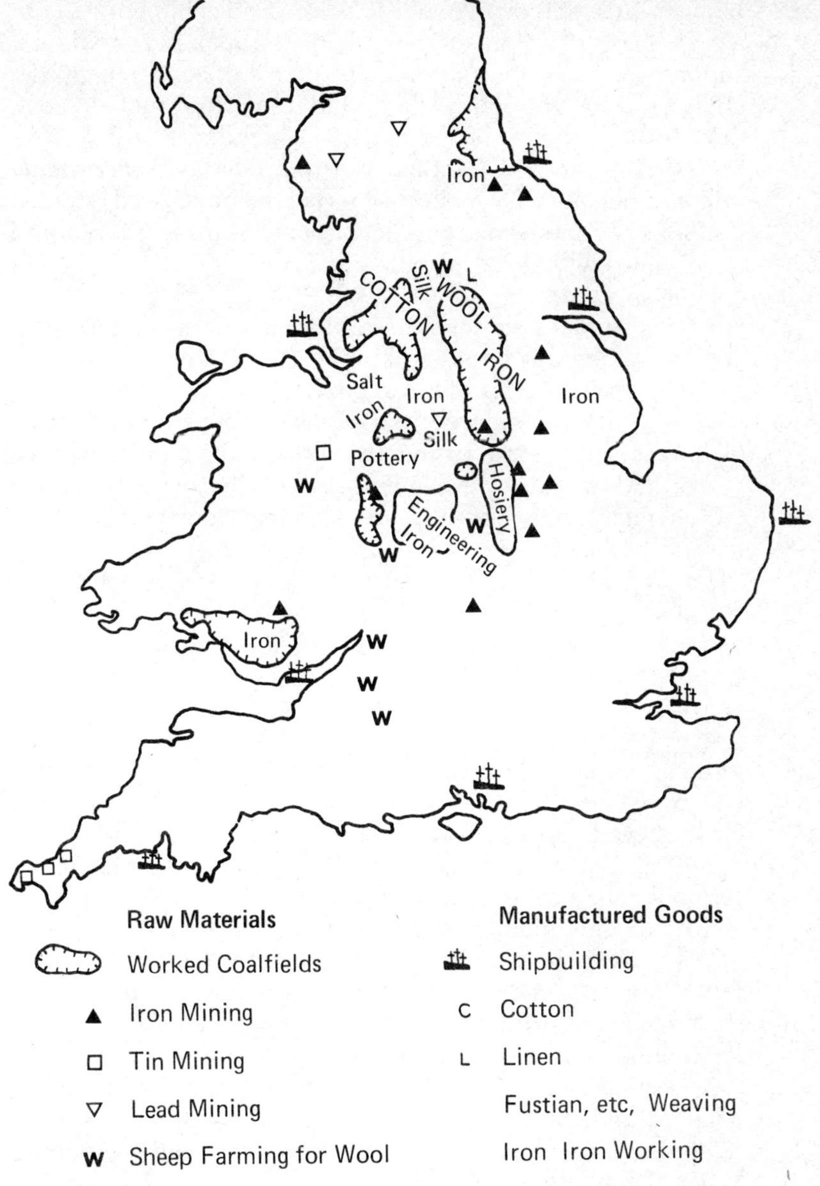

Fig. 5b Chief Industries and Manufactured Goods in the Early Years of the Industrial Revolution

English Ambassador at the Court of the Great Mogul, wrote home in 1616 that cloth and lead were 'dead commodities' and would 'never drive this trade'. All in all, the market could not support further capital development. In spite of a general decline, however, the old freedoms and franchises still held good among some at least of the miners of Mendip, and it was reported as late as 1815 that there were peculiar laws still in being amongst the miners, who had a court of their own, and retained the power of banishing any delinquent from the district and confiscating his house and tools.

In contrast to these old-established mining enterprises, copper-mining and brass-making were virtually unknown in England until the reign of Elizabeth I. Their development was a deliberate act made largely in the interests of national defence. For brass is a material eminently suited to the making of guns and ordnance of all kinds, and brass is an alloy of copper and of zinc—which comes from the ore calamine. Copper was known to exist, but it was necessary to prospect for calamine.

Following the pattern of textile-working, German workmen, familiar with copper-mining and brass-manufacture in their native land, were brought to England in the fifteenth century. But it was not until 1567 that German capital combined with German skill to mine and forge 'perfect copper' from the Newlands mine near Keswick. On the strength of this a monopoly mining company was incorporated in 1568 as the Mines Royal. Calamine, the other essential to brass-manufacture, which had for long evaded search, was discovered about the same time in Somerset at the west end of the Mendips—fitting compensation for the decline of Mendip lead. In January 1568 brass was made and another monopoly company was incorporated for its manufacture under the name of The Mineral and Battery Works. But the quality of the brass was not of the highest, the financial return was not enough for the German investors, the monopoly lapsed, and the copper-mining part of the venture declined also. The Mines Royal and the Society of the Mineral and Battery Works are typical examples of the attempt to establish industries under the protection of a patent. When the monopoly lapsed some small-scale production continued, the largest works in the eighteenth century being at Warmley, in Gloucestershire, where some 800 people were employed. At the end of the century there was an even larger enterprise in Anglesey, employing some 1 200 people, but for the most part the copper and brass workers, like the small-scale iron and steel workers, existed in little domestic enterprises in the Midlands, the North of England and Wales, producing pots, pans, kettles, trays, nails, pins, wire and such small metal goods. The grandiose project of gun and ordnance factories came to nothing.

Alum, which was very important as a mordant, or fixing agent, in the dyeing of cloth and as a dressing for tanned leather, was produced from native alumstone in increasing quantities in the sixteenth and seventeenth centuries. In the reign of James I there were large alum houses at Whitby, made of wood, to which the alumstone was brought, to be smelted over brick furnaces fired by coal and wood. The scale and number of these alum houses increased enormously in the following decades, when many thousands of pounds of capital and hundreds of workmen were involved.

Of other large enterprises, paper-making, after two abortive attempts, was established at Dartford with water-driven mills before the end of the sixteenth century. Sir John Spielman was knighted by the Queen at Dartford in 1588, and given a licence for ten years for 'the sole gathering of all rags and other articles necessary for making paper'. After 1590 hemp for sails also became a well-established industry. Before that date it had been in the hands of the French, who supplied sails both for the ships of the sea-dogs and for the Spanish galleons.

Another industry in which considerable capital was sunk by the end of the seventeenth century was salt-making. The small-scale evaporation of salt had continued through the Middle Ages, even though large quantities were imported, and with the increasing use of coal at the end of the sixteenth century it became practicable to construct large salt-evaporating furnaces, run on capitalist lines, at the mouth of the Wear and of the Tyne, where hundreds of men and thousands of pounds were employed.

At the other end of the scale were a group of small industries which expanded rapidly in the century between 1540 and 1640. Particularly around London, domestic industries were moving from the homes of the workpeople to workshops or small factories, and were showing many of the signs of capitalist production: the workers were becoming wage-earners; machines and other forms of production were becoming more elaborate;

more capital was sunk in the enterprise. Most of the industries affected were already established in a non-capitalist form, but by the middle of the sixteenth century the scale was changing. Round London by 1640, for example, there were little capitalist brew houses and little factories for making soap and alum and the important saltpetre (a constituent of gunpowder) where many Londoners worked for wages,[15] and from whose ranks came many of the left-wing supporters of the Civil Wars.

CHAPTER XVI

Population and Prices

Agrarian changes and industrial development were taking place to the accompaniment of a general expansion in population, in prices, in trade and commerce, and even in the known world itself. The population, which had grown very slowly after the Black Death, began to recover in the middle of the fifteenth century. Figures are not reliable, and are undergoing constant revision, but it seems likely that, after a slow start, the population of England and Wales leaped forward between 1500 and 1600, growing from about 2·5 or 3 million at the beginning of the century to some 4 million at the end, and that between 1500 and 1640—that is, between about the Tudor accession and the outbreak of the Civil Wars—it completely doubled, being at the later date over 5·5 million. After that the rate of increase slowed down, there being possibly 5·8 million people in England and Wales in 1700.[1] The increase was in spite of the fact that, although no major epidemic of the proportion of the Black Death had hit the country, there were outbreaks like the 'sweating sickness' of the 1520s, the influenza epidemic of the mid-century, plague at the end, and plague again in the early seventeenth century, when the coronation of James I was twice postponed.

The expansion of population was accompanied by a steep, though somewhat erratic, rise in prices. This began slowly at the end of the fifteenth century, was attracting attention by 1510, and then gathered such momentum that between 1510 and 1560 prices more than doubled. There was a slower advance between 1560 and 1590, but the movement accelerated in the last decade of the century, nearly doubling again between 1580 and 1597. There was then a slight drop, but prices failed to

The Estimated Population of England, 1086–1801

year	*million persons*
1086	1·1
1300	3·5
1348	3·7
1400	2·1
1430	2·1
1525	2·3
1545	2·8
1603	3·75
1640	5·5
1700	5·5
1731	6·0
1760	6·5
1801	8·8

The population figure given above for 1801 is for England and Wales and is taken from the first official census.

return to even the 1590 mark and remained at this high level for the first thirty years of the seventeenth century. There was a further marked rise in the 'thirties, a smaller rise in the 'forties, prices reaching their peak in the four years 1648, 1649, 1650 and 1651. Taking the price-level between 1451 and 1475 as 100, it stood at 685 in 1597, 839 in 1650, and, after a fluctuating fall, was still at 671 in 1700.

Agricultural prices were affected first, rent and the price of wool showed the biggest and most consistent increase, prices in the neighbourhood of towns, particularly London, appeared to rise earlier and more quickly than elsewhere. On the whole the price of food rose more than that of manufactured goods, wages began to rise in the 1540s but lagged behind prices. There are no very clear figures to help a full assessment of the rise, but an examination of the prices of certain consumables compared with builders' wage-rates confirms this pattern and indicates that the price index of articles of ordinary consumption in a labourer's household rose from 100 in 1508 to 231 in 1547 and 285 in 1551.[2] Between 1510 and 1580 they had more than trebled, and more than quadrupled between 1510 and 1600.[3] At the same time contemporary Acts of Parliament, public pronouncements, wage assessments and private diagnoses testify to the price-rise and its effects. Complaints of high prices and of 'dearth', which signified shortage coupled with high prices, went, indeed, right through the agrarian discontent and the tillage laws of the period. It is only necessary to think of Latimer's sermons or, for example, the Act of 1534 which spoke of the doubling in price 'of all manner of corn, cattle, wool, pigs, geese, hens, chickens, eggs and such other'.[4] Wage assessments are also evidence of the price-rise, as when the J.P.s of the City of London in 1586 had 'an especiall consideracion and regard unto the high and verie chargeable prices of all kinde of victualls, fewell rayment and apparrell bothe linnen and wollen and alsoe of howsrente'.[5]

It was natural that the conversion of arable land to pasture and the enclosing of commons should by some people be held responsible for the price-rise, on the grounds that it reduced the amount of food available. Another reason commonly assigned for the inflation was the debasement of the coinage, particularly that carried out by Henry VIII and Edward VI between 1544 and 1551. This was coupled with illegal clipping and counterfeiting, which put more coin on to the market. Queen Elizabeth had no doubt that her father's and brother's action in debasement had done her a bad turn in this respect, causing her expenses to rise threefold,[6] while one of the reasons given in the Proclamation announcing the reform of the coinage in 1560 was that 'all maner of prices of thynges in this Realme, necessarye for sustentacion of the people, growe dayly excessive,' with which it coupled the everlasting complaint against inflation at all times and in all places that the rise in prices hurt particularly everyone who lived by fixed incomes, 'speciallye of Pensioners, souldyers, and all hyred servauntes, and other meane people that lyve by any kynde of wages, and not by rentes of landes, or trade of marchaundyse'.[7] The release of the treasure and the land of the monasteries similarly had an inflationary effect as it reached the market for the first time. The sale of monastic land after 1540, and particularly between 1543 and 1547 when land was sold, and frequently was sold again, and yet again, on the rising market stimulated inflation still more.

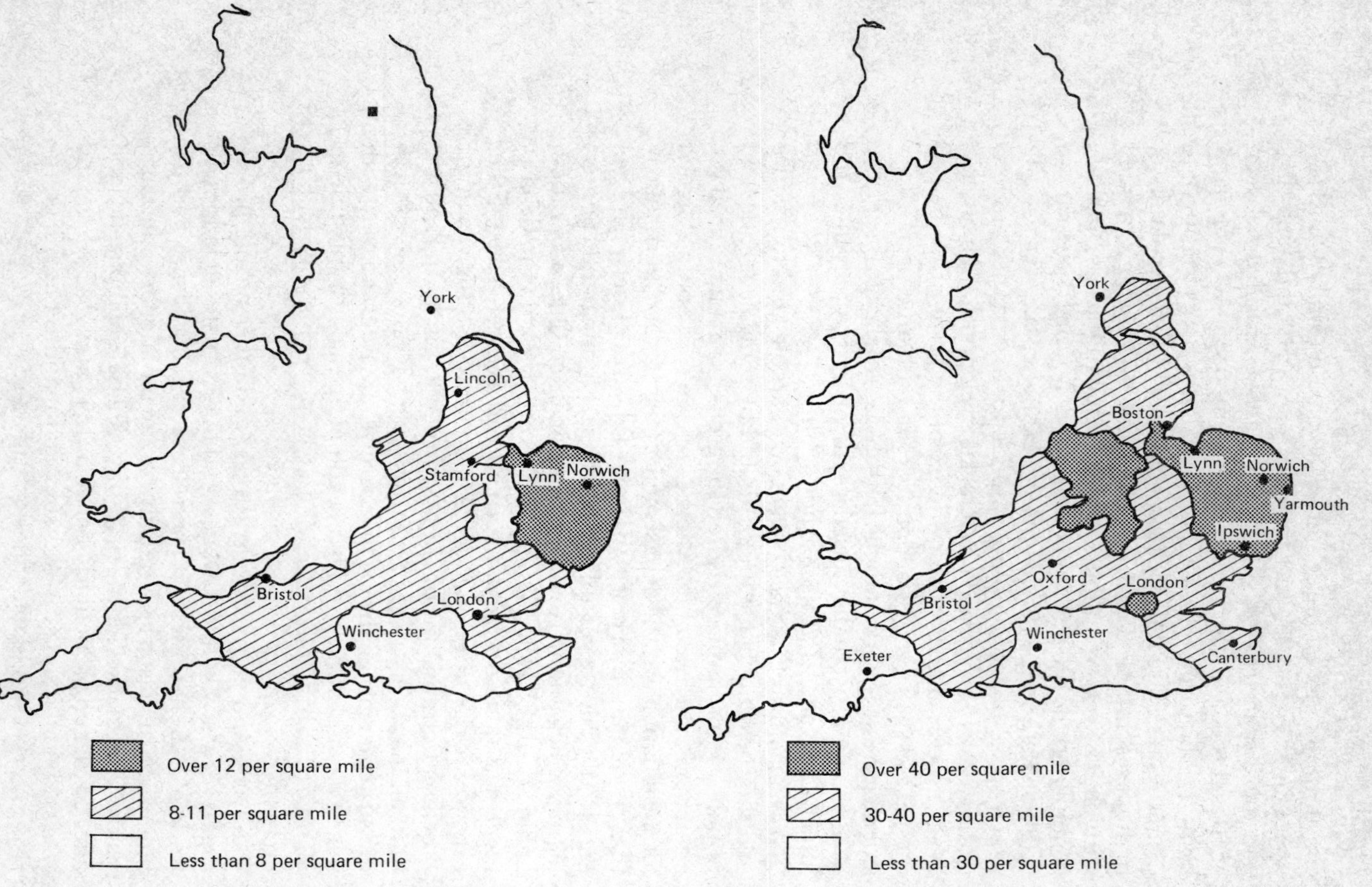

Fig. 6a Distribution of Population, 1086

Fig. 6b Distribution of Population, 1377

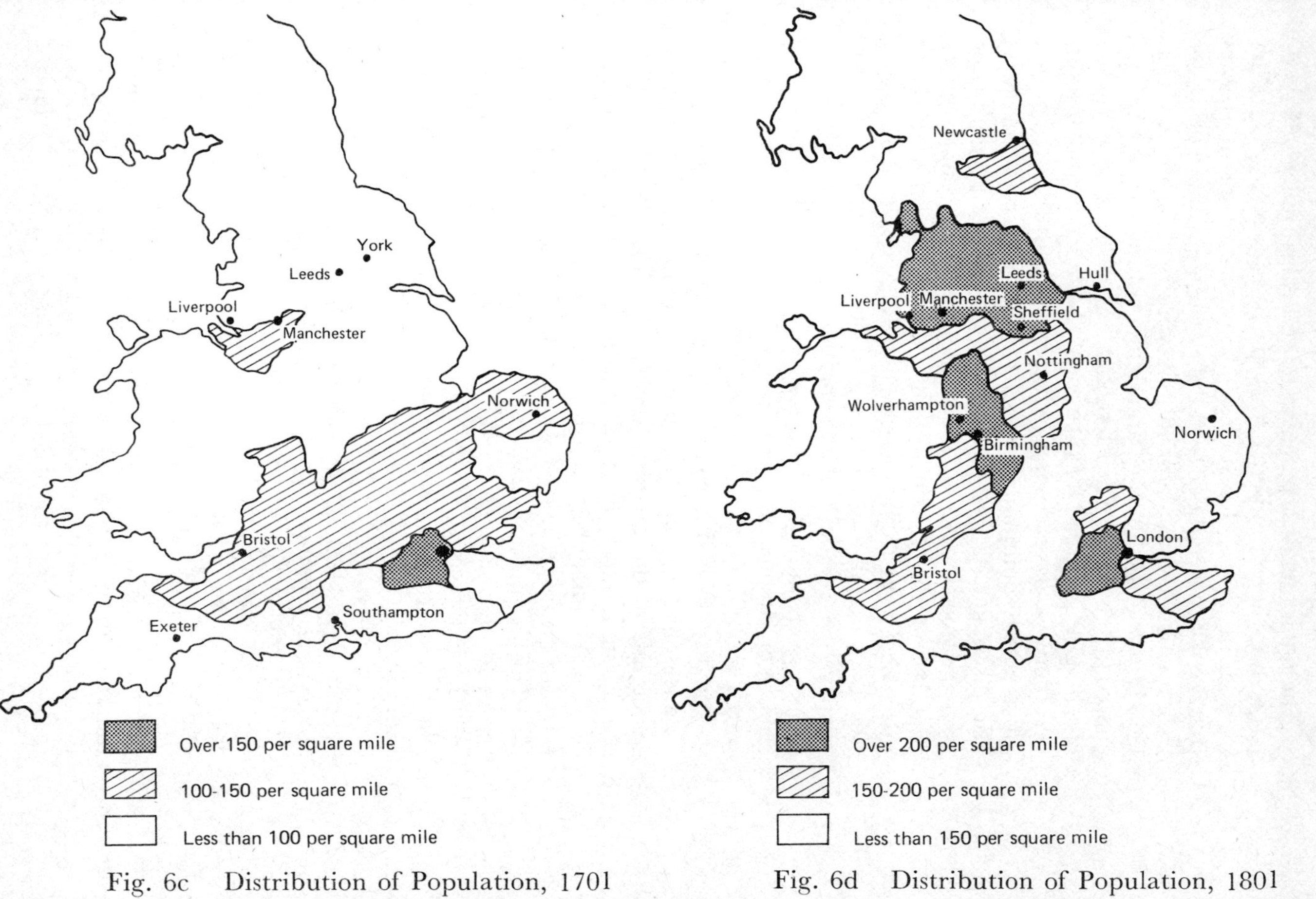

Fig. 6c Distribution of Population, 1701

Fig. 6d Distribution of Population, 1801

The outcry against patents and industrial monopolies was largely on the grounds that they pushed up prices.[8] Middlemen of all kinds—'forestallers', 'regraters', the 'caterpillars that crept between the bark and the tree'—enhanced prices for their own gain. Speculators did likewise, and had the same effect. Usury—'the buyenge and sellinge of money for tyme'[9]—caused prices to rise. The Merchant Adventurers were accused of selling dear abroad for their own advantage, with the result that there was a corresponding increase in the price of imported goods which communicated itself to home products. There was also discussion as to the role foreign exchange played in the level of domestic prices: if money flowed in to a country prices would rise—'the prices of victuals and other wares in like sort is raised according to the increase of treasure';[10] it followed that 'the Exchange is the gouernere of prises of all warres interchangeablye vented'.[11] A memorandum prepared for a Royal Commission on the Exchanges of 1564 was emphatic that 'the risynge or fallynge of the Exchange dothe gouerne the prise of wares'.[12]

The discussion of the effect of the rate of exchange and the balance of payments upon prices assumed the fundamental hypothesis of the quantity theory of money that 'plenty of money in a kingdom doth make the native commodities dearer'.[13] It was a short step to assume that the treasure flowing into Europe from the New World was a factor in the price-rise. The Doctor in the *Discourse of the Common Weal* gave as one reason for the rise in prices 'the infinite sums of gold and silver, whych are gathered from the Indies and other countries, and so yearely transported unto these costes'. Malynes was even more explicit:

> According to the plentie or scarcitie of the monie, then, generally things became dearer or good cheape, whereunto the great store or abundance of monie and bullion, which of late years is come from the west Indies into Christendom, hath made every thing dearer according to the increase of monie, which . . . hath caused a great alteration and inhauncing of the price of every thing.[14]

Population increase was only lightly touched upon as a cause of inflation, although much contemporary discussion assumed its importance, a writer of 1645, for example, speaking of food prices 'which rise still with the increase of people'.[15] Harvest failures, and the fitting-out of expeditions of war or privateering, were recognized as contributing to the price-rise through a decreased supply or an increased demand.

All these factors affected prices, although it is difficult to assess their order of importance. Silver reaching England from the New World was for a long while considered to be the prime cause. But how and when did it reach England, and in what proportions, and how long did it take to be coined? It seems likely that the upward swing of prices began before much could have come into circulation. The debasement, to which contemporaries attached so much importance, is similarly open to question, for the years of the great debasement fell between 1544 and 1551, and inflation was well on the way before this. Besides, so far as the computation can be made, prices did not increase in proportion to the reduction of silver in the silver coin, nor in proportion to the increase in face value of the coinage in circulation. Moreover, any of these arguments, based upon an increase of the circulating media, would need to take into account the increasing number of Bills of Exchange made necessary at a time of commercial and industrial expansion. The question is not whether, or to what extent, there was an increase in the various media of exchange but whether they increased disproportionately to total national production. And such a computation is exceedingly difficult to make.

There remains the population increase which began, so far as can be ascertained with any degree of certainty, about the same time as the price-rise. London, in particular, sustained a continuing and enormous expansion, and the rise in prices was often spoken of as being particularly severe in the neighbourhood of the capital. In the absence of a corresponding increase in productivity, the population rise could well have caused of itself a very substantial rise in prices. Since the population of the whole of Europe was increasing, and the price-rise was common to the whole continent, it is likely that the simple effect of a population pushing up demand was in a large way responsible for the rise. When to this is added the accumulation of the other factors each of which was partly responsible, at different times and in different ways, a tentative explanation is reached. To this must certainly be added the enormous gusto and exuberance of the age, in which there were not only more people, but more people doing more things, buying more, importing more, going to the theatre more, making more journeys, voyaging more, trading more, manufacturing more. Quite apart from there being more money in circulation, the

Inflation in Tudor and Stuart England[1]

The Index numbers represent the price of a composite unit of consumables in Southern England. An average of the years 1451–1475 = 100.

Year	*Index Number*	*Year*	*Index Number*
1510	103	1640	546
1560	265	1645	574
1580	342	1646	569
1590	396	1647	667
1595	515	1648	770
1597	685	1649	821
1598	579	1650	839
1599	474	1651	704
1600	459	1655	531
1605	448	1660	684
1610	503	1665	616
1615	561	1670	577
1620	485	1675	691
1625	534	1680	568
1630	595	1685	651
1635	597	1700	671

[1]From E. H. Phelps-Brown and Sheila V. Hopkins, 'Seven Centuries of the Prices of Consumables Compared with Builders' Wage Rates' in *Economica*, N.S. XXIII, Nov. 1956.

velocity of circulation was increasing enormously, with the effect of a constantly increasing pressure upon prices.

The price-rise made a heyday for the speculator, and many fortunes were also made from trade and agriculture, from industry and the law (for enterprise and land purchase breed litigation, as well as requiring the services of the law). People with flexible incomes gain most or lose least from rising prices, and landlords who could raise their rents and merchants and manufacturers who could raise their prices either made a profit or protected themselves from the worst effects of inflation—and in so doing sent up prices still further. Sometimes, indeed, even the clothiers fell foul of the economic situation, particularly those in the West Country, who repeatedly found their market collapsing, but generally it was the working-man, whose wages were not rising with prices, and all those who in a time of level prices might just have made ends meet, who were the greatest sufferers. The State attempted to help them, but this, and the trade vicissitudes which accompanied the inflation, is another story.[16]

Overseas trade, meantime, stimulated by and itself stimulating the price-rise, was developing in all directions. For centuries Britain had hung on the outskirts of the known world, her contacts, not only with the East but with much of Europe, being made largely through the merchants of other lands.[17] But it was inevitable that in time English merchants should themselves undertake some of the lucrative carrying and shipping trade. The Merchants of the Staple were quite early in a privileged position, with a monopoly of the wool export.[18] Other merchants, dealing in various commodities, began also to undertake their own shipments. At first these voyages were irregular, and many cargoes were lost. But the very perils of the situation, the risk of total loss as well as the prospect of considerable gain, induced some of these merchants to band themselves together, and the Company of Merchant Adventurers was formed. As their bold name suggests,[19] they did not confine themselves to one commodity or to one shipping route but 'adventured abroad', trading with much of northern Europe, the Rhineland, and the Baltic. They exported lead, tin, corn, beer and, above all, cloth, and their wealth and power expanded as the cloth industry grew. One commodity they did not touch was wool, which remained the monopoly of the Staplers, but as the wool export yielded to that of cloth, so the Merchant Adventurers ousted the Staplers and became the chief importers of a wide variety of goods—Rhenish wine and gunpowder from Germany, tapestry and linen from the Netherlands, spices and drugs from Portugal, silks and velvets from Italy, shipbuilding materials from the Baltic. Like the gilds, they won recognition from English monarchs, Henry VII confirming and enlarging their privileges in a charter of 1505 which, among other things, gave them the right to appoint a governor and twenty-four assistants to run the Company and its affairs.

In the middle of the sixteenth century, when the Crown determined to make the duty on the export of cloth compensate for the drop in the wool revenue, the Merchant Adventurers were made responsible for collecting the cloth taxes and their

European headquarters became the channel through which the cloth passed. This was a virtual bypassing of the Merchants of the Staple, yet the Staplers could not give to the Crown the immediate financial help which the Adventurers gave when they paid off the Government and Crown debts at their full value at a time when the English coinage was badly debased. A grateful Crown granted incorporation to the Adventurers in 1564, and confirmed their privileges in 1586.

The Merchants of the Hanse, who for three hundred years had dominated English foreign trade, also suffered in the interests of the Merchant Adventurers, their privileges being continually whittled down or suspended in the course of the sixteenth century. They appealed to James I, hoping that a new dynasty would help them, but James needed money no less urgently than the Tudors, and again confirmed the rights of the Adventurers. In 1611, when the Merchant Adventurers, who had been compelled to leave Antwerp at the coming of the Spanish in 1567, were invited to settle permanently in Hamburg, in the heart of Hanse territory, it was a body blow from which the Hansards never recovered. They retained the Steelyard residence in London, with a few fiscal immunities, but the League was a shadow of its former self. The Merchant Adventurers were masters of the field. The doom of the Venetian galleys had come with restrictions on the export of wool, their departure hastening the decline of Southampton and helping to establish the pre-eminence of London, whence the cloth fleets of the Adventurers sailed for the marts of Europe.

The Adventurers were still organized fundamentally as a craft gild: admission to the Company was by patrimony (through relationship with a member), by redemption (the payment of an entrance fee), or by apprenticeship for possibly eight years, and an indenture fee as high as £200 or £300. Their secretary at the beginning of the seventeenth century boasted that these apprentices were 'for the most part gentlemen's sons or men's children of good meanes or quality'; they were generally sent abroad 'to learne good fashions, and to gaine experience and knowledge in trade, and the maners of strange Nations, thereby the better to know the world betimes'.[20] By this time they were drawn from many different gilds and companies, and included Staplers who had changed from wool to the cloth-export business. Although, in the manner of the craft gilds, they continued to be based upon various English towns, the branches were loosely affiliated into a whole which elected its own officers. They were described by their secretary as consisting of

> a great number of wealthy and well-experimented merchants dwelling in divers great cities, maritime towns and other parts of the realm . . . linked and bound . . . together in company for the exercise of merchandise and sea-fare, trading in cloth, kersey, and all . . . commodities vendible abroad.[21]

The Company hired ships, or built its own, on which it assigned space to members, it controlled sailings so that one member could not steal a march upon another; it operated a stint, assigning to each merchant the quantity of goods he might ship; it aimed at keeping prices high and steady; it even guaranteed the quality of goods it sold; it directed trade, in order to control it, to certain mart towns; it operated a rigorous set of rules to govern the conduct of members and their operations. So important was this aspect of their organization that the Merchant Adventurers, and companies modelled on them, were known as 'regulated companies'. But, although so linked for commerce and protection, the members traded each on his own capital, responsible for his own gains or losses.

Yet monopolists are never widely loved. In the increasing ferment of trading activity that came with geographical expansion 'interlopers' and 'free traders' of all kinds—men belonging to no company, yet ready to 'adventure' with what capital they had, men anxious to form Companies outside the monopoly of the Merchant Adventurers—were beating at the door. To them the Adventurers were a fraternity of engrossers. In 1604 a Committee was appointed to consider the questions of monopoly and free trade. It sat for five days, hearing evidence from a wide variety of people, while outside the committee-room doors a great concourse of clothiers and merchants from all parts of the kingdom, bitterly divided between themselves, struggled to be heard. The Committee made its report to the House of Commons on 21st May, carefully marshalling the arguments on both sides, but coming down in favour of free trade and commenting that the Merchant Adventurers 'being the spring of all monopolies and engrossing the grand staple commodities of cloth into so few men's hands, deserves least favour'. The Report of the Committee on Free Trade was a remarkable anticipation of later political and economic writing, and was couched in language which Adam Smith himself would have approved: 'All free Subjects', it said,

> are born inheritable, as to their Land, so also to the free Exercise of their Industry . . . Merchandize being the chief and richest of all other, and of greater Extent and Importance than all the rest, it is against the natural Right and Liberty of the Subjects of England to restrain it into the hands of some few.[22]

The Merchant Adventurers kept their adversaries at bay, in spite of the Report, largely through their assistance to the Crown, but by the time of the Civil Wars later in the seventeenth century it seemed their end had come, along with the other monopolists castigated so scathingly by the Long Parliament. But Parliament and Protectorate, like Tudors and Stuarts, needed money, and the Merchant Adventurers, lending indifferently to one and the other, withstood the tumbling of the monopolists in return for £30 000 lent to the Long Parliament and a further loan to Cromwell, who renewed their Charter in 1656. They weathered the Restoration in return for more money, and it was not until 1689, in face of the continued expansion of trade and the continuing pressure of interlopers, that the cloth trade was thrown open to all. The Merchant Adventurers nevertheless continued to prosper and kept their European headquarters at Hamburg until 1807, when the French occupied the town in the course of the Napoleonic Wars and the Adventurers were forced to flee.

It was easy to cry out against the Adventurers' monopoly of England's chief export. But the Company performed certain services. The Merchant Adventurers themselves claimed that they advanced the art of navigation; they 'employed and bred up many worthy masters of ships and mariners, and built many tall, warlike and serviceable ships'. Their channelling of exports and imports prevented fraud in Customs; they were conscientious collectors of the taxes; they were in a position to give sound advice concerning English trade. By breaking the power of foreign merchants, particularly the Hansards, they did a service not only to themselves but to all concerned in English foreign trade. Through trade they strengthened diplomacy; they delayed the sailing of the Spanish Armada for a year under the guidance of the financier Sir Thomas Gresham, himself an Adventurer, by manipulating the foreign exchanges against Spain. More tangibly, they lent money to the Crown and raised loans for the State. Nor did they neglect to use their wealth in acts of 'piety and charity'. The charge levelled against them that they engrossed all trade to London was only partly true. The emphasis upon London occurred not only because it was the natural focus for many Merchant Adventurers, but because it was the capital and a good port, and on a naturally good sea route to Flanders and the mart towns of Antwerp and Hamburg. It could not be denied that it was better placed for the cloth-trade than, for example, Bristol or Southampton.[23] Nor could the Adventurers be accused of hindering the development of English shipping, which by 1629 had grown from the 50 000 tons of 1572 to 115 000 tons.

Yet the Merchant Adventurers' monopoly was being undermined in a number of ways before it was formally abolished. New companies in the sixteenth century were allowed to export cloth; the Eastland Company, in the Adventurers' own territory in the Baltic, also brought back the same shipbuilding materials. Above all, as trade expanded beyond Europe, embracing 'new' territories to the East and to the West, the Merchant Adventurers' ascendancy declined. They were a 'great old tree which hath borne good fruit, but now is mossy and too full of branches'.[24]

CHAPTER XVII

The New World

England stood somewhat outside the more spectacular geographical discoveries. Christopher Columbus was a Genoese, sailing under Spanish authority, when he touched the Bahamas in 1492 and later reached the shores of America. Central America, and most of South America, including Mexico and Peru, fell to the Spanish Conquistadores, all more anxious to bring home gold and silver from these fabulous lands than to build up trade. The Portuguese, however, were thinking in terms of trade, trying to find a way by sea round Africa that would break the Venetians' monopoly of trade from the East. Prince Henry the Navigator worked patiently for years, sending Portuguese vessels ever farther south down the uncharted coast of Africa, past Cape Bojador, the southernmost limit of territory then known to man, and on to new lengths of coast, until finally Bartholomew Diaz in 1487–8 rounded the Cape of Good Hope. Ten years later Vasco da Gama sailed right round the Cape and reached India. In another ten years the Portuguese had pushed on to Molucca and the East Indies, gaining control of the East Indian trade and supplanting Venice. This was sailing from west to east. In 1519 Magellan, a Portuguese but sailing in the Spanish service, followed the wake of Columbus, passed through the Straits which afterwards bore his name, and came to the Indies from the east across a calm ocean he called the Pacific. He was killed in a skirmish in the Philippines, storm and shipwreck destroyed his ships. Only the *Victoria* survived to reach home in 1522—the first ship to circumnavigate the world.

John and Sebastian Cabot, meanwhile, encouraged by Henry VII, had sailed from Bristol in 1497 and 1498, reaching North America at Cape Breton Island on the first voyage, and on the second touching Greenland, Newfoundland, and Nova Scotia. The English, like the Portuguese, also tried to reach India by a new route and embarked upon the famous and ill-fated quest for a North-West Passage. It was an incredibly daring enterprise, that three times met with disaster, but had the effect of opening up part of Russia to the explorers.

Although her share in the geographical discoveries was small, England was affected by them in many ways, and was one of the first to send settlers to the New World. The settlement of Virginia, named after Elizabeth, the Virgin Queen, was first attempted by Sir Walter Raleigh in 1584; settlers reached Bermuda and other West Indian islands shortly afterwards. In 1620 the Pilgrim Fathers left Plymouth in the *Mayflower*, intending to make for Virginia, but they landed farther north and founded the New England colonies instead. Maryland followed in 1634, Carolina in 1663, Pennsylvania in 1681.

The northern colonies were temperate and well-wooded, and the settlers applied themselves to agriculture and fishing, and to some forms of industry, becoming, in particular, expert shipbuilders and mariners. In the hot West Indian colonies sugar was cultivated in large plantations, with a little cotton and some indigo and tobacco. Indigo was valued as a blue dye, similar to the woad which for centuries had been one of England's most coveted imports. Sugar was known as a scarce luxury imported from the East, supplementing the honey which throughout the Middle Ages had been the chief form of sweetening. When it was seen that the sugar-cane would flourish in the southern parts of the New World all settlers, of whatever nationality, hastened to plant it. Soon large plantations in the West Indian islands were helping to feed the seemingly insatiable demand of Europe. Cotton was already known in the New World—gifts of the plant and woven cloth had been brought to the early explorers by the natives—but the crops were at first small. The time had not yet come for the full cotton harvest to be in demand.

In the southern mainland colony of Virginia tobacco was the chief crop, though here too sugar and a little cotton were grown. Columbus had seen natives rolling and smoking the leaves of this plant, and the habit was probably practised in England as early as the 1560s. It had become immensely popular, and Virginia built up a considerable prosperity on the cultivation and export of tobacco. There was some feeling, however, that the colonists should not be encouraged to rely on the cultivation of such a non-essential commodity, and James I had added his comments in characteristic fashion. The habit of smoking—'this precious stink'—was

> a custom loathsome to the eye, hateful to the nose, harmful to the brain, dangerous to the lungs, and in the black stinking fume thereof nearest resembling the horrible Stygian smoke of the pit that is bottomless.

'Is it not both great vanity and uncleanness', he wrote,

> that at table, a place of respect, of cleanliness, of modesty, men should not be ashamed to sit tossing of tobacco pipes, and puffing the smoke of tobacco one to another, making the filthy smoke and stink thereof to exhale athwart the dishes, and infect the air, when very often men that abhor it are at their repast? Surely smoke becomes a kitchen far better than a dining chamber, and yet it makes a kitchen also oftentimes in the inward parts of men, soiling and infecting them, with an unctious and oily kind of soot, as hath been found in some great tobacco takers, that after their death were opened.[1]

The main problem of the southern colonies and the West Indian islands was to find labour to work on the plantations—labour able to withstand long hours of work under a scorching sun. Their problem was solved by the use of Negro slaves from Africa. The use of Negro slaves in the colonies of European peoples was begun by Portugal in the sixteenth century. England joined the trade in 1562, when John Hawkins took his first cargo of slaves from the Gold Coast to sell to Spanish colonists in Central America. The trade was profitable. In 1663 the monopoly of the English trade in slaves was granted to the Company of Royal Adventurers of England trading with Africa, and a century later England was doing about half the total trade, with cargo space for nearly 50 000 slaves. It was a three-cornered trade between an English port—Liverpool, Bristol or London being the chief—the west coast of Africa, and one of the colonies. The miserable Africans were kidnapped, bought from unscrupulous slave-dealers, made over by a tribal chief as punishment for some misdeed, or simply got rid of in this way in the course of war and tribal feuds. In whatever way they were acquired, their plight was dreadful in the extreme. No one knew how many died in the closely packed bowels of the ships that took them to a strange land. No one cared whether families were kept together, or to whom the Negroes were sold: all that mattered was the price. Nor was there anyone to question the conditions of their lives when they became slaves to a white master. England's record in the slave trade remains a permanent stain, but she made some amends by leading the movement for the abolition of slavery. It was a long, hard fight, in which the colonists saw themselves ruined, and it was not until the nineteenth century that first the slave trade, and then slavery itself, was abolished throughout the British Empire.

The new map of the world that took shape with the geographical discoveries put England more firmly on the trade routes than before, and her shipping, her commerce and her mariners responded to the new opportunities. Her sea-dogs met and frequently overcame the Spaniards, now hated as rivals in religion as well as trade, and captured treasure swelled the chests of Elizabeth and her pirate adventurers; one of them, Francis Drake, sailed round the world in two and a half years between 1577 and 1580—the first Englishman to do so. The climax came with the defeat of the Spanish Armada in 1588. When the remnant of that mighty fleet crawled, crippled, back to Spanish waters it was obvious that England, in spite of a late start, had emerged triumphant. The issue was not quite so simple as that of trade versus plunder, but there was a moral in the fact that Spain had simply taken treasure from South America while England was settling the West and trading with the East.

To do so under her own resources had become increasingly necessary when the Portuguese had fallen under the power of Spain, who had annexed their Empire to its own. When the power of Spain declined, weighed down by the illusory power of her treasure, England's opportunity was there. But she was not quite quick enough. Holland was the first to get a footing in Ceylon and the East Indian islands, though England was the first to obtain concessions in India. The Dutch had for centuries been hardy navigators, rivals to the British in the Baltic, on the fishing banks, and in North America. When they also met as rivals in the Far East it was apparent that the Spanish-English enmity would be succeeded by a Dutch-English struggle.

By the time the Merchant Adventurers had lost their monopoly, merchants as a whole had become very conscious of the risk run by individual traders, particularly when they adventured to distant lands in the teeth of hostile rivals. The cost of financing an enterprise, also, was often more than an individual could bear. At the same time, in attempting to strike a bargain in unfamiliar surroundings with strange people the individual trader could well be at a disadvantage. Joint ventures in difficult times had not been unknown, so the principle of joint stock was not entirely new. At first merchants would join together for the duration of a single voyage, like the 240 who in 1553 took shares of £25 each for trading into the White Sea and Russia. This they called the Russia, or Muscovy, Company. In 1581 the Levant Company, trading to Turkey and the East, was also joint-stock, the Queen contributing £40 000 to the venture.

Skirmishes with the Dutch in the East, in the course of which the Dutch got the monopoly of pepper and raised its price, induced a group of English merchants to form another company to carry on trade direct with India. They met together in 1599 and decided 'that a trade so far remote cannot be managed but by a joint and united stock', the merchants contributed £30 000, and petitioned Queen Elizabeth for permission to form a joint-stock East India Company with licence to transport foreign coin, and freedom from Customs and subsidy on exports for six voyages. The Queen granted the charter on 31st December 1600 to 'certain adventurers for the discovery of the trade for the East Indies . . . which heretofore this realm hath been supplied with at the hands of strangers'. The Company was to be a monopoly, being 'the whole, entire and only trade' to and from the East Indies. All other subjects were forbidden 'directly or indirectly' to 'visit, haunt, frequent or trade, traffic or adventure by way of merchandise into or from any of the East Indies' except by permission of the Company. The Company was licensed to carry out of the country the sum of £30 000 provided a similar amount was returned after each voyage.

The East India Company was given the right of internal self-government, with a Governor, deputy Governor and twenty-four assistants; there were 218 members, coming from many trades and callings and including members of the Levant and

Russia Companies. Membership depended upon the purchase of at least one share and the payment of an admission fee. As well as business, matters of health and religion—'for that religious government doth best bind men to perform their duties'—were supervised by the governors, and they were given power to make 'reasonable' laws to exercise their authority. Sailors 'for the better advancement' of their salaries were credited with shares in the enterprise equivalent to two months' wages. The principle of joint stock was at first confined to each voyage, but obvious advantages lay in a permanent joint stock, and this was created in 1657.

Trading with India and the East Indies raised many difficulties. In the first place, it was not at all clear what England could offer in return for the commodities she took. Woollen cloth was pressed, but not unnaturally had a small sale, and the Company complained that it was eaten by moths and white ants. Lead and tin were taken by the East in small quantities only. The Romans had faced the same problem, and the spices and silks of the East had, indeed, seldom been exchanged for anything but treasure. The East India Company's charter permitted them to solve the problem in the same way, and the bullion which they exported formed the basis of the India trade. When this was held against the Company their reply was that they brought back in goods, many of which were re-exported, far more than they took out.

The East India Company won concessions from Indian rulers and established trading factories in India at Surat, Madras, Calcutta and Bombay. It even pushed out to Persia in one direction and China and Japan in the other. Its profitability so delighted James I that in 1609 he renewed its charter 'for ever'. However, like the Merchant Adventurers, having friends in every camp, the Company took the precaution of having it renewed by Cromwell also. By 1614 it possessed twenty-four ships, and the armed East Indiaman became a feature of the trade.

The Dutch formed an East India Company less than two years after the English, and their rivalry dominated the Eastern trade for most of the seventeenth century. From the three naval wars between the two countries England emerged victorious, although not decisively so. Trade with the East expanded, there was room for both nations, and by the eighteenth century the Dutch were masters of the East Indies, while England was firmly established in India. Here she found herself in conflict with another European rival—France, who established an East India Company in 1664.

The Anglo-French conflict, like the Anglo-Dutch, spread over the West and the East, to North America as well as to India. Unlike the Dutch wars, however, the French wars were fought mainly on land, embracing Europe, North America and India. France was brought down in Europe in 1713 by a coalition of nations that feared the ambitions of Louis XIV; by 1763 the British had beaten her in a struggle for the settlement of what became Canada; in the same year the British stood victorious over France in India, and the British East India Company was left in control of a large part of the Indian subcontinent. Britain was also reaching out to other continents and islands to the east and to the west, in particular to New Zealand and Australia, partly surveyed by Captain Cook in 1769. Although the American colonies would break away and secure their independence in 1776, Britain's trade increased, her power grew and the foundations of her Empire were firmly laid.

The motive behind the struggle is vividly expressed by the trade figures, the £4·6 millions of 1622 being £24·5 million in 1760—a more than fivefold increase. Exports over the same period grew from about £2·5 million to some £14·7 million, of which £3·7 million were re-exports; imports grew from about £2·1 million to around £9·8 million over the same period; exports had increased more than six times (or five times if re-exports are excluded), while imports more than quadrupled.[2]

This expansion of England's trade had also changed it. Henry Belasyse, describing in 1657 England's economic enterprise, was able to say

> The cheife and first is cloth, which maketh all Europe almost England's servant and weare our livery. The next is our tinn or pewter, which is excellent in Cornwall . . . Leather is excellent in England, and of great asteeme abroad . . . Stockings belong to shooes and our worsted stockings are in great request all Europe over . . . Coales is another great necessary commodity which Smiths at least cannot be without, and as men are shodd with our leather, so horses by our iron and coales. For even iron too which locks up all other treasure, comes out of England.[3]

In 1657 when Belasyse wrote woollen manufactures constituted about 80 per cent of total exports. In 1697 they were about half,

English overseas trade immediately before the Industrial Revolution in £1 000[1]

Year	*Total Trade*	*Imports*	*Exports*	*Re-exports*
1697	6 735	3 344	2 295	1 096
1760	24 528	9 833	10 981	3 714

Chief exports from England (official values) immediately before the Industrial Revolution,[1] *showing how the pattern was already changing*[2]

	1697	*1760*
Coal	£33 000	£136 000
Iron and Steel	£98 000	£539 000
Non-ferrous and manufactured	£171 000	£499 000
Woollen goods	£1 481 000	£5 453 000
Cotton goods	£11 000	£167 000

[1]From B. R. Mitchell and Phyllis Deane, *Abstract of British Historical Statistics*, Overseas Trade 1, p. 279, and Overseas Trade 5, pp. 293–4.

Values of most important East India imports, yearly averages, in £000[2]

	1699–1701	1722–24	1752–54	1772–74
Pepper	103	17	31	33
Drugs	14	8	45	40
Tea	8	116	334	848
Coffee	9	123	50	22
Calicoes	367	437	401	697
Silks and mixtures	107	146	96	76
Raw Silk	42	50	94	156
Grand Total of ALL	756	966	1,086	1,929

[2]From Ralph Davis, 'English Foreign Trade, 1700–74', in *Economic History Review*, 2nd ser., XV (1962).

in 1760 they comprised not much more than a third. Other manufactured goods accounted then for some 20 per cent of exports and still included leather goods, tin and copper ware (though the pewter export was diminished) and particularly a growing quantity of the small metal ware of Birmingham and the Midlands. The heavy raw material exports had not yet reached the peak they would attain later and accounted for only about 5 per cent of total exports. Of these, coal exports had shown the most conspicuous growth, nearly trebling between 1660 and 1760, though constituting at the later date still only 1·5 per cent in value of total exports. Tin and lead together accounted at the same period for about 5 or 6 per cent of exports, and iron for about 8 per cent.

Most of the rest of the export trade in 1760 consisted of re-exports. The development of the re-export trade—from the West and from the East through England to Europe—was, indeed, one of the most remarkable and one of the most profitable developments in the English trading pattern between the middle of the seventeenth century, when re-exports constituted about 3 or 4 per cent of total exports, and the beginning of the eighteenth century when they amounted to about 30 per cent—which was not so much less than the 47 per cent of manufactured woollen goods which were exported at that time. These re-exports comprised both the valued old commodities of the East—spices such as cloves, mace and particularly pepper, of which four-fifths of the English export was exported to Europe; calicoes, of which two-thirds were re-exported; and increasing quantities of coffee and tea. From America and West Indian plantations came sugar, of which about a third was re-exported, tobacco, of which two-thirds were re-exported, rum, and a little raw cotton.[4]

While re-exports to Europe grew, the greatest growth in exports was to non-European countries, which by the middle of the eighteenth century took about 20 per cent of the whole. At that time some 17 per cent of the woollen textiles, and 73 per cent of the manufactures exported, went outside Europe.[5] The American Plantations took in particular large quantities of cutlery, glassware, iron, copper and brassware of all kinds, domestic and other. They as yet could offer no competition in the manufacture of such commodities, and it was part of England's policy to keep them from doing so.[6] Even in the East the story was the same, while the African continent, paying largely in slaves, imported small metal wares from the English Midlands.

Imports naturally reflected the changed export pattern. In 1760 England still took from Northern Europe some of the old staples—shipbuilding materials, including timber, flax, hemp, iron and steel, skins and furs; hops from Germany, wines and fruit from Southern Europe. But by 1700 the change had been apparent, in that 32 per cent of her imports came from non-European sources, and by the middle of the century nearly half came from outside Europe. These imports consisted of the spices, coffee, tea, calicoes, rum, sugar and tobacco, a great deal of which was required for re-export. But enough was retained to alter English habits considerably. The import of tobacco, for example, which was a mere 20 000 lb in 1619, was 1 000 000 lb in 1630, and 22 000 000 lb at the end of the century. Allowing for the two-thirds re-exported, this still left more than 7 000 000 lb for home consumption. The sugar import, negligible before the Civil Wars, was some 150 000 cwt in 1670, and over 370 000 cwt at the end of the century. Allowing for a re-export of about one-third, this left about 250 000 cwt to meet the increasing demand for sweetness.[7] What was probably an under-sweet diet in the days when sweetness came primarily from fruits and honey now put an over-emphasis upon sweetening. Coffee-drinking, a more or less middle-class pursuit which began in the middle of the seventeenth century, reached its peak in the middle of the eighteenth, and thereafter yielded in general popularity to tea. Tea had been a novelty to Pepys: 'I did send for a cup of tee (a China drink) of which I never had drank before', he noted in his diary for 25th September 1660. Its import increased some 120 times between 1700 and 1750 as tea-drinking reached all sections of the community—encouraged by the production of earthenware teapots and earthenware tea-cups.

Saltpetre, indigo for dyeing, wines, calicoes, silks, rice, fish from the Newfoundland fisheries, a little raw cotton (soon to grow to a mountain) swelled a large and diversified import trade. Official trade figures had to be supplemented, as in previous epochs, by smuggling. Import duties and taxes were inordinately high, and the profits from illicit trading proportionately attractive. Cargoes that were light in weight and bulk compared to their price, like rum and tea, were particularly lucrative. Smuggling probably reached its height in the course of the American War of Independence, when it is estimated that, with the connivance of large numbers of the local population, the smuggled entry amounted to £2 or £3 million a year or 25 per cent of the total legal imports.[8]

For the longer hauls West and East bigger vessels were required. For the Western trade, particularly when cotton and sugar came in large quantities, size was very important. In the Eastern trade, though cargoes were mainly not bulky, the splendid East Indiaman continued to hold sway. The total of English-owned merchant shipping grew from probably 50 000 tons in 1572 to 115 000 in 1629, 230 000 in 1686 and about 420 000 tons in 1751.[9] Dock-building and the continued improvement of ports was a necessary accompaniment. Not only the profits of trade itself, but the shipping charges, the port dues, the handling charges, the insurance—all swept money liberally into the pockets of the mercantile interest.

Of all the ports which benefited from the growth of foreign trade, London gained most of all. Apart from the monopoly of the woollen cloth export, it had already been accused in the sixteenth century of engrossing the trade of the whole kingdom. According to Defoe in the seventeenth century, it 'sucked the vitals of trade in this island to itself'. In 1700 London handled four-fifths of the nation's imports, 70 per cent of its exports and 86 per cent of re-exports. It was also calling upon a wide hinterland to satisfy its demands for food and other consumption goods, and for the raw materials of its industry. By the seventeenth century London was importing corn from the Midlands and from Kent, and in times of scarcity looked much farther afield; she took cheese and butter from Essex and Suffolk, from Norfolk and Lincolnshire, from as far north as Durham and Northumberland; eggs and poultry came from Bedfordshire and Northamptonshire, mutton from Gloucestershire and Northamptonshire, beef from the Midlands. The London tanner, who formerly had looked to the Weald for his bark and to London itself for his hides, now collected his bark from Sussex and Hampshire and sought his hides in the eastern counties, and even farther away.

Of other towns, Bristol had remained a thriving city through the Middle Ages. Sturmy and other merchants sailed from her port, the Merchant Adventurers showered on the City evidence of their wealth in their houses, their benefactions, their institutions. By the early sixteenth century she was declining, with much of the trade of her hinterland directed to London, but the sailing of the Cabots and the export of Mendip lead prevented her complete destitution, and as the New World opened up Bristol, geographically well placed, regained much of her lost trade and past prosperity. In 1760 she was next to London in size, although with a population of 60 000 she fell in that respect far behind the capital. York, which at the time of the Black Death had been the second city in the kingdom, was declining economically by the seventeenth century, partly because the larger ships now in use could not get upstream to the city, partly because the wool trade was moving westward into the West Riding. She did, however, continue to participate in the Baltic trade, her exports including herrings and some of the West Riding cloth. She also remained an important centre of communications; she was on the coaching route between north and south, and was a popular and fashionable town on the eve of the Industrial Revolution, even if no longer economically one of the most important.

Southampton, whose prosperity was bound up with Venetian galleys, Portuguese carracks and Gascon wine, declined at the end of the sixteenth century as trade swung more to English vessels and to the port of London. She did not really revive until the nineteenth century. Another town, Exeter, almost unknown nationally at the time of the Black Death, was the third port in size and importance by the end of the seventeenth century, and the fifth in size of all towns. Her prosperity was associated with the dyeing and finishing and subsequent export of serges which were spun and woven in her hinterland from the fleece of the local sheep which, though formerly considered too coarse for export, was now eminently suited to the serges which improved technique had made popular. Celia Fiennes in 1698 was amazed at the 'incredible quantity' of serges made and sold.[10] Defoe in the first quarter of the following century, when the commercial prosperity of the town was at its height, was similarly impressed by the Exeter serge market.[11] Newcastle grew prodigiously on the coal trade, both coastwise and overseas, from the sixteenth century onward. Norwich, continuing the skill in cloth-making which the Low Country immigrants had taught her, remained one of the chief cloth towns for home consumption and for export, reaching the height of her prosperity in the eighteenth century, when she ranked third in size, coming only after London and Bristol.

CHAPTER XVIII

Money, Exchange and Banking

The machinery of exchange that sufficed for simple transactions was inadequate for the more complicated production and exchange that had developed. The institution of joint stock[1] met one aspect of the problem, but there were others, in a way more fundamental, that concerned money, currency and exchange, and involved questions of time, risk and reward. As enterprises became larger more capital was required, and the gap between production and sale became longer. Questions of sinking capital to buy a machine or to improve a piece of land, of running capital to pay for raw materials or wages, posed their own problems, the one requiring investment, the other a supply of money regularly available. Similarly, even with joint stock, money had to be found to invest in a trading venture and commitments had to be met while awaiting the outcome. It became increasingly necessary to plan for the future, to pledge money in advance, to hold it on call, to pass it simply and easily from one person to another. But first it was necessary to come to grips with the medium of exchange, with money itself.

The total amount of money throughout the Middle Ages was small. There were no banknotes, no cheques, coins were normally made of silver refined from the lead of English mines[2] or imported for the purpose and sometimes mixed with a little alloy. Gold was used only occasionally. The actual minting of coins was the jealously guarded prerogative of medieval rulers, who granted the right to others only as a concession, town charters, for example, nearly always including the right to a mint. In the thirteenth century there were as many as fifty or sixty recognized mints in different parts of the country, but by the end of the sixteenth century most local minting had come to an end.

In spite of the proliferation of mints, it was the silver penny, coined at the end of the eighth century by the royal mint of Offa, King of Mercia, which throughout the Middle Ages remained the coin most commonly used and most highly prized abroad as well as at home. Smaller denominations were made by breaking or cutting the coin into halves and quarters.

By the end of the thirteenth century not only silver pennies but silver halfpennies, farthings, groats (worth about fourpence) and half-groats had been coined. Gold was first used successfully in the time of Edward III, in the middle of the fourteenth century, for the florin and the noble—the latter bearing a ship, and intended particularly for foreign trade. A handsome golden sovereign 1·6 inches in diameter, and so called because it bore a picture of the monarch, was minted in 1489 by Henry VII. A silver shilling appeared in 1548, half- and quarter-shillings, shortly afterwards. By the end of the Tudor period there were also gold and silver crowns and silver half-crowns. A golden guinea was coined in the time of Charles I, being so named because the gold of which it was made came from the Guinea coast of Africa. In spite of this considerable variety, the quantity of coin in circulation had been supplemented by many heavy leaden tokens. These clumsy and inconvenient objects were superseded in 1640 by the minting of a copper coinage. But silver remained the fundamental measure until the eighteenth century, when gold took over and the silver coinage dwindled.

Periodic overhaul of the currency was necessary, partly because coins wear out, partly because of the constant debasement that occurred and partly for the simple reason that the quantity of precious metal available in the Middle Ages did not keep up with the growing demand for money. Various recoinages increased the quantity of money struck from the same amount of precious metal by decreasing its intrinsic value, either through lightening its weight or by mixing it with alloy. Such recoinage, not increasing the amount of money in circulation beyond the increase of goods and services available, did no harm to the currency, nor did it result in a serious rise in prices. Nor should it be confused with the activities of forgers who were clipping metal from the more valuable coins and reminting others with a larger admixture of alloy, thus giving themselves considerable gain. Rulers on the whole protected their coinage, but in times of difficulty it was tempting for them also to resort to debasement. This was the case with Henry VIII. Putting debased coin on the market in excess of what the economy required at a time when the silver recently released from the monasteries was also getting into circulation, the King stimulated an all-round rise in prices in which he himself was the chief, albeit but temporary, gainer.[3] It was a time when forgers also flourished. A big recoinage was carried through in 1560–1 to get rid of the debased, clipped and mutilated coins which were distorting the market, silver from the New World being used for the purpose. A century later the country was again faced with the same phenomenon—clipped and bad money, money of varying weight and thickness. People found it necessary, so it was said in 1695, to settle the price of the very money they were to receive for their goods before they could price the goods themselves. In 1696–8 another recoinage was effected.

But, even when sound, the coinage alone was quite inadequate to carry the needs of the commercial world: the total amount of money remained small; the counting out of coin was cumbersome in the extreme, and merchants spent long hours in their counting-houses engaged on this exercise alone. First to supplement coin and bullion were the Bills of Exchange which had developed largely from the sales of English wool.[4] But buyers might be unable to meet their obligations at the time promised in the Bill; or sellers might be in urgent need of ready cash before a settlement took place. Intermediate lending might then occur, a loan being made on the security of the Bill: before the implications of these developments could be worked out, however, the divisive question of usury had to be resolved.

The lending of money very early came under discussion. In lending itself there was nothing new. Among the small peasant proprietors and open-field workers of the Middle Ages borrowing and lending had been an accepted part of the yearly round: 'In a world where seasons are uncertain and six months intervene between sowing and harvest, the need of advances was not the invention of man'.[5] Ecclesiastical and secular pronouncements, legislation, cases brought before local courts for non-payment of debts are ample evidence of the prevalence of the habit. But the question remained: could money, should money, ever be lent for interest? Two Church Synods in 787 forbade interest or usury, Edward the Confessor did likewise, but it was accepted by William the Conqueror, and there settled in England about the time of the Conquest many Jews who already were established in Europe as merchants, traders, money-changers and money-lenders. They dealt in the currencies of many countries, and it was probably they who introduced the Bills of Exchange which became so common. It was not this, it was their role as lenders of money for interest upon which contemporary attention was focused. In the early Middle Ages they lent on a wide scale, often upon the security of landed estates. In this way they not only became wealthy but often became big landowners as well, when they foreclosed upon the estates of a defaulting debtor. They were probably at their most powerful in England in the twelfth century. All foreigners were disliked, often persecuted, sometimes massacred, and the Jews called down upon themselves more venom than most. There were repeated pogroms, often sparked off by some story of excessive greed. Though occasionally they lived upon the landed estates they had acquired, it was usual to find them in the Jewries of English towns, where they lived a life apart. A Jew known to lend money at interest was forced to wear a plate upon his breast proclaiming himself an usurer, or else depart the country. Finally, in 1290, all were compelled to leave, and were not allowed back until the time of Cromwell, when, unofficially, they were again allowed to settle.

After the Jews, the role of money-lender and dealer was taken over by the Italians, principally by those merchants known as Lombards who came from the prosperous towns of northern Italy. They were familiar figures as dealers in English wool and tax-gatherers for the Pope. Besides lending money at interest, they undertook certain rudimentary banking functions, like remitting money to their own country, making out or discounting Bills of Exchange, and holding money for customers—all at high interest. They were also pawnbrokers, and introduced the sign of the three golden balls to indicate where goods could be pawned for money. It is said that the rooms where these goods lay in pawn were known as Lombards' rooms—which in course of time became lumber rooms. The great days of the Lombards were in the thirteenth and fourteenth centuries, when they gave their name to a London street and to various banks whose descendants still exist as Lombard banking houses. Thereafter their fortunes declined, and they were banished the country by

Elizabeth I.

The Church, meantime, continued to believe that economic conduct, like all conduct, was subject to the moral law and should be judged by moral standards: on the whole, lending to relieve necessity was Christian duty that looked for no reward. In line with this doctrine was the opinion that regarded money and the act of lending money as 'barren'. Trade was necessary to exchange, and mutual gain resulted; producers of goods, landowners who worked their land, enriched society in many ways. These were 'honourable callings', producing 'natural riches', for which a reward expressed in money was just. But those who dealt only in money were dealing with a mere instrument. In contrast to trade and production, theirs was but 'artificial wealth', they added nothing, and could therefore receive no reward. Right through the Middle Ages and into the Tudor period laws and ordinances against the taking of usury testify to the strength of these beliefs. But, as society became more complex, it was also recognized that the lending of money for commercial purposes was different from lending to relieve necessity, and might merit a controlled reward. That the situation in a commercial centre could be very difficult is demonstrated by the special tribunal formed by the City of London in the fourteenth century to consider the merits of cases where interest was asked for.

It was commonly considered that the Reformation and Protestantism in general were responsible for a change in the Christian view of usury. Protestantism, of its very nature, was more able than the Catholic Church to divorce religious ethics from business transactions; indeed, it 'grew to a proverb that usury was the brat of heresy'.[6] Theory, however, was most effectively undermined by the developing economic system itself, which was insatiable for ever more capital. As Francis Bacon said, trading with borrowed capital was so universal that if the lenders called in their money the trade of the country would be at a standstill.[7] And call it in they would if they received no return for risking their savings. This was more than 'tiding over': it was putting money at risk for the benefit of the borrower, and it was but equitable that the lender should partake of the gain. Lending to an improving landowner or to an industrialist setting up a small workshop or factory was similar in principle. But whether, or at what rate, the needy gentleman, borrowing in order to continue his life of conspicuous waste, was to be charged interest on his folly was not always considered as a separate question.

At the end of the fifteenth century legislation began to adapt itself to the new situation. The strict law against usury of 1487 was repealed in 1495, and although usury was still condemned, it was allowed in certain circumstances. In 1545 the taking of interest was fixed at 10 per cent. There was a fresh attempt at prohibition in 1552, but the legality of usury was recognized anew shortly afterwards, and by the seventeenth century it was merely a case of producing fresh justification for what was already permitted. The seventeenth-century lawyer John Selden asserted: 'Tis a vain thing to say money begets not money, for that no doubt it does'.[8] Only money locked up was unproductive; 'to receive profit from the loan of money is as equitable and lawful as receiving rent for land', declared John Locke.[9] Borrowing and lending had indeed become so widespread, and the lenders so fully aware of the value of their lending, that the only questions were: at what rate should interest be fixed, and should the State enforce it? In 1624 a limit of 8 per cent was laid down. It was reduced to 6 per cent in 1651, and to 5 per cent in 1713. Sir Josiah Child advocated a reduction to 4 per cent on the model of the Dutch, who kept their interest rates low and were undeniably the most prosperous nation in Europe. But it was Misselden, not only in the title of his book but in the sentiments he uttered, who in 1622 ushered in the economic doctrines of the age to come: 'As it is the scarcity of money that maketh the high rates of interest', he wrote in *Free Trade*, 'so the plenty of money will make the rates low better than any statute for that purpose'.

Meanwhile the role of moneyer devolved increasingly upon the native scriveners and goldsmiths. The scriveners were, perhaps, the first to become important in commercial affairs, drawing up bills of exchange and bonds, acting as intermediaries between borrowers and lenders, occasionally taking money for safe-keeping or on promise of a 'return' or interest. But if the scriveners' experience in drawing up legal documents made them important in one way, the goldsmiths' association with the precious metals made them important in another. After the Lombards left it was in fact the goldsmiths who became increasingly important as bankers. They kept supplies of foreign money, 'culled' and weighed English coins and by the sixteenth century, with their familiarity with the precious metals, their strong-rooms and strong-boxes, they were becoming the main repositories of money and valuables. In the troubled times of the seventeenth century, when no institution was invulnerable and no private dwelling appeared safe, the strong-rooms of the goldsmiths were closed protectingly on many a family fortune.

It was natural that in less troubled times the goldsmiths should not leave this money lying idle, but should lend it on security. The changing climate of opinion that legalized usury encouraged them to lend at interest, sometimes as a straight loan, sometimes in the form of discounting bills of exchange. During the Interregnum they were said to be supplying Cromwell's wants 'upon great advantages', and merchants, landowners and later the Crown became indebted to them. The practice of lending became so profitable that, so far from charging a fee for looking after people's money, the goldsmiths were paying to have it left with them, offering as much as 6 per cent interest to depositors. There was no shortage of takers; on the contrary, there was competition to invest. Most men, wrote Sir Josiah Child, 'as soon as they can make up a sum of £50 or £100 send it in to the goldsmith'.[10]

The goldsmiths' activities increased the velocity of exchange by putting into circulation money which would otherwise have been idle. They also added to the actual means of exchange. Hitherto money, in the form of coin and bills of exchange, had been the chief, if not the only, circulating media. Now the goldsmiths issued not only receipts for the money deposited with them but 'notes' or promises to pay based upon these receipts. The notes were not addressed to a particular person, and could therefore change hands freely, thus becoming the first banknotes. Another convenient form of payment developed when the depositor addressed a request to the goldsmith to pay a certain sum to a person named: this was the origin of the banker's cheque. Thus the goldsmiths developed into modern banking and discount houses, performing the chief functions of the modern bank—deposit, discount, note-issue, investment, payment and loan.

There were criticisms of the goldsmiths: they lent money at exorbitant rates, they provided inadequate security to depositors, they even clipped or debased the coin that passed through their hands, they paid more regard to their own profit than their customers' money. There was some truth in this—goldsmith bankers certainly amassed fortunes—but the crash, when it came, was not altogether their fault. The sequence of events concerned the Crown closely. When Charles II succeeded to the throne in 1660 there were many debts to meet, ranging from his own personal extravagances to back pay for Commonwealth soldiers. Extra Parliamentary sources of revenue had been stopped in the course of the Civil Wars, but Parliament immediately voted supplies. These, however, took time for collection, and the need was urgent. Where should the King turn but to the goldsmiths who already had been supplying Cromwell? They were willing enough to lend upon the security of the taxes to come, and at a rate of interest at first mentioned as 8 per cent but later left to the King's bounty.

At first all went well, and the King came again and again to the goldsmiths. As he did so, the revenues anticipated as security became more and more distant, and the goldsmiths' charges went up and up to 10, 20, 30 per cent. Pepys thought it 'a most horrid shame' that in 1663 goldsmiths were getting 15 or 20 per cent and making £10 000 a year out of the King's extremities. The goldsmiths began to be resented, not only for the high rate of interest they were charging but also because of their harshness in collecting the taxes they farmed. These feelings may have helped the panic withdrawals that took place at the first sign of crisis. The first run on the banks was in June 1667, when, while peace negotiations were dragging on with the Dutch, de Ruyter coolly sailed into the Medway virtually unopposed, burnt several ships and towed away the largest English vessel of the fleet. Charles induced a temporary calm by proclaiming that all payments from the Exchequer would be made as usual. But when he himself on 2nd January 1672 issued an order suspending such payments for a period of twelve months there was panic indeed among all those who had deposited with the goldsmiths and whose money therefore was at loan to the King on a non-existent security.

About £1 300 000 was owing to about ten goldsmiths, and perhaps some 10 000 people in all were affected when the goldsmiths in their turn suspended payments. Bills of Exchange were dishonoured, merchants declared themselves bankrupt, trade received a severe setback, private citizens were ruined. 'The common faith of a nation violated', wrote a contemporary.[11] 'The credit of this bank being broken did exceedingly discontent the people, and never did his majesty's affairs prosper to any purpose after it', wrote Evelyn in his diary. The King agreed to assign the income from the hereditary excise to meet the debt, and interest at 6 per cent was paid for a few years, but that was all.

In spite of their failure, the goldsmith banks had shown the way. Now, on all sides, and for diverse reasons, the idea of a national bank was taken up, on the lines of national banks at Venice, Genoa and, most importantly, at Amsterdam. The idea gained ground of a paper currency which a national bank could agree to underwrite; one writer (probably thinking of the goldsmiths' 30 per cent) even proclaiming that a national bank would yield so much profit that all taxation could be abolished. Matters became urgent with the outbreak of war with France in 1688, but it was another six years before a scheme was really taken seriously. Then the proposals of a Scotsman, William Paterson, with the close support of a merchant named Michael Godfrey, began to bear fruit.

As finally worked out with the Treasury, £1 200 000 was to be lent to the Government in return for an annual interest of £100 000—which was a rate of 8 per cent, together with £4 000 for expenses of management. The money was raised by public subscription in only ten days in June 1694, and on 27th July the bank's charter of incorporation as the first English joint-stock bank was granted. It was to have the privileges of a bank for twelve years, after which the Government reserved the right to annul the charter on one year's notice. The real genius of the enterprise was that the loan to the Government was not the actual £1·2 million subscribed, but was in the form of bills or notes bearing the Bank of England's promise to pay. In this way the Bank kept both its capital and its interest, and the issue of paper money became indeed one of its prime functions—'to furnish the kingdom with an imaginary coin to serve the uses of that which is really so', as a pamphlet of 1697 expressed it. Paper money had many advantages. It was easy to transport and to count, and, if backed by unimpeachable authority, would retain its value permanently—unlike coin, which could be clipped or otherwise debased. In issuing paper money the Bank had always to determine, as indeed the goldsmith bankers had done before them, that it had sufficient currency backing to meet demand if the notes were presented for payment. The Bank of England made mistakes in this respect, there were over-issues, but not until the Bank Charter Act of 1844 were the limits of note-issue firmly prescribed.

Besides issuing paper money, the Bank of England discounted bills, it bought and sold bullion, it made payments on behalf of its depositors, it advanced money upon security. It did not at first have a monopoly, though this was conferred for all practical purposes by the two Acts of 1697 and 1709. Nor did it have branches in the provinces. Provincial merchants continued to make their own arrangements for the transaction of business, many transferring their cash to the safety of the Bank in London. In these affairs one bank would probably act as agent for others, and so what was virtually a country banking business came into operation. The origins of some of the country banks speak for themselves: Smith, a mercer, started the Nottingham bank; Coutts, a corn-dealer, started an Edinburgh bank; Gurney, a worsted manufacturer, started the Norwich bank; an ironmaster in Birmingham, a bookseller in Bristol started banks. These had none of the primary banking functions of the Bank of England, but they eased the wheels of commerce, their numbers grew, and by the end of the eighteenth century they were recognizably the banks we now know.

The age was one of speculation, in both senses of the word. The project which led to the foundation of the Bank of England was but the beginning of an avalanche of schemes which brought with them a flood of monetary speculation and engulfed hundreds of thousands of people. Daniel Defoe called it the Projecting Age. Some of the schemes were good; others, in the words of Defoe, were 'a mere nothing', blown up until the projector had made the maximum profit and taken himself off, whereupon they collapsed. Among the more genuine, as well as interesting because it foreshadowed the ideas of Robert Owen, was the bank of credit. Merchants deposited goods with the bank, on the security of which they were allowed bills of credit to the extent of two-thirds or three-quarters of the market value of the goods, and on which they paid 6 per cent interest. It was thought that by thus 'raising a credit on their own dead stock' manufacturers and others would practise a little self-help and get the wheels of commerce turning. The idea seemed good, but the actual project lasted for only a few months of 1696. There was also a land bank, which had a brief spell of life in 1696 and foreshadowed the ideas of some of the Chartists, a lottery loan, a tontine (a form of annuity) and many more.

At the centre of the speculative orgy was the South Sea Company. This Company was incorporated as a joint-stock company by an Act of Parliament of 1710 which gave it the monopoly of English trade to South America and other lands in the South Seas which the Spaniards were endeavouring to preserve for themselves. The terms by which the Company received this privilege took some time to work out, but the chance to break the Spanish monopoly was welcomed, and stimulated an enormous interest in the South Seas generally. While negotiations were still in progress excitement was rising and £100 worth of stock was already selling for £126 in 1719. When in April 1720 the South Sea Company Act was passed by which the Company agreed to take over a large part of the national debt (on which it would receive an interest of 5 per cent, decreasing to 4 per cent after seven years) as the price of its monopoly, mania started in earnest. £100 shares jumped to £310—to £500—to £890—and at the end of June were changing hands at over £1 000. The King, his mistress, the courtiers, vied with merchants, landowners, politicians and any who could lay their hands on sufficient money to buy a share. What chicanery went on behind the scenes is impossible to discern. The South Seas became the fashionable topic. The quick-witted rushed in to sell South Sea garments, South Sea ornaments, South Sea jewellery, even to provide South Sea servants. The statesman Robert Walpole, though alive to the danger, could not himself refrain from investing in South Sea shares.

All this was sufficient encouragement for speculators of all kinds, who played on the mixture of avarice and credulity which was now rampant. There was no project, it seemed, for which people would not subscribe money in expectation of gain. One was 'for the discovery of perpetual motion', another 'for importing a number of large jack-asses from Spain'. One which received a thousand subscriptions of £2 each in five hours was 'for carrying on an undertaking of great advantage, which shall in due time be revealed'. But the time never came, for the projector decamped with his £2 000!

> At length Corruption, like a gen'ral flood . . .
> Shall deluge all, and Av'rice creeping on
> (So long by watchful Ministers withstood)

Spread like a low-born mist and blot the sun;
Statesman and Patriot ply alike the stocks,
Peeress and Butler share alike the Box,
And Judges job, and Bishops bite the town
And mighty Dukes pack Cards for half a crown.[12]

But confidence can break as quickly as speculation can soar. Flimsy or dishonest share-promotion was no help to the South Sea Company. As it tried to discredit these worthless rivals to its own plans, as more and more fictitious or paper-light schemes collapsed, the obloquy and the panic fell upon its own shares. At the same time there was little of solid worth to back them. The hoped for trade with Spanish America was not noticeably enhanced, trade with Spain itself declined, and the Plantations, particularly Jamaica, suffered from the monopoly of the South Sea Company. The panic of attempted selling that ensued was as wild as the orgy of buying had been, and thousands of speculators from all ranks of society were ruined as the value of South Sea shares fell to nothing. Robert Walpole, however, had already made £40 000 by selling his at the right time, and there were doubtless others who had got out in time. It was more generally satisfactory that the breaking of the monopoly of the South Sea Company left the way open for individual trading with South America when other circumstances were favourable.

But there was one project which did come off—a proposal to search for a Spanish treasure ship sunk in the South Seas forty years previously. Sir William Phipps hit on the right spot, and brought home a cargo of pieces of eight valued at nearly £200 000. His enterprise, legitimately combining capital with knowledge and skill, with ingenuity, risk and a modicum of good luck, might perhaps be remembered as much as the corruption and jobbing that surrounded the South Sea Bubble, as part of the age as a whole.

CHAPTER XIX
Mercantilism

While monetary and banking systems were helping the expanding economy in one way, a series of expedients collectively comprising what later economists termed Mercantilism, or the Mercantile System, was seeking to advance it in another.

In its simplest form, mercantilist doctrine held that a state must be self-sufficient, that its political power must be underpinned by economic power, that its wealth and power depended upon trade and industry as well as upon fighting men and fortifications, that the state itself could determine where economic advantage lay and that it could, and should, legislate accordingly. The concept took centuries to emerge, it was nowhere explicitly stated, yet it was inherent in the first import duties, the first taxes on trade, the earliest attempts of any society to direct its commerce. Any chance of success depended upon the central authority being sufficiently powerful to implement its directives. So, while a state could be bolstered by economic strength, economic strength depended upon a powerful state.

The various expedients which constituted the mercantile system grew up piecemeal throughout the centuries, until they reached a flood with the expanding trade of the seventeenth and eighteenth centuries. They consisted then of import duties, taxes, bounties, prohibitions, shipping regulations (the Navigation Acts), legislation which comprised the so-called Old Colonial System, and was designed to direct the economic activity of the Plantations solely to the benefit of the mother-country, and the remnants of many other efforts to control economic affairs in the interests of the State. The term itself was not used until Adam Smith, referring in 1776 to certain practices he wished to change, and certain beliefs he had no confidence in, spoke in *The Wealth of Nations* of the mercantile system of earlier generations. Adam Smith wished to substitute free trade and free enterprise generally for the mercantile system, and in the antithesis between the two lies, perhaps, the best definition of mercantilism.

Throughout the Middle Ages countries measured their wealth in terms of the gold and silver they accumulated, and since there was an overall shortage of the precious metals, Governments were repeatedly forbidding their export without clearly understanding why they should be flowing out. The position in England was so serious in 1382 that a Committee of Officers of the Mint was appointed to consider the alarming outflow of currency and bullion. In its Report Richard Aylesbury declared that if the position was to be improved England must sell to foreigners no less than she bought from them:

> We maintain that if the merchandise which goes out of England be well and rightly governed, the money that is in England will remain and great plenty of money will come from beyond the sea, that is to say, let not more strange merchandise come within the realm than to the value of the denizen merchandise which passes out of the realm.[1]

This was the first time that the relation between the trade balance and money or bullion had been clearly expressed. The necessity for a favourable balance of trade has remained a cardinal aim of British policy ever since, and was the plank upon which the whole of mercantilist policy rested.

But the immediate outcome of Aylesbury's advice was the Act of 1382, again prohibiting the export of gold and silver, and there were constantly reiterated prohibitions or partial prohibitions throughout the fifteenth century and beyond. Thus it would seem that Aylesbury's message had not been understood. Aware of this, another critic, in another way, pressed the point again in an anonymous homily in verse of nearly 1 200 lines published in 1436 and entitled *The Libelle of Englyshe Policye*.[2] It contained much economic criticism, and advised that we should import only goods of solid worth, and forswear the 'niffles' and 'trifles' which robbed us of our bullion without being productive in any way. A few years later a similarly inspired verse pamphlet *On England's Commercial Policy* made similar points.[3]

There was more commercial legislation in the decade 1430–40, but neither legislature nor Mint nor poet nor pamphleteer produced the desired result, and there were continued complaints that policy was ineffective. Some at least of the Yorkist unrest against the Lancastrian kings was caused by economic troubles, and in the middle of the fifteenth century the Yorkists drew up a list of economic grievances which included the continued outflow of treasure.[4] Effective action lagged until a Government was established which was strong enough to enforce legislation, and it was only when Henry VII reiterated the older economic measures that some attention was given to their enforcement. They were not original, not even strikingly effective, measures, yet for the first time they added up to something like a policy. The bullion laws were repeated in the form of a veto on the export of bullion, showing that the old association of prosperity and the precious metals was still there. At the same time, Henry encouraged the trade that was the more fundamental by means of commercial treaties with Spain, the Empire, France and the Netherlands. He gave his patronage to voyages of discovery westward. He encouraged shipbuilding by paying bounties on the building of large ships.

A rudimentary navigation policy had begun in the year of the Peasants' Revolt, but had never been seriously enforced. The benefits accruing from the carrying trade, and the advantages to the country which controlled it, had by then been perceived: if England did her own carrying she took profit from other countries, ships and merchant sailors were ready to become a fighting fleet, and so commercial gain and sea-power marched hand in hand. This was the very epitome of mercantilist doctrine, though any such conception was far removed from the understanding of the men who passed the first Navigation Act in 1381. This Act laid down that 'none of the king's liege people do from henceforth ship any merchandise in going out or coming within the realm of England, in any port, but only in ships of the king's liegance'. It was not only difficult to enforce such an Act, but the strength of English shipping hardly made it practicable to do so, and a century passed before another

Navigation Act was passed. The Tudor Act of 1485 laid down that wines of Gascony and Guienne were to be imported only in English, Irish or Welsh ships, and a further Act three years later prescribed that the master and mariners of these ships must be English subjects.

But it was extraordinarily difficult to maintain a consistent navigation policy, as subsequent events demonstrated. Edward VI partly repealed the Act of 1485 on the grounds that it enhanced the price of wine without benefiting the Navy, and the whole navigation policy came into disrepute in face of reprisals, particularly when the Emperor Charles V placed a retaliatory ban on English ships. There were various ad hoc instructions from trading companies or the Privy Council in the course of the sixteenth century for the employment of native shipping, and James I tried to enforce a navigation policy by Proclamation, but there was no fresh legislation and much conflicting interest, with unemployed seamen complaining that foreigners engrossed all the shipping, commercial interests fearing reprisals, consumers predicting higher prices and shortages, shipbuilding interests favouring their own monopoly and merchants generally being torn both ways.

A Commission set up in 1622 to consider the causes and remedies of the decay of trade[5] was instructed specifically to inquire 'how our laws do now stand in force for the prohibition of merchandise to be imported in foreign bottoms' and it came down on the side of mercantilist policy, urging in its Report the employment of more English ships. Charles I called again for a more vigorous navigation policy, but the situation was influenced more than anything else by the development of the English colonies in America and the West Indies.[6]

Economic speculation meanwhile continued. An anonymous writer in 1549, who had obviously well assimilated Aylesbury's dictum, laid down once more the theory of the balance of trade: 'The onlie meanes to cause mouche Bullione to be broughte oute of other realmes unto the kinges mintes is to provide that a great quantite of our wares maye be carriede yerly into beyonde the Sees and lese quantitie of ther wares be brought hether a gaine'.[7] A few years later was published another anonymous pamphlet which put the case even more clearly and is often regarded as the first real statement of mercantilism as a national policy. *A Discourse of the Common Weal of this Realm of*

England asserts that 'we must always take heed that we buy no more of strangers than we sell them for so we should empoverish ourselves and enrich them. For he were no good husband that hath no other yearly revenues but of husbandry to live on, that will buy more in the market than he selleth again'. Echoing *The Libelle of Englyshe Polycye*, the writer criticizes the nature of these imports: 'trifles . . . that we might either clean spare, or else make them within our own realm, for the which we pay inestimable treasure every year, or else exchange substantial wares and necessary for them, for the which we might receive great treasure', and he proceeds to list many items from puppets and penhorns to paper and pins, from brooches and buttons of silk to hawk's bells and toothpicks.[8]

By this time the 'over balance' or the adverse balance of trade rather than the loss of bullion was recognized as the evil to be avoided, and trade was seen to be the basis upon which bullion and money movements rested. But there were different kinds of trade. The most advantageous exports were raw materials like tin, coal and leather (above what we needed for our own production); manufactured goods and re-exports. Imports should be confined to naval supplies, essential raw materials like woad or madder for dyeing, and what were considered near-essential foodstuffs which varied, according to the season, from corn and herrings to sugar and spices and—always—wine. Manufactured goods should be confined to those which were useful, and which we could not manufacture ourselves. The old admonition of *The Libelle* and *A Discourse* was everywhere accepted, and the import of frivolous and luxury inessentials was condemned. An Act of Elizabeth I 'for the avoiding of divers foreign wares' embodied this view and the list of forbidden imports was very long, ranging from girdles and gloves to leather and laces, to saddles and stirrups, to pins and rapiers and daggers and knives. The list of prohibited articles was extended at various times. Less crude was *The Book of Rates* of 1611, which relied upon import duties rather than prohibition to reduce imports, at the same time exempting from taxation such foreign raw materials as were used in home production, abolishing or reducing duties on native products sent abroad, and paying bounties on such exports as needed encouragement.[9]

An extra dimension was given to mercantilism generally, and the navigation system in particular, by the development of

England's colonies in America and the West Indies, which were building up a trade and some manufacture of their own. To England the colonies were her possessions—her *Plantations*, to give them the name by which they were normally known. They were 'planted' by her, and existed for her benefit. The settlers, for their part, felt a close bond with England, which was still the mother-country. England supplied much of the capital for their development; they could look to her for protection in time of trouble; she safeguarded their trade routes; she respected their monopoly of fishing by excluding English fishermen from the New England banks, she sent them her own manufactures; she was not only a market for their raw materials, and for such manufactured goods as they produced, but was sometimes a protected market. The growing of tobacco, for example, was forbidden in England and virtual embargo was put on the import of tobacco other than colonial. Nevertheless, the colonies and their inhabitants had their own lives to lead and their own fortunes to make, and there was bound to be a conflict of interest if England's mercantilist policies impinged upon their activities.

The first attempt to bring the colonies within the ambit of the English mercantile system was aimed at the lucrative tobacco trade. In 1621 it was laid down that tobacco from the colonies should be landed in England before proceeding for sale to other countries. Three years later it was enacted that the tobacco must not be carried in foreign ships but only in those of the Plantations or of England. In 1633 an Act forbade aliens to engage in trade with Virginia—forbade them, that is, to trade in tobacco. In 1647 it was laid down that *all* goods 'of the growth' of the Plantations must be exported in English bottoms. Three years later ships of foreign countries were forbidden to trade with the English Plantations without licence. The legislation was not only repetitive but confusing, and gave the impression of being ineffective. In 1651 an effort was made to bring it all together into one comprehensive Act, which may be regarded as the quintessence of Navigation policy. It laid down that goods exported from Asia, Africa or America should come to England only in English or colonial ships; and that all goods exported from Europe should come to England, Ireland or the Plantations only in English or colonial ships or ships of the country of origin. Nine years later an 'enumerating clause' attempted to confine the trade of the colonies to the mother-country alone, specifying that certain enumerated commodities, including sugar, tobacco, cotton-wool, ginger and indigo could be sent by the colonies only to England, Ireland, Wales, or to another colony. The same Act required that the master and at least three-quarters of the crew of an English or colonial ship should be English. Two years later such ships were required also to be built in the king's dominions. The Staple Act of 1663 attempted to assert the control of England still further: no European manufacture could be shipped direct to the colonies, but had first to be taken to England or Wales and shipped from there.

It is doubtful whether this crescendo of control conferred a large or lasting benefit upon the mother-country. On the other hand, it is possible that the colonies gained something from their unwilling partnership. Their ships had the same privileges as those of England, they were even encouraged to build their own ships, and New England did in fact build up a flourishing shipbuilding industry behind the shelter of the Navigation Acts. Some mitigation came also not through intent but through the difficulty of enforcing the Navigation Acts. Smuggling was easy on the little-known coasts of the colonies, and no one was going to question the country of origin of a ship running in to some 'exchange' area on, say, the Newfoundland coast. In other cases restrictions defeated their own end. Rice was for a time added to the enumerated commodities of 1661, which meant that it could not be sent direct from the colonies to Europe but had to go to England first. The result was that the rice started to go bad, and the regulation had to be repealed. Even in so far as they were successful, certain undesirable results followed from the Navigation Acts. English trade with the Baltic, for example, declined because of the ban on Dutch ships, which were especially adapted to work in those waters. As a result England became short of vital shipbuilding materials, the price of English ships increased, and to this extent the Navigation Acts defeated their own ends. Yet they did put a greater responsibility than before upon English ships, English shipbuilding and English merchant sailors, and to this extent they helped to increase her share in the carrying trade, and helped to achieve the favourable balance of payments which was now central to mercantilist policy.

Another aspect of mercantilism was evident as the colonies

began to manufacture goods for themselves. England intended a partnership in which the production of the colonies should complement her own. Naval stores such as hemp, flax, timber, pitch and turpentine, as well as food and tobacco, were therefore acceptable products on which duties were reduced or completely withdrawn on import into England; a system of selective bounties was even tried for a time. But woollen goods and iron manufactures that would compete with her own were a different matter. An Act of 1699 contained a clause saying that no wool or woollen manufactures could be exported from the colonies, either to another colony or to another country. In 1732 an attempt was made to prevent the colonial hatmakers from exporting hats made from the beaver skins in good supply in the colonies, the London Feltmakers complaining that 'being supplied with beaver skins at less expense than the petitioners' they were 'enabled not only to supply the foreign markets but even to send over hats to Great Britain'.[10] In the case of iron, England wanted to encourage the import from the colonies of unwrought iron but to discourage any manufacture. So an Act of 1750 allowed pig iron and bar iron to be imported into England from the colonies duty-free, but forbade the erection of any manufacturing plant in the colonies. The colonies, on the other hand, were expected to, and did, take from England woollen manufactured goods, including apparel, and ironware.

The colonies' own reaction to England's navigation policy is indicated in the title of the pamphlet they issued in 1689: *The Groans of the Plantations*. But they were themselves responsible for certain contradictions and difficulties. The northern colonies found it to their advantage to import sugar, molasses and rum from French and other foreign sugar colonies. The British sugar colonies objected, and asked for the enforcement of the Navigation Acts in this respect. In response, the Molasses Act of 1733 laid heavy duties on foreign molasses imported into the colonies or Great Britain, so forcing the northern colonies to forgo the more attractive import from the French colonies. As in other cases, smuggling was rife, and the Act was largely disregarded.

In 1664, with the main features of mercantilism already present—a favourable balance of trade, the Navigation Acts, the old colonial policy, the regulation of imports and exports—there was published *England's Treasure by Forraign Trade, Or,*

The Ballance of Our Forraign Trade is the Rule of our Treasure, a small book which in its title neatly summed up mercantilist belief and in its contents ranged over the whole mercantilist policy. It had been written some forty years earlier by Thomas Mun, who had died in 1641. Mun was born in 1571, became wealthy as a London merchant, engaged in the Levant trade, in 1615 became a director of the recently formed East India Company and was a member of the Standing Committee on Trade and Plantations, which was the original Board of Trade. He had already published, in 1621, *A Discourse of Trade from England unto the East Indies: Answering to diverse Objections which are usually made against the same.* The objections arose from the export of bullion which the East India Company, by the terms of its charter, was permitted to make.[11] Mun's writing was primarily an apologia for the East India Company, whose actions in this respect appeared to be against the bullionist policy of the extremer form of mercantilism. Mun set out to prove that in the end it would benefit England, for it was total trade and not trade with one particular country which was important. The goods brought back from the Indies exchanged for more bullion or treasure than was taken out, and could in no wise be classed a losing trade.

In *England's Treasure* Mun enlarged and generalized the argument. It was the balance of *international* trade upon which the flow of treasure depended, and action must be guided by a simple policy 'wherein we must ever observe this rule, to sell more to strangers yearly than we consume of theirs in value'. The 'strangers' were merchants collectively, and not of any one country, and thus, in taking the final step in the evolution of mercantilist theory, its proponents had come back to Aylesbury. The loose talk that had intervened of 'losing' trade or 'gaining' trade with this country or that was for ever discredited. The country's treasure was in foreign trade as a whole, and the end it must seek was an overall favourable balance of trade.

The broad ends to which mercantilism was directed—power and plenty, economic self-sufficiency, wealth and the favourable balance of trade—remained desirable even when mercantilism as a means of achieving them was no longer popular. The State had never been powerful enough to enforce mercantilist legislation, and it slipped into disregard as the economic system expanded. There had indeed always been so many loopholes and so many evasions that there was never a time when a full mercantilist system was in operation. It was left to laissez-faire in an entirely changed set of economic circumstances to attempt the same ends with different means. If laissez-faire appeared more successful than mercantilism, this was due as much to Britain's lead in industrial techniques, her coal and her iron, and her access to raw cotton, as to the new approach. Laissez-faire, it has been said, 'did almost without effort what mercantilism had set out to do but failed to achieve'. But it did so in a new environment. Mercantilism should be judged, not in the light of the Industrial Revolution and from the standpoint of the nineteenth century, but by the standards of its own time. Would laissez-faire in the seventeenth or eighteenth century have dealt any more successfully than mercantilism with the problems of those times? It can at least be answered that the country which stood poised to take advantage of the new situation, which had come to its position through many centuries of Government intervention and attempted control, was well enough equipped in capital, in enterprise, in man-power and in technique, to take and keep for over a century the lead in industry and commerce, in trade and in shipping. She could not have been badly served by the generations of mercantilists, in one form or another, who attempted to shape her development.

CHAPTER XX

Intervention and Control

The assumption that governments could and should intervene in economic and social affairs was taken for granted from the Middle Ages to the nineteenth century: in this respect mercantilism was merely trying to do for commercial affairs what medieval rulers had always assumed they should do over a wider field. The chief difference between medieval and later controls was that in earlier times there were more controlling agents and consequently less uniformity. The State and the towns, the Church and the gilds, all took their responsibilities for granted and, however much practice might vary, however inefficient the administration, the principle of collective responsibility was never lost sight of. There were even examples of town planning by medieval rulers and the laying down of dimensions for house-building,[1] as well as repeated injunctions against the use of thatch and other combustible materials in towns. For much of the medieval period, however, the State was the weakest of the controlling agents. The Church pronounced upon usury[2] and the care of the poor and afflicted.[3] The gilds exercised a wide control from within their organization over quality and price, wages and working conditions, ill health and old age.[4] The towns, while generally co-operating with the gilds, also spread their own authority over an equally wide field. Thus the town of Chester felt itself responsible for seeing that its citizens had 'good and wholesome victual at reasonable prices'. The mayor of Coventry nailed the 'just price' of victuals to the church door. The concept of the 'just price' was, indeed, one which the medieval citizen thought he could arrive at, and believed he should enforce. Anyone who tried to enhance this price for his own profit or to create an artificial scarcity was condemned. The forestaller who bought before the market in order to buy cheap and sell dear; the regrator who purchased at one price and sold at a higher; the engrosser who bought in bulk and then held back to get a higher selling price, were all subject to severe penalties. The forestaller was denounced in Bristol as 'a manifest oppressor of the poor and a public enemy of the whole commonalty and country . . . oppressing his poorer and despising his richer neighbours'.[5] Regrating was often prevented by allowing no buying or selling before the ringing of the market bell. Search was made to discover goods concealed for future sale by the engrosser.

If prices had to be 'right' and 'just', so commodities had to be available, and in particular the provision of corn in time of scarcity was an integral part of public policy. Many big cities, including London, sent away to buy corn when it was scarce and stipulated its sale at a reasonable price to the poor, while those who had a surplus were commanded to bring it forward for sale. Conversely, public corn granaries were established to store corn in times of plenty, so that it was available in times of shortage. The central Government, from an early time, supplemented these efforts by permitting the export of corn only in times of plenty and repeatedly forbidding it in bad years, as in 1361, or, as in 1437, allowing it only when it did not exceed a certain price.

The Assize of Bread and the Assize of Ale were Government expedients aimed at protecting the consumer's essential food from fraudulent practices. The first Assize of Bread was probably that of 1266, but it was based on earlier Anglo-Saxon laws; it instituted a sliding scale which regulated the weight of bread according to the price of wheat, so that instead of the price of a loaf varying, its size varied instead. In calculating the weight of the loaf a fixed sum was added to the price of the wheat to cover the baker's working expenses, which included labour, fuel, light, yeast, salt. The baker's profit came in the form of two peck loaves for every baking from a quarter of wheat, together with the discarded bran. The Assizes which fixed the weights were held several times a year.[6] It was a conscientious attempt to regulate prices and profits in accordance with the cost of production, but the difficulties of detecting a transgressor, the opportunities for evasion, the frequency of fraud are reflected in the medieval hatred of the miller and the baker: the miller kept back grain for his own use, the baker diverted dough into his own trough. It was not always easy to make the millers and the bakers attend the Assize of Bread. At Coventry 'the Commons rose and threw loaves at the mayor's head in St. Mary's Hall because the bakers kept not the assize, neither did the mayor punish them according to his office'.[7] And even if they attended it was difficult to enforce the law. Punishment, if caught, was by the pillory or the stocks, or most commonly the baker was dragged through the streets on a hurdle with the offending loaf tied round his neck. The Assize of Bread continued until it was abolished in London in 1822, and in the rest of the country in 1836.

The Assize of Ale was similarly based upon earlier laws confirmed by statute in 1266; it instituted a sliding scale regulating the price of ale according to the price of wheat, barley and oats. Again enforcement was difficult, particularly since there were probably more brewers than bakers: in London in 1309 there were said to be no less than 1 300.[8] The punishment for false measure or excessive price was again the pillory or the tumbril. If the ale was found bad, or of inferior quality, it was poured over the head of the offending brewer. In general, the pillory and the stocks were there for the punishment of overcharging or selling inferior quality of any product. Both were by law required to be kept at every fair and market place.

Another sphere in which central authority acted early was in the standardization of weights and measures, without which trade was badly hampered. As early as Anglo-Saxon times attempts had been made to enforce the 'just weight' and the 'just measure' and Magna Carta in 1215 said 'Let there be one measure of wine throughout our whole realm, and one measure of ale, and one measure of corn . . . and one width of cloth . . . of weights also let it be as of measures'. In 1340 it was repeated that 'from henceforth one measure and one weight shall be throughout the realm of England'.

A prescribed width was not the only regulation to which the woollen-cloth industry was subject. It attracted, indeed, a greater amount of direction and control from the gilds, from the towns, and from the State than any other industry or occupation: its establishment was subject to encouragement of various kinds,[9] the length of a bale as well as its width was prescribed, and efforts were made, as with bread and ale, to control its quality. It was forbidden, for example, to mingle different kinds of wool in the same cloth, the quality had to be as good in the middle as at the edges, and over-stretching was forbidden. Officials of gild, of town, and of the State all, at various times and various places, attempted to enforce these and other regulations.[10] Some of the requirements the clothiers were genuinely unable to observe, for woollen cloth, of its nature, is not uniform. In 1537, for example, clothiers protested to the Lord Chancellor that it was impossible to keep the width of cloth that the law required, and although the Chancellor bade them 'take heed and beware' the Act was suspended. In 1622 the Government admitted that the 'number and contradiction' of the various laws made it impossible to enforce them, yet in 1792 it was estimated that 311 laws relating to the control of wool and woollen cloth were still on the Statute Book.[11] Similarly, throughout the tillage debates[12] the Government took for granted that it was competent to determine the merits of proposed enclosure or conversion to pasture. The Privy Council under Tudors and Stuarts acted repeatedly to protect the corn supply, to keep down the price of corn and, in particular, to take action against 'the ingrossers of corne that seeke all excessive and ungodly lucar by whording up of corne and making more scarcety then there is'.[13] A good corn-supply represented, indeed, the self-sufficiency which was one of the pillars upon which mercantilism stood – the other being a favourable balance of trade—'Husbandry and tillage', said a Statute of 1598, is a cause that the realm doth more stand upon itself, without depending upon foreign countries'. In 1586 the Scarcity Book of Orders—'Orders devised by the especiall commandement of the Queenes Majestie for the reliefe and stay of the present dearth of Graine within the Realme'—was issued, under which it was expected that Justices of the Peace would be able to control the price of corn, prevent hoarding and ensure that no sale took place but in the open market. In the bad harvests at the end of the sixteenth century, with wheat prices doubling and even trebling, the Scarcity Book of Orders was reissued. It is not clear how successful it was in keeping down the price of corn, but the Government had sufficient faith in it to issue it again, and yet again, in 1605, 1608, 1622 and 1630. Yet it is likely that too often its intentions were thwarted by the very officers who should have been activating them, if not through inefficiency then through vested interest, for the Justices themselves, according to the Privy Council, were frequently the very 'corne masters' they were trying to check, neglecting 'the execution of suche good orders as have bin devised' and 'acting not for the public good but to inhance the prices of corne'.[14]

While the woollen-cloth industry, with its taxes, prohibitions, sumptuary legislation and invitations to foreign workmen is an outstanding example of Government intervention to encourage an infant industry[15] other projects also were fostered, often by means of what were termed patents of monopoly. These were a form of charter conferring monopoly rights and other privileges upon the recipient, and were not basically different from other charters. In some instances a good case could be made out for monopoly. The most unexceptionable form of patent was in the case of an invention—where 'any man out of his own Wit, industry or indeavour finds out anything beneficial for the CommonWealth', as Bacon put it.[16] A period of monopoly control to develop his project unhindered seemed reasonable. Similarly, the granting of a patent to develop an industry in its infant days or to assist in developing a backward one might be justifiable. Monopolies for glass-making, for paper-making and for the production of alum and saltpetre, the mining of copper and the production of brass were granted early in the reign of Elizabeth.[17] But even the most desirable monopoly could fail in its purpose: within its protection prices became too high, other interests were excluded and the monopoly became, in the words of the Parliament of 1604, 'a private or disordered engrossing for the enhancing of prices, for a private purpose, to a public prejudice'.[18] At the same time it was all too easy to reward a favourite, or pay a creditor, or raise money, by granting a patent of monopoly. The money then became more important than the project itself, with the result that unnecessary and even frivolous monopolies added to the number. At the end of Elizabeth's reign there were monopolies for the making of pins and playing cards, for tobacco-growing, for wine and soap and starch and leather. Sir Walter Raleigh was granted the monopoly of licensing ale-houses. There were monopolies for printing the Psalms of David, for making spangles, for printing all manner of songs in parts. Someone was given the monopoly of buying and transporting ashes and old shoes for seven years, another of sowing woad in England.[19]

The outcry against monopolies was so considerable that Elizabeth was compelled to let the Parliament of 1601, summoned to contribute to the cost of war, denounce monopolists instead as 'bloodsuckers of the Commonwealth', and she was obliged to retreat gracefully from some of her grants. In 1610 James I confirmed by Proclamation the ending of monopoly. Later in his reign, nevertheless, occurred one of the most famous, as well as one of the most ill-fated, grants of monopoly. It concerned the cloth trade, and was instigated by Alderman Cockayne. The Cockayne project had a superficial attraction. Instead of sending white or unfinished cloth abroad, as was customary, it should be dyed and dressed at home, thus employing more men and women, and substantially increasing native self-sufficiency. The idea was not new, but had always been foiled by the opposition of the Merchant Adventurers and of the clothiers. But Cockayne was plausible—'If to be done with a pen or an argument at Council Table, Mr Alderman Cockayne will do it'[20]—and James was gullible. So Cockayne got the monopoly he asked for, a Proclamation of 1614 forbade the export of any broadcloth undyed or undressed and, the Merchant Adventurers still refusing to participate, a new Company was granted a charter in 1616 for the export of undyed or undressed cloth. But the Netherlanders, with a great industry geared to the finishing trade, could achieve much better results than the English, and foreign customers preferred their work. Moreover, if they were not to import our unfinished cloth they could send nothing in return. To protect their own finishing trade, they began a cloth-production of their own. On all counts English trade, and in particular the cloth industry, suffered. Clothiers complained of unsold cloth, clothing workers of depression and famine, King James that he had been 'much abused'. 'Time', he remarked characteristically, 'discovereth many inabilities which cannot at first be seen'.[21] The project was abandoned, leaving a legacy of disruption.

But the idea of monopoly died hard, where some were abolished others grew, and some of the old ones took on fresh life in the hands of new favourites: the licensing of ale-houses, for example, once the prerogative of Sir Walter Raleigh, had passed to dependants of the Duke of Buckingham and then into the hands of the family of Sir Thomas Wentworth. The Statute of Monopolies of 1624 pronounced illegal all monopolies 'for the sole buying, selling, making, working or using of anything', but there were many specific exemptions, and in addition a general exemption of monopoly companies and corporations as opposed to individuals with a monopoly; for, as it was said, to include companies would be to pronounce illegal all industrial gilds and any corporate bodies. Charles I, in the period of personal government, took full advantage of these exemptions to grant many lucrative monopolies to companies and corporations, and monopolists were among those most heavily castigated by Paliament when at last it met—'they dip in our dish, they sup in our cup'. Industrial monopolies were abolished in 1639 in the legislation that preceded the Civil Wars. But the commercial monopoly of the Merchant Adventurers remained. It was as far beyond the reach of a Parliament which required its financial aid as it had been beyond the reach of Elizabeth and the Stuarts, and it remained inviolate for the same reasons under Cromwell and the Protectorate.[22]

While monopoly grants were doing some harm and some good and at the same time replenishing the privy purse the State was taking advantage of the growing wealth of the country in increased taxation. Taxes assumed many forms. There were taxes on goods brought into the country, which could be revenue-raising as well as protective, and taxes on goods taken out of the country which could be revenue-raising as well as encouraging; land taxes, taxes on personal belongings; poll taxes—at one time graduated according to rank, at another time universal; a hearth tax; a window tax; stamp duties on deeds and instruments and law proceedings and news-sheets; taxes on houses, on trades, on births, on burials, on marriages; taxes on bachelors under which a duke in 1695 paid over forty times as much as a gentleman and a gentleman paid six times as much as the man lower in the social scale. The excise was established by Parliament in 1643 during the Civil Wars, and proved so profitable it was never abandoned. Even Elizabeth I had been reluctant to tax beer because 'it was certain that, should she grant never so small a fee, the people would say their drink was "excised" as it was in Flanders, and would repine at it'. Repining there was in plenty, but not only beer and ale but spirits, wine, tea, coffee, salt, spices, tobacco, malt, timber, coals, were all taxed as the principle spread. The confusion was such as to evoke Sydney Smith's famous outburst of 1820.

Over the wider field of economic affairs generally the State also kept watch. It was perplexed and agitated above all by the vicissitudes of trade which brought periodic unemployment and fluctuating prices. These had always been present, but the widening of the market made them more frequent, the greater dependence of workmen upon industry made the situation more serious. By the Tudor period the trade-cycle was a recognized phenomenon, and there were periods of intense unemployment throughout the sixteenth and seventeenth centuries: the years 1528, 1586, 1622 and 1629 were particularly bad. The position was exacerbated by the rising prices which, in common with most of Europe, England was experiencing in Tudor and early Stuart times.[23]

The Tudors, like their medieval forebears, assumed they could legislate for most things, and as they were much concerned to preserve a contented population, they conceived it their duty to deal with the economic situation. In particular they tried to protect the clothing workers from the worst effects of trade depression, and commanded the clothiers to 'keep their workpeople on work' in slack times and pay them a prescribed minimum wage. When the clothiers retorted that merchants would not buy they sent for the merchants and commanded them to step up their orders. The merchants retorted that foreigners would take no more English cloth, but Wolsey in 1528 in a justly famous and completely irrelevant admonition rebuked them sharply:

> Sirs, the King is informed that you use not yourselves like merchants, but like graziers and artificers; for where the clothiers do daily bring cloths to your market for your ease, to their great cost, and there be ready to sell them, you of your wilfulness will not buy them as you have been accustomed to do. What manner of men be you? I tell you that the King straitly commandeth you to buy their cloths as beforetime you have been accustomed to do, upon pain of his high displeasure.[24]

The Privy Council in the crisis of 1586 again attempted to press this policy upon both merchants and clothiers, and its intervention in social and economic affairs continued under the Stuarts until the outbreak of the Civil War. Several times gentlemen were ordered to return to their homes in the country so that in times of distress they might by their example, by their hospitality, relieve the troubled situation—in 1603, a time of plague and distress; in 1607, a time of disturbance in the North and Midlands over enclosure; in 1608, when there was a very bad harvest; in the period between 1620 and 1624, a time of trade stagnation, bad harvests, and incipient insurrection. It was a policy strongly upheld by James I. 'A country gentleman in town', he said, 'is like a ship at sea, which looks very small; a country gentleman in the country is like a ship in a river, which looks very big.'

The crisis that began in 1620 was one of the worst with which the Government had to deal. It was particularly severe in the textile industry, where it lasted for over four years. Thousands of workmen in all the textile areas became unemployed as the export trade declined and the price of wool fell. In desperation the poor of these counties gathered in bands of forty or fifty and went to the houses of the rich demanding meat and money, and they took provisions before they were put on sale in the market. The Privy Council commanded the J.P.s to require the clothiers to keep their workpeople at work. The J.P.s replied that the clothiers themselves were on the verge of ruin, and that unsold cloth accumulated in their barns. The clothiers of Gloucestershire, nevertheless, consented to keep their workpeople at work for another fortnight. Everything was tried—merchants were ordered to buy cloth, wool-dealers to sell wool as cheaply as possible, creditors to restrain their demands on the clothiers. Sandys in 1621 spoke movingly in the House of Commons of the necessity to safeguard 'the poor man's labour, his inheritance', and early in the following year the Privy Council laid down the rule by which wool-grower, clothier, and merchant alike should be governed, that 'whosoever had a part of the gaine in profitable times must now in the decay of Trade . . . beare a part of the publicke losses'.[25] A few months later the first Commission on Unemployment was appointed.

The brief of the twelve commissioners was to find the causes of, and suggest remedies for, the decay of trade and they directed themselves primarily to the cloth industry, hearing evidence from clothiers, merchants, Customs officials, landowners and others. Their long Report attributed the crisis to faulty and bad workmanship; the burden of duties and tariffs, both home and foreign; the uncertainties generated by foreign wars; the monopoly of the Merchant Adventurers; the scarcity of money and the lower value of foreign currency compared with English;

the wearing of silk and imported materials rather than woollen cloth. The remedies proposed were an embargo on the export of raw wool; a revision of the tangled legislation governing cloth-production; the establishment of a corporation in every county to prevent bad or faulty manufacture; restrictions on middle-men; the compulsory wearing of native cloth; the abolition of duties on wool. Over the wider economic field they urged the encouragement of fisheries and the employment of English shipping; the reform of trading companies; monetary control; and, they said, pinning their hopes upon the Mercantilist precept, 'the most important remedy . . . is to provide against the overbalance of trade'.[26]

The Privy Council, meanwhile, was constrained to bolster the clothiers with public assistance, instructing the Justices of the Peace to raise 'public stocks for the employment of such as want work'. That they were not altogether philanthropic in this command is made clear by their announcement of the same year:

> that they would not endure 'that the cloathiers . . . should, att their pleasure and without giving knowledge thereof unto this Board, dismiss their workfolkes, who, being many in number and most of them of the poorer sort, are in such cases likely by their clamors to disturbe the quiet and government of those partes wherein they live.[27]

Burleigh had spoken similarly a quarter of a century before: 'by lack of vent tumults will follow'.

But the Government was also trying to operate a wages policy which would apply to good times as well as tiding over bad. The Statutes of Labourers had intended to control wages after the Black Death by maximum rates, or by those obtaining before the plague. In 1390 an Act gave authority to J.P.s to assess wages 'by their discretion according to the dearth of victuals'. A statutory maximum was again fixed by the Act of 1445, and was continued by the early Tudors. At the beginning of Elizabeth's reign Justices were given a free hand to fix this maximum; by the Statute of Artificers[28] of 1563 the statutory maximum was discarded altogether and Justices were ordered to adjust wages to the time and to the season and to 'yield unto the hired person both in the time of scarcity and in the time of plenty a convenient proportion of wages'. That the laying down of wage-scales was taken seriously is indicated by the fact that wage assessments exist for every decade of Elizabeth's reign. Much was done to enforce them, particularly by the Privy Council, who kept in touch with the localities and gave much advice and exhortation. Under the early Stuarts the Privy Council was similarly active, and the system of wage-assessment continued, though perhaps it had become too automatic and failed to take account of fluctuating prices. Wiltshire weavers, for example, in 1614 complained of 'the small wages given them by the clothier, being no more than what was accustomed to be paid forty years past, notwithstanding that the prices of all kind of victual are almost doubled from what they were'. The Privy Council expressed the view to the Wiltshire J.P.s that it was fitting they should call the clothiers before them to examine the truth of the complaint 'and finding it to be as informed, to use your best endeavours for the proportioning of their wages unto the state of these present times'.[29] Meanwhile in the Act of 1604 two important additions had been made to the wages policy. The first substituted a minimum wage for a maximum wage, laying down that if any person 'shall not pay so much or so great wages . . . as shall be set down . . . every . . . person . . . so offending shall forfeit . . . to the party grieved ten shillings'. The other made the significant pronouncement that no Justice of the Peace who was also a clothier might have any hand in the rating of wages. Wage-assessments continued during the Interregnum and the Restoration, but they gradually died out. One of their weaknesses was that they tended in their operation to apply to agricultural workers only, and not to industrial workers. Moreover, any uniform wage system required a strong central authority, and as the power of the monarch and of the Privy Council declined there was only *laissez-faire* to take its place.

The Tudors tried also to come to terms with the situation in a wider way. Much of the concern of the Statute of Artificers was to maintain an adequate supply of agricultural labour: in spite of the development of industry the land was still basic, both in its produce and in the men it nurtured. Agricultural workers between the ages of twelve and sixty years were therefore to remain on the land and not to enter another occupation, while those with no fixed employment were to become agricultural labourers. In time of harvest 'all . . . persons as be meet to labour' could be conscripted for agricultural work at the discretion of the Justice of the Peace. The only persons who could be apprenticed to a trade were those whose parents had an annual income of more than 40*s*. from land. Having laid down these limits upon employment, the Statute then proceeded to limit mobility by enacting that unmarried persons, or those under the age of thirty, should not leave their calling. In industry a period of seven-year apprenticeship was reinforced, the number of apprentices was not limited, but in respect of the wool, tailoring and shoemaking industries it was prescribed that every master who had three apprentices should have one journeyman.

The workman was protected in several ways. In industrial work he was protected against casual labour by the provision that there should be no hiring for less than a year. All people hired by wages for the day or week were to keep specified hours of work; but these were so vague as to be virtually useless as protection for the worker. Finally, to provide a satisfactory wage, particularly in view of rising prices, Justices of the Peace were to rate wages in accordance with prices by laying down a periodic maximum wage. It is doubtful whether a maximum wage can ever help the workman, but the Statute of Artificers (which remained on the Statute Book for two and a half centuries, during which time it was whittled down, evaded and distorted by various interests in various ways) remains a landmark. It is a tribute to the efforts of a State, still in its formative period, to come to grips with the problem of a rising population, a developing industry, a changing social structure and a great inflation. The careful notes made by Burleigh on social and economic matters and the debates in the House of Commons, as well as the legislation itself, show a regard for the well-being of the population as a whole, and an ability to survey the whole scene. The weakness of the Tudor, and indeed of much later, legislation was in its execution, where it relied upon the unpaid, and often prejudiced, amateur Justice of the Peace or the Church Warden. Elizabethan statesmen put the interest of land and landlords so high that agricultural workers were not allowed to leave their work on the land. Their consciousness of 'class' or 'degree' was such that they could bind the agricultural worker to the soil and allow only more prosperous citizens to take up a trade. But if they are judged by the standards of their own time they did well. If they are judged by the standards of nineteenth-century *laissez-faire* it is not at all certain that they would lose by the comparison.[30]

CHAPTER XXI

The Poor Law

In spite of all that could be done there remained a residue of people living below the lowest acceptable standard of life. The problem had exercised society since early times, and poor relief had taken many forms. Although by the beginning of the seventeenth century a national Poor Law had been evolved which was to remain law until 1834, it had by no means superseded other forms of poor relief which continued their independent existence.

To the Christian Church almsgiving had been recognized from early times as part of the Christian life. It was cherished, not only as a duty necessary to salvation, but as a blessing to the giver as well as to the receiver. King Alfred 'bestowed alms and largesses on both natives and foreigners of all countries'. Fitzstephen, describing London in the reign of Henry II, praised its 'laudable customs' in giving alms and hospitality. In the fifteenth century the chroniclers are still recording acts of largesse as being worthy of highest praise. The Bishop of Ely 'gave daily at his gates, besides bread and drink, warm meat to two hundred poor people'. Edward, Earl of Derby, fed 'aged persons twice every day, sixty and odd, besides all comers thrice a week'. And John Stowe himself saw two hundred people fed at Thomas Cromwell's gate, twice every day, with bread, meat and drink. Hospitality, particularly to the stranger, ranked high among forms of almsgiving, and the principle of welcoming all strangers was integral to the monasteries.

Christian almsgiving by the living was naturally accompanied by benefactions from the dead, and funds and institutions for the use of the poor and the sick accumulated in various forms. William the Conqueror distributed his wealth among the churches, the clergy and the poor, the precise sums being set down as he spoke them on his deathbed. Richard Lionheart gave a quarter of his treasure to his servants and the poor.[1] The scale of the bequest varied enormously. Elena Langwith, a widow, in 1467 included in her will charitable gifts of coal to the poor.[2] Alderman Richard Gardener, of the City of London, in 1488 left, in default of an heir, the sum of ten pence daily to five poor men in honour of the five wounds of Jesus Christ and to five poor women in honour of the five joys of the Blessed Virgin Mary.[3] Money was left for the education of poor children—'to John Southcot, to find him a school', read a legacy of 1367.[4] Provision would be made for the marriage of a portionless girl, landlords would make provision for poorer tenants. At the other end of the scale was the foundation and endowment of schools, hospitals and almshouses. Generally the endowment would take the form of assigning certain revenues for specified purposes, and as capital accumulated in the later Middle Ages new endowment increased and existing benefactions prospered; scarcely any will of the moderately well-to-do did not include some benefaction to charity. The legacy would frequently be accompanied by the stipulation that the recipient would attend the funeral, recite obits, light candles, or otherwise commemorate the dead.

These benefactions for the care of the sick, the old, the destitute, generally under the charge of a master or warden, always religious in character, with two or three priests or sisters in attendance, for a long while carried the chief load of institutional poverty and sickness. Their reputation was high, if not always for what they did for the poor, then for what they did for the donor, and they attracted further endowment. There was probably also a great deal of spontaneous, everyday help, of its nature not recorded.

But while individuals were interpreting the teaching of their religion in this way, the Church itself maintained a permanent connection with almsgiving. Since the earliest days of the Christian Church it had been customary for a community to support its priest through payment of a tythe, originally a tenth part of its land or produce, and for a third or a quarter of the tythe to be put to the use of the poor. The Church also organized festivities on behalf of the poor of which the Church Ale and the Church House became the most popular. To the Church Ale parishioners would donate malt or barley, and ale would be brewed and foodstuffs brought to what frequently developed into a great feast with games and merrymaking, lasting several days, at which all paid for what they consumed, the proceeds going to the poor. The Church House became a centre for entertainments of various kinds, on the same principle.

But greatest testimony of all to Christian almsgiving came from the monasteries. They gave alms at their gates, hospitality and shelter within their walls, ranging from a night or two to passing strangers to long periods for the unfit. It was part of their doctrine, incorporating the rules of their Church and the most ancient laws of hospitality, that no one should be turned away. The infirmary generally stood by the monastic buildings themselves, and here the sick would be nursed. The able-bodied might stay on more or less permanently in return for a modicum of work. While not all monasteries interpreted their duty as entailing more than a pittance, and while some people regarded the monastery as a means of permanently avoiding work or as one source of free food in a chain of many such establishments, there is no doubt that many people in real need praised God for the monastery.

More discriminating were the fraternities and gilds which, by their Friendly Society functions, as well as by bequests, looked after their own sick and unfortunate. Sometimes a specific bequest would be administered. Sometimes the gild would form an association for providing shelter for destitute members, which could range from hiring a cottage to providing almshouses or hospitals. The almshouses of St Thomas at York, for example, were connected with the fraternity of Corpus Christi and permanently kept ten poor people, as well as eight beds for poor strangers. By the fourteenth or fifteenth century all the bigger and more important gilds had their own almshouses and hospitals. In many of the towns, also, there was a practical combination of Christian spirit, community of purpose and discrimination in almsgiving. There were 'leper tolls' in several cities—at Chester on all foodstuffs brought to market; at Southampton on all imported wine; at Carlisle on brewers and 'Sunday bakers'; throughout Cumberland there was a 'leper tithe' on corn. A town would build almshouses, a house or two for the aged and infirm, pay a pension to widows or other deserving poor, make itself responsible for certain orphans.

In spite of all that was being done, however, the whole question had assumed new dimensions by the end of the fourteenth century with the disintegration of the manor and the visitation of the Black Death. The increase in the numbers of destitute was coupled with fear as the 'sturdy beggar' roamed the countryside, and the Government, while attempting to control wages,[5] at the same time tried to come to grips with the problem of destitution. The 'sturdy' or 'valiant' beggar—he who is able to work but will not—is distinguished from the unfit and alms are forbidden him. 'And because many sturdy beggars', proclaimed the Ordinance of Labourers of 1349,

> so long as they can live by begging for alms, refuse to labour, living in idleness and sin and sometimes by thefts and other crimes, no man, under the aforesaid penalty of imprisonment, shall presume under colour of pity or alms to give anything to such as shall be able profitably to labour, or to cherish them in their sloth, that so they may be compelled to labour for the necessaries of life.

In other words, almsgiving must be strictly discriminatory.

The separation of the able-bodied from the unfit remained fundamental to English poor-law policy. One of the first methods of making the distinction was laid down in the Ordinance of 1360 which prescribed the branding of the sturdy beggar with the letter F for felon. A Statute of 1388, with memories of the Peasants' Revolt only seven years behind it, added the further injunction that the sturdy beggar should be removed from the place where he was found begging and returned to such parish or village as could be made responsible for him. Like the distinction between the sturdy beggar and the deserving poor, the law of Settlement was to remain at the core of poor-law policy for centuries. It was equally difficult to implement, or even to establish where a 'settlement' lay. The Act of 1388 decided that it should be in the town where a man was born, the place where he was resident at the time of the promulgation of the Act, the town whence he came, or some other town within the hundred, rape or wapentake. The offence for not removing to one of these places within forty days of the proclamation of the Statute was the stocks or imprisonment, as well as forcible ejection. The legitimate traveller needed to carry with him a letter, sealed with the king's seal and imprinted with the name of the town or village where it was issued, stating the reasons for his journey. The seal was in the charge of the J.P. or some approved man of the district, and the cost of making, sealing and delivering the letter was limited to one penny. A person on the move at the end of the fourteenth century would thus be examined for the tell-tale letter F and asked to produce the mitigating sealed letter. The possession of the one, or lack of possession of the other, would land him in the stocks or in prison.

But the problem was growing faster than could be dealt with. On the one hand there was a falling off of help as older benefactions fell into decay, their incomes 'withdrawn and spent in other uses', while the old rules for the division of tythes were falling into desuetude as livings fell into the hands of absentees, or priests became less careful of their charges. On the other hand, there was a constant replenishment of the stream of vagrancy, which by the Tudor period had become a flood. The end of the Wars of the Roses, the Statute against Retainers, enclosure, the move to sheep-farming, all threw unattached people on to the country; trade, piracy and adventure brought a flotsam and jetsam of wanderers to English shores; in the disintegration of the gilds many people were detached from their moorings; fundamental changes in commercial and industrial affairs produced disorganization and unemployment; the very enlargement of the overseas market made the country more vulnerable to trade depression; and the steep and continuing price-rise ruined many people, or reduced to penury many who would otherwise have remained above destitution.

Various enactments failed to come to grips with the problem. But an Act of 1536 was on a wider scale. Besides repeating the distinction between the impotent and the able-bodied poor, it divided the able-bodied into three classes: those unwilling to work, who would be punished; those willing to work, who would be kept in 'continual labour'; and children between the ages of five and fourteen, who were to be apprenticed to masters of husbandry and other crafts. The 'impotent poor' were prohibited from begging, no one was to give them alms except through the common poor-box, but parishes and towns were instructed to collect voluntary alms every Sunday and holy day, the clergy exhorting the people to be generous. In this exhortation lay the germ of a compulsory poor-rate, while the prohibition of begging, the separation of the impotent poor and the sturdy beggar and the apprenticing of pauper children remained basic to subsequent poor-law policy.

But, even as the Act of 1536 was becoming law, the situation was being made worse by the dissolution between 1536 and 1539 of first the smaller and then the bigger monasteries, while the income from chantries and other charitable institutions with religious connections was being diverted to other uses. Thousands of poor people were turned from the monastery gates. Whether genuinely indigent or not, they added to the pauper stream, and their ranks were swollen by monks and other inmates of the monasteries thrown out into the world for perhaps the first time to seek a living. Moreover, the monastery was in many cases the lifeline of the people in neighbouring towns or villages. The people of Furness described how they had supplied provisions to Furness Abbey and received in return 'almost as much as they supplied'—sixty barrels of single beer or ale, thirty dozen loaves of coarse wheat bread, iron for their ploughs, and other farm tools, and timber to repair their houses . . . everyone having a plough was allowed to send two people to dinner in the refectory one day a week from Martinmass to Pentecost, all tenants were allowed to send their children to school in the monastery, and to dinner or supper in the refectory each day; and if any child was 'apt for learning' he was given a post in the monastery.[6]

The Act of 1547 reacted to the worsening situation with unparalleled severity. A sturdy beggar could be made a slave for two years, being branded on the breast with the letter V for vagrant. If he ran away from the master to whom he was sent he was branded on the forehead or cheek with the letter S and was made a slave for ever. If he ran away yet again the penalty was death as a felon.[7]

The towns, meantime, were of necessity trying to help themselves. London in particular was affected by the dissolution of the monasteries and was faced with the loss of four lazar-houses and fifteen hospitals, including some of the richest and largest. The citizens begged the king that some of these might be preserved, with the result that St Bartholomew's and St Thomas's for the sick, and Bethlehem hospital for the lunatic, were refounded. Christ's Hospital, a new foundation for orphan children, was founded in 1553. To help those who were neither sick nor orphaned London in 1547 levied what amounted to the first compulsory poor-rate on each citizen according to his means. The levy was for a year only, but it put the capital ahead of any other city, and of the nation as a whole.[8] The following year certain profits of the City were assigned to the relief of the poor, and the sum of 500 marks was assessed proportionately to their size upon the City Companies. Two years later the voluntary principle was tried again and the people of London were called to their parish churches and this time asked how much they would give to parish relief upon a weekly basis.

The London citizens were also endeavouring to get the use of 'a wide, large, empty house of the King's Majesty's, called Bridewell'. On the principle of the Act of 1536, they had classified their poor into three groups—'the succourless poor child', 'the sick and impotent', and 'the sturdy vagabond or idle person'. The third group would be the largest, and it was for them that they begged the use of the Palace of Bridewell. The citizens described their scheme in some detail. The inmates should be set on profitable work which would vary according to the condition of the person. Some would make caps; the weaker or less skilful would make feather-bed covers or be occupied in spinning, carding, knitting, winding silk or drawing wire; 'the stubborn, and fouler sort' would make nails and other ironwork. It was hoped that City merchants would supply the raw materials and pay for the finished goods for resale 'and always as the wares are wrought to renew the stock. And thus shall there never lack matter whereon the idle shall be occupied'.[9] The Palace of Bridewell was granted to the City of London and by 1555 the citizens felt content that 'there is no poor citizen . . . that beggeth his bread but by some mean his poverty is provided for'. Christ's Hospital contained 280 poor children and orphans; in St Thomas's Hospital some 260 people were cared for; in St Bartholomew's a hundred beds were fully maintained; in the hospital of Bethlehem about fifty or sixty lunatics were housed, and over and above this the City gave alms to about five hundred poor people in their own homes. Now Bridewell, or the House of Correction as the citizens named it, would set on work all who were fit to labour.

But the very measures taken by London aggravated her problem by attracting more of the destitute and homeless to the capital. However devout the citizens, they could not contain the flood. The problem of the sturdy beggar and of the Elizabethan underworld was nation-wide, but in London, swollen in this way, it assumed titanic proportions, as contemporary literature makes clear. For a period the State had been content to let the towns take the initiative. Now it was evident that some wider policy was necessary.

In the decade from 1566 to 1576 there were many parliamentary discussions on the Poor Law. Enclosure was being debated, and the Committees appointed to consider enclosure turned their attention also to the allied question of vagrancy and the poor. A Bill proposed in 1571 was considered 'oversharp and bloody' by Mr Sandys, who thought that every man could be relieved in his own house if trouble were taken. Sir Francis Knollys wanted to follow the example of London and erect a Bridewell in every town. An amended Act became law in 1572. If not 'oversharp', it was still sharp towards the sturdy beggar. For a first offence he was to be whipped and bored through the ear, unless someone would stand surety and keep him in his service for a year. For a second offence he would be adjudged a felon and would be hanged, unless, again, he found surety. For a third offence he would be hanged as a felon—and there was no mitigating clause.

Who was this sturdy beggar? How would he be known? The Act of 1572 is at pains to describe him in some detail: he could be any able-bodied person who was not working, any stage player unattached to a regular Company, any unlicensed pedlar or tinker, anyone practising palmistry or 'other lyke fantasticall Imaginacions' or making money through fraudulent games or competitions. The whole of the English fair, it seems, would be suspect. The same Act went on to say that since it is as necessary to help the aged and impotent as to repress the vagabond, a compulsory poor-rate, levied on all alike, would be instituted, the Justices of the Peace making the assessment and appointing collectors and overseers.[10] The State thus followed the example set by the capital in 1547. The decade ended with the Act of 1576, which again followed London and provided for a House of Correction in every county, stocks of wool, flax, hemp, iron or other material to be provided in every town by the justices.

In the years between 1594 and 1597 harvests were again bad, and corn prices quadrupled. There was riot and distress in many parts of the country. Social and economic problems of many kinds occupied the attention of Parliament and no fewer than seventeen Bills dealing with the poor and the vagrant were introduced into the Parliament in 1597. Thirteen of these were referred to a Committee on which served some of the most famous in the land: Sir Francis Bacon, Sir Edward Coke, Sir Walter Raleigh. In the Lords Burghley and Archbishop Whitgift were active. Two Acts resulted, An Acte for the Reliefe of the Poore and An Acte for Punyshment of Rogues, indicating that the Government was continuing to think along the same lines of division. The Acts enunciated the main principles of English poor relief which were re-enacted and codified in 1601, but not materially changed for two and a half centuries. The Acte for the Reliefe of the Poore came first. It divided the poor into four categories, on the principles already many times laid down: adults able to work, who were to be provided with stocks of materials upon which to work in Houses of Correction; adults unable to work through age or infirmity, who were to be looked after in infirmaries; children of paupers, who were to be apprenticed to a trade; and the sturdy beggars. These last were not to beg outside their own parish on pain of being declared rogues. Funds for the projects envisaged were to be raised by taxing every inhabitant, assessment to be made by parochial officers with the agreement of two Justices of the Peace. Richer parishes might be rated to help poorer, and there was to be in addition a county rate. The State had finally come to the principle of compulsory rating over the whole country, but administration was still in the hands of the churchwardens, together with four overseers appointed by the J.P.s. The whole of the poor-law service was in the hands of unpaid, voluntary workers. The overseers particularly had heavy responsibilities; they were to set the poor children to work, to bind them apprentice, to provide the stocks of hemp, flax and other materials that would occupy the adult unemployed,[11] to relieve the impotent. Perhaps most important of all—together with the Justices of the Peace they had the responsibility of classification, and upon their decision rested the treatment which was given.[12]

The second Act of 1597—An Acte for the Punishment of Rogues—repealed all previous legislation on the subject. There were to be Houses of Correction for sturdy beggars, set up at the discretion of the Justices in session, where they would be made to work. Vagabonds were to be punished by whipping, and were to be sent to the gaol or House of Correction belonging to their place of settlement, after which they would be put to service if able-bodied, or sent to the almshouse if unfit.[13] The High Sheriffs and Justices of all the counties of England and Wales were required by the Privy Council in 1598 to put this Poor Law into operation.

The Statute of 1601 was but a re-enactment, with slight alterations, of the two Statutes enacted in 1597. It added, however, a useful provision of help for maimed soldiers, the money to be raised by county rate on the parishes. The Act of 1601 also made it clear that it did not intend State help to supplant voluntary aid, and inquiry was to be made into breaches of trust concerning charities. There was nothing but amendment until 1834, and this was on the whole retrogressive. An Act of 1609 commanded the erection of one or more Houses of Correction in every county to set 'rogues or such other idle persons on worke', with no mention of the deserving unemployed. Instead of real *work* houses for the unemployed the Houses of Correction were becoming places of detention for the idle rogue. The unemployed came to dread them, and their evil reputation grew until, it was said, the very name of Bridewell was odious in the ears of the people. The contribution of the Restoration to the development of the Poor Law was the institution of the Law of Settlement in a new form. The Settlement Act of 1662 laid down that anyone whom it was felt *might* become chargeable could be sent back to his place of settlement, a restrictive principle that gave powers of discrimination and persecution to the Justice of the Peace.[14] The framework of the 'old poor-law' was completed by the Workhouse Test Act of 1723 which made provision for the erection of a workhouse in every administrative area and made the receipt of relief dependent upon entering the workhouse.[15]

CHAPTER XXII

The Voice of the People

The proportions assumed by the problem of poor relief were partly the result of the maladjustment of society to economic developments. The enclosure of open fields and of common land, the expansion of sheep farming, the persistence of copyhold tenure, the development of capitalist industry, the monopoly of trade and commerce by the chartered companies, the sale of patents and monopolies which could be hurtful to those excluded, the growth of a privileged livery in the gilds, high taxation, import and export duties, were merely some of the most obvious developments which depressed the standard of living and hurt the pride of hitherto independent workmen. Under Charles I wealthier people had to deal also with forced loans and the seizure by the King of depositors' money held for safety by the goldsmiths in the Tower of London.[1] The landowning class as a whole were hit by the revival of feudal dues like fees for knighthood (whether wanted or not), fines for infringement of royal forests (enlarged for the purpose), while the extension of the profitable sinecure of wardship and the sale of peerages and other honours on a large scale was bitterly resented by those who had no part in the bargain.

At the same time religious differences were splitting the nation. Henry VIII's break with Rome had led to the establishment of a Church of England. Protestantism and the Bible in English had opened the doors to an individual interpretation of the Scriptures that resulted not only in a stern organized Presbyterianism but in a variety of Independent forms of worship which eschewed any church organization, and an ever greater variety of sects. Even laymen would preach as the spirit moved them. Praise-God Barebones was a well-known character who would lay down his leatherworker's tools to preach to great crowds outside his shop in Fetter Lane in London; and there were hundreds more of such simple souls who, because they were often the economically under-privileged, appeared to be giving a message that was socially as well as spiritually revolutionary. The more orthodox pulpit, too, was still—as it had been in the Middle Ages—the platform of 'Puritan' preachers whose message was denunciation of all who attempted religious coercion.

By the time of Charles I not only was religious unorthodoxy growing but Charles himself, with his Archbishop William Laud, was feeding the fires of Puritanism by strengthening the place of bishops in Church organization and dogma and reintroducing ritual and ceremony, which to him was no more than 'order' and 'decency' in worship but which to many people smacked of the Church of Rome. The clash was all the more serious since non-conformity was met with intolerance and persecution. The 'Puritan martyrs' were accompanied to their trials and their prisons or places of punishment by huge crowds whom they harangued in biblical phrases easily understood by the people. Those who were fined, imprisoned, pilloried and mutilated for conscience sake were the best propagandists for the Puritan cause.

The issue was also constitutional since it involved the position of Parliament and the right of the Sovereign to act without Parliamentary authority. As one of the speakers in the debates in the Long Parliament put it: of the three main matters with which they were concerned—privileges of Parliament, matters of religion and the property of goods and estates—it was the first in which the other two were comprised.

This was the material for civil war, although when fighting broke out the alignment was by no means clear cut. Traditional loyalty, family connections, the mystique of kingship, took many to the side of the King who had bitterly opposed him previously. On both sides were large and small landowners, old landed families and new, merchants, industrialists and lawyers; rising gentry and falling gentry, aristocratic families and ordinary working people. It was almost a misnomer to talk of King *versus* Parliament, for some 43 per cent of the Long Parliament were for the King, 55 per cent for the Parliament, while some 2 per cent remained uncommitted.

As the struggle proceeded the opponents of the King fell out among themselves. The Army felt that the Parliament was compromising with the King. The Army was stronger than Parliament but was in its turn harassed by elements both within and outside its ranks who wanted to push reform further than the Army wanted to go. These were the people called Levellers, and their leader was a young Puritan called John Lilburne. In his person he was typical of a large section of the population. He was second son of a smallish landowner, and had therefore no patrimony but was apprenticed to a cloth merchant in the City of London. He had been nurtured in the Puritan tradition, had a decent education at a small grammar school, but knew little Latin and less Greek. In London he rapidly came under the influence of the sectarian preachers and was more vocal than most in his opposition to the bishops. When he was about twenty he suffered a spectacular martyrdom by being whipped through the streets at the cart's tail from the Fleet prison to Westminster where, his back raw and bloody from the weals of the three-pronged whip, he stood in the pillory, haranguing the crowd and scattering leaflets among them. He wholeheartedly followed Parliament, and when fighting broke out, with many other apprentices of the City of London he joined the regiment of Robert, Lord Brooke.

After the battle of Naseby in June 1645, which virtually ended the First Civil War, Parliamentary supremacy appeared to be established and many felt that the issues for which they fought had been won. But there were others who now found themselves in a worse position than when they entered the wars. In *England's Birthright Justified* Lilburne stated their case—their livelihood gone, their possessions wasted away, their families in want, religious intoleration and Press censorship as severe as it had been before the fighting. The groups that met with Lilburne in the inns and conventicles of the City now coalesced into the Leveller party, paying subscriptions, organizing petitions to Parliament, sending out emissaries to gather recruits. And all the time Lilburne and his friends were writing one pamphlet after another whose very titles were sufficient to stir to action: *The Freemans Freedome vindicated; Liberty vindicated against Slavery; The Oppressed Mans Oppressions declared.*

Among those listening were the soldiers who had fought and

won the war. By the spring of 1647 these men were becoming restive. Many were Independent in religion or of extremer sectarian belief and they still felt insecure in their worship; they knew that in their absence their farms were going to ruin, their little businesses were decaying, their jobs were going to someone else. They knew that harvests had been bad, that there was a scarcity of food, that prices of all kinds were soaring, that their wives and families were falling into destitution. But their greatest grievance was that they were not being paid their wages. By March 1647 the foot-soldiers were eighteen weeks in arrear, the horse and dragoons forty-three weeks. In the Eastern Association, whose backbone was the sturdy Independent freeholders who had followed Cromwell into the wars for conscience' sake, the Leveller pamphlets were circulating. Lilburne was imprisoned in the Tower for his opposition to Parliament, but this merely added one more plank to his platform and did nothing to stem the flow of words which, in one pamphlet after another, were smuggled out to the army. Parliament added fuel to the flame of discontent by proposing to disband the army without paying its arrears.

In the clash between Army and Parliament that followed the Leveller literature played an important part. There is plenty of evidence of the pamphlets circulating among the soldiers, where no doubt the literate read aloud the most inflammatory exhortations to those unable to read. Goaded beyond endurance, the soldiers of horse in the spring of 1647 elected representatives or agents (or 'agitators' to use the contemporary word) from each regiment to press their case. The foot regiments followed a month later, choosing committees of agitators for every troop and company. The Army Command, although agreeing to the agitators' demand for a Council of the Army on which two commissioned officers and two private soldiers elected from each regiment would serve, used the situation to its own advantage and by the autumn Lilburne and the Levellers were attacking the army command as previously they had attacked Parliament.

King, Parliament, Army Command had all failed—there remained only the people. If the people were to be given power to manage affairs as they wished it was necessary, however, to give them control of Parliament. To this end political reform must precede social reform and so there came into existence the remarkable written constitution which was published as *An*

Agreement of the People. This required an extension of the suffrage (the right to vote being then vested in the 40*s.* freeholder in the country and a miscellaneous collection of mostly influential people in the towns); equal electoral districts according to the number of inhabitants; the dissolution of the existing Parliament and thereafter biennial Parliaments; and the 'reserving' of certain spheres of action from Parliamentary jurisdiction so that no legislature, for example, would have powers of compulsion in matters of religion.

The *Agreement of the People* was discussed by the Council of the Army at Putney in the autumn of 1647. Edward Sexby, one of the organizers of the soldiers, spoke for the rank and file: 'Wee have engaged in this Kingdome and ventur'd our lives, and itt was all for this: to recover our birthrights and priviledges as Englishmen, and by the arguments urged there is none. . . . I wonder wee were soe much deceived'. Cromwell spoke as a practical man who already sensed the difficulties of governing. He took his stand on the fact that they had not entered upon civil war in order to introduce an extension of the suffrage, that the consequences of such a change would be boundless. How do we know, he asked, that it would not lead on to another change—and another—and another? Where would it end? They must be bound by the engagements they had made. But an unknown soldier, simply referred to as a 'Bedfordshire man', maintained that only if an engagement were just should it be kept. If it were unjust, it should be broken. Then Henry Ireton was on his feet to urge that the keeping of covenant was the basis of civil society and of property in land and goods; the breaking of it would be anarchy. 'All the maine thinge that I speake for', said Ireton, 'is because I would have an eye to propertie', and he argued that the right to vote must devolve upon men of property, men with a stake in the country. But Colonel Rainsborough, the only officer of the higher command to be wholeheartedly with the men, was passionate:

> I thinke that the poorest hee that is in England hath a life to live as the greatest hee; and therefore . . . I thinke itt's clear, that every man that is to live under a Government ought first by his owne consent to putt himself under that Government.

The debates were inconclusive. The year 1648 saw Leveller activity swinging back to civilian organization, with meetings and great petitions to Parliament in which women were as vocal as the men. Their organization was betrayed by spies, Lilburne was again imprisoned. Times were bad. A new tax—excise—had been levied on goods of every description, including food and drink. Heavy monthly assessments were being made on the counties to support the Army. Free quarters continued. Plunder, damage to crops and other property was common. There had been exceptionally bad harvests since 1646, and the price of bread had more than doubled. The price of meat increased by about 50 per cent between 1645 and 1648. Rents were everywhere falling; internal trade languished; foreign trade declined; people were put off work in the industrial areas; bureaucracy tormented people; the 'Committee man' lined his own pockets instead of serving the public; war profiteers were 'swolne great' by their neighbours' losses; the Leveller pamphlets were bitterly class-conscious. 'O you Members of Parliament and rich men in the City', exclaimed 'many thousand Tradesmen',

> that are at ease, and drink Wine in Bowls, and stretch yourselves upon Beds of Down, you that grind our faces, and flay off our skins, Will no man amongst you regard, will no man behold our faces black with Sorrow and Famine? . . . What then are your russling Silks and Velvets, and your glittering Gold and Silver Laces? are they not the sweat of our brows, and the wants of our backs and bellies?

The Second Civil War broke across Leveller activity. The Army's victory was followed by the trial and execution of Charles I in January 1649. But the Council of State which took the place of the monarchy made little difference. *Englands New Chains* was the title of the Leveller pamphlet which marked the change. Soon all London was chanting the Leveller question: 'We were before ruled by King, Lords, and Commons; now by a General, a Court Martial, and House of Commons: and we pray you what is the difference?'

Mutiny in the army was suppressed, Lilburne was put on trial for life and finally banished to Jersey. The Protectorate fell with the death of Cromwell and the monarchy was restored, though sufficiently hedged in for the commercial and landowning classes to feel secure. The Levellers, like the Diggers, had failed to bring redress to the workmen of town or country. Lilburne, saddened and in poor health, was brought back from

Jersey to imprisonment in Dover Castle. At the end his turbulent spirit turned to the Quakers and he was allowed in his last years to attend and to speak at Quaker meetings in Kent.

The Quaker movement was growing at this time. George Fox, the son of a weaver and the apprentice of a shoemaker, had been spreading Quaker beliefs from 1647 onwards, while the Levellers were formulating the *Agreement of the People*, and Winstanley was feeling his way towards the practical communism that would bring the Diggers out on to the commons. Quakerism derived from the religious individualism of the sects; it eschewed all organized religion, even the sermon, leaving people to speak as the spirit moved them. It was against all coercion or violence, maintaining a passive resistance in the face of opposition or persecution. In this Quakerism was diametrically opposed to the stormy opposition of the Levellers.

Neither Levellers nor Diggers survived into the Restoration, and they left no direct mark upon subsequent movements. The Levellers, precociously born out of the turmoil of the civil wars, reflected but a faint shadow of themselves in the Chartist movement of the nineteenth century; the Diggers bequeathed something to the Owenites. It was the Quakers who in the end made the greatest impression upon the country, busying themselves with good works and surviving persecution to endure as a recognized and respected religious organization.

What the Levellers wanted, who they were, can be seen in their numerous pamphlets, in their petitions, in their newspaper, *The Moderate*, in the speeches of their leaders. They wanted freedom of religion, the abolition of tythes and the end of any enforced maintenance of the clergy; they wanted freedom of speech and of the Press; they wanted the law translated into English so that all might understand it; they wanted proceedings simplified and speeded up so that long, ruinous suits might be ended; they wanted the revision of punishment so that it might more nearly fit the crime, and in particular a reassessment of the position of debtors. Coupled with law-reform was prison-reform, and, out of their own bitter experience, they asked that gaolers' fees be abolished, their brutality stopped, and the prisons themselves made cleaner and healthier. They demanded the end of the monopoly of the Merchant Adventurers, the abolition of the excise, the repeal of any duties upon goods or restrictions upon trading.

All this was far beyond the simple programme of the Diggers. But the Leveller demands for agrarian reform showed a basic affinity with the Diggers: they asked for the opening of the enclosure of fens and common land for 'the free and common use and benefit of the poor' and for the abolition of any servile tenure that remained, particularly of copyhold tenure 'the badge of slavery', whose uncertainties might at any time be used to penalize a tenant holding his land by copy of ancient court roll.

The Levellers' social programme included the relief of the poor, the maintenance of almshouses, and the provision of schools. They asked that 'all ancient charitable donations towards the constant relief of the poor . . . and all hospitals [almshouses] . . . may be restored and safely preserved', that new almshouses should be established at the public charge, and they suggested that all the glebe land in the kingdom should be earmarked for this purpose. They also suggested that money be raised out of confiscated royalist and Church estates to help those who had fallen on hard times during the wars. With schools, as with almshouses, they demanded that all ancient foundations which had been converted to other uses or fallen into decay should be restored as free schools for the use of poor children, and, moreover, that all parts of the country without schools should have a competent number founded at the public charge 'that few or none of the freemen of England may for the future be ignorant of reading and writing'.

The Leveller movement was not a proletarian movement—indeed, a proletariat hardly as yet existed—but it appealed to all those who were barely preserving their independence. In their own words, the Levellers were 'the middle sort of people'. When Lilburne made his appeal to the hobnails and the clouted shoes and the leather aprons he meant all those who worked, small masters as well as employees, and was not speaking primarily of the dispossessed. The Levellers were not communists or socialists, and spoke specifically against 'abolishing propriety, levelling men's estates, or making all things common', and they denounced the 'erronious tenets of the poor Diggers' in this respect. Whereas the Diggers belong to the long line of communist or socialist idealists the Levellers were the forerunners of the highly individualist doctrine of the true Liberals—duties and privileges for all within a society of private ownership. In this respect they could find little amiss with

Ireton's statement during the debates at Putney: 'All the maine thinge that I speake for is because I would have an eye to Propertie'. But the revolution which Ireton represented, which was accomplished by means of civil war and confirmed by the Restoration settlement of 1660, was not one which helped either Levellers or Diggers. It strengthened parliamentary government, but not so as to include them; it destroyed the last vestiges of feudalism, but, apart from copyhold tenure (which was yielding to the work of lawyers like Sir Edward Coke) these had pressed not upon the Levellers or Diggers but upon their masters. It sanctified 'contract'—the complement of property—but this was a concept from which few Levellers or Diggers could derive any benefit. The Levellers and Diggers were neither the heirs of a dying feudalism nor the progenitors of the new order that was coming to life. It was another class of men upon whom the mantle fell, men and women who had been accumulating wealth and power from trade and industry, from the dissolution of the monasteries or the sale of Crown lands, as reward, by speculation or even shadier means, from intermarriage, from the sequestration of estates during the Civil Wars, from the very achievements of those wars in securing them from economic harassment or political coercion.

CHAPTER XXIII

Education

By the time the civil wars let loose their flood of polemic the English language had attained its full beauty and flexibility, and the art of printing, first practised in England by Caxton at the end of the fifteenth century, was widespread. Literature had developed from Chaucer and Langland (who were probably alive at the time of the Black Death and certainly alive at the time of the Peasants' Revolt) to Shakespeare and the brilliant cohort of scarcely less distinguished writers. The Bible had been translated from Latin into English by John Wyclif at the end of the fourteenth century, by William Tyndale and Miles Coverdale in the first decades of the sixteenth century, and by Protestant exiles in Geneva. Yet, while the written word was well served, the size of the reading public remains uncertain. It must be assumed that the Great Bible which was chained in the churches for all to read actually *was* read, and that the 150 editions of the Geneva Bible were for people who could read. Sir Thomas More as early as 1533 said that half the population could read an English translation of the Bible, and a century later, on the eve of the Civil Wars, there is evidence enough that Bible-reading was one of the formative influences of the time. It remains uncertain, nevertheless, not only how many people could read but how wide was the range upon which they drew. Apart from the Bible, popular broadsheet ballads and news-sheets had a considerable circulation, and many half-literate people may have spelled them out. But how many people read the plays of Shakespeare? Or did the populace who thronged to the Globe and other theatres expect only to see and hear plays and not to read them? Who read Milton? Who read the 100 000 copies of Bunyan's *Pilgrim Progress* which were printed within ten years of its publication in 1678? Who comprised the large public for the tales of Lilliput published by Swift in 1726? Who read Daniel Defoe's *Robinson Crusoe* with such enthusiasm that, published in 1719, it ran to four editions in the course of three months? Richardson—Fielding—Smollett: as England stood on the threshold of revolutionary economic changes and the first generations of proletarians were forming in factory and mine, was it only a leisured upper class who read their long, romantic, satirical and often socially pointed novels?

There are some pointers to the kind of book which the humblest people possessed (besides the Bible) and, therefore, most likely read. John Bunyan's first wife, for example, brought him as her sole marriage dowry two books—Arthur Dent's *The Plaine Man's Path-way to Heaven*, and Lewis Bayly's *The Practise of Pietie*, describing 'How to read the Bible with profit and ease once over every yeere'. Dent's book ran to twenty-five editions between 1601 and 1640, Bayly's to forty-five between 1612 and 1640. Three thousand copies of a sermon could be printed in a few months, Foxe's *Acts and Monuments* (better known as *Book of Martyrs*), published in 1562, was one of the most quoted books among Puritans. It was one which, besides his wife's dowry, had a great influence upon Bunyan. He himself was an example of a simple and poor working-man, a tinker by trade, who attained the little formal education he had at his parish school. His own book, *The Pilgrim's Progress*, was one of the most potent influences upon simple people from the end of the seventeenth century until long afterwards. A little later there is evidence that 'the number man' would bring weekly or monthly parts of educational books or novels to the fair or market for people who had contracted to take them.

As distinct from questions regarding the reading public, there is ample evidence that the passionate interest in playgoings of Shakespeare's time included all classes of the community, particularly of the capital. There is no doubt of the ability of all classes to follow a theme, catch an allusion, and enjoy spoken English. Evidence of close political reasoning and ability to grasp abstract argument is afforded by the pamphlets which were issued in the course of the Civil Wars of the seventeenth century. Those produced by the Levellers particularly, addressed specifically to soldiers and to working men and women, envisage a high intelligence. Yet they are not direct evidence of literacy, for many of them were doubtless read aloud. Their production shows that people could follow an involved argument, and appreciate the magnificent rolling prose of the seventeenth century, rather than that they themselves could read.[1]

Evidence of literacy based upon the amount and type of education available is no more reliable than that based upon the amount and type of literature available. Schooling during the Middle Ages rested with the Church. Every cathedral was required by canon law to have a grammar school in which Latin was taught, as well as rhetoric and dialectic and sometimes arithmetic, geometry, astronomy and music as well, and a school was normally attached to a church or monastery. Most of the pupils of these schools were intended for the Church. Higher education at the universities, the big foundations at Oxford and Cambridge starting in the twelfth and thirteenth centuries, was almost entirely a preserve of the Church. This emphasis upon clerical learning was part of a general dichotomy which was accepted throughout the early Middle Ages: the churchman or 'clerk' was trained to speak and write in Latin, to make accounts, to carry on the business of the country, while the knight was trained in all the virtues of chivalry—physical prowess, bravery, the succour of the weak, gentleness to women, unyielding struggle with his enemies.

It would seem, nevertheless, that as early as the time of King Alfred in the ninth century there were educated men not intended for the Church, and by the fourteenth and fifteenth centuries lawyers, manorial officers and town officials were necessarily becoming part of a growing class of educated laymen. Many of these took their education side by side with churchmen, but by this time there were also increasing numbers of grammar schools founded by bequest for the population generally. Though many of these schools were founded for the purpose of instructing boys in the rudiments of Greek and Latin grammar, this could hardly have been done without a knowledge of the written word in English. Free grammar schools were also being established by the gilds and by the towns, instruction in English and elementary arithmetic or accounting being fundamental to their purpose. There existed also chantry schools where the scholars as part of their duty sang obits for the soul of their dead benefactor. While many of these were for children intended for the Church, there were also many little village song-schools attached to the local church which drew in a wider range of children, and there were independent foundations, simpler than the grammar schools, endowed by wealthy benefactors for the education of village children. There were also schools where a few pence sufficed to pay a small stipend to a village schoolmaster; or the priest would himself act as teacher to the children of his parish, instructing them in reading and writing as well as in the Catechism. A small bequest to a village boy to pay the few pence necessary 'to get him a school' was quite common.

The existence of schools open to all is indicated by the author of *Pierce the Ploughman's Creed*, written probably in the last decade of the fourteenth century: 'Now may every cobbler set his son to school, and every beggar's brat learn from the book'. It is confirmed by the Statute of 1406, which forbade parents of less estate than 20*s*. a year from land to apprentice their children in towns, but added the interesting proviso: 'that every man and woman, of what estate or condition whatsoever, shall be free to set their son or daughter to take learning at any manner of school that pleaseth them within the realm'. Sufficient schools clearly existed for the State to take cognizance of them, but an estimate of their numbers is difficult indeed. It is possible even that in the turbulent ending of the Middle Ages many schools, with almshouses and other charitable institutions, fell into decay, and that there were fewer schools at the end of the fifteenth century than at the beginning.[2] But if the beginning of the Tudor period marked a nadir in education, its lusty development helped a revival. It has even been suggested that there was nothing short of an educational revolution in England between 1550 and 1640.[3]

On the one hand, the education of the aristocracy was widening through their use of private tutors, and their travel abroad, where they could share in the excitements of the European Renaissance. Certain schools began to be regarded as their preserve—Eton, founded in 1440 by Henry VI, and Westminster (or St Peter's College), an old school refounded first by Henry VIII and then, in 1560, by Queen Elizabeth. They tended after this to go to one of the colleges of Oxford or Cambridge. By the end of Elizabeth's reign the statesman with the learning of the clerk, the courtier with the attributes of chivalry, the poet with a command of the English language, were frequently one and the same person.

The sons of the gentry, meantime, who would go into the Church, the Law, or some kindred profession, were seeking a similar education at one of the less exclusive grammar schools which would prepare them for the Inns of Court or the University. The newly rich, or those who had recently acquired land, would naturally seek to equip their children with an education which was not inferior, and all in all there was a general pressure upon the educational services. Older foundations that had fallen into decay or were swept away in the dissolution of the monasteries and chantries were refounded. New schools were established, such as John Colet's St Paul's School in 1509–10, and the 'Blue Coat School' in Newgate Street, attached to the older Christ's Hospital, in 1553. The continued diversity of the scale and aim of education is indicated by the bequest, at one end of the scale, from a husbandman of Wigston in Leicestershire, who in the 1580s left twenty shillings for his son in order 'that he be kept to scoole tyll he cane wrytt and reade' to that of Sir William Paston, who founded a grammar school at North Walsham, Norfolk, in 1606 for 'the training, instructing, and bringing up of youth in good manners, learning . . . the true service of Almighty God . . . the dutiful obedience and subjection to their natural Prince and other Magistrates . . .'[4] The number of parsons and curates teaching a few boys the rudiments of Latin and their native tongue probably increased during the Interregnum as dispossessed Anglican clergy set up as schoolmasters, while in 1661 Richard Lawrence, a Commonwealth soldier, founded a 'charity school' for twenty boys. Dr Busby, who was headmaster of Westminster School from 1638 to his death in 1695, gave £5 or £6 annually for instructing poor children from the parish. It has been estimated that between 1480 and 1660 over a quarter of all charitable giving went into education, and that by the middle of the seventeenth century there was a school for every 4 400 of the population.[5]

Even on the university level there was a new departure in a foundation in London endowed by Sir Thomas Gresham at the end of the sixteenth century for the dissemination of 'useful knowledge', which in contrast to the existing universities was lay and not clerical, with emphasis upon scientific teaching conducted in English. Gresham College functioned as a kind of extra-mural establishment, with close ties with the older universities, who provided teachers and lecturers. It embraced the interest of a wide class of student, being part adult education centre, part working-men's college, and through the eminent scientists who lectured there it attracted also many scholars as well as merchants, shopkeepers and financiers, and it became a lively centre of scientific learning and discussion. Poorer people at the same time were gaining access to higher education in a different way. Two Cambridge colleges whose entrance lists have been studied—Caius College and St John's—show artisans and shopkeepers, yeomen farmers, husbandmen, and a group who are entered as 'plebeian'—boys who were probably there by benefit of some endowment or who were working their way through college by serving the richer members.[6]

But while there is a general indication of wider education, and more opportunities for education, there is still no firm basis for an estimate of the degree of literacy in Tudor and Stuart times. If a felon could read a sentence from the Bible he could claim benefit of clergy, and his punishment would then be branding instead of hanging. That many did so is a general pointer to literacy. Another pointer is given by the Committee on Free Trade in 1604, which found 'Learning Preferrments' to be 'common to all and mean', and therefore of no attraction to the gentleman's son. Another is that a third of the adult males who signed a Protestation of Loyalty in Surrey in 1642 used their names rather than marks.[7]

But by the end of the seventeenth century charitable bequests were again falling into decay, and the foundation or upkeep of schools for poorer people was languishing. New foundations indicated a different spirit. In 1698 the Society for Promoting Christian Knowledge—the SPCK—was founded by the Rev. Dr Bray and others. Its objects were 'to promote religion and learning in the plantations abroad and to propagate Christian knowledge at home'. Two years later, making use of the name employed by a Commonwealth soldier in 1661, and in the same spirit in which Sir William Paston founded his grammar school in 1606, the charity school movement proper was founded by Colonel Colchester and Thomas Bray. Its avowed object was 'the education of poor children in the knowledge and practice of the Christian religion as professed and taught in the Church of England' and 'teaching them such other things as are most suitable to their condition'.

School hours were to be from seven to eleven and from one o'clock to five in summer and from eight to eleven and from one o'clock to four in winter. The first business of the master was to instruct the children in the church catechism 'which he shall first teach them to pronounce distinctly and plainly, and then, in order to practice, shall explain it to the meanest capacity . . . twice a week'. He was to

> 'teach them the true spellings of words and distinction of syllables, with the points and stops, which is necessary to true and good reading and serves to make the children mindful of what they read. As soon as the boys can read competently well the Master shall teach them to write a fair legible hand, with the grounds of arithmetic, to fit them for service or apprenticeship.

The girls, meantime, besides reading, were to knit their stockings and gloves, make, mark and mend their clothes, while the more apt would be taught to spin and even to write.

The teacher was rewarded by the payment by results method so derided in the nineteenth century. He received 2*s*. 6*d*. for each child who mastered the alphabet; 2*s*. 6*d*. for each child who could spell; 5*s*. for each one who could read well and distinctly and say the Catechism; and 15*s*. for each one who could write and cast accounts. The total estimated cost a year for each child at the school was £75. Their ages varied between seven and twelve years, and they were provided with a uniform which they were required to wear. In 1707, 69 of these schools flourished in and around London, accommodating 2 813 children; by 1711 there were 119 schools and 4 687 children; by 1727 they had spread all over England, and a total of nearly 1 400 schools taught over 22 000 boys and nearly 6 000 girls. Various little private-enterprise schools scattered over the country completed what existed as education for poorer people on the eve of the Industrial Revolution.

CHAPTER XXIV

The Landlord State

Fundamental to the history of England from the Black Death to the Industrial Revolution has been the land. In spite of the importance of trade and the growing importance of industry, in spite of the often very substantial spoils of office which hung in some unclassified but remunerative limbo between politics and economics, it was the land which was basic to wealth, to prestige, to power. Land was a reward for services rendered, a guarantee of service to come; it was a source of wealth in itself, it was an investment, its possession was the key to public office at the centre and prestigious service in the locality; it brought respect, service, graceful living, recreation as well as profit; it was requisite to a place in Parliament; it accompanied and sometimes brought ennoblement; it bred and nurtured a good race of men fit for the country's business and the nation's defence.

In feudal times the power of the sovereign and of his feudal barons was expressed directly in terms of land. In the break-up of feudalism land changes affected big landowners and small, but on the whole change was slow.[1] In times of civil war change was more rapid, the victorious party rewarding its adherents with land and confiscating the estates of its opponents. The Wars of the Roses were such an occasion, Henry Tudor himself being an example of one who accumulated estates through being on the winning side, the Stonor family being an instance of those who lost heavily through being allied with the losers. The seventeenth-century civil wars and Interregnum present another instance of land confiscation and sale. The fact that much of it was bought back by its former owners, while mitigating the degree of change involved, underlines its importance. The dissolution of the monasteries and the sale of monastic land constituted another major change. Much of it changed hands several times on the speculative market before coming to rest in the hands of corporations, peers, courtiers, royal officials, lawyers, industrialists and newly risen gentry. Monarchs in times of financial difficulty regarded Crown land as a realizable asset, even Elizabeth, at the end of her reign, selling on a large scale. Land also came on the market for many other reasons; the impoverishment of a landowner, the lack of an heir, high taxation such as took place in the Interregnum and later seventeenth century, inability to cope with a large estate. While it did not necessarily follow that such sales brought new classes to the land, there is no doubt that commercial wealth helped to effect the purchase. Often it was more attractive to both sides to intermarry rather than sell or buy, and City wealth joined aristocratic acres in the marriage contract: merchants 'often change estate with gentlemen, as gentlemen do with them, by a mutual conversion of the one into the other'.[2] At the same time more enterprising landowners were themselves embracing the practical side of estate management, as Harrison noted, becoming 'graziers, butchers, tanners, sheepmasters, woodmen . . . thereby to enrich themselves and bring all the wealth of the country into their own hands'.[3] Change, for whatever reason, was constant, sometimes as slow as the break-up of feudalism, sometimes quickening so much as to appear revolutionary to contemporaries.

A period of more rapid change was noted in the middle of the sixteenth century, when those alive at the time became aware of a landowning class later described by Sir Walter Raleigh as 'situated neither in the lowest grounds . . . nor in the highest mountains . . . but in the valleys between both'.[4] Contemporaries called them 'gentlemen', or 'gentry'. They could be distinguished from those below them in the accepted hierarchy by their right to armorial bearings, and it is significant that in the century following one of the major land-transfers—the dissolution of the monasteries—the number of gentle families reported by heraldic visitations considerably increased.[5] These families were not of noble title, though their ties with the aristocracy were frequently close; their interests in trade and commerce were generally strong. Their rise to become important landowners was by no means one-sided. They were sometimes welcomed, sometimes met half-way, even if they sometimes changed places with the aristocratic landowner. Their ties were indeed frequently so close that there was sometimes little difference between a gentry family and an aristocratic family, the one being absorbed into the other. The recognition of the importance of the gentry, as well as of their recent rise, is clear enough from contemporary literature. They even had manuals of conduct written for their benefit. One speaks of 'the true and new art of gentilizing'. They advise on apparell—'comely not gaudy'. A woman must prefer honour before pleasure, must beware of self-praise, must 'cloathe not her look with a disdainfull scorn, nor cloud her brow with an imperious frown' but believe gentry to be 'best graced by affability'. The gentleman similarly 'scorns pride, as a derogation to Gentry'. But on the practical side he

> wonders at a profuse foole, that he should spend when honest frugalitie bids him spare; and no lesse as a miserable Crone, who spares when reputation bids him spend. . . . *Learning* he holds not only an additament, but ornament to *Gentry*. . . . He intends more the tillage of his minde, than his ground; yet suffers not that to grow wilde neither.[6]

The gentry did not normally live in the same kind of state as the aristocracy, and were therefore less vulnerable to inflation. Probably, also, they were able to weather the stress of high prices, bad times and high taxation better than the smaller freeholders, who had less to fall back upon. They were peculiarly and tenaciously pervasive. While under the English system of primogeniture their land passed to their eldest sons, their younger sons went not only into the Church and the law and other professions but into trade and commerce and, less frequently, into industry. At the same time, while some of them rose to be big landowners, undoubtedly there were so-called gentry families who, through ill-luck or bad management or through biting off more than they could chew, sunk into the ranks of the smallholder or went back to trade. Sometimes there was little difference between a gentry family and a prosperous yeoman family, and it was said with truth that to be a 'gentleman' was but 'to carry the port, charge and countenance of a gentleman'.[7] A yeoman farmer could stretch his estate to live in such a way. Conversely, a gentleman farmer could live frugally, like a yeoman, and husband his estate by so doing.

The aristocracy, meanwhile, although probably spending more on the traditional upkeep of their way of life, were compensated not only by the salaries but by the perquisites of Court office. Against these there had to be set the expenses of appearing at Court and living in the capital, yet the fruits of office could be rich. Robert Cecil, first Earl of Salisbury, made £4 000 a year from the sale of offices in his gift, £480 a year as master of the Court of Wards, £2 100 from the sales of wardships, £7 000 a year from the farm of the silk customs. This total of £13 580 should be compared with the £7 000 which was his annual average receipt from his land.[8] But, if he enjoyed the fruits of office, the aristocrat did not leave the fruits of commerce to be plucked solely by the gentry. It has been estimated that, of the families in the peerage between 1560 and 1640, fully two-thirds were engaged in colonial, trading, or industrial enterprise, and that these did not necessarily coincide with recent creations. Edward Stafford, third Duke of Buckingham, who prospered in the early sixteenth century, was such a one.

The younger sons of the aristocracy, like those of the gentry, were also entering the professions, going into the Church, engaging in trade, the difference on that level between gentry and aristocracy becoming blurred. Conversely, the newly arrived gentry family, however its land was acquired, became after a couple of generations assimilated into the landed classes. The story hardly changes over the centuries—the rise by office, Court favour, trade, industry, marriage, to the acquisition of land or more land. The aristocracy, as a class, was as old as the lord of the manor, but individual peerages could be newer than a rising gentry family. The Tudors rewarded their favourites with noble titles, but they acted with discretion; the first two Stuarts made a lucrative business of ennoblement, creating between them over a hundred peerages at as much as £10 000 apiece, their new lordships receiving the honour, as Pym put it in the House of Commons, 'according to the heaviness of their purse and not for the weightinesse of their merit'. On the other hand, a family like that of William Stump, the famous Wiltshire clothier, could achieve the same end through marriage—in his case on an even larger scale, even if it took three generations to do so, for three of his great-grand-daughters married into the peerage, becoming Countesses of Rutland, of Suffolk, and of Lincoln respectively.[9]

It is apparent that no class had the monopoly of advantage or determination. If some gentry were more able to weather the rise in prices because they lived more frugally, had less to 'keep up', and because they could supplement their landed income by their commercial assets, the aristocracy had the fruits of office, as well as their interests in commerce, to oil their estates. If there were spendthrift peers who squandered an inheritance there were spendthrift upstarts who frittered away their newly acquired wealth. If the middle classes wanted to farm their new land for profit—and it is not certain that this was why they wanted to be landowners, prestige and founding a landed family being often equally (or more) important—there is no reason to believe that the older-established landowners did not do likewise, as the efficiency of the monastic houses, and the careful Estate Treatises, demonstrate. Nor was the conversion of arable to pasture when sheep were profitable, or enclosure itself, confined to new families. Any attempt to generalize upon class and a more rapid rise of new gentry families acquiring after centuries of the blending of landed and commercial wealth there appeared, between about 1540 and 1640, to be a more rapid rise of established gentry families within the landowning class and a more rapid rise of new gentry families acquiring land for the first time. The controversy as to whether or not the gentry at this time were acquiring land at the expense of the aristocracy, at the expense of smaller landowners, or of both has been temporarily laid to rest on the assumption of continuing flux and of 'rising' and 'falling' families at all times, both within and between all classes. Meanwhile, detailed work on landholding in various parts of the country, which alone can provide the correct answers, continues to provide examples that involve all classes.[10]

Peers and gentry were not the only classes on the land. Very important were the smaller freeholders, with whom may be included the inheritable copyholders and other tenant farmers of secure tenure, who together formed the 'yeomen of England'—the sturdy, independent farmers upon whom Elizabeth I loved to say she relied, and in whom Cromwell found the 'men of a spirit' who formed his Ironsides. They were the owner-occupiers who, living unostentatiously, could possess more solid wealth than a gentleman, or who, conversely, might adopt the style and port of a gentleman and educate their sons with those of the gentry, and some of whom, like the Peels in the eighteenth century, turned their talents to industry to become the first generation of Industrial Revolution factory-owners. Perhaps together they occupied 25 per cent of the cultivated land of England during the Tudor period and early seventeenth century, farming in units of as little as thirty or as large as a hundred acres. This could be enclosed or open-field land; they could be as active as bigger landowners in buying more land or in contriving to get scattered strips in one piece. They would even let at rent as well as farming themselves. They sometimes became so wealthy, said Harrison, 'that many of them are able and do buy the lands of unthrifty gentlemen'.[11] They could farm for sheep, for arable, or for a combination of both. They frequently farmed several farms, each of which might bring in, as in a case in Suffolk, from £40 to £80 a year.[12] In the reign of Elizabeth there was general testimony to their prosperity. They 'live wealthilie', said Harrison, and 'keepe good houses' with 'costlie furniture'. They improved their houses in many ways, including the building of the newly fashionable chimneys. If they paid rent they had enough money tucked away to pay six or seven years of the next lease.[13] Their prosperity was partly due to their self-sufficiency, baking their own bread, brewing their own beer and, in general, living upon the produce of their own land. It was good, solid living, but not extravagant. The yeoman, moreover, rarely squandered good money on journeys to London, still less on speculation. It was the kind of life that enabled him to weather inflation better than most. By the end of the seventeenth century, nevertheless, the yeomen had passed the peak of their prosperity, and were yielding to pressures of various kinds: one was the political value of their land, a 40*s*. freehold being sought as bringing the right to vote; another was the development of farming techniques which favoured the bigger unit.

For by this time all who could do so were intent upon increasing the size of their estates. By the end of the seventeenth century the movement to the Great Estate was beginning, and it was well on the way by the middle of the eighteenth century with the extension of landed estates and the intensification of ownership within manors. New stewards, like their medieval forebears, were advising their masters in reasoned and detailed estate treatises. Buy land! urged Edward Laurence, the agent of the Duke of Buckingham, and he elaborated his advice in *The Duty of a Steward to his Lord*, published in 1727. The steward, he said, 'should endeavour to lay all the small farms, let to poor indigent people, to the great ones'. He was careful to advise his lord to wait until the death of a tenant, but the tenant's family was not considered.

By the second half of the eighteenth century a group of some few hundreds of the greatest landowners, including most of the aristocracy, who had owned between them some 15 to 20 per cent of the cultivated land of England in the late fifteenth century, now owned some 25 per cent of it, which they held in large estates of some 10 000 to 20 000 acres. Some of this they farmed themselves, some they let at lease, generally on short term so that it could be called in or the rent raised if they considered this desirable. On the whole, and as a class, they had gained since the Tudor accession, while, on the other hand, less land was in ecclesiastical possession, less in the possession of the Crown than there then was. At the same time, it is possible that by the beginning of the eighteenth century the purchase of land by wealthy merchants had become less attractive, as investment in Government stock became more tempting, that after about 1730 there was less movement by new families into land, and that by the middle of the century the structure of ownership had become fairly static.

The peasant, whose fortunes we have traced from the time of the Black Death, when he was farming his strips in the open fields as a villein bound to the soil, was now free in the eyes of the law, but in many ways only questionably better off. We heard him demand the end of serfdom in 1381. We heard the same cry, more faintly, in 1549. We heard the outcry against enclosures, but there was then no accompanying demand for personal freedom, for villeinage had practically disappeared. It had not gone down before revolt or revolution but before the slow erosion of the movements we have discussed. Occasionally decisive action was called for, as when Henry VII at the beginning of his reign cut one of the knots of legal controversy by enacting that 'no land holden in villeinage . . . shall ever make a man a villein', while Elizabeth I in 1575 freed 200 bondmen (the Tudor name for villein) in the Duchy of Lancaster. But generally the transformation had been less emphatic; more villeins won their freedom in the towns; more took land on lease and became indistinguishable from freemen; others were accepted into the Church and given minor office. They merged into the rest of the population, and the last villein passed away early in the seventeenth century. Nevertheless, in the middle of the eighteenth century open-field villages existed, particularly in the Midlands, much as they had done at the time of the Black Death. There was to be one more upheaval in the enclosure that accompanied the so-called Agrarian Revolution before the medieval village would have ceased to exist altogether.

The political significance of land had been somewhat overlaid in early modern times by its economic importance. The Livery Companies were stressing both aspects when in 1697 they limited membership of the Livery to those possessing landed estate.[14] For land still remained necessary to a seat in the House of Commons, and, apart from a varying borough franchise, was the qualification for a vote. These representational rights assumed a new importance as the State became increasingly powerful.

At the time of the Black Death, in England as in Europe, the pattern of life was determined by feudalism, the Christian religion as represented by the Church of Rome, and the Latin tongue. By the time of the Industrial Revolution economic activity and social life were contained within a framework provided by the State, there was a Church of England, and the English language—full, versatile, malleable—had everywhere replaced Latin, except in certain legal documents.

The nation-state that now stood at the centre of national life differed from feudalism in many ways. The most clearly marked difference between the two is that whereas the modern State provides a central point of authority, in feudal times there were many—in practice often as many as there were manorial lords—in spite of the fact that in theory the King was supreme. This change of emphasis from power at the periphery to power at the centre came about in many ways. Partly it was due to a slow dissolution of the old ties as population grew, activities became more diversified, new opportunities for action and new horizons of thought opened up. Improved communications, an expansion of trade, were obvious centripetal forces; the growth of towns, while not helping national unification, yet cut across the feudal structure; powerful centralizing force was the unification of justice and of law and order. Feudalism succumbed in part to the natural desire of the monarch to break the power of his feudal barons and stop their constant warfare. It broke down because kings needed money, and could not rely upon their barons to give it to them, evoking instead some authority to underwrite a more regular source of income. It broke down in face of internal strife which tore the nation apart and of external war which required a unity of effort. It disintegrated because human society will not for ever exist on a basis of constraint. When Bosworth Field ended the last of the barons' wars Henry VII emerged as master of an embryo nation-state. He assisted its development by limiting the power of feudal lords to maintain armed followers dependent upon themselves; he strengthened the Justices of the Peace at the periphery and the Great Council at the centre, making both more dependent upon himself. At the same time he found ready to hand an instrument which had been in existence long before the Black Death: Parliament.

The development of Parliament began when King John in 1213 ordered the sheriffs of each county to send four 'discreet' men of the shire to speak with the king on public business. In 1254 two knights chosen from each county were summoned to a Great Council at Westminster to report on the amount of monetary aid their districts would give the king. In 1265 Simon de Montfort, the feudal lord who for a short while was ruler of England, called a Parliament which, to strengthen his own position, included representatives of the towns; in 1275 Edward I summoned a Parliament to approve the wool tax known as the Great and Ancient Custom on wool. Parliament continued to meet at intervals, but only when the king summoned it, and it became customary to include representatives of both the counties and the towns. The monarch's power continued to grow, and by the end of the Tudor period there was a strong state headed by a powerful monarch, whose instrument was the Privy Council, supported by a Parliament, which still met only on his summons, and by a ramification of local officers, mostly unpaid amateurs, supposedly carrying into effect a national law. This was the weakness of the Tudor monarchy, and remained a weakness of government until the nineteenth century. Feudal power had been absorbed, the power of the towns had been broken, but in the new synthesis the local drive and initiative of the manor officer and the town burgess had not been effectively replaced.

Strong though the Tudor monarchs were, other developments were again at work, challenging the nature of the monarchy. Parliament was one of the greatest of these, and the relationship between monarch and Parliament was changed irrevocably in the heat of civil war. Although the Restoration of Charles II in 1660 restored the monarchy, it was not the monarchy of Elizabeth, nor even the monarchy of his father. With fears of arbitrary government laid to rest, with the last remnants of feudal obligation brushed away, the ruling class—part commercial, part landed—now swept forward to ever greater prosperity within the framework of a constitutional monarchy underpinning a nation-state. That state was now the all-powerful Leviathan of which Thomas Hobbes wrote in 1651: *Non est potestas super terram quae comparetur ei*—there is no power on earth to compare with it. If Hobbes personalized Leviathan in the sovereign he at the same time described Leviathan as 'a Commonwealth, or State . . . which is but an artificial man; though of greater stature and strength than the natural, for whose protection and defence it was intended'.[15] It was in this sense that Leviathan was accepted by the New Order which replaced feudal society.

Feudal society had been a society of carefully graded degree wherein each knew his duties and his rights. That these rights and duties depended basically upon custom made them more rather than less acceptable, their very immutability giving them sanction. This concept of status went right through society from top to bottom, and applied not only legally and economically but to all a person did and was trained to be. A knight governed his life by the code of chivalry, a clerk by the learning he absorbed, an ecclesiastic by the laws of the Church, a villein by the custom of the manor, a mechanic by the rules of his gild. Society was held together by the fact and the knowledge of status or degree, as Shakespeare knew well:

> Take but degree away, untune that string,
> And, hark, what discord follows![16]

That the distinction could be finely drawn was demonstrated by Wolsey's rebuke to the clothiers in 1528: 'You use not yourselves like merchants, but like graziers and artificers'.[17]

But this conception was being changed by economic and

religious developments. An uneasy sense of economic mutation was expressed by the Committee on Free Trade in 1604: if they have no opportunity to merchandize abroad, they ask, 'what else shall become of Gentlemen's younger Sons, who cannot live by Arms, when there is no War, and Learning Preferrments are common to all, and mean? So that nothing remains fit for them, save only Merchandize . . . unless they turn Serving-men, which is a poor Inheritance'. A society which is economically fluid produces changing patterns of wealth which produce new social relationships. A society open to the restless questioning which Protestantism encouraged is inimical to the idea of immutable degree. Where the individual fends for himself economically, and stands up to God as an individual, the idea of personal contract freely entered into becomes the binding cement of society. Such ideas had been common currency in the debates which preceded and accompanied the Civil Wars. Cromwell was gropingly expressing this at Putney when he opposed the *Agreement of the People* on the grounds that it was contrary to the 'engagements' made at the beginning of the conflict.[18] Now it was said not only that civil society itself had come into being through contract but that the object of that contract was the preservation of property. Echoes of Putney sound again, this time in the voice of Henry Ireton: 'All the maine thinge that I speake for is because I would have an eye to propertie'.[19]

But the Committee on Free Trade had already perceived that the uncontrolled accumulation of property in unequal proportions could be damaging to the Commonwealth. 'The more equal Distribution of the Wealth of the Land', they said,

> is a great Stability and Strength to the Realm, even as the equal Distributing of the Nourishment in a Man's body; the contrary whereof is inconvenient in all Estates, and oftentime breaks out into Mischief; when too much Fulness doth puff up some by Presumption, and too much Emptiness leaves the rest in perpetual Discontent, the Mother of Desire of Innovations and Troubles.

James Harrington developed the idea. In 1656 in his sketch of an ideal Commonwealth, Oceana, he maintained that there was a 'balance of forces' between property and political power—or, as a later generation would say, between economic and political power. The accumulation of property by some at the expense of others resulted in oligarchy or dictatorship. An equal division of property resulted in a balanced political constitution or a democracy. An imbalance between economic and political power would, moreover, lead to war and disturbance, as in the Civil Wars of the seventeenth century. Harrington, like most of his contemporaries, thought mainly in terms of landed property, and his proposal was to limit landholding to estates of the annual value of £2 000. To maintain the balance it would be necessary to prevent the accumulation of land, which should therefore be divided upon the death of a landowner between all his children.

It could hardly be expected that a society which was busy accumulating property and adding to its estates in every way possible would be guided by Harrington's dictum. It was rather John Locke who was the prophet of the new age. He preached both the necessity of property and the preservation of property without any limit. He went further. The preservation of property was the chief end of civil society. It was indeed for this, for the preservation of property, that men made a social contract and entered into civil society in the first place. That being so, 'the preservation of property being the end of government, and that for which men enter into society, it necessarily supposes and requires that the people should have property.'[20] It was the voice of the individual, it was the negation of socialism or communism or any form of common ownership, it was the doctrine that would carry capitalism triumphant upon its back into the New Order of the nineteenth century.

But a doctrine without action, a theory without concrete manifestation, is a tiger without claws. The importance of property was given practical expression in the legal system, the judiciary, in social relationships, in command of the armed forces, in hereditary membership of the House of Lords and, most clearly and obviously, in the electoral system. The county franchise devolved upon those with an annual income of 40*s*. or more from their own land; in the towns a mixed franchise, of little uniformity, gave for the most part electoral rights to property-owners. The qualification for membership of the House of Commons, having always rested upon property, was in 1711 expressly tied to an income from land of not less than £300 a year. The overt and uninhibited use of property as the cornerstone of civil society was the ultimate mark of the change that had occurred: feudal lords had been no less anxious than their descendants to preserve their property, but it would not have occurred to them to express themselves in this way. The men who justified their possessions in terms of first principles, and created a state to underpin their interests, had seen enough of civil war and rebellion, and relied instead upon a monarchy and a Parliament of their own making.

The close relationship between commercial wealth and landed wealth, manifest in a variety of ways, was one of the driving forces of English social and economic development, whose momentum lasted until the influx of industrial wealth threatened to overturn the balance. The struggle between the old and accepted amalgam of land and commerce, on the one hand, and the upstart wealth of the Industrial Revolution on the other, was played out largely in the field of politics, when new wealth forced its way into Parliament not only by acquiring land, as the Tudor gentry had done, but by Parliamentary reform. Meanwhile, however, in the countryside the squire played his autocratic role throughout the eighteenth century and most of the nineteenth. In the novels of Fielding and Smollett and Jane Austen he comes to life. He is Lord of the Manor writ large, the Game Laws preserving his shooting as the Forest Laws protected the hunting of his forebears. Local justice and the fixing of wages are in his hands as Justice of the Peace. His aristocratic neighbours lead similar lives on a grander scale, and, as Lords-Lieutenant of the counties, back up his activities as J.P. They are all 'gentlefolk'. Their substantial houses stand in their spacious 'parks', carefully laid out after the fashion set by Dutch William and Mary or in the 'romantic' style of 'Capability' Brown. They all go regularly to church—when they are at home, and not 'visiting' or attending to business or politics or the social round in the capital. Like the medieval lords who fed the poor at their gates, their womenfolk bring succour to the poor and to the sick. For the most part they are not unkind, or even intentionally autocratic. They simply accept a class division in society, with an acceptance as total as that of any medieval lord.

At the centre the State had now interpreted its role as one of active interference and busy calculation in what was best for trade and industry and for the property-owners whose instrument it was. The result was the tangle of taxation, the maze of legislation known as mercantilism.[21] But since property was expressed so largely in land it was only to be expected that agrarian legislation also would protect the landed interest. The abolition, in the course of the Civil Wars, of old, irksome feudal obligations was confirmed in the Restoration Settlement of 1660. Enclosure continued slowly, and there was no further attempt by the State to stop it. The Corn Laws which had had, on the whole, the object of protecting the consumer[22] by not allowing prices to *rise above* a given level, now protected the producer by not allowing prices to *fall below* a given level. A sliding scale of import duties kept out imported corn when prices were low, a sliding scale of bounties on export provided a wider market except in time of scarcity when, as in 1698 and several times during the eighteenth century, the export of corn was forbidden. For nearly two hundred years a series of Acts expressing this policy in various forms appeared and reappeared on the Statute Book. Their effect is not easy to judge. They encouraged self-sufficiency, improvements in farming, and a greater reliance upon arable farming as a corrective to the over-balance of pasture. But poor people often suffered. 'The Act which is good for the farmers, is not beneficial to the town', wrote a correspondent from Falmouth in 1673, expressing a basic and unavoidable conflict of interest. The poor people, he said, 'begin to murmur'.[23] Their murmurs were louder in the nineteenth century, but it was not they but a powerful party of wealthy industrialists who, after an avowedly class struggle with the landlords, repealed the main body of Corn Laws in 1846. The last of the Corn Laws went in 1869.

Plague was intermittent throughout most of the period. It was basically only when the flea-carrying black rat was driven out by the brown sewer rat that the pestilence was halted. But the only outbreak to assume anything like the proportions of the Black Death was the last. The Great Plague raged from the spring of 1665 to the end of 1666 and was at its worst in London, where some 7 000 deaths occurred in one week alone. The course of events was not unlike that of 1348–9. The Court and Government left the capital for Hampton Court and then for Salisbury; many clergy deserted their posts, but others took their places; some doctors fled the scene, others remained to little better practical effect; the same mixtures of superstition and ancient herbal remedies were applied with no more success. When at last the plague had receded, through no cause then known, the Great Fire broke out in London, said to have started in a baker's shop near London Bridge. Fire was not uncommon in cities, which, in spite of injunctions to the contrary, were still built of a high proportion of wood and thatch, and in the particular dryness of the season the fire of September 1666 swept through the City for four whole days, destroying churches, public buildings, property of all kinds and some 13 000 houses.[24] There were few deaths, and the destruction of so much that was dirty and insanitary paved the way for Christopher Wren's magnificent churches.

Paradoxically, the eighteenth century which hung with such determination on to commercial legislation let the reins run slack around social improvement. The opportunity to rebuild after the Great Fire was expressed more in churches than in houses, and the condition of all towns was rapidly becoming worse than it had ever been: of all that it might have learned from the past nothing had taught the country how to deal with the dirt created by people living closely together. As the population increased and pressed in upon the towns cholera and typhoid fever took the place of plague, and the country was unequipped to deal with either. Neither had it the will nor the equipment to deal with the poor law. Nor did it act any longer as a brake upon employers. When workmen organized self-help in the form of Friendly Societies the State took no action, but when workmen tried to organize their own resistance to excessively long hours of work or low rates of wages the State replied as in 1726 and 1749 by forbidding their combination. Shortly commercial legislation would in its turn be swept away by the teachings of a new prophet, Adam Smith, and a doctrine of *laissez-faire*, previously unknown to any ruler,[25] would cast away the remnants of mercantilism and industrial control. Yet, such are the paradoxes of history, that even while that was being done a new social legislation would be forced into existence through the very enormity of the social problems created by the Industrial Revolution.

The population of England and Wales had reached only some 5·8 million in 1700, and was not more than 6½ million in 1760.[26] There was nowhere as yet any sign of the population explosion that accompanied the Industrial Revolution. The birth-rate and the death-rate were both high, the death-rate only beginning, in 1760, to show that decline which played a major part in the later expansion. It is likely that by the middle of the eighteenth century some three-quarters of the population of the towns were already engaged in one way or another in non-agricultural pursuits.[27] Apart from industrial development, shipping and everything connected with trade and commerce and transport required labour, and at any large port there were mariners and dock-workers, insurance and shipping clerks, customs officers and carters. Yet, when all has been said, the country still pressed in on the town, no one was far away from open country and few families were completely cut off from the land. England's industry had developed, indeed, over the previous four centuries, but compared with the real and rapid transformation that would follow the pace had been slow and the changes small-scale.

Outside the towns there were fewer open fields, more enclosure, the proportion of arable land to grazing was somewhat smaller than at the time of the Black Death. More land had been taken into cultivation and the great trees of the most accessible woodland had been felled—it was not visibly apparent that the forests were now preserved not for the chase but for their timber. But, in spite of all that had been done, there were vast tracts of land still untamed where neither sheep nor plough had penetrated and whose timber resources were virtually unused. At the same time there were deeper scars on the countryside where the coal- and iron-mines had dug deeper and spread further. The rivers were much the same as they were, except for more and better bridges, and a somewhat spasmodic cleaning and dredging of some stretches. Roads showed little improvement, particularly in the bad weather of winter.

Life and manners, as well as the physical appearance of much of the country, would be quite unrecognizable to most of the people who were alive at the time of the Black Death, and a greater change than was generally realized was smouldering beneath the surface in 1760. Yet there were still large areas, particularly in the North, the Midlands, and the South-West, where the medieval farmer could still feel at home in spite of the passage of four hundred years. There had been change and development, indeed, but also an underlying continuity from generation to generation. This continuity was to be shattered, except in isolated parts of the country, by the impact of revolutionary change, in which the descendants of the medieval farmer and small townsman would be left defenceless in a new society they barely understood. There was to be a long and bitter struggle ahead before a new equilibrium had been reached. By then the handicraftsman, the open-field village, the shepherd on the lonely down, had all but passed away and only 'history' remained to tell their story.

Notes

CHAPTER I. THE BLACK DEATH

1 The Chronicle of Henry Knighton, a Canon of Leicester.
2 Giovanni Boccaccio, introduction to *The Decameron*.
3 'The Annals of Ireland' by Friar John Clyn, edited from the MS in the library of Trinity College, Dublin, with introductory remarks by Richard Butler in *Irish Archaeological Society*, 1849, *p*. 37.
4 *cf*. Shakespeare, *Timon of Athens*, Act IV, Scene iii,

> Be as a planetary plague, when Jove
> Will o'er some high-vic'd city hang his poison
> In the sick air:

5 A gum or resin from the bark of certain trees.
6 Small medical cakes or lozenges.
7 An antidote compounded of many ingredients.
8 For these and other contemporary monastic records see Francis A. Gasquet, *The Black Death of 1348 and 1349*, and G. G. Coulton, *The Black Death*.
9 A. Hamilton Thompson, 'The Pestilences of the Fourteenth Century in the Diocese of York', *Archaeological Journal*, lxxi (1914), *pp*. 97–154; G. G. Coulton, *op. cit.*, Chapter II and *pp*. 63–4. Coulton concludes, however, that less than 18 per cent of bishops died of the plague.
10 E. Robo, 'The Black Death in the Hundred of Farnham', *English Historical Review*, xliv (1929), *pp*. 560–72.
11 C. E. Boucher, 'The Black Death in Bristol', *Transactions of the Bristol and Gloucester Archaeological Society*, vol. 60 (1938), *pp*. 31–46.
12 J. C. Russell, *British Mediaeval Population*, *pp*. 229–35; John Saltmarsh, 'Plague and Economic Decline in England in the Later

Middle Ages' in *Cambridge Historical Journal*, vol. VII (1941), *pp.* 23–41.

13 For example, J. E. Thorold Rogers, *A History of Agriculture and Prices* and *Six Centuries of Work and Wages*.

CHAPTER II. LAND AND PEOPLE

1 M. M. Postan, 'Some Economic Evidence of Declining Population in the later Middle Ages' in *Economic History Review*. vol. 2, (1950), *pp.* 221–46.
2 Barbara M. Harvey, 'The Population Trend in England Between 1300 and 1348' in *Royal Historical Society Transactions*, 5th series, vol. 16 (1966), *pp.* 23–42.
3 J. C. Russell, *British Medieval Population* (1948).
4 Ibid., *pp.* 142–3.
5 *Polychronicon Ranulphi Higden.*
6 See L. F. Salzman, *English Trade in the Middle Ages,* Chapter XI; also Arthur Raisbrick and B. Jennings, *A History of Lead Mining in the Pennines*.

CHAPTER III. THE MANOR AND THE OPEN FIELDS

1 The following account is based on C. S. and C. S. Orwin, *The Open Fields*, 3rd ed. (1967), *pp.* 32–52. See also Preface to the same edition by Joan Thirsk.
2 C. S. and C. S. Orwin, op. cit., Plates 9, 10, 11.
3 Fynes Moryson, *Itinerary* (1617), quoted Ernle, *English Farming Past and Present* (1932 ed.), *p.* 9.
4 See 'The Farming Regions of England', Chapter I of *The Agrarian History of England and Wales,* Vol. IV, *1500–1640*, ed. Joan Thirsk (1967), *pp.* 1–112.
5 Orwin, op. cit., Part II, 'The Open Fields of Laxton'; J. D. Chambers, *Laxton: the Last English Open Field Village*.
6 Orwin, op. cit., Chapter III, particularly *pp.* 39–43; and C. S. Orwin, 'Observations on the Open Fields' in *Economic History Review*, vol. 45 (1930), *p.* 220.
7 Warren O. Ault, 'Some Early Village By-Laws', in *English Historical Review,* vol. xlv (1939), *p.* 220.
8 H. S. Bennett, *Life on the English Manor, 1150–1400, pp.* 45 and 45–9 passim.
9 Sugar was an expensive luxury imported from the East.
10 Mead and metheglin were almost entirely fermented honey and water, metheglin being a spiced variant of mead.
11 A type of coarse cloth.
12 Reaping by request.
13 A grant upon request, a boon day.

14 *Seneschaucie* [the office of Seneschal], anon., *c.* 1276.
15 *Hosebonderie*, anon., *c.* 1276.
16 *Seneschaucie.*
17 Walter of Henley, *Hosbondrye.*
18 *Hosebonderie* (anon.).
19 See *pp.* 247–8.
20 *The Court Baron*, edited for the Selden Society by F. W. Maitland and W. P. Bailden *pp.* 54–5, and passim; *Select Pleas in Manorial and other Seignorial Courts*, edited for the Selden Society by F. W. Maitland, passim.

CHAPTER IV. WOOL, WOOD AND LEATHER

1 Eileen Power, *The Wool Trade in English Medieval History*, *pp.* 29–30.
2 See *p.* 139.
3 Eileen Power, op. cit., *pp.* 21–3.
4 Power, op. cit., Lecture II, passim.
5 *Fleta* (*c.* 1300), *p.* 167.
6 Power, op. cit., *p.* 27.
7 Power, op. cit., *pp.* 30–1.
8 L. F. Salzman, *Building in England down to 1540*, *p.* 249.
9 Ibid., *p.* 318.
10 John Evelyn, *Sylva* (1664).
11 G. G. Coulton, *Medieval Village, Manor, and Monastery*, *p.* 223.
12 G. T. Lapsley, 'The Account Roll of a Fifteenth-Century Iron Master' in *English Historical Review*, xiv (1899), *p.* 514.
13 L. F. Salzman, *English Industries of the Middle Ages* (1923 ed.), *p.* 39.

CHAPTER V. QUARRYING AND MINING

1 See L. F. Salzman, *English Industries of the Middle Ages* (1923 ed.), Chapter V passim.
2 Ibid., *p.* 96.
3 W. H. St. John Hope, 'On the sculptured alabaster tablets called Saint John's Heads' in *Archaeologia*, Vol. LII (2), (1876), *pp.* 679ff.
4 L. F. Salzman, op. cit., p. 91.
5 W. Cunningham, 'Notes on the Organization of the Masons' Craft in England' in *Proceedings of the British Academy*, Vol. VI, 1913, *pp.* 167–77.
6 J. Clapham, *A Concise Economic History of Britain from the Earliest Times to 1750*, *p.* 136.
7 Salzman, op. cit., *pp.* 173–80.
8 John Brand, *History and Antiquities of Newcastle*, Vol. II (1789), *p.* 254 and note.

9 See *pp*. 253–7.
10 Salzman, op. cit., *pp*. 25–6.
11 M. S. Giuseppi, 'Some Fourteenth-Century Accounts of Ironworks at Tudeley, Kent', in *Archaeologia*, 2nd S. XIV (1912).
12 G. T. Lapsley, 'The Account Roll of a Fifteenth-century Iron Master' in *English Historical Review*, vol. XIV (1899), *pp*. 509 ff.
13 Now in the Victoria and Albert Museum, London.
14 William Houlbrook, *A Black-Smith and no Jesuite* (1660).
15 *Sussex Archaeological Collections*, vol. LXVII (1926), *p*. 51.
16 Vannoccio Biringuccio, *De la Pirotechnica*, 1540, trans. by Cyril Stanley Smith and Martha Teach Gundi, published by The American Institute of Mining and Metalurgical Engineers (1942, 1943, 1959) quoted by Lister, *Decorative Cast Ironwork in Great Britain*, *pp*. 215–16.
17 L. F. Salzman, *English Industries of the Middle Ages*, *p*. 63.
18 The 'Italian Relation', *The Relation of the Island of England*, (*c*. 1500), Camden Society Publications No. 37, *pp*. 42–3.
19 Lawrence Weaver, *English Leadwork*, *p*. 213.
20 *The Rhymed Chronicle of Edward Manlove*.
21 George R. Lewis, *The Stannaries*, *p*. 212.
22 'The Italian Relation', op. cit., *pp*. 43 and 11.
23 William Harrison, *Description of England* (ed. 1968), *p*. 367. A garnish consisted of twelve platters, twelve dishes and twelve saucers.
24 Op. cit.
25 *Victoria County History*, Somerset, Vol. II, p. 368.

CHAPTER VI. THE BREAK-UP OF THE MANOR

1 See G. R. Owst, *Preaching in Medieval England* and *Literature and Pulpit in Medieval England*, passim.

CHAPTER VII. TOWNS AND INTERNAL TRADE

1 F. W. Maitland, *Domesday Book and Beyond*, *p*. 203, and see the whole of Essay I, section 9, 'The Boroughs'.
2 See M. McKisack, *Parliamentary Representation of the English Boroughs during the Middle Ages*.
3 Outsiders, whether from overseas or not, were variously referred to as 'foreigners', 'aliens', 'strangers'. While a 'foreign merchant' would most likely—but not inevitably—be from overseas, an 'alien' or a 'stranger merchant' could be simply from another town.
4 For example, in the first Statute of Westminster, 1275 (applying to

native merchants) and its extension in 1353 to cover aliens.

5 See *pp.* 134–5.
6 Charles Gross, *The Gild Merchant,* Vol. I, *p.* 32.
7 Gross, op. cit., I, *p.* 33.
8 Ibid., *p.* 33.
9 Bland, Brown and Tawney, *English Economic History: Select Documents, 1000–1846, pp.* 158–59.
10 Bland, Brown and Tawney, op. cit., *pp.* 159–60.
11 *Collected Works*, Vol. III, *p.* 179.
12 Ibid., *p.* 226.
13 L. F. Salzman, *English Industries of the Middle Ages* (1923 ed.) *pp.* 260–1, 275.
14 These were not generally favoured, as being destructive of small fish and a danger to boats.
15 E. Lipson, *The Economic History of England* (1966 ed.), Vol. I, *p.* 273.
16 'Considerations delivered to 'the Parliament', 1559 (Tawney and Power, *Tudor Economic Documents*, Vol. I, *p.* 330).

CHAPTER VIII. THE DEVELOPMENT OF FOREIGN TRADE

1 See *p.* 65.
2 See *pp.* 111–2.
3 L. F. Salzman, *English Trade in the Middle Ages, pp.* 217–22 passim.
4 Her end is described in *A Collection of Voyages and Travels*, printed for John Churchill MDCCIV, Vol. III, Monson's 'Naval Tracts', *pp.* 442–3.
5 Salzman, op. cit., *pp.* 249–50.
6 Henry VIII's Charter to Trinity House, 1514, *Tudor Economic Documents*, Vol. 2, *pp.* 90–3.
7 C. L. Kingsford, *Prejudice and Promise in XVth Century England*, Lecture IV and Appendix; L. F. Salzman, *English Trade in the Middle Ages*, Chapter XI passim.
8 The tun, which came to mean the measure of a ship's size, originally indicated the number of wine-casks or tuns of wine a ship could carry.
9 Salzman, *English Trade, p.* 231.
10 Ibid., *p.* 241.
11 See *p.* 116.
12 L. A. Clarkson, *The Pre-Industrial Economy in England, 1500–1750, p.* 157.
13 W. Cunningham, *The Growth of English Industry and Commerce* (5th ed., 1914), *p.* 195; George Unwin, *Studies in Economic History: Collected Papers* (1966 ed.), *p.* 386—who gives 1376 as the date of the establishment of the Hanseatic League; *Cambridge Economic History*

of Europe, Vol. II. *Trade and Industry in the Middle Ages* (1952), *p.* 191.
14 Ralph Davis, *The Rise of the English Shipping Industry*, Chapter I, and *p.* 222.

CHAPTER IX. THE WOOL TRADE

1 Lydgate, 'Horse, Goose and Sheep' in *Political, Religious and Love Poems*, ed. by F. J. Furnivall for Early English Text Society, vol. XV (1866), *p.* 30.
2 See Eileen Power, 'The Wool Trade in the Fifteenth Century', in *Studies in English Trade in the Fifteenth Century*, edited by Eileen Power and M. M. Postan, *pp.* 42–3.
3 *The Cely Papers, 1477–1487.*
4 See Eileen Power, *The Wool Trade in English Medieval History*, Lecture IV.
5 See also *pp.* 146–7.
6 Power, 'The Wool Trade in the Fifteenth Century', in *Studies in English Trade in the Fifteenth Century*, ed. Power and Postan, *p.* 41.
7 Power, 'The Wool Trade in the Fifteenth Century', *p.* 48.
8 *The Libelle of Englysh Polycye*, ed. Warner, *p.* 24.
9 See *p.* 147.
10 See *pp.* 138–48.

CHAPTER X. THE GILDS

1 See Lucy Toulmin Smith, (ed.) *English Gilds, the Original Ordinances of more than one hundred Early English Gilds* and her Introduction.
2 See *pp.* 92–5.
3 For an exception, see Masons, *pp.* 63–4.
4 Lipson, *Economic History of England* (1966 ed.), Vol. I, *p.* 309.
5 Lipson, op. cit., *p.* 309, note 5.
6 See *pp.* 256–7.
7 'The Italian Relation', *Camden Society Publications*, No. 37, *pp.* 24–6.
8 Bland, Brown and Tawney, *English Economic History: Select Documents 1000–1846, p.* 142.
9 Toulmin Smith, op. cit., *p.* 284.
10 Bland, Brown and Tawney, op. cit., *p.* 137–8.
11 Lipson, *The Economic History of England* (1966 ed.) vol, I, *p.* 353.
12 Ibid., *p.* 330.
13 Sylvia Thrupp, *A Short History of the Worshipful Company of Bakers of London, pp.* 41, 45.
14 Toulmin Smith, op. cit., *p.* 285.
15 Lipson, op. cit., *pp.* 359–60.
16 Lipson, op. cit., *p.* 348.

17 Toulmin Smith, op. cit., *p*. 183.
18 Toulmin Smith, op. cit., *p*. 182.
19 Report of Her Majesty's Commissioners appointed to inquire into the Livery Companies of the City of London (1884), *Parliamentary Papers*, vol. xxxix, Part I, *p*. 12.
20 See for example L. Toulmin Smith, *York Plays* and Introduction.
21 Report of Her Majesty's Commissioners appointed to inquire into the Livery Companies of the City of London (1884), *Parliamentary Papers*, vol. xxxix, Part I, *p*. 21.

CHAPTER XI. THE WOOLLEN-CLOTH INDUSTRY

1 E. Carus Wilson and O. Coleman, *England's Export Trade, 1275–1547*.
2 The term 'broadcloth' is here used in its technical sense. There were many types of cloth, of which the broadcloth was one. But all were converted into broadcloths for purposes of calculation.
3 See *p*. 88.
4 See E. M. Carus-Wilson, 'The Woollen Industry' in *The Cambridge Economic History of Europe* (1952).
5 See *pp*. 199–207.
6 See *pp*. 159–72.
7 *The Question of Wool Truly Stated* (1788), *p*. 21.
8 *Prince Butler's Tale: Representing the State of the Wool-Case or the East-India Case truly Stated* (1699).
9 See *pp*. 159–72.

CHAPTER XII. CLOTHIERS AND WORKPEOPLE

1 Daniel Defoe, *A Tour Through England and Wales*, Vol. II (Everyman ed.), *pp*. 193–5, 204–8.
2 Lipson, *Economic History of England*, Vol. II (1931), *p*. 16.
3 See Eileen Power, *The Paycockes of Coggeshall* and 'Thomas Paycocke', which is Chapter VI of *Medieval People*.
4 Sometimes called John Smalwoode, and sometimes said to be descended from Simon de Winchcombe, a rich draper of Candlewyk Street, London. The name Winchcombe probably derived from the Cotswold wool town of that name, but John Winchcombe lived in Newbury from his earliest years. He died in 1520; the date of his birth is unknown.
5 *The Works of Thomas Deloney*, ed. Francis Oscar Mann.
6 'Benedict Webb, Clothier' by Esther Moir in *Economic History Review*, Second Series, vol. 10 (1957–8), *pp*. 256–64.

7 Bland, Brown and Tawney, *English Economic History: Select Documents: 1000–1846*. *pp*. 356–7.
8 Ibid., *pp*. 357–8.
9 Lipson, *The Economic History of England*., Vol. II, *p*. 105.
10 *Journal of the House of Commons*, vol. XXX, *p*. 214.
11 P. Gregg, *Social and Economic History of Britain*, *pp*. 39–40.
12 A. P. Wadsworth and J. de L. Mann, *The Cotton Trade and Industrial Lancashire 1600–1780*, *p*. 15.

CHAPTER XIII. 'THE GREAT MULTITUDE OF SHEPE'

1 See P. J. Bowden, *The Wool Trade in Tudor and Stuart England* and Table on *p*. 117.
2 Hales's charge to the Enclosure Commissioners of 1548, reprinted in Tawney and Power, *Tudor Economic Documents*, Vol. 1, *pp*. 39–44.
3 A. H. Johnson, *The Disappearance of the Small Landowner*, *pp*. 48, 58.
4 Philip Massinger, *A New Way to Pay Old Debts*, Act II, scene 1.
5 *Utopia*.
6 Ibid.
7 Thomas Bastard, 'Chrestoleros' in *Tudor Economic Documents*, Vol. 3, *p*. 80.
8 See M. Beresford, *The Lost Villages of England*.
9 'The Decaye of England only by the Great Multitude of Shepe', 1550–53 in *Tudor Economic Documents*, Vol. 3, *pp*. 51 ff.
10 Notes of the Marquess of Salisbury in ibid., Vol. I, *p*. 89.
11 'History of Henry VII' in *Works*, ed. Spedding, Ellis and Heath (1858), Vol. VI, *pp*. 93 ff.
12 D'Ewes, *The Journal of all the Parliaments during the Reign of Queen Elizabeth* (1682 ed.), *p*. 674.
13 Ibid., *p*. 674.
14 Ibid., *p*. 674.
15 Ibid., *p*. 674.
16 *Tudor Economic Documents*, Vol. I, *p*. 41.
17 M. Beresford, 'Habitation versus Improvement' in *Essays in Honour of R. H. Tawney*, ed. F. J. Fisher, *p*. 45.
18 D'Ewes, op. cit., *p*. 675.
19 Beresford, op. cit., passim.

CHAPTER XIV. ENCLOSURE VERSUS OPEN FIELDS

1 *Surveyenge*, see Tawney and Power, *Tudor Economic Documents*, Vol. 3, *p*. 22.
2 Ibid., *p*. 23.
3 Ibid., *p*. 24.
4 Tawney and Power, *Tudor Economic Documents*, Vol 1, *pp*. 16–18.

5 *The English Improver Improved* (1652).
6 S. Taylor, *Common Good: or the Improvement of Commons, Forests, and Chases by Inclosure* (1652); Adam Moore, *Bread for the Poor . . . Promised by Enclosure of the Wastes and Common Grounds of England* (1653).
7 See *p*. 171.
8 *A Vindication of a Regulated Enclosure*, *p*. 9.
9 *England's Interest and Improvement.*
10 See *p*. 297.
11 See F. J. Fisher, 'The Development of the London Food Market, 1540–1640' in *Economic History Review*, vol. 5 (1935), *p*. 52.
12 R. H. Tawney, *The Agrarian Problem in the Sixteenth Century, pp*. 318–20.
13 See R. M. Tawney, op. cit., passim.
14 *Victoria County History*, Warwickshire, Vol. II, *pp*. 161–2.
15 Gerrard Winstanley, *The New Law of Righteousness*, Jan., 1649.
16 *A Declaration from the Poor Oppressed People of England*, *p*. 273.
17 *A Declaration of the Grounds . . . why we the Poor Inhabitants of . . . Wellinborrow . . . have begun . . . to Dig . . . the Common . . .* (March 1650), *p*. 650.
18 See *pp*. 268–76.
19 *The Compleat Copyholder* (1641).

CHAPTER XV. THE DEVELOPMENT OF INDUSTRY

1 *The Itinerary of John Leland in or about the years 1535–1543* ed. by Lucy Toulmin Smith, Vol. V, *p*. 139.
2 A. L. *Relation of some abuses against the Commonwealth composed especiallie for the Countie of Durhame.* B. M. Add. MSS 18 147. Quoted VCH Durham, Vol. II, *p*. 280.
3 Ralph Davis, *The Rise of the English Shipping Industry*, chapter I.
4 Michael Drayton, *Polyolbion*, Song xvii, ll 396 ff.
5 A standard = about 165 cu ft of timber. But the standard was, in practice, the equivalent of one tree, and the composition aimed at was twelve trees in each acre, their crowns spreading laterally above the short coppice of chestnut, hazel, hornbeam, etc. that was constantly cut.
6 J. U. Nef, *The Rise of the British Coal Industry*, Vol. I, *p*. 25.
7 Ibid., Vol. I, *pp*. 19–20.
8 Thomas Savery, *The Miner's Friend: or an Engine to raise Water by Fire described and the Manner of fixing it in Mines* (1702).
9 *Lives of the Norths*, ed. Augustus Jessopp (1890), Vol. I, *p*. 176.
10 See *pp*. 257, 261–7.
11 J. U. Nef, 'The Progress of Technology and the Growth of Large Scale Industry in Great Britain, 1540–1640' in *Economic History Review*, vol. V (1934), *pp*. 11–12, 20.

12 L. A. Clarkson, *The Pre-Industrial Economy in England 1500–1750*, *p.* 114.
13 *Britannia* (ed. 1695), *p.* 505.
14 Sir Christopher Wren's Accounts preserved at St Paul's, printed in Ernest Straker, *Wealden Iron, pp.* 207–8.
15 See J. U. Nef, 'The Progress of Technology, and the Growth of Large-Scale Industry in Great Britain 1540–1640' in *Economic History Review*, Vol. 5 (1934).

CHAPTER XVI. POPULATION AND PRICES

1 The most recent estimated figures for England are 1430—2·1m; 1522–5—2·3m; 1545—2·8m; 1603—3·75m. Julian Cornwall, 'English Population in the Early Sixteenth Century' in *Economic History Review*, Second Series, 23 (1970), *pp.* 32–44.
2 E. H. Phelps-Brown and Sheila V. Hopkins, 'Seven Centuries of the Prices of Consumables compared with Builders' Wage Rates', in *Economica*, N.S. XXIII, *p.* 312. Reprinted in Ramsey's, *Price Revolution*.
3 Ramsey, op. cit., Appendix B.
4 Bland, Brown, and Tawney, *English Economic History; Select Documents 1000–1846*, *p.* 265.
5 Tawney and Power, *Tudor Economic Documents*, Vol. 1, *p.* 366.
6 'Memorandum on the Reasons Moving Queen Elizabeth to Reform the Coinage', 1559, in Tawney and Power, op. cit., vol. 2, *p.* 193.
7 Tawney and Power, op. cit., vol. 2, *p.* 196.
8 See, for example, 'Policies to Reduce this Realme of England unto a Prosperous Wealthe and Estate', 1549, in Tawney and Power, op. cit., vol. 3, *p.* 319; and *pp.* 250–2.
9 Memorandum Prepared for the Royal Commission on the Exchanges,' 1564, in Tawney and Power, op. cit., vol. 3, *p.* 349.
10 *A Discourse of the Common Weal of this Realm of England* (1549), ed. Lamond (1893), *p.* 187.
11 Memorandum Prepared for the Royal Commission on the Exchanges', 1564, in Tawney and Power, op. cit., Vol. 3, *p.* 347.
12 Ibid., *p.* 348.
13 Thomas Mun, *England's Treasure by Forraigne Trade* (1664), *pp.* 43–44.
14 Gerrard de Malynes, 'A Treatise of the Canker of England's Commonwealth (1601), in Tawney and Power, op. cit., Vol. 3, *p.* 387.
15 *A Discourse consisting of Motives for the Enlargement and Freedom of Trade* (1645), *pp.* 6, 22.
16 See *pp.* 249, 253–7.

17 See *pp.* 103–23 passim.
18 See *pp.* 118–23.
19 To 'adventure' was, indeed, to engage in foreign trade.
20 John Wheeler, *Treatise on Commerce* (1601), *p.* 24.
21 Ibid., *p.* 19.
22 *Journals of the House of Commons*, Vol. I, *p.* 218, reprinted in Bland, Brown and Tawney, *English Economic History, Select Documents 1000–1846*, *pp.* 443–53.
23 See Wheeler, op. cit., passim, for a defence of the Merchant Adventurers.
24 *House of Commons Journals*, 5th May 1624, I, *p.* 698.

CHAPTER XVII. THE NEW WORLD

1 *A Counterblast to Tobacco* (1604), facs. Amsterdam and New York 1969.
2 The figures are based upon official values—i.e., upon unchanging prices—and are a truer basis for comparisons over a period than fluctuating money values. They are, however, particularly before the use of customs-house ledgers showing imports and exports, highly defective. The customs house ledger came into general use around 1696.
3 *An English Traveller's First Curiosity: or the Knowledge of his owne Country. Hist. MSS Comm. Various*, ii, 193, 200.
4 Ralph Davis, 'English Foreign Trade, 1660–1700' in *Economic History Review*, Second Series, Vol. 7 (1954–55).
5 L. A. Clarkson, *The Pre-Industrial Economy in England, 1500–1750*, *p.* 127.
6 See *pp.* 240–3.
7 Davis, op. cit. The figures are for imports into London.
8 W. A. Cole, 'Trends in Eighteenth Century Smuggling', *Economic History Review*, Second Series, Vol. 10 (1957/58), *p.* 409.
9 Clarkson, *The Pre-Industrial Economy in England*, *p.* 157.
10 *The Journeys of Celia Fiennes*, ed. Christopher Morris (1947) *p.* 245.
11 *A Tour Through England and Wales*, Vol. I, *p.* 222 (Everyman ed. 1928).

CHAPTER XVIII. MONEY, EXCHANGE AND BANKING

1 See *p.* 216.
2 See *p.* 74.
3 See *p.* 199 ff.
4 See *p.* 121.

5 R. H. Tawney, Introduction to *A Discourse Upon Usury* (1572) by Thomas Wilson, *p*. 19.
6 *Brief survey of the growth of usury in England with the mischiefs attending it* (1673).
7 *Of Usury*.
8 *Table Talk*, compiled and published in 1689 by Selden's secretary.
9 *Works* (1801 ed.), Vol. V, *pp*. 36–7.
10 *A New Discourse of Trade*, 1690.
11 T. Turnor, *The Case of the Bankers and their Creditors* (1675).
12 Alexander Pope, *Epistle to Lord Bathurst*, ll. 135–41.

CHAPTER XIX. MERCANTILISM

1 *Opinions of Officers of the Mint on the State of English Money*, reprinted in Bland, Brown, and Tawney, op. cit., *pp*. 220–3.
2 See the edition edited by Sir George Warner (1926). It was not unusual for serious economic or political treatises to be written in verse and the *Libelle* undoubtedly had more appeal than a prose work. It probably circulated widely in Government circles.
3 'Political Songs and Poems relating to English History', ed. Thomas Wright, *Rolls Series* (1861), vol. 14b, *pp*. 282–7.
4 'Collections of a Yorkist Partisan 1447–52', Article 12, in Kingsford, *English Historical Literature in the Fifteenth Century*, *pp*. 235, 362–3.
5 See *pp*. 254–5.
6 See *pp*. 212–23 passim.
7 *Policies to Reduce this Realme of Englaunde unto a Prosperus Wealthe and Estate*, in Tawney and Power, *Tudor Economic Documents* vol. 3, *pp*. 311–45.
8 Extracts are in Tawney and Power, op. cit., Vol. 2, *p*. 219, and Vol. 3, *pp*. 305–8. It now seems certain that the author of the *Discourse* was not John Hales, as formerly assumed, but Sir Thomas Smith. See M. Dewar, 'The Authorship of the "Discourse of the Common Weal"' in *Economic History Review*, Second Series, vol. 19 (1966), *pp*. 388 ff.
9 *The Rates of Marchandizes as they are set downe in the Booke of Rates*.
10 *House of Commons Journals*, vol. xxi, *p*. 802.
11 See *p*. 216.

CHAPTER XX. INTERVENTION AND CONTROL

1 Maurice Beresford, *New Towns of the Middle Ages*.
2 See *pp*. 226–9.
3 See *pp*. 258–60.
4 See *pp*. 130–5.

5 E. Lipson, *The Economic History of England,* Vol. I, *pp.* 300–1.
6 Sylvia Thrupp, *A Short History of the Worshipful Company of Bakers of London.*
7 M. D. Harris, 'Lawrence Saunders' in *English Historical Review,* vol. IX (1894), *p.* 635.
8 Lipson, op. cit., Vol. I, *p.* 294.
9 See *pp.* 140–1, 145–6.
10 See *pp.* 130–1.
11 Lipson, op. cit., Vol. III, *p.* 319.
12 See *pp.* 166–72.
13 *Acts of the Privy Council,* 1596–7, *pp.* 94–5.
14 *Acts of the Privy Council,* 1596–7, *p.* 95. After the Restoration policy changed, the aim being not so much to protect the consumer by keeping down prices as to encourage the production of corn; see *p.* 297 for post-Restoration Corn Laws.
15 See *pp.* 140–1, 145–6.
16 D'Ewes, *The Journals of all the Parliaments during the reign of Queen Elizabeth* (1682), *p.* 644.
17 See *pp.* 196–7.
18 *House of Commons Journals,* i, *p.* 985.
19 Bland, Brown, and Tawney, *English Economic History: Select Documents, pp.* 440–3.
20 *House of Commons Journals,* i, *p.* 491.
21 *State Papers Domestic,* James I: 1, Proclamations Collection No. 50A, August 12, 1617.
22 See *pp.* 210–11.
23 See *pp.* 199–207.
24 E. Hall, *Chronicle* (ed. 1809), *pp.* 745–6.
25 9th February, 1621/2, *Acts of the Privy Council July 1621–May, 1623, pp.* 132–3.
26 The Report is well summarized in Lipson, op. cit., vol. III, *pp.* 307–10.
27 9th February, 1621/2, *Acts of the Privy Council July 1621–May, 1623, p.* 132.
28 Sometimes called the Statute of Apprentices.
29 *Acts of the Privy Council 1613–1614, pp.* 457–8, and see *pp.* 652–3.
30 Much of the Statute is given in Bland, Brown and Tawney, op. cit., *pp.* 325 ff.

CHAPTER XXI. THE POOR LAW

1 William Tegg, *Wills of their Own.*
2 R. R. Sharpe, *Calendar of Wills Proved and Enrolled in the Court of Husting, London,* Vol. II, *pp.* 585–6.
3 Sharpe, op. cit., Vol. II, *p.* 591.

4 Tegg, op. cit., *p.* 7.
5 See *pp.* 253–7.
6 Thomas West, *The Antiquities of Furness* (ed. 1822), *p.* 195.
7 This part of the Act was repealed two years later.
8 'The First Compulsory Poor Rate in London, 1547' in Tawney and Power, *Tudor Economic Documents,* Vol. II, *pp.* 305–6.
9 'The Citizens of London to the Privy Council on Their Suit to the King for Bridewell, 1552' in Tawney and Power, op. cit., Vol. II, *pp.* 306 ff.
10 Part of the Act is given in Tawney and Power, op. cit. Vol. I, *pp.* 328–31.
11 The idea that tradesmen would provide raw materials (see *p.* 264) had broken down.
12 The Act is printed in *Tudor Economic Documents*, Vol. II, *pp.* 346–54.
13 The Act repeats the vivid description of the people against whom it was legislating in terms of the Act of 1572. It is printed in Tawney and Power, op. cit., Vol. 2, *pp.* 354–62.
14 Reprinted in Bland, Brown and Tawney, op. cit., *pp.* 647–9.
15 Reprinted in Bland, Brown and Tawney, ibid., *pp.* 650–2.

CHAPTER XXII. THE VOICE OF THE PEOPLE

1 See *pp.* 229–30.

CHAPTER XXIII. EDUCATION

1 See *p.* 271.
2 W. K. Jordan, *Philanthropy in England, 1480–1660, pp*, 285–6.
3 Lawrence Stone, 'The Educational Revolution in England 1560–1640' in *Past and Present*, No. 28 (1964), *p.* 68.
4 Stone, op. cit.
5 Jordan, op. cit., *p.* 279.
6 Stone, op. cit., *p.* 67.
7 Ibid., *p.* 43.

CHAPTER XXIV. THE LANDLORD STATE

1 See *pp.* 81–8 passim.
2 William Harrison, *Description of England* (1577), ed. 1968, *p.* 115, and *pp.* 162–4.
3 Ibid., *p.* 204.
4 R. H. Tawney, 'The Rise of the Gentry' in *Economic History Review*, vol. 11 (1941).

5 A. G. Dickens, *The English Reformation*, *p*. 229.
6 R. Braithwaite, *The English Gentleman* (1633), *The English Gentlewoman* (1633).
7 Harrison, op. cit., *p*. 114.
8 Lawrence Stone, 'The Fruits of Office' in *Essays in the Economic and Social History of Tudor and Stuart England*, ed. F. J. Fisher, *pp*. 89–116.
9 Lawrence Stone, *The Crisis of the Aristocracy*, *p*. 759; G. D. Ramsay, *The Wiltshire Woollen Industry in the Sixteenth and Seventeenth Centuries*, *pp*. 36–7.
10 The controversy is well documented. See Bibliography, *p*. 327.
11 Op. cit., *p*. 118.
12 Letter from a 'Suffolk Gentleman' quoted Ernle, *English Farming, Past and Present*, 4th ed. (1932), *p*. 292.
13 Harrison, op. cit., *pp*. 201–2, 528, and William Webb (1621), quoted Ernle, op. cit., *p*. 83.
14 See *p*. 137.
15 *Leviathan*, Introduction.
16 *Troilus and Cressida*, Act I, Scene 3.
17 See *p*. 253.
18 See *p*. 272.
19 See *p*. 272.
20 See particularly *Second Treatise on Government, An Essay Concerning the True Original, Extent and End of Civil Government*, Chapter XI.
21 See *pp*. 236–45.
22 See *p*. 249.
23 E. Lipson, *Economic History of England*, Vol. II, *p*. 453.
24 See description of the fire by Samuel Pepys in his *Diary*, Everyman edition, Vol. II, *pp*. 87–91.
25 But see *pp*. 171, 174–5. People—e.g., Sir Walter Raleigh and the Committee on Free Trade—had been groping on the edge of such an idea without reaching the conclusion that it made for the general good.
26 L. A. Clarkson, *The Pre-Industrial Economy in England*.
27 See Table, *p*. 200, and Note.

Select Bibliography

I WORKS USEFUL FOR THE WHOLE OR A LARGE PART OF THE PERIOD COVERED BY THIS BOOK

Collections of Documents, etc.

BAGLEY, J. J., and ROWLEY, P. B.: *A Documentary History of England*, 2 vols., 1066–1931 (Penguin, 1965–6).

BLAND, A. E., BROWN, P. A., and TAWNEY, R. H.: *English Economic History: Select Documents, 1000–1846* (G. Bell, 1914; reissued 1930).

COULTON, G. G.: *Social Life in Britain from the Conquest to the Reformation* (Cambridge Univ. Press, 1918).

MAITLAND, F. W. (ed.): *Select Pleas in Manorial and other Seignorial Courts* (Selden Society Publications, 1889).

MAITLAND, F. W., and BAILDON, W. P. (eds.): *The Court Baron* (Selden Society Publications, 1891).

POWER, EILEEN, and REED, A. W. (eds.): *English Life in English Literature*, 5 vols. (Methuen, 1928).

SHARPE, REGINALD R.: *Calendar of Wills Proved and Enrolled in the Court of Husting, London, A.D. 1258–A.D. 1688*, 2 vols. (1889).

TAWNEY, R. H., and POWER, EILEEN: *Tudor Economic Documents*, 3 vols. (Longmans, 1924; reissued 1951).

THIRSK, JOAN, and COOPER, J. P.: *Seventeenth-century Economic Documents* (Clarendon Press, 1972).

Original narratives or descriptions (in chronological order)

HIGDEN, RANULF: *Polychronicon* (first half of fourteenth century; English trans. by John Trevisa in second half of that century; new trans. by John Taylor, Clarendon Press, 1966).

FROISSART, JEAN: *Chronicles* (1325–1400); first dated ed. 1504, first English trans., by Lord Berners, 1523–5; a shortened version of Berners in one vol. ed. G. and W. Anderson (Centaur Press, 1963);

a new translation and selection by G. Brereton in paperback (Penguin, 1968).

Paston Letters—correspondence, etc., of the Paston family of the fifteenth century, selected and edited by N. Davis (Oxford Univ. Press, 1971).

The 'Italian Relation', *The Relation of the Island of England, c.* 1500, in Camden Society Publications, No. 37.

HARRISON, WILLIAM: *Description of England* (1577; 1587): ed. by Georges Edelen, slightly abridged, in one vol. in Folger Shakespeare Library (Cornell Univ. Press, 1968).

FIENNES, CELIA: *Through England on a Side-saddle*, 1684–1702, ed. by Christopher Morris as *The Journeys of Celia Fiennes* (Cresset Press, 1947; rev. ed. 1949).

DEFOE, DANIEL: *A Tour through England and Wales* (Everyman ed., 2 vols. 1928), from *A Tour thro' the Whole Island of Great Britain* (1724–6).

Secondary Sources

ASHLEY, SIR W. J.: The *Economic Organization of England* (Longmans, 1914; 3rd ed. 1949, with three supplementary chapters by G. C. Allen).

BAGLEY, J. J.: *Historical Interpretation, Sources of English History,* 2 vols, 1066 to the Present Day (Penguin, 1965, 1971).

BEAN, J. M. W.: *The Decline of English Feudalism, 1215–1540* (Manchester Univ. Press, 1968).

BENNETT, H. S.: *The Pastons and their England* (Cambridge Univ. Press, 1922; paperback 1968).

——: *Life on the English Manor, 1150–1400* (Cambridge Univ. Press, 1937, 1968).

——: *Six Medieval Men and Women* (Cambridge Univ. Press, 1955; paperback 1970).

CLARKSON, L. A.: *The Pre-Industrial Economy in England, 1500–1750* (Batsford, 1971).

COULTON, G. G.: *Medieval Panorama,* 2 vols. (Cambridge Univ. Press, 1938; Collins, 1961).

——: *Medieval Village, Manor, and Monastery* (H. Hamilton, 1960; first published in 1925 as *The Medieval Village*).

CUNNINGHAM, WILLIAM: *The Growth of English Industry and Commerce,* 3 vols (Cambridge Univ. Press, 1882; repr. F. Cass, 1968).

DARBY, H. C.: *An Historical Geography of England before A.D. 1800* (Cambridge Univ. Press, 1936).

FISHER, F. J. (ed.): *Essays in the Economic and Social History of Tudor and Stuart England* (Cambridge Univ. Press, 1961).

HARDING, ALAN: *A Social History of English Law* (Penguin, 1966).

JUSSERAND, J. J.: *English Wayfaring Life in the Middle Ages*, trans. from the French by Lucy Toulmin Smith, 1889, 2nd ed. rev., 1920; 4th edd. Benn 1950 and Methuen 1961, have fewer illustrations than 2nd ed.

KINGSFORD, C. L.: *Prejudice and Promise in Fifteenth Century England* (Clarendon Press, 1925).

LIPSON, E.: *The Economic History of England,* 3 vols. (A. & C. Black, 1915, and many subsequent editions).

MARSHALL, D.: *English People in the Eighteenth Century* (Longmans, 1956).

OWST, G. R.: *Literature and Pulpit in Medieval England* (Cambridge Univ. Press, 1933; rev. ed. Blackwell, 1961).

——: *Preaching in Medieval England* (Cambridge Univ. Press, 1926).

POOLE, AUSTIN LANE (ed.): *Medieval England*, 2 vols., new and revised edition of Barnard's *Companion to English History* (Clarendon Press, 1958).

POSTAN, M. M.: 'Revisions in Economic History, The Fifteenth Century' in *Economic History* IX (1938).

——: *The Medieval Economy and Society; an Economic History of Britain 1100–1500* (Weidenfeld and Nicolson, 1972; Penguin, 1975).

POWER, EILEEN: *Medieval People* (Methuen, 1924; Penguin, 1938).

RAMSEY, P. H.: *Tudor Economic Problems* (Gollancz, 1963).

SALZMAN, L. F.: *English Life in the Middle Ages* (Oxford Univ. Press, 1926).

——: *England in Tudor Times* (Batsford, 1926).

TAWNEY, R. H.: *Religion and the Rise of Capitalism* (Murray, 1926; Penguin, 1938).

TURBERVILLE, A. S. (ed.): *Johnson's England* (Oxford Univ. Press, 1933).

——: *English Men and Manners in the Eighteenth Century* (Clarendon Press, 1926; 2nd ed. 1929).

WILSON, CHARLES: *England's Apprenticeship, 1603–1763* (Longmans, 1965).

Historical Association leaflets and pamphlets cover a wide field. Some are mentioned in this bibliography under the appropriate subject heading. A full list may be obtained from The Historical Association, 59A Kennington Park Road, London SE11 4JH.

'Studies in Economic History', edited for the Economic History Society by M. W. Flinn, also have a wide range, and several are listed here in their appropriate places. A full list of titles may be obtained from the Economic History Society or from the publisher, Macmillan.

II THE LAND, AGRICULTURE, ETC.

The Estate Treatises and other contemporary works (in chronological order)

Fleta (end 13th century) edited with a translation by H. G. Richardson and G. O. Sayles in Selden Society Publications, vols. 72, etc. (1955–).

WALTER OF HENLEY: *Hosbondrye*, about 1276.

Hosebonderie (author unknown) (before 1300).

Seneschaucie, or The Office of Seneschal (author unknown), about 1276.

The *Rules* of Robert Grosseteste (before 1300).

The last three are appended to Walter of Henley's *Hosbondrye*, and all four are translated and edited by Dorothea Oschinsky as *Walter of Henley and Other Treatises of Estate Management and Accounting* (Oxford Univ. Press, 1971). An earlier edition by Elizabeth Lamond (Longmans, 1890) is simpler to handle, but out of print and available only in libraries.

FITZHERBERT, ANTHONY or JOHN: *The Booke of Husbandrie* (*c.* 1523).

BLITH, WALTER: *The English Improver Improved or the Survey of Husbandry Surveyed, Discovering the Improveableness of all Lands* (1652).

EVELYN, JOHN: *Sylva; or a Discourse of Forest Trees and the Propagation of Timber* (1664; facsimile of this ed. published by Scolar Press, 1972).

TULL, JETHRO: *The new Horse-Houghing Husbandry* (1731); William Cobbett edited and published this work in 1822.

TUSSER, THOMAS: *A Hundreth Good Pointes of Husbandrie* (1557).

——: *Five Hundred Points of Good Husbandry* (1573).

Collections of Farming Books

FUSSELL, G. E.: *The Old English Farming Books from Fitzherbert to Tull*, 1523–1730 (Crosby Lockwood, 1947).

——: *More Old English Farming Books, from Tull to the Board of Agriculture, 1731–1793* (Crosby Lockwood, 1950).

SECONDARY SOURCES

The Agrarian History of England and Wales (general editor H. P. R. Finberg), Vol. IV, 1500–1640, edited Joan Thirsk (Cambridge Univ. Press, 1967).

AULT, WARREN O.: 'Some Early Village By-laws' in *English Historical Review*, No. 45 (1930).

——: 'Village By-laws by Common Consent', In *Speculum*, Vol. 29 (1954).

——: 'Gleaning and the Problems of Harvest', in *Economic History Review*, Vol. 14 (1961).

——: *Open-field Farming in Medieval England* (Allen and Unwin, 1972).

BERESFORD, MAURICE: 'Habitation versus Improvement', in *Essays in the Economic and Social History of Tudor and Stuart Times*, edited by F. J. Fisher (Cambridge Univ. Press, 1961).

——: *History on the Ground, Six Studies in Maps and Landscapes* (Lutterworth Press, 1957; revised edition Methuen, 1971).

BERESFORD, MAURICE, and HURST, J. G. (eds.): *Deserted Medieval Villages* (Lutterworth Press, 1971).

——: The *Lost Villages of England* (Lutterworth Press, 1963).

CAMPBELL, MILDRED: *The English Yeoman under Elizabeth and the Early Stuarts* (Yale Univ. Press, 1942; Merlin Press, 1961).

HILTON, R. H.: *The Decline of Serfdom in England* (Macmillan, 1969).

——: *A Medieval Society* (Weidenfeld and Nicolson, 1966).

HOSKINS, W. G.: *The Making of the English Landscape* (Hodder and Stoughton, 1955).

——: *The Midland Peasant: The Economic and Social History of a Leicestershire Village* (Macmillan, 1957; paperback 1965).

JOHNSON, ARTHUR HENRY: *The Disappearance of the Small Landowner* (1909; reprint Oxford Univ. Press and Merlin Press, 1963).

KERRIDGE, ERIC: *Agrarian Problems in the Sixteenth Century and After* (Allen and Unwin, 1969).

MINGAY, G. E.: *English Landed Society in the Eighteenth Century* (Routledge, 1963).

ORWIN, C. S. and C. S.: *The Open Fields* (Clarendon Press, 1938; 3rd edition 1967).

POSTAN, M. M.: 'Agrarian Life of the Middle Ages', in the *Cambridge Economic History of Europe*, 2nd. edition (1966).

——: 'The Famulus', in *Economic History Review*, Supplement 2.

POWER, EILEEN: 'Peasant Life and Rural Conditions', in the *Cambridge Medieval History*, Vol. VII (1932).

PROTHERO, R. E. (LORD ERNLE): *English Farming, Past and Present* (Longmans, 1912; 6th edition with Introduction by G. E. Fussell and O. R. McGregor, Heinemann, 1961).

TAWNEY, R. H.: *The Agrarian Problem in the Sixteenth Century* (Longmans, 1912).

THIRSK, JOAN: *Tudor Enclosures*, Historical Association Pamphlet General Series, No. G. 41 (1959).

——: 'The Common Fields', in *Past and Present*, No. 29 (1964).

——: 'The Origin of the Common Fields', in *Past and Present*, No. 33 (1966).

TITOW, J. Z.: *English Rural Society 1200–1350* (Allen and Unwin, 1969).

III TOWNS

BAKER, TIMOTHY: *Medieval London* (Cassell, 1970).

BERESFORD, MAURICE: *New Towns of the Middle Ages* (Lutterworth Press, 1967).

BIRD, RUTH: *The Turbulent London of Richard II* (Longmans, 1949).

FISHER, F. J.: 'The Development of the London Food Market 1540–1640', in *Economic History Review*, Vol. V (1935).

GREEN, A. S.: *Town Life in the Fifteenth Century,* 2 vols. (Macmillan, 1894).

MITCHELL, R. J., and LEYS, M. D. R.: *A History of London Life* (Longmans, 1958; Pan, 1967).

PEARL, V.: *London and the Outbreak of the Puritan Revolution, 1625–1643* (Oxford Univ. Press, 1961).

SABINE, ERNEST L.: 'Butchering in Mediaeval London', in *Speculum,* 1933.

——: 'Latrines and Cesspools of Mediaeval London', in *Speculum,* 1934.

THRUPP, SYLVIA: *The Merchant Class of Medieval London, 1300–1500* (Univ. of Chicago Press, 1948; Univ. of Michigan Press, 1967).

IV INDUSTRY

AGRICOLA, GEORGIUS: *De Re Metallica* (1556, translated from the Latin of the first edition by H. C. and L. H. Hoover, 1912).

COURT, W. H. B.: *The Rise of the Midland Industries, 1600–1838* (Oxford Univ. Press, 1938).

NEF, J. U.: 'The Progress of Technology and the Growth of Large-Scale Industry in Great Britain 1540–1640' in *Economic History Review,* 5, 1934.

SALZMAN, L. F.: *English Industries of the Middle Ages* (Constable, 1913; new enlarged edition Clarendon Press, 1923; reissued Pordes, 1964).

THIRSK, JOAN: 'Industries in the Countryside', in *Essays in the Economic and Social History of Tudor and Stuart England,* ed. F. J. Fisher (Cambridge Univ. Press, 1961).

Brass and Copper

HAMILTON, HENRY: *The English Brass and Copper Industries to 1800* (Longmans, 1926; 2nd ed. F. Cass, 1967).

Building, etc.

KNOOP, D., and JONES, G. P.: *The Medieval Mason* (Manchester Univ. Press, 1933; 3rd. ed. rev., 1967).

SALZMAN, L. F.: *Building in England Down to 1540* (Clarendon Press, 1952).

Coal

NEF, J. U.: *The Rise of the British Coal Industry* (Routledge, 1932; F. Cass, 1966).

STONE, L.: 'An Elizabethan Coal Mine' in *Economic History Review,* 2nd Series, 3, 1950.

Iron and Steel

AYRTON, M., and SILCOCK, A.: *Wrought Iron and its Decorative Use* (Country Life, 1929).

CROSSLEY, D. W.: 'The Management of a Sixteenth Century Iron Works' in *Economic History Review*, Second Series, 2, 1966.

GIUSEPPI, M. S.: 'Some Fourteenth-Century Accounts of Ironworks at Tudeley, Kent' in *Archaeologia*, Second Series, XIV, 1912.

LAPSLEY, G. T.: 'The Account Roll of a 15th Century Iron Master' in *English Historical Review*, No. 55, 1899.

LISTER, RAYMOND: *Decorative Wrought Ironwork in Great Britain* (Bell, 1957).

——: *Decorative Cast Ironwork in Great Britain* (G. Bell, 1960).

RAISTRICK, A.: *Dynasty of Ironfounders: The Darbys and Coalbrookdale* (Longmans, 1953).

SCHUBERT, H. R.: *A History of the British Iron and Steel Industry from c. 450 A.D. to A.D. 1775* (Routledge, 1957).

STRAKER, ERNEST: *Wealden Iron* (G. Bell, 1931; David and Charles, 1969).

Lead

GOUGH, J. W.: *The Mines of Mendip* (Clarendon Press, 1930; rev. ed. David and Charles, 1967).

HOUGHTON, THOMAS: *The Compleat Miner* (1687).

LETHABY, W. R.: *Leadwork* (Macmillan, 1893).

WEAVER, SIR LAWRENCE: *English Leadwork* (Batsford, 1909).

Leather

CLARKSON, L. A.: 'The Organization of the English Leather Industry in the Late Sixteenth and Seventeenth Centuries' in *Economic History Review*, Second Series, 13, 1960.

WATERER, J. W.: *Leather in Life, Art and Industry* (Faber, 1946).

——: *Leather Craftmanship* (Bell, 1968).

Salt

BRIDBURY, A. R.: *England and the Salt Trade in the Late Middle Ages* (Clarendon Press, 1955).

CALVERT, A. F.: *Salt and the Salt Industry* (Pitman, 1929).

Stone, marble, alabaster

PRIOR, EDWARD S., and GARDINER, ARTHUR: *An Account of Medieval Figure Sculpture in England* (Cambridge Univ. Press, 1912).

ST JOHN HOPE, W. H.: 'On the Sculptured Alabaster Tablets called Saint John's Heads' in *Archaeologia*, Vol. LII (2), 1876.

Tin

HEDGES, E. S.: *Tin in Social and Economic History* (Arnold, 1964).

Lewis, G. R.: *The Stannaries* (Houghton Mifflin, 1906; Constable, 1908).

V. WOOL AND THE WOOL TRADE, WOOLLEN CLOTH AND THE TRADE IN WOOLLEN CLOTH

Bowden, P. J.: *The Wool Trade in Tudor and Stuart England* (Macmillan, 1962).

The Cely Papers, 1477–1487, the Correspondence and Memoranda of the Cely Family, Merchants of the Staple, ed. H. E. Malden for the Camden Society, 3rd series, No. 1 (1900).

Deloney, Thomas: *The Pleasant History of . . . Jack of Newberie* (1626) in the *Works of Thomas Deloney*, ed. Francis Oscar Mann (Clarendon Press, 1912).

Heaton, H.: *The Yorkshire Woollen and Worsted Industries* (Oxford Univ. Press, 1920; 2nd edition 1966).

Lipson, E.: *The History of the Woollen and Worsted Industries* (A. & C. Black, 1921; reissued F. Cass, 1965).

——: *A Short History of Wool and its Manufacture* (Heinemann, 1953).

McClenaghan, B.: *The Springs of Lavenham* (Ipswich, 1924).

Power, Eileen: 'Thomas Betson' and 'Thomas Paycocke' in *Medieval People* (Methuen, 1924; Penguin, 1937).

——: *The Wool Trade in English Medieval History* (Oxford Univ. Press, 1941).

——: 'The Wool Trade in the Fifteenth Century' in *Studies in English Trade in the Fifteenth Century*, edited by Eileen Power and M. M. Postan (Routledge, 1933).

Ramsay, G. D.: *The Wiltshire Woollen Industry in the Sixteenth and Seventeenth Centuries* (Oxford Univ. Press, 1943; n.e. F. Cass, 1965).

Wilson, E. M. Carus, and Coleman, O.: *England's Export Trade, 1275–1547* (Clarendon Press, 1963).

VI TRADE, TRANSPORT AND COMMERCE

Defoe, Daniel: *An Essay Upon Projects* (1697; facs. Scolar Press, 1969).

Hales, John (? or Sir Thomas Smith): *Discourse of the Common Weal of this Realm of England* (1549), ed. E. Lamond (1893).

Libelle of Englyshe Polycye (1436), ed. Sir George Warner (Clarendon Press, 1926).

Wheeler, John: *A Treatise of Commerce* (1601). Facsimile; ed. with introduction and notes by G. B. Hotchkiss (Facsimile Text Society and New York Univ. Press, 1931).

Andreades, A.: *History of the Bank of England, 1640–1903* (trans. C.

Meredith, 1909; 4th ed. with new Introduction by Paul Einzig, F. Cass, 1966).

CARSWELL, JOHN: *The South Sea Bubble* (Cresset Press, 1960).

CLAPHAM, SIR JOHN: *History of the Bank of England* (Cambridge Univ. Press, 1944).

DAVIS, RALPH: 'English Overseas Trade 1660–1760' in *Economic History Review*, Second Series, vol. 7, 1954.

——: *The Rise of the English Shipping Industry* (Macmillan, 1962).

DOWELL, STEPHEN: *History of Taxation and Taxes in England* (Longmans, 1884; 2nd ed. rev., 1888).

OUTHWAITE, R. B.: *Inflation in Tudor and Early Stuart England* (Macmillan, 1969).

POWER, EILEEN, and POSTAN, M. M.: *Studies in English Trade in the Fifteenth Century* (Routledge, 1933).

RAMSAY, G. D.: *English Overseas Trade During the Centuries of Emergence* (Macmillan, 1957).

RAMSEY, P. H.: *The Price Revolution in Sixteenth Century England* (Methuen, 1971).

RICHARDS, R. D.: *Early History of Banking in England* (King, 1929).

SALTMARSH, JOHN: 'Plague and Economic Decline in England in the Later Middle Ages', *in Cambridge Historical Journal,* VII (1941).

SALZMAN, L. F.: *English Trade in the Middle Ages* (Clarendon Press, 1931; Pordes, 1964).

SCAMMELL, G. V.: 'English Merchant Shipping at the end of the Middle Ages' in *Economic History Review*, Second Series, vol. 13, 1961.

SCOTT, W. R.: *The Constitution and Finance of English, Scottish and Irish Joint-Stock Companies to 1720* (Cambridge Univ. Press, 3 vols., 1910–13).

STENTON, SIR F. M.: 'The Road System of Medieval England', in *English Historical Review,* 7, 1936, pp. 1–21.

WILLAN, T. S.: *River Navigation in England, 1600–1750* (Oxford Univ. Press, 1936).

——: *The English Coasting Trade 1600–1750* (Univ. of Manchester, 1938).

WILLARD, J. F.: 'Inland Transportation in England During the Fourteenth Century', in *Speculum,* 1 (1926).

——: 'The Use of Carts in the Fourteenth Century', in *History,* vol. 17, 1932.

WILSON, THOMAS: *A Discourse Upon Usury* (1572) with Introduction by R. H. Tawney (G. Bell, 1925; n.e., F. Cass, 1962).

A reproduction of the Gough map is obtainable from the Bodleian Library.

Mercantilism

CHILD, SIR JOSIAH: *A New Discourse of Trade* (1693).

MISSELDEN, EDWARD: *Free Trade; or the Means to make trade flourish* (1622).

MUN, THOMAS: *England's Treasure by Forraign Trade* (1664; repr. of 1664 ed. made by Basil Blackwell in 1928 and 1949).

HECKSCHER, E. F.: *Mercantilism*, trans. Mendel Shapiro (Allen and Unwin, 1935).

——: 'Mercantilism, Revisions in Economic History' in *Economic History Review*, vol. 7, 1936.

HORROCKS, J. W.: *A Short History of Mercantilism* (Methuen, 1925).

WILSON, CHARLES: *Mercantilism*, History Society Pamphlets, General Series, G. 37 (1958; repr. 1967).

VII THE GILDS

GROSS, CHARLES: *The Gild Merchant* (Clarendon Press, 1890; reissued 1927).

HEAL, SIR AMBROSE: *The London Goldsmiths 1200–1800* (Cambridge Univ. Press, 1935).

HERBERT, W.: *History of the Twelve Great Livery Companies of London* (1833).

KAHL, WILLIAM F.: *The Development of London Livery Companies* (Boston, Mass., 1960).

KRAMER, STELLA: *The English Craft Gilds* (Oxford Univ. Press, 1928).

PRIDEAUX, SIR W. S.: *Memorials of the Goldsmiths' Company* (London, 1896).

SMITH, LUCY TOULMIN: *English Gilds, The Original Ordinances of more than one hundred Early English Gilds* (Early English Text Society, Vol. XL, 1870).

THRUPP, SYLVIA: *A Short History of the Worshipful Company of Bakers of London* (London, 1933).

UNWIN, GEORGE: *The Gilds and Companies* (1908; 4th ed., with a new Introduction by William F. Kahl, F. Cass, 1963).

VIII POPULATION, PRICES AND CALAMITY

BEAN, J. M. W.: 'Plague, Population and Economic Decline in the later Middle Ages', in *Economic History Review*, Second Series, vol. 15 (1963).

CORNWALL, JULIAN: 'English Population in the Early Sixteenth Century, in *Economic History Review*, Second Series, vol. 23 (1970).

GOULD, J. D.: *The Great Debasement* (Clarendon Press, 1970).

HARVEY, BARBARA M.: 'The Population Trend in England Between 1300 and 1348' in *Royal Historical Society Transactions*, 5th Series, vol. 16, 1966.

KING, GREGORY: for his population tables see Sir G. N. Clark, Appendix to *The Wealth of England from 1496–1760* (Oxford Univ. Press, 1946).

OUTHWAITE, R. H.: *Inflation in Tudor and Early Stuart England* (Macmillan, 1969).

POSTAN, M. M.: 'Some Economic Evidence of Declining Population in the later Middle Ages' in *Economic History Review*, Second Series, vol. 2, 1950.

RAMSEY, P. H.: *The Price Revolution in Sixteenth Century England* (Methuen, 1971).

RICH, E. E.: 'The Population of Elizabethan England', in *Economic History Review*, Second Series, vol. 2, 1950.

RUSSELL, J. C.: *British Medieval Population* (Univ. of New Mexico Press, 1948).

SALTMARSH, JOHN: 'Plague and Economic Decline in England in the Later Middle Ages' in *Cambridge Historical Journal*, VII, 1941.

The Black Death

BOCCACCIO, GIOVANNI: *The Decameron.* There are many translations. See those of J. M. Rigg (1903, new edition 1953; or that of G. H. McWilliam, Penguin, 1972).

COULTON, G. G.: *The Black Death* (Benn, 1928).

DEAUX, G.: *The Black Death 1349* (H. Hamilton, 1969).

GASQUET, F. A.: *The Black Death of 1348 and 1349* (G. Bell, 2nd ed., 1908).

ZIEGLER, P.: *The Black Death* (Collins, 1969; Penguin, 1970).

Other Calamities

BELL, W. G.: *The Great Plague in London in 1665* (John Lane, 1924; 2nd ed., 1951).

——: *The Great Fire of London* (John Lane, 1920).

WILSON, F. P.: *The Plague in Shakespeare's London* (Clarendon Press, 1927; Oxford Univ. Press, 1963).

IX EDUCATION AND MANNERS, ETC

BRATHWAITE, R.: *The English Gentleman* (1630).

——: *The English Gentlewoman* (1631).

CAMPBELL, R.: *The London Tradesman* (1747; Facs. David and Charles, 1969).

DEFOE, D.: *The Complete English Tradesman* (1725).

PEACHAM, H.: *The Compleat Gentleman* (1622).

TUSSER, THOMAS: *A Hundred Poyntes of Good Husserie* (1557).

JORDAN, W. K.: *The Charities of Rural England, 1480–1660* (Allen and Unwin, 1961).

——: *Philanthropy in England, 1480–1660* (Allen and Unwin, 1959).

LAWSON, J.: *Medieval Education and the Reformation* (Routledge, 1967).

MARSHALL, DOROTHY: *The English Domestic Servant in History* (Historical Association Leaflet, General Series, G. 13, 1949).

POTTER, GEORGE: Chapter on Education in *Cambridge Medieval History*, vol. VIII (1936).

SIMON, JOAN: Education and Society in Tudor England (Cambridge Univ. Press, 1966).

STONE, LAWRENCE: 'Literacy and Education in England 1640–1900' in *Past and Present,* No. 42 (1969) and 'The Educational Revolution in England, 1560–1640' in ibid., No. 28 (1964).

THOMAS, KEITH: 'Work and Leisure in Pre-Industrial Society' with discussion, *Past and Present*, No. 29, 1964.

THOMPSON, A. HAMILTON: 'Song Schools in the Middle Ages', (*Church Music Society, Occasional Papers,* No. 14, 1942).

The Gentry, etc. (studies in chronological order)

TAWNEY, R. H.: 'Harrington's Interpretation of his Age' in *Proceedings of the British Academy,* 1941.

——: 'The Rise of the Gentry 1558–1640' in *Economic History Review,* vol. 11, 1941.

STONE, LAWRENCE: 'The Anatomy of the Elizabethan Aristocracy' in *Economic History Review,* 13, 1948.

TREVOR-ROPER, H. R.: 'The Elizabethan Aristocracy: An Anatomy Anatomized' in *Economic History Review,* 2nd Series, 3, 1951.

STONE, LAWRENCE: 'The Elizabethan Aristocracy, a re-statement' in *Economic History Review,* Second Series, vol. 4, 1952.

TREVOR-ROPER, H. R.: 'The Gentry 1540–1640' in *Economic History Review Supplement* I, 1953.

TAWNEY, R. H.: 'The Rise of the Gentry', a Postscript', in *Economic History Review,* Second Series, vol. 7, 1954.

COOPER, J. P.: 'The Counting of Manors' in *Economic History Review,* Second Series, vol. 8, 1956.

HEXTER, JACK H.: 'Storm Over the Gentry' in *Re-appraisals in History* (Longmans, 1961).

SIMPSON, ALAN: *The Wealth of the Gentry 1540–1660* (Cambridge Univ. Press, 1961).

STONE, LAWRENCE: *The Crisis of the Aristocracy 1558–1641* (Oxford Univ. Press, 1965).

——: *Social Change and Revolution in England, 1540–1640* (Longmans, 1965).

COLEMAN, D. C.: 'The Gentry Controversy and the Aristocracy in Crisis, 1558–1641' in *History*, vol. 51, 1966.

X THE POOR LAW, ETC

BAGLEY, J. J. and A. J.: *The English Poor Law* (Macmillan, 1966).

BEARD, C. A.: *The Office of Justice of the Peace in England* (1904).

LEONARD, E. M.: *Early History of English Poor Relief* (Camb. Univ. Press, 1900; F. Cass, 1965).

MARSHALL, DOROTHY: *The English Poor in the Eighteenth Century* (Routledge, 1926).

PUTNAM, B. H.: *The Enforcement of the Statutes of Labourers during the first decade after the Black Death, 1349–1359* (Columbia College N. Y., 1891).

WEBB, S. and B.: *English Poor Law History: Part I, The Old Poor Law* (Vol. 7 of *English Local Government*) (Longmans, 1927).

XI THE PEASANTS' REVOLT AND OTHER DISTURBANCES

DOBSON, R. B.: *The Peasants' Revolt of 1381* (Macmillan, 1970).

HILTON, R. H.: *Bond Men Made Free: medieval peasant movements and the Rising of 1381* (Smith, 1973).

——: 'Peasant Movements before 1381' in *Economic History Review*, Second Series, vol. 2, 1949.

OMAN, SIR CHARLES: *The Great Revolt of 1381* (Clarendon Press, 1906; new edition by E. B. Fryde, 1969).

PETIT-DUTAILLIS, CHARLES: *Studies and Notes Supplementary to Stubbs' Constitutional History, Vol. II: Causes and General Characteristics of the Rising of 1381.* Translated from the French by W. T. Waugh (Univ. of Manchester, 1914). Reissued in one vol., 1930.

BINDOFF, S. T.: Ket's Rebellion, 1549 (Historical Association pamphlets, General Series, G. 12 (1949, reprinted 1968).

BRAILSFORD, H. N.: *The Levellers and the English Revolution* (Cresset Press, 1961).

FLETCHER, ANTHONY: *Tudor Rebellions* (Longmans, 1968; second edition, 1973).

GREGG, PAULINE: *Free-Born John: a Biography of John Lilburne* (Harrap, 1961).

SABINE, GEORGE H.: *The Works of Gerrard Winstanley, with an Introduction* (Cornell Univ. Press, 1941).

XII UTOPIAS, ETC.

BACON, FRANCIS: *New Atlantis* (written before 1617, first published 1627, edited by H. Osborne, University Tutorial Press, 1937, and other editions).

CHAMBERLEN, PETER: *The Poore Man's Advocate* (1649).

HARRINGTON, JAMES: *The Common-wealth of Oceana* (written 1656); and see BLITZER, C.: *An Immortal Commonwealth, the Political Thought of James Harrington* (Yale University Press, 1960).

TAWNEY, R. H.: 'Harrington's Interpretation of His Age' in *Proceedings of the British Academy,* 27 (1941).

HARTLIB, SAMUEL: *A Description of the famous Kingdome of Macaria* (1641).

MORE, SIR THOMAS: *Utopia* (first published in 1516 in Latin; first French translation 1550; first English translation 1551. Of the many English translations one in paperback is that by Paul Turner, Penguin, 1965).

Index

PERSONS

PLACES

SUBJECTS

0831
687988.